STUDIES IN
IMPERIALISM

D0088274

General editor John M. MacKenzie

Established in the belief that imperialism as a cultural
phenomenon had as significant an effect on the dominant as
on the subordinate societies, Studies in Imperialism seeks to
develop the new socio-cultural approach which has emerged
through cross-disciplinary work on popular culture, media
studies, art history, the study of education and religion,
sports history and children's literature. The cultural
emphasis embraces studies of migration and race, while the
older political and constitutional, economic and military
concerns are never far away. It incorporates comparative
work on European and American empire-building, with the
chronological focus primarily, though not exclusively, on the
nineteenth and twentieth centuries, when these cultural
exchanges were most powerfully at work.

Reporting the Raj

MANCHESTER
UNIVERSITY PRESS

Reporting the Raj

THE BRITISH PRESS AND INDIA
c. 1880–1922

Chandrika Kaul

MANCHESTER
UNIVERSITY PRESS
Manchester and New York

distributed exclusively in the USA
by PALGRAVE

Published by **MANCHESTER UNIVERSITY PRESS**
OXFORD ROAD, MANCHESTER M13 9NR, UK
and ROOM 400, 175 FIFTH AVENUE, NEW YORK NY 10010, USA
www.manchesteruniversitypress.co.uk

Distributed exclusively in the USA by
PALGRAVE, 175 FIFTH AVENUE, NEW YORK, NY 10010, USA

Distributed exclusively in Canada by
UBC PRESS, UNIVERSITY OF BRITISH COLUMBIA,
2029 WEST MALL, VANCOUVER, BC, CANADA V6T 1Z2

British Library Cataloguing-in-Publication Data
A catalogue record for this book is available from the British Library

Library of Congress Cataloging-in-Publication Data applied for

ISBN 0 7190 6175 X hardback
    0 7190 6176 8 paperback

First published 2003

11 10 09 08 07 06 05 04 03   10 9 8 7 6 5 4 3 2 1

Typeset in Trump Mediaeval
by SNP Best-set Typesetter Ltd., Hong Kong
Printed in Great Britain
by Bookcraft (Bath) Ltd, Midsomer Norton

*For my mother
and to the memory of
my great-grandmother, Dimma*

CONTENTS

[vii]

CONTENTS

Appendices

LIST OF TABLES

LIST OF ILLUSTRATIONS

[x]

GENERAL EDITOR'S INTRODUCTION

Language offers many clues to the history of power and influence. The fact that the key word in representing the technology of printing came to be applied to the daily and periodical papers developing so vigorously from the eighteenth century neatly reflects this. Indeed, no cultural phenomenon has been more ubiquitous and, many would say, more powerful, than the press. Yet, while there have been many studies of the organisation and the economics, the personalities and the preoccupations of the press in Britain, very little work has been done on the relationship between press and empire, or upon the early efforts of government to manipulate and control its output.

This is surprising because the modern press developed at precisely the time that imperialism, empire, and colonies were becoming a major concern. The removal of fiscal controls, the development of new printing technologies and forms of transmission of information, and the emergence of special correspondents and specialist editors all took place as the British Empire was expanded and consolidated. The press fed off empire voraciously and, in doing so, came to have an influence upon affairs. This was not just a metropolitan phenomenon. As anyone who has examined the British 'provincial' papers knows, empire was a prominent feature of the papers of towns and cities everywhere, including those in the major centres of Scotland or Ireland. Moreover, a colonial press, often shrugging off efforts at official control, appeared throughout the British Empire, and equally became a force to be watched, to be courted, to be influenced, and also to be owned. By the last decades of the nineteenth century, any politician or official who ignored, or was contemptuous of, the press throughout the British Empire, did so at their considerable peril.

Chandrika Kaul's study focuses on the key relationship between the press and India. As well as exploring the vital technical changes of the period, she examines the manner in which Fleet Street editors and journalists developed a particular set of attitudes towards the British Raj in India. But these attitudes were not permitted to flourish unhindered and uninfluenced. The concept of 'news management', after faltering starts, came to be a significant factor in the three-way relationship of the British Government, the Indian administration, and the personalities of the press. Indeed, an understanding of the complex of personalities involved in each arm of this relationship is vital. The style and wording of press content, the ideas and pressures it attempted to convey to its readership, all emerged from the predilections of these personalities and the considerable conceit that many had in respect of their influence and authority. Of course both the networks and the growing scale of the press complex ensured that such developments were self-sustaining and mutually reinforcing. But they also reflected a considerable advance in the power of the bourgeoisie and its anxieties to reflect and influence the popular attitudes in an age of a growing franchise.

GENERAL EDITOR'S INTRODUCTION

Personalities, constitutional changes, and key incidents, as mediated to and by the press, abound in the pages that follow. By using a wide range of newspapers and journals, as well as large numbers of private and official papers, Chandrika Kaul unveils the complicated relationships of government and the press over India. In many ways, these form the foundation of the similar sets of connections that obtain to this day. Moreover, it becomes clear that some of the ideas and perceptions relating to India and Indians which continue to prevail have their origins in the carefully modulated press attitudes of the late nineteenth and early twentieth centuries. This book marks a significant development in studies of the press and it is to be hoped that it will be followed by many more examining the relationship between the 'fourth estate' and the processes of imperialism in all its ambitions and anxieties, follies and fallacies.

John M. MacKenzie

ACKNOWLEDGEMENTS

Research and the writing process are at once an intensely personal as well as a widely shared experience. This book is no exception. My interest in the British press and India was given initial focus by my mother, Minoti Chakravarty-Kaul, who suggested I work on the Ilbert Bill for my final honour school dissertation at Balliol College, Oxford. She has been a constant source of inspiration and loving support over the subsequent years, which have witnessed that interest evolve into a larger project for a doctorate at Nuffield College, as well as forming part of a wide-ranging study of the press, communications and empire that has provided the basis of my research and teaching.

Oxford has been the intellectual home of this book, and my special thanks and gratitude are reserved for my mentors there. My supervisors, John Darwin and David Butler, gave unstinting encouragement and advice. Judith Brown, Michael Brock and Lawrence Whitehead read various sections of the doctorate and made helpful comments. Maria Misra and Michael Bromley (Queensland University) were critical but fair examiners who enthusiastically supported publication. Bob Moore, Bernard Porter and Elizabeth Redgate, colleagues at the University of Newcastle upon Tyne, offered intellectual support and friendship at a critical juncture in the writing process.

Numerous individuals as well as institutions and their staff have given freely of their time and expertise, and, where appropriate, have allowed me to quote from their holdings: Eamon Dyas (and Melanie Aspey) at TNL Archives; the John Rylands University Library, Manchester, and the Central Library, Manchester; Keith Wilson and archivists at the Brotherton Library, Leeds, and the Earl Bathurst; the Clerk of the Records, House of Lords Record Office; the British Library Newspaper Library, Colindale; the India Office Library and Records and the Manuscript Section of the British Library; the Bodleian Library and the Keeper of Western Manuscripts, University of Oxford; Nuffield College Library; the Robinson Library, University of Newcastle upon Tyne; the National Archives and the Teen Murti Nehru Memorial Museum and Library, New Delhi; the British Library of Political and Economic Science; the offices of the *Spectator* and the offices of Associated Newspapers, London; Birmingham University Library; the Wren Library, Trinity College, and Cambridge University Library; the late John Grigg; Anna Mathias; Dr Jeremy Hogg; T. J. Fraser; Colin Lee; and the secretary, the Round Table. Special thanks are due to the Reuters Archives team, led by John Entwistle, along with Donald Read, Justine Taylor and Adrian Steele, who have been unfailingly good-humoured and generous in their support over several years, and made the hours spent at Reuters offices pleasurable as well as productive. Milton Gendel allowed me to consult family papers, and both he and Mrs Gendel were generous hosts during my stay in Rome. David Astor, Iverach

ACKNOWLEDGEMENTS

MacDonald, John Linton and the late David Ayerst kindly took time to share their thoughts and experience with me. Thanks are also due to the following publishers for permission to use extracts from my articles: Frank Cass for 'A new angle of vision: governmental information management and the Indian empire, 1900–22', *Contemporary Record*, 8: 2 (1994); Routledge for 'Imperial communications, Fleet Street and the Indian empire, *c.* 1850s–1920s', in M. Bromley and T O'Malley (eds), *A Journalism Reader* (1997); and Macmillan for 'Popular press and empire: Northcliffe, India and the *Daily Mail*, 1896–1922', in P. Catterall *et al.* (eds), *Northcliffe's Legacy* (2000).

Permission to reproduce photographs and illustrations has been given by the *Punch* Archives, the British Library, Reuters Archives, News International Syndication, Alpha Photo Press Agency and James Nisbet publishers.

My thanks are also due to the several institutions that have provided financial support over the years, most recently the British Academy with a research grant to enable the completion of the book; Beit Senior Research Scholarship, University of Oxford; Inlaks Foundation scholarship; Foreign and Commonwealth Office scholarship; Charles Wallace India Trust; and Nuffield College.

As any author would readily acknowledge, the role of the publisher is crucial, and I have been singularly fortunate in my association with Manchester University Press. John MacKenzie has provided rigorous intellectual stimulation and perceptive comments, for which I am most grateful. I would also like to thank the external reader for fine-tuning my work through helpful suggestions. The history editor at MUP, Alison Whittle, and her assistant Jonathan Bevan, have been models of patience and creative support.

Peter Lane, Jason Tomes and Konstantina Pitsiakou have been generous friends and have given timely technical assistance, while Margaret Yee has been a constant source of spiritual sustenance. There is one person who, above all, has been involved with this book and with my life in more ways than I can begin to appreciate, and to him are reserved my special thanks – my husband, Ian St John.

C.K.

LIST OF ABBREVIATIONS

These are used in the endnotes. The place of publication is London unless stated otherwise. 'The press', unless otherwise specified, refers to the London press/Fleet Street/the metropolitan press/the British national press. The main news agency is cited as 'Reuters', except in references, when the version used by the writer is retained. In general the terms 'Government of India' and 'the India Office' distinguish between the British administrators in India and those in London respectively. 'The government' or 'the imperial government' refers to the sum of the two different organisations and, depending on the context, also the British Government in general.

BL	British Library, London
Bodl.	Bodleian Library, Oxford
BP	Beaverbrook Papers, HLRO
BUL	Birmingham University Library
CC/no.	Chelmsford Collection, IOLR
CHP	Valentine Chirol Papers, TA
CUL	Cambridge University Library
CurC/no.	Curzon Collection, IOLR
DNB	Dictionary of National Biography
D-S/no.	Dunlop-Smith Collection, IOLR
EngHR	*English Historical Review*
FMLB	Foreign Manager's Letter Book, TA
Fortnightly	*Fortnightly Review*
Gazette	*Westminster Gazette*
G–B	Glenesk–Bathurst Papers, Brotherton Library, Leeds
E. W. M. Grigg	Grigg Correspondence, TA
HAG	H. A. Gwynne Papers, Bodl.
HBC/no.	Harcourt Butler Collection, IOLR
HLRO	House of Lords Record Office
Home Poll A, B or Deposit	Home Political Papers series A, B, and Deposit, NAI
HP	Hardinge Papers, CUL
ICS	Indian Civil Service
IESHR	*Indian Economic and Social History Review*
INC	Indian National Congress
IOLR	Oriental and India Office Library and Records, BL
JCH	*Journal of Contemporary History*
JICH	*Journal of Imperial and Commonwealth History*
JPT/no.	J. P. Thompson Diaries, IOLR
JSA	*Journal of the Society of Arts*
MAS	*Modern Asian Studies*

LIST OF ABBREVIATIONS

MC/no.	Montagu Collection, IOLR
MG	*Manchester Guardian (Guardian)*
MGA	Manchester Guardian Archives, John Rylands Manchester University Library
Mitchell's	*Mitchell's Press Directory*
MLB	Manager's Letter Book, TA
MorC/no	Morley Collection, IOLR
MP Trinity	Montagu Papers, Trinity College, Cambridge
NAI	National Archives of India, New Delhi
P&P	*Past and Present*
RA	Reuters Archives, Reuters Ltd, London
RC/no.	Reading Collection, IOLR
Reynolds's	*Reynolds's Weekly Newspaper*
RJ	Roderick Jones Papers/File, RA
RpvtC/no.	Reading (Private) Collection, IOLR
RT	Round Table Papers, Bodl.
Sell's	*Sell's Directory of the World's Press*
SP	John St Loe Strachey Papers, HLRO
SpA	*Spectator* Archives, *Spectator* offices, London
TA	*The Times* Archives, TNL Archives, London

CHAPTER ONE

Introduction

In the summer of 1909 Lord Curzon, Chancellor of Oxford University and previously Viceroy of India, welcomed journalists attending the first Imperial Press Conference to a luncheon in All Souls College. After referring to Oxford's contribution to the empire and the Indian Civil Service, he noted how 'We also train no inconsiderable number of Pressmen . . . who, much more than any other officials, will be in the future the speaking links – the "live rails" . . . for connecting the outskirts of the Empire with its heart'.[1] Curzon's remark introduces several of the key themes of this book. It illustrates the growing political recognition of the role of the press and reveals the symbiotic operation of political, journalistic and academic elites *vis-à-vis* empire. For the press too, the conference, convened at the initiative of Fleet Street, reflected an increasing self-assurance and consciousness of its position within the empire, its proceedings being conceived as a 'Parliament of the Empire's Press' and as 'a replica in a freer style' of the Imperial Naval Conference taking place the same year.[2] Lord Burnham, proprietor of the *Daily Telegraph* (hereafter *Telegraph*), went so far as to claim that the two press conferences (a second was held in Ottawa in 1920) carried 'Imperial solidarity to a further point in newspaper affairs than it has as yet been found possible to do in our Parliamentary relations'.[3]

Reporting the Raj provides the first detailed analysis of how Fleet Street functioned as the speaking link and live rail of the Raj during the late nineteenth and early twentieth-century heydey of the empire. These years witnessed several critical developments within the institutional structure of the medium and in its relationship with the political process – including vast improvements in the efficiency of imperial communications, an expansion in the scale and diversity of the national press, and growing sensitivity amongst politicians of its influence within the context of a more democratic political organisation. Systems of imperial management and control were forced to adapt to the new communication realities.

The growth of the press and the enhanced communication links between metropole and periphery increased the potential accessibility of Indian news, while the reforms, crises and controversies of the first two decades of the twentieth century ensured that Indian affairs were brought more prominently before the British public. It has been insufficiently recognised that what was at stake for governments was not simply opinion within the subcontinent but political opinion in Britain itself. Political commentators were right when they claimed that no election would be won or lost over India. But it would be misleading to infer that officials were unconcerned about public perceptions of imperial actions. For press coverage as a form of mass communication did matter, and governments wished, as they do now, to mediate how events and issues were reported. Efforts at news management through the press had the potential to reach a variety of publics, from the politically informed elite – Gladstone's 'upper ten thousand' – to the lower middle and working classes. Politicians and administrators were also concerned to prevent the communications media from misrepresenting the official position and playing to the advantage of their opponents. Finally, domestic politicians had before their mind the repercussions of press reporting of political debate within Britain on opinion in the subcontinent – both Anglo-Indian and indigenous. Thus, even if elections were not fought directly on Indian issues, governments were conscious of the implications for public and party confidence should they appear to be mishandling imperial affairs.

As a consequence the India Office (and also the Government of India) were forced to take steps to influence British press coverage of the subcontinent. Prior to 1914 such media manipulation tended to be unsystematic. The India Office possessed no formal machinery for guiding the press, though individual politicians and administrators appreciated the value of cultivating relations with the media and a reciprocal relationship did develop often based on personal friendship. Although similar methods continued during and after the war, they were intensified and placed on a more formal basis, being explicitly incorporated into government strategy. In this process Edwin Montagu, Secretary of State for India 1917–22, played a central role. Montagu saw political reform and news management as joint constituents of a 'new angle of vision' in the approach to Indian governance. Yet his domestic political weakness also caused him to attach particular importance to efforts to shape newspaper reporting of his actions. An on-going revolution in media and communications, a transformed political situation within Britain and India, and the character and political imperatives of the Secretary of State, therefore combined to place India Office–press relations on a new footing. *Reporting the Raj* analyses these developments in terms of three inter-related areas: communications and empire within the context of imperial policy *vis-à-vis* India; the domestic imperatives of Indian policy, particularly the interaction of the India Office with Fleet Street, and the political coverage of the subcontinent by the press and its response to critical issues facing the Raj during and immediately after the war – this last being undertaken by means of case studies, chosen to highlight significant aspects of the press–politics nexus, official news management, and the flavour of press reporting itself.

Communications and empire

Systems of communications play a vital role in shaping political, institutional and cultural structures, affecting the 'trajectory of social evolution and the values and beliefs of societies'.[4] In general, governments, considered as networks of decision and control, are dependent on processes of communication, that is to say, their ability to receive, process, and disseminate information.[5] This is especially so in the case of empires, with the extensive spatial dimensions inherent in this form of political organisation. And it is indeed the case that communications played a crucial role in creating, mediating and sustaining the evolution of the British imperial experience. Technologies such as steam boats, railways and submarine cables allowed metropolitan politicians to combine with imperialists in the periphery to consolidate and expand British interests – though they could also allow 'men on the spot' to demand immediate assistance from the centre or to appeal direct to British political opinion in support of their policies.[6] They provided the infrastructure of imperial expansion and trade, while the bureaucracy of empire was bound together by an information network of political, military and commercial intelligence – what Lloyd George referred to as the 'steel frame' of empire. But communications were more than mere mechanisms. They brought into being for the first time what Marshall McLuhan was later to call the 'global village' – or in our case an imperial village. Ideas and cultural values were transmitted around the world, linking metropolis and periphery in a dynamic relationship and bringing into existence an informed political opinion on imperial affairs – in the colonies as well as in London. This was a factor of capital importance since conceptions of how empire should be run were formulated to a large extent in the metropolis on the basis of the information, images and conceptions generated by and filtered through communication.

Moreover, the inherent dynamism of communication technology has meant that communications have been a determining factor in the evolution of political institutions. Modern study of this process began with the work of the Canadian economist and historian based at the University of Toronto, Harold Adam Innis. Innis contended that media are never neutral, and that patterns of social relations are intimately linked to the systems of communication in given eras – an idea later taken up by McLuhan and encapsulated in his aphorism 'the medium is the message'.[7] Thus in *Empire and Communications* (1950) and *The Bias of Communication* (1951) Innis sought to demonstrate how developments in modes of communication shaped the political and social history of the West. Large-scale political organisations, like empires, should be evaluated, he argued, in terms of the dimensions of 'space' and 'time'.[8] A medium of communication has

> an important influence on the dissemination of knowledge over space and over time and it becomes necessary to study its characteristics in order to appraise its influence in its cultural setting. According to its characteristics it may be better suited to the dissemination of knowledge over time than over space, particularly if the medium is heavy and durable and not suited to transportation, or to the dissemination of knowledge over space than over time, particularly if the medium is light and easily transported. The relative emphasis on time or space will imply a bias of significance to the culture in which it is imbedded.[9]

Though not a technological determinist, Innis devoted attention to the consequences of new information technologies, such as printing, for the extension of society in space, and its impact on political and cultural norms, contending that British imperial expansion in the nineteenth century was sustained as much by printing and cheap pulp paper as by the gunboat, and that its changing character in the twentieth century 'has been, in part, a result of its influence on public opinion'.[10]

The centrality of communication media to both culture and social structure implied that the principal axis of change, of the rise and fall of empires, would be alterations in the methods of communications, though he emphasised the 'facilitating' and 'hastening' characteristics of the communicational impact, rather than a straightforwardly determining one. The motivating force, according to Innis, was the search for power. Developments in communications technique occur within institutional contexts which sustain inequalities in access to power. As such communications, and the information which they process, reinforce inequalities as elite groups have privileged access to knowledge – and the power it brings. However, Innis's study of the impact of communications on the distribution of power was, perhaps, insufficiently dynamic. It is not a one-off effect but the beginning of a process of negotiation and struggle. Whilst it is true that the immediate impact of a new technology is to consolidate the position of an established elite, other groups will also seek access to that technology and the information and influence it yields. As a result, innovations in communications can have considerable and unexpected effects upon social organisation and the distribution of power. Indeed, Innis himself highlighted the double-edged character of improved communication technology, which by facilitating the production and dissemination of critical national literature and languages acted, in turn, to undermine imperial power – a process beginning in America in 1776. 'With printing, paper facilitated an effective development of the vernaculars and gave expression to their vitality in the growth of nationalism . . . the newspaper strengthened the position of language as a basis of nationalism'.[11] The power of the newspaper was reflected in the success of the American Revolution and in the adoption of the Bill of Rights guaranteeing freedom of the press.[12] In similar ways, 'language under the influence of mechanization of the printed word and the spoken word' – what Benedict Anderson has called 'print-capitalism' – had caused the British empire to be increasingly exposed to nationalist forces, which took up these tools to articulate their case and create the 'imagined communities' that Anderson eloquently describes.[13]

Developing upon the insights provided by Innis, this book seeks to analyse the key role of communication technologies and techniques on the conduct of politics in relation to India, viewing it as one important determinant in a situation of imperial domination. Emphasis is also placed upon the process by which existing groups negotiated the distribution and forms of power, representation, and knowledge. Technological innovation did not automatically induce new forms of social and political practice. Much depended on the form and adaptability of the old procedures, as well as such contingent factors as the presence of external threats to society and the imagination and endeavour of leading individuals. To take one example. While inventions like compositing and rotary machines, created the conditions for the press to become a mass-production capitalist industry for the first time, the consequences of these developments for journalism and British society more generally cannot be considered independently of the handful of forceful and even visionary personalities. Men such as the Harmsworth brothers (later Lords Northcliffe and Rothermere) and Max Aitken (later Lord Beaverbrook) did not only exploit the potentialities of new technology. They deliberately set out to create a new style of populist news presentation as a means to a new sort of political power.

Press and empire

The press lay at the heart of the processes of communication in the late nineteenth and early twentieth centuries, helping to create and sustain what Habermas referred to as the 'public sphere' at a time when empire permeated the political ethos of Britain. Any conception of contemporary public debate on empire would therefore be incomplete without an understanding of the contribution of the press. Queen Victoria's Diamond Jubilee celebrations provoked Beatrice Webb to note in her diary: 'Imperialism in the air – all classes drunk with sight-seeing and hysterical loyalty'.[14] The growth of the empire was, says MacDonald, 'watched with pride by a largely sympathetic press'.[15] Imperial issues were a continuing preoccupation with editors of the quality papers, while proprietors of the popular press learned 'the value of imperial drama as a way to sell their product'.[16] Contemporary press directories like *Sell's* and *Mitchell's* reveal the existence of a plethora of imperial publications. Fleet Street ran spirited imperial campaigns and exerted increasing pressure on government through the second half of Victoria's reign. A vivid example was Lord Esher's use of the *Pall Mall Gazette* to press Gladstone into sending Gordon to the Sudan in 1883, a cry taken up by other papers.[17] Many editors were deeply committed to the cause of empire and viewed their papers as vehicles for imperial publicity – men such as G. Dawson, H. A. Gwynne, J. A. Spender, J. St Loe Strachey, Sidney Low, Leopold Maxse and J. L. Garvin. Gwynne reflected in 1911, upon assuming the editorship of the *Morning Post*, 'I have given of the best part of my life and intend to devote the rest of it to promote the objects I hold dear – a united Empire, England secure on land as on sea.'[18] Strachey wrote in 1922, 'To me the alliance of the self-governing Dominions, which constitute the British Empire, has a sacred character . . . I feel further that throughout Africa, as throughout India, we have done an incomparable service to humanity by our maintenance of just and stable government.'[19]

Such sentiments found a wide resonance in Fleet Street. Pioneers of the new popular journalism expressed similar views, though these arguably served different ends. Northcliffe, proprietor of the *Daily Mail* (hereafter *Mail*) – the first mass-circulating daily newspaper – held strong imperialist convictions, yet his abiding interest in the empire was combined with shrewd business acumen as he perceived its commercial potential. Colonial conflicts were especially profitable. As MacKenzie notes:

The popular press exploited this spectatorial fascination with colonial warfare, and its power was such that not only the jingoist *Daily Mail* but also labour papers like *Reynolds's News* were swept up into it. In 1898 the Labour *Leader* complained that the working class were more interested in celebrating Omdurman than in supporting the Welsh coal strike.[20]

The Boer War saw the circulation of the pro-war *Mail* soar, whereas the *Manchester Guardian* (hereafter *Guardian*) continued to lose readers and W. T. Stead's tenure at the *Review of Reviews* was associated with declining revenue and sales – at least in part because of their unrelenting opposition to the conflict.

Some of the relationships between empire and Edwardian journalism have been traced by Startt, particularly with respect to the debate surrounding the future of South Africa and tariff reform. He suggests that it was the quality, rather than the popular, papers that were central to Edwardian politics, and 'helped to make the Empire one of the two or three commanding subjects of the time and extended the parameters of discussion about it'.[21] However, though Startt acknowledges that journalists generally took pride in the achievements of the Raj, he does not consider newspaper coverage of India, contending that it 'never became a continuing controversial subject', remaining, like the dependencies, a 'special case' and 'largely in the domain of the experts'.[22] Yet, as we shall show, Indian issues could and did generate significant press coverage, and the Raj's prominence in the press – both quality and popular – grew throughout this period, and, especially in the war and immediate post-war years. *Reporting the Raj* aims to put Britain's largest imperial possession back into the history of the British press, while also examining the politics–press nexus and what MacKenzie has labelled the 'centripetal' forces exercised on Britain by her empire.

In its emphasis upon the role of the British press in shaping the conduct and policy of the India Office, and its wider contribution to the formation of metropolitan images of India, this study adds to the growing body of research dealing with the impact of the imperial experience on Britain. It is increasingly being recognised how closely empire was interwoven with social conditions and British cultural institutions, its significance persisting into the inter-war period, when empire was portrayed as a source of pride and as a means of arresting national decline.[23] As it emerged in the late nineteenth century the imperial cult, says MacKenzie, was made up of 'a renewed militarism, a devotion to royalty, an identification and worship of national heroes, together with a contemporary cult of personality, and racial ideas associated with Social Darwinism'.[24] A large number of non-government agencies discovered that imperial patriotism was also profitable, and imperial values were projected by such diverse means as music halls, missionary societies, Churches, book publishers, magazines and juvenile literature, school texts, cinema and organisations like the Boy Scouts. In *Britannia's Children*, for instance, Castle has examined the representations of subject peoples in history textbooks and children's periodicals, and argues that the 'sheer volume and invasive nature of imperial propaganda directed at the rising generation did help to shape images of self, and certainly of the "others"'.[25]

A growing body of literature, associated with such authors as Said, Spivak, Suleri, Bhabha, Mills, McClintock and Bratlinger, has explored the means by which images of the 'East' (including India) were constructed in the West. The press, as a mass literary form, was a key agent in this process and its role in generating conceptions of India within Britain has yet to be fully explored. This, however, is not the focus of *Reporting the Raj*, which is concerned not with general coverage of Indian society and culture, but with press reporting of Indian political affairs and, in particular, press analysis of imperial policy and the consequent attempts by the government to shape that reporting.

By the turn of the twentieth century it was the London press that was the most significant in terms of the coverage of India. Most provincial papers routinely replicated extracts from Fleet Street. The major metropolitan dailies had far larger circulations and, given the structure of political society, the London press was tantamount to the national press. 'For better or worse, its voice was heard most audibly by policymakers, congregated in the capital, and its resources were those to which they attached paramount significance.'[26] The analysis which follows is based upon a comprehensive survey of twenty-four major national papers and reviews (including the important provincial daily, the *Manchester Guardian*), which have been selected with a view to providing a representative picture of this press, in terms of both political affiliation and the character and style of journalism.

The shape of the book is determined, at one level, by themes that preoccupied the press, especially during the climactic years 1917–22. Attention has throughout been focused upon the views expressed in the press and attitudes exhibited by pressmen in their private correspondence, while the press itself is situated in its broader historical context. Fleet Street provides a unique record of informed opinion and enables us to observe its evolution under the pressure of circumstances. Imperial events impacted on the domestic consciousness when they were debated in Parliament and appraised by Fleet Street. The press played an important role in generating public perceptions of political and social change and imperial policy. While not always living up to its reputation as a fourth estate, it was an indispensable part of the political process and, particularly in pre-broadcasting days, the main link between politicians and the electorate. For the press, too, intimate contacts with government were essential, for 'without friends in the Government, and with no sources of "inside" information, [it] spoke with little authority on political issues, and lacked influence and prestige'.[27]

In writing a political history of the Raj, newspapers are especially valuable in enabling the reconstruction of contemporary perspectives on events without the tendency towards teleology evident in subsequent historical accounts which, aware of the outcome, supply an artificial coherence to developments. Newspapers allow us to follow the manner in which contemporaries reacted to events as they unfolded over time. Yet the images of 'reality' as reflected in the press was a kaleidoscopic construct, the coverage of each paper being determined by a variety of factors. These included the news values of the paper (a *Times* scoop was not always the same as a scoop for the *Daily Express*, hereafter *Express*); the costs of information; the varying sets of relationships between newspapers and their perceived readerships; and the assumptions and idiosyncrasies of individual editors, proprietors and journalists.[28] Above all, it should be remembered that imperial news, both in its gathering and in its discussion, had to operate within an imperial political context. Fleet Street was a free press at the heart of an imperial system of coercion, and to that extent it was inevitable that the press both reflected and reinforced prevailing images of order and power.

Governments attempted to influence Fleet Street's coverage of India partly through such official channels as Blue Books and parliamentary debates. However, we are primarily concerned with the more informal channels through which Secretaries of State strove to publicise their views and persuade the press of their interpretation of events: a process which has since come to be termed 'news' or 'information management'. Contemporaries sometimes referred to informal and formal news management techniques, together and separately, as propaganda. The word had not (before 1914) acquired pejorative overtones, and was used to signify the process by which governments (or their opponents) communicated with their audiences. Taylor defines publicity as 'the supply or release of information of a factual nature which is designed to provide the public in general with an opportunity for each individual member to formulate opinions for himself and to act according to his own conscience'. Propaganda, by contrast, is:

an attempt to influence the attitudes of a specific audience, through the use of facts, fiction, argument or suggestion – often supported by the suppression of inconsistent material – with the calculated purpose of instilling in the recipient certain beliefs, values or convictions which will serve the interests of the author, usually by producing a desired line of action.[29]

During the period of this study the distinction was blurred, though there was, already, a tendency for governments to describe their own efforts at persuasive communication as 'information' and 'publicity' and those of their opponents as 'propaganda'. As the Viceroy, Lord Reading, remarked in 1921, 'publicity by government is essential when propaganda is disseminated, as it is, by opponents'.[30]

The existence of 'public opinion' involves mass communication, with the press its leading exponent, and it has been plausibly argued by Elihu Katz that 'public opinion, in effect, *is* communication'.[31] It is, nevertheless, beyond the scope of this book to examine the broader themes of public opinion and imperial propaganda or address the full range of issues confronting India.[32] There will not, more specifically, be an attempt to discover what part the press played in the formation of popular opinion regarding India. The intention is, throughout, a more limited one: namely to survey press opinion on specific Indian issues – constitutional reform, unrest and monarchy – and to trace the manner and extent to which this opinion was subject to influence by politicians. The purpose is to discern as far as possible the techniques of media management actually deployed, and assess the extent to which they were successful. The government's ability to control information and news is evaluated by noting the circumstances within which these attempts yielded dividends and those in which they did not. Could the India Office, at this time, manufacture consensus amongst Fleet Street, or did newspapers retain independence in their judgement on events? The case studies are selected with a view to providing a succession of differing perspectives on this same set of issues, thus making it possible to capture some of the leading features of the problems of press coverage and control. The focus is thus the London press, both as an institution and as a mirror of events. We have confined our attention to the political coverage of India, and this was indeed the main preoccupation of the press. Politics made news, and it was the political issues and personalities connected with India that attracted newspaper attention.

Throughout the main emphasis is also upon the ideas and motives of the leading members of the India Office and the view of India taken here is the view from Whitehall and Westminster. There were closer connections between the worlds of Indian politics and London journalism than has been generally realised, and the book discusses how these connections worked in practice, as well as the role of different newspapers in major controversies, analysing where possible the policy-making process within the paper. Another concern has been to identify and discuss the external influences on the press, the organisational framework for news collection (including the seminal role of telegraphs and Reuters news agency), the impact of governmental pressure and directives, and the demands of party or personal loyalty. Following Koss, attention has been paid to the points of intersection between politics and the press, within the context of India. Several themes have emerged from these investigations. Co-operation between the India Office and the press was a facet of political life throughout the period, though it varied in importance and significance, depending on the Secretary of State and the domestic political situation, becoming particularly crucial during the war and immediate post-war years. The operational paradigm is one structured around an underlying partnership between politicians and pressmen as imperialists, rather than one based upon a division of functions between the ruling power and the critical scrutiny of an independent press. Journalists aspired to exert influence and give and withhold their support for politicians and policies. Yet, while the vitality and integrity of Fleet Street were reflected in the spectrum and quality of its coverage, the press was amenable to political persuasion over a range of issues, and was influenced by the general political climate as well as the practical need to harmonise its relations with the government. The India Office, especially under Montagu, strove hard to establish a mutually advantageous relationship with the press and to utilise its columns to further personal and official initiatives. As Lee astutely observes, 'A political system controlled by those who believe the press a valuable weapon in political warfare will provide evidence of attempts by politicians to use the press for political ends. That such attempts might prove fruitless does not detract from the fact that they have been made.'[33]

Government, war and propaganda, and news management

The use of propaganda as a systematic instrument of national and foreign policy was a twentieth-century phenomenon, and more precisely one whose origins can be located in the First World War – the bulk of the major theoretical work being done between 1918 and the end of the 1960s.[34] One of the classic discussions of this new dimension to propaganda was by Harold Lasswell, who attributed the growth of propaganda in the first part of the twentieth century to:

[11]

the social disorganisation which has been precipitated by the rapid advent of technological changes . . . Literacy and the physical channels of communication have quickened the connection between those who rule and the ruled . . . Most of that which formerly could be done by violence and intimidation must now be done by argument and persuasion.[35]

Lambert, in another early study, drew a distinction between direct and indirect methods of propaganda, contending that the latter were generally more successful because they could not be identified easily and therefore the press, 'whose existence is based on a public demand for news and information, affords the most obvious channel for propaganda'.[36] Propaganda could encompass a wide range of activities, from an attempt to influence a journalist to state-funded education and advertising programmes, and, moreover, its character and official use changed considerably over the first decades of the twentieth century. Indeed, this transition in the nature of propaganda was concentrated precisely in the wartime period that constitutes the focus of this book, while the subsequent inter-war years saw its intensity and cynical deployment reach still higher levels. Thus when administrators and politicians referred to propaganda in 1918 the associations of the word were different from those that it possessed in 1914 or had acquired by 1939.[37]

For these reasons an effort has been made to avoid referring to India Office attempts to shape news reporting as 'propagandist'. Of course, in both motives and methods its activities shared elements of the wider evolution of state propaganda, and this was still more the case with the government in India. Thus there were aspects of the Lasswellian formula governing the strategy of the propagandist discernible in their approach – 'to intensify the attitudes favourable to his purpose, to reverse the attitudes hostile to it, and to attract the indifferent, or, at the worst, to prevent them from assuming a hostile bent'.[38] Nevertheless, within Britain the actions of the India Office, and in particular Montagu, were not of the systematic and sometimes crude forms implied by the word propaganda and there were no direct attempts to control the thoughts of the masses. The opinion they wished to shape was the press opinion formulated by the editors, leader writers and proprietors of Fleet Street, who were perceived to be in a position to influence a 'newspaper-ridden people',[39] and here any heavyhandedness was likely to be almost certainly counterproductive. If anachronistic terms are to be employed, it is the techniques of modern media management – spin doctoring and rebuttal – which form perhaps the more appropriate model.

To appreciate the institutional response of the India Office in the sphere of news management and publicity, it is important to situate it within its British context, since, as Husain notes, it 'did not merely function as an Indian administrative machine but also as a machine for general imperial administration in London'.[40] Taylor's work on the Foreign Office provides a valuable model. Traditionally the most secretive of government departments,[41] the Foreign Office ironically proved the first to 'open its doors to the press', with the war providing the catalyst. The Foreign Office News Department was based on:

> a belief in the value of indirect techniques of persuasion . . . The chief targets of the News Department's propaganda were, therefore, the opinion makers and influential members of society, the principle being that it was more effective to influence those in a position to influence others than to attempt a direct appeal to the mass of the population.[42]

Taylor contends that formal relations between Whitehall and the press came to be seen as a 'necessary expedient' as the war progressed and departments were forced to 'abandon their traditional aloofness' towards journalists. Press offices provided a neutral meeting ground for the two professions, and the wartime contacts between Whitehall and the press could not simply be terminated at the end of hostilities. Indeed, increased official communication with the press was but one facet of a wider development as the arrival of new media meant that 'publicity became an established fact of British political and diplomatic life'.[43] An increase in the number of official press departments was a marked feature of government during the inter-war period: by 1938 there were more than a dozen. While Whitehall opinion varied considerably as to the desirability of persisting with propaganda in peacetime, there was a small coterie of Foreign Office officials who argued strongly for its continuance. They maintained that, because the return of peace had been accompanied by an escalation of the use of propaganda by foreign governments, there was a need to project a more balanced picture of British aims and policies.[44] Similar concern with the activity of opponents, in this case Indian nationalists and their supporters, was one of the factors prompting the India Office to continue its publicity operations while other government departments suspended theirs during the retrenchment of the 1920s.

Politics–press nexus

More generally, too, the India Office inhabited a political world that was rapidly changing. Between the 1880s and the end of the Great War the development of the mass-circulating newspaper press, and new techniques of information transmission, caused communications to play a more important role in political practice than ever before. The impact of these changes was reinforced by the fact that this was also a period of far-reaching political change, and this coincidence of developments in the spheres of communication technology and politics is crucial to our understanding of the evolving politics–press nexus. In the first place, the spread of telegraph communications and international news agencies broke the government's effective monopoly of access to foreign news. Second, the coming of mass-circulation newspapers directed towards a popular readership brought political news before a large class of people who had hitherto been beyond the reach of Westminster politics.

In these circumstances news control became an increasingly important element in the conduct of foreign and imperial policy. British official control of telegraph communications and press censorship was revealed during the Boer War, and again on a still larger scale during the First World War. This, combined with developments in cinema and wireless, contributed to a growing awareness of mass persuasion or 'propaganda' as a new technical expertise involving the manipulation of the media. As Pronay and Spring observe:

> There can be little doubt that in their perception of the political conditions and needs which had come into being after 1918, the political leaders of the period saw a direct link between politics and propaganda, and that they acted on their perceptions. This is a fact which the historian needs to take into account like other facts.[45]

The early twentieth century also witnessed a continuance of the shift, already under way by the 1880s, from the 'close community-based' politics of the mid-Victorian period to a 'more nationally class-based' politics.[46] The Parliament of 1900 rested on the votes of 3.5 million, expanding to 21 million (including 8 million women) by 1918. The arrival of a mass electorate would, it was commonly believed, open the door to demagogues and newspaper proprietors who would appeal to the poorly educated and excitable new electors. Conscription, introduced for the first time in 1916, brought with it fears that the conduct of a rational foreign policy would be hampered, with the government forced to depend upon the will of the masses as opposed to the pre-war educated elite of opinion makers. Another portentous development was the growth of the labour movement as a political and ideological force, with the potential use of the general strike reinforcing a sense of menace. In this situation the effectiveness of the new methods of propaganda and counter-subversion, tested successfully during the war, persuaded many politicians to support moves to incorporate 'propaganda' into politics. Conservatives, in particular, feared they had most to lose from the widening of the electorate, which was presumed to be largely socialist, and many were therefore persuaded of the necessity for 'political education'. Publicity efforts increased in 1918 when electoral registration was accepted as a duty of the state – 'thereafter direct publicity became the only means of contact with the voters'.[47] The government itself increasingly appealed to public opinion, motivated, according to Morgan, by the belief that public opinion 'existed', and that the 'only real problem was of communicating the truth to it without ambiguity, and then reaping the reward in public support and a lease of power'.[48] Although the belief that political legitimacy derived ultimately from popular support had grown during the nineteenth century, post-war politics were to an unprecedented extent swayed by new kinds of popular pressures. Above all, it was the uncertainty concerning the many new voters which influenced politicians, especially given that traditional party distinctions had been blurred and even dissolved during the war, with a Liberal–Conservative coalition facing a mixed opposition made up of Labour, Liberal, and independent Conservative MPs.[49] Thus developments in communications technology, newspaper organisation and the political process itself all combined to ensure that the ability of the national press to exert political leverage increased from the late nineteenth century until it reached, during the war, 'perhaps its highest point of influence'.[50]

To view the politics–press nexus from the perspective of the press highlights its symbiotic character. The propensity of the press to seek alliances with political interests was, of course, nothing new and had existed in varying degrees since its beginnings in the 1620s, motivated initially by sheer survival, and later by financial gain and the means to garner influence and prestige. Governments, in turn, utilised and subsidised newspapers, whilst subjecting them to a variety of punitive fiscal controls – the so-called taxes on knowledge – until the mid-nineteenth century.[51] The late nineteenth century witnessed a struggle for press power as politicians displayed 'an increasingly acute sensitivity to newspaper criticism, however much they might discount the impact or belittle the source'.[52] The declining fortunes of Liberalism were reflected in its press. The 'new journalism', which was regarded as 'depoliticising' the press, was especially worrisome to Liberals, who saw the press as an educative institution, safeguarding liberty and democracy. Therefore 'to become non-political or even less politically orthodox, was, in effect, to capitulate to the Unionist ascendancy'.[53] However, the political dimension remained a significant for most papers. In his study of the 1910 general elections Blewett estimated that at least seventeen metropolitan dailies backed the parties.[54] Further, even those papers which ostensibly eschewed a strong political line were not necessarily anti-political: 'There was,' argues Koss, 'nothing to prevent a paper which postured at being above or outside party from promoting party causes, participating in party wrangles, or serving political ambitions.'[55]

In terms of professed political association Fleet Street, by the early twentieth century, was preponderantly Conservative. In 1910 the Conservatives had a big lead in terms of circulation in the morning press – around 2.5 million, compared with the Liberals' 0.8 million – though the press was no more united than its party. For evening papers the figures were in the range of 0.6 million and 0.3 million to the Conservatives and Liberals respectively. Only amongst Sunday papers did the Liberals have a clear lead, with something like 4.75 million to the Conservatives' 0.6 million.[56] By 1914 the Liberal Party could count on only three London morning papers, as opposed to the Conservatives' seven, and two evening papers, against the latter's four.[57] Many observers acknowledged that the important role of the newspaper was in keeping rather than winning the voter: 'by action analogous to that of water dripping on a stone, [it] keeps him loyal to the party'.[58] Modern studies have confirmed this view.[59] Journalists were always liable to enter the political sphere and many had a foot in both camps. Harold Spender, successively of the *Daily News*, *Guardian* and *Morning Leader*, became in 1909 secretary of Lloyd George's Budget League, C. P. Scott, while editor of the *Guardian*, was an MP for ten years and President of the Manchester Liberal Federation. There was an increasing number of professed 'journalists' in the Commons after the 1880s – partly because journalism helped pay the bills of an impecunious MP (a large proportion of Irish and Labour MPs were identified as 'journalists'). By 1906 Thomas calculates that journalists were the third largest occupational group in the Commons, after the law and services.[60] It was a similar story with proprietors: before 1880 there were six or fewer newspaper proprietors in the Commons; in 1880 the figure more than doubled to fourteen and rose subsequently to between twenty and thirty. Although representation and association were not guarantees of 'influence', the connections were important both for politicians, who gained outlets for opinion, and for journalists, who were given access to information and an opportunity to communicate their ideas.

The Edwardian period saw a number of divisive political controversies, not only between parties but also within them, and neither the Conservative nor the Liberal press was consistently of one mind on many of the important issues. Influential editors like Garvin of the Unionist *Observer* and Massingham of the Liberal *Nation*, while valued for their views within the party context, were capable of fermenting controversy and arguing against a party position.[61] Furthermore, the popular press manifested an interest in subjects besides politics, rather than a loss of interest in politics as such, and Curran contends that the press barons:

> did not break with tradition by using their papers for political propaganda; their distinctive contribution was rather that they downgraded propaganda in favour of entertainment. Nor did they subvert the role of the press as a fourth estate: on the contrary it was they who detached the commercial press from political parties and, consequently, from government.[62]

Though the industrialisation of the press had been going on apace from well before the turn of the century, there was more than a shade of truth in the remark of Kennedy Jones, manager of the *Mail*, to John Morley: 'You left journalism a profession, we have made it a branch of commerce.'[63] Financial success was the overriding goal of the new breed of proprietors, and it was solvency and profits, as demonstrated by the mass-circulating *Mail*, that made 'independence' a tangible proposition for the press. Northcliffe, contends Seymour-Ure, 'cut the knot of political subsidy that so often joined papers to parties. Instead, he wove a cat's-cradle of advertising subsidies.'[64] To achieve economic viability *and* political power it was necessary to win a large enough circulation to attract advertisers without alienating the politically important elite. The competition of the mass-circulation press made such papers as the *Westminster Gazette* (hereafter *Gazette*) commercially obsolete. The fate of the Liberal daily *The Tribune*, which folded within two years of its commencement in 1906, illustrates the manner in which commercial and political pressures affected the more radical of the political journals.[65] The experience of the Labour papers during this period reveals a similar plight. Increasing circulation with insufficient advertising was the *Daily Herald*'s (hereafter *Herald*) nightmare, as George Lansbury wrote: 'The more copies we sold, the more money we lost.'[66] Economic and technical changes were also weakening the older journalistic basis of the political press. Such papers catered for a smaller constituency than could now secure financial viability. They had either to find external support or lower their price and increase advertising revenue, and this meant aiming for compromise and the middle ground. The small-circulation press survived, but with changes. Of those which had preserved their traditional standards, most papers had done so at the expense of their financial, and thus political, independence.

Every editor, with the exception of Scott, Maxse and Strachey, was under the control of a proprietor, and several important papers relied on political benefactors to keep them solvent. Indeed, under pressure from the 'new journalism' the quality press was compelled to seek financial support from wealthy patrons with political motives, like Cadbury, Rowntree and Thomasson. The Cadburys bought the *Daily News* in 1901 and Lloyd George sat on its board for some years. Lloyd George acquired the *Daily Chronicle* (hereafter *Chronicle*) with the help of Lord Dalziel and party funds and made an unsuccessful attempt to buy *The Times* after Northcliffe's death. The *Globe* and the *Standard* were in receipt of Conservative subsidies. The *Pall Mall Gazette* 'continued to gnaw at the Astor family fortune', the *Gazette* was 'a burden cheerfully borne by Newnes'.[67] Political benefactors, parties and syndicates were thus prepared to carry on subsidising papers. So the Northcliffe revolution, which ultimately freed newspapers from dependence on such contributions, initially had the effect of reviving the political financing of the press.

The notion of the power and influence of the press has been an underlying theme in the above discussion. Yet, although widely referred to then and since, studied considerations of the question have tended to arrive at sceptical conclusions concerning the extent of press influence. Lee, for example, has argued that the increasingly Conservative leanings of the press in the late nineteenth century did not give the Conservative Party any tangible benefits, or exercise much influence on voters or politicians. 'This failure, perhaps more than the decline of the old Liberal press at the same time, was due witness to the advent of both a "new journalism" and a "new politics".'[68] Curran is similarly convinced that there was 'no close correspondence between the climate of opinion in the country and the political character of the press'.[69] Certainly, that the press did not have the power to control how someone voted was demonstrated by Gladstone's defeat in 1874 – the year in which the Liberals had the greatest lead in the press they ever enjoyed.[70] Similarly, the Liberal landslide of 1906 occurred when the London Unionist dailies had an aggregate circulation three times that of their Liberal rivals.[71]

What is less contestable is that readers and writers alike believed that the press had pervasive influence. 'Mistaken or not,' contends Koss, 'this conviction created its own reality.'[72] The journalism of the quality press undoubtedly played a part in shaping opinion amongst the politically informed elites. But how important was this influence? During the nineteenth century many came to see the press as a powerful factor in politics – an unofficial fourth estate in the constitution. Journalists encouraged this idea, since it added authority and prestige to what had previously been a less than respectable trade. As late as 1829 Walter Scott could write to his son-in-law Lockhart, 'Your connection with any newspaper would be a disgrace and degradation. I would rather sell gin to poor people and poison them that way.'[73] But it was also, paradoxically, fostered by the nineteenth-century parliamentary culture. A diverse range of public men utilised the political press to bring pressure to bear on affairs of state. 'Seizing upon the press out of hope, out of desperation, or simply out of habit, they sedulously fostered newspapermen's self-images.'[74] While the press could not always shape party policy, both the popular and the quality press helped to expound it. Furthermore, Gwynne argued that, though the power of the press had been exaggerated, in terms of its impact on individual careers it could achieve much: 'It can kill men. It can make men.'[75]

The popular press did not exert a direct influence upon elite opinion formation. Its influence, if it existed, was indirect, exerted via the massed numbers of its readers. Northcliffe, for instance, liked to believe that his circulation success was 'balanced by an equal power to influence public and political opinion'. Williams, however, doubts this claim, believing that he voiced rather than formed the political prejudices of his readers.[76] On the other hand, Spender was of the opinion that Northcliffe was 'immensely important, however much solemn people might try to blink or evade the fact. He and his imitators influenced the common mind more than all the Education Ministers put together; of all the influences that destroyed the old politics . . . he was by far the most powerful.'[77] Here again perceptions helped to create reality. In Inwood's words, it was 'not the fact that Northcliffe controlled public opinion, but the fact that many politicians thought he did, that gave him his power. The *Daily Mail* did not persuade politicians, but it frightened them, and Northcliffe acquired an influence over those who feared him.'[78]

As is apparent, there is an important difference between press and public opinion, and it is with the former that we are concerned. The two are nonetheless connected, and in considering the history of the period the dimensions of this relationship have to be borne in mind. During the nineteenth century there were few opportunities for public opinion, in the sense of the views and attitudes held by large numbers of the population, to be recorded outside general elections. Elections themselves were held infrequently, with the electors usually being asked to choose between parties rather than specific issues, and in any case many either could not or did not vote. Accordingly there was a strong temptation to regard newspaper opinion as a proxy for a wider public opinion.

Of course, in the absence of knowledge of public opinion, any suggestion that newspapers were barometers of public opinion must remain unproven and the issue is one which has generated much controversy amongst historians. However, while historians can debate the relationship between press and public opinion, this luxury was not open to politicians. For them press reporting, by the fact of its volume, relentlessness and articulateness, could not be ignored. In the absence of alternative insights into public attitudes, there is no doubt that many politicians acted on the assumption that press opinion was tantamount to public opinion. For some this identification was itself unwelcome: Peel, writing to Croker in 1820, described public opinion as 'that great compound of folly, weakness, prejudice, wrong feeling, right feeling, obstinacy and newspaper paragraphs'.[79] To others, like James Mill and Jeremy Bentham, public opinion was the opinion of the enlightened and informed classes – a safeguard against misrule and the characteristic of a democratic state. Yet to twentieth-century writers, especially after the Great War, public opinion was equated with the masses and the crowd; the non-rational emotional aspects were emphasised and the competence of public opinion was questioned. However, welcomed or not, it was primarily press opinion that politicians responded to and sought to influence.[80] In the case of Indian affairs this preoccupation with press opinion was still more marked, since in most cases it was – quite reasonably – believed that there were no definitely held public beliefs on details of Indian government. It was a relatively small group of informed writers in the quality press which interpreted the government's handling of Indian issues for the wider class of politically interested readers and fellow politicians.

An additional – and somewhat contradictory – factor influencing contemporary perspectives on the press and public opinion was the idea that newspapers did not simply mirror the opinion of their readers but also shaped it. In other words, public opinion reflected newspaper opinion, a belief which then and since has reinforced the concern of politicians with press coverage. Harding, in a 1937 survey, claimed that there was some reason to believe that in times of crisis people turned more to their newspapers and other media for guidance than was normally the case. Though there were limits to such power, to deny that newspapers 'have an influence, and a very great influence, on public opinion is fantastic'. The press, 'talking to a vast public, about a wide range of topics, with some extra prestige . . . with immensely greater adroitness, and with better sources of information, must be extremely potent moulders of opinion'.[81] Another early writer, A. L. Lowell, argued that much of the influence of the press was exerted by the process of 'directing attention'. An effect was produced by 'coloring the news', not by distortion or lies but by according 'greater prominence to those things which conform to the paper's point of view'.[82]

Equally, the opposite held true – the power to 'suppress' by omission could influence response. Every newspaper, Lippman similarly observed, was the result of a series of selections, and it was in the combination of these elements and the paper's ability to evoke a personal reaction from the reader that 'the power to create opinion resides'.[83] Certainly, no historian wishing to gauge public opinion during the Crimean or Boer Wars could neglect the impact of the contemporary press. Waley has argued along such lines in his study of British public opinion during the Abyssinian War, while studies of the role of the press in the Great War have revealed comparable consensus.[84] These historiographical analyses all find a place in the discussion of the press response to India via in-depth case studies.

Public opinion, as Boyce concludes, is 'mainly what contemporaries perceived it to be'.[85] Many were convinced that the press influenced the public, and it is implausible to assume that there was no connection between the two. What is of importance is that a substantial number of politicians believed that there existed a correlation between press and public opinion and acted upon the belief.

Fleet Street and the Indian empire

Much debate has been generated in recent years regarding the cultural representations of, and British attitudes to, India and Indians, created in literary and pictorial genres, travelogues, records and memoirs. Surprisingly, there has been no systematic study of the national newspaper press in relation to Britain's largest imperial possession, and those who have worked on imperial themes, like Startt, or on specific papers, like Wilson's history of the *Morning Post*, have tended to overlook India as a special, and indeed relatively less important, case.[86] Only a handful of modern studies have dealt in detail with such issues. In a thesis tracing the history of the empire during the years following the Seven Years War as witnessed from the perspective of the press, J. P. Thomas argues that Company in-fighting 'became of interest to the periodicals, and the periodicals themselves became of immense interest to the infighters as a theatre for their quarrels'.[87] Peter Marshall paints a similar picture in connection with domestic newspaper response to the Company's battles with Tipu Sultan in the 1790s.[88] Palmegiano's article on the coverage of the Mutiny or Great Rebellion of 1857–58 in specialist periodicals such as *Blackwood's* and *Bentley's Magazine* found reinforcement of contemporary stereotypes such as the cultural and racial divide between East and West, the valour – physical and moral – of the Christian soldier, with material being targeted at home audiences having professional and family connections with the subcontinent.[89] In an attempt to promote the study of nineteenth-century print media in relation to India, D. Peers contends that British periodicals exhibited a marked rise in interest in the subcontinent from the 1820s onwards, with India and the public fascination with wars playing an 'increasingly important role in the developing military press'.[90] Peers and Finklestein claim that newspapers and periodicals 'present sites of reference potentially more influential and valuable in discussions of otherness, colonial, national, ethnic, gender and professional identities, than those often sought and sometimes found between book covers'.[91]

In an earlier study K. K. Aziz utilised a small sample of quality newspapers and weeklies in his analysis of the response of British public opinion to the development of Muslim nationalism in India after 1857. He concludes that 'on the whole' this opinion was 'not well informed' on Muslim India, the blame lying equally with the Muslims and British. One reason why the Muslim case went by default, he claims, was that Muslims had 'practically no press in India', and that British newspapers and agencies 'had to recruit from a journalistic pool where Hindus predominated'.[92] While Aziz's study contains many suggestive points, their development is rather limited. The relationship between the press and public opinion is not fully explored and the discussion of the interaction between the press and politics is similarly undeveloped.

Press and politics within India

Whilst the interaction between politicians and Fleet Street has not been analysed with reference to the subcontinent, the relationship between the Raj and the Indian press has been a significant sphere of study. Ironically, though the British introduced the modern form of newspapers to late eighteenth-century India,[93] the relationship between journalists and officials was always uneasy and often hostile. As Griffiths notes, 'the battle for the liberty of the Press was not as might have been expected, fought by Indians in defence of their own freedom. It was rather a struggle between non-official Englishmen and the Company.'[94] Interestingly, this paralleled, and no doubt also reflected, the social and political constraints under which the press was functioning in Victorian Britain and its campaigns against punitive government sanctions. Margarita Barns's classic account (1940) analysed the development of modern newspapers as both an expression and a determinant of a growing public opinion within the subcontinent, and there have been several subsequent studies of the political context of the growth of the press, the role of the Raj, and the successful utilisation of newspapers in the service of nationalism.[95]

In *Banned*, an incisive account of the exercise of political control, Barrier has traced the government's deployment of censorship and propaganda, including the use of the print media. Whereas government had previously 'preferred a low-key policy of informal influence over the press instead of direct subsidies and persistent application of penalties', by the end of 1905 the situation had changed 'dramatically'. This was due to a variety of factors, including the mass politicisation of the nationalist movement, their utilisation of the expanding print media, and in response the attempt by government to belittle the Indian National Congress (INC) as a competent political adversary. Barrier claims that Parliament and Secretaries of State 'exhibited no consistent attitude toward freedom of the Indian press. Rather, home concerns depended on the party in power, the personalities of India Office officials, and the situation both in Europe and in India.' Similarly, the government in India appreciated that their actions would receive 'careful review and occasional public debate' in Britain and this fact 'narrowed the options' open to it.[96]

More recently Bayly has contended that there emerged in the nineteenth century 'an all-India information order'.[97] He examines the extent to which 'intelligence failures and successes' contributed to the Rebellion of 1857 and contends that it was 'at the point of intersection between political intelligence and indigenous knowledge [that] colonial rule was at its most vulnerable'. 'The British were now reaping the consequences of the information revolution which they had set into train. To a much greater extent than any earlier Anglo-Indian encounter, this was a modern war of propaganda.'[98] The survival of the British was predicated in large part on their mobilisation of a worldwide system of communications and their reliance on the electric telegraph.[99] As we shall see, Bayly's recognition of the paradoxical impact of information in the context of the Mutiny points to what was, in fact, a fundamental and wide-ranging paradox relating to the role of information and communications in the system of British rule in India.

The most comprehensive survey of relations between the Indian press, the Government of India and the nationalist movement in the subcontinent has been made by Milton Israel. Focusing upon the ' "national" communications institutions' involved in the Indian struggle for independence between the wars and the officials, journalists and propagandists who participated in this enterprise, he argues that during the first half of the twentieth century the press–politics nexus in India developed along the lines identified by Koss in Victorian England:

[23]

politicians sought the control of newspapers and newspapermen went into politics. And in both societies there appeared to be an insatiable interest in political news . . . But the nature of the Anglo-Indian colonial society and the development of organized nationalist politics made the comparison difficult for the Government of India to accept.[100]

For the government a priority was the establishment of an information system that would allow it to compete with the developing communications network of the nationalist movement. However uncomfortable with the 'new environment of debate and popular understanding', the government saw that public opinion had 'become important' and it was accordingly 'determined to influence it'.[101] Such perspectives complement our preoccupation with the response of the British at home and help to elucidate the motivations of both ruler and ruled in their interaction with the media. *Reporting the Raj* is concerned with the print culture of empire in Britain. However this culture not only linked metropolis and periphery but was seized upon as a crucial element in the developing national consciousness.

Conclusion

Henry Sumner Maine once remarked that British rulers in India were like men bound to make their watches keep time in two longitudes at once[102] – prompting the Secretary of State, John Morley, to wonder how this could be done. In attempting an answer, he vehemently dismissed the notion that wise rule in the subcontinent would be 'overthrown by the folly of democracy here'. Instead, he argued, 'if we realise the enormous weight, complexity, delicacy, and hazards of all the obligations . . . that arise from our connexion with the great Asiatic continent, Indian questions need far more close, and especially more consecutive attention from politicians, press, perhaps even from cabinets, than has hitherto been the fashion'.[103] Morley made these remarks in the context of a review of *Indian Unrest*, by Valentine Chirol, the veteran journalist whose book was based on his in-depth series of articles in *The Times* (1910) that had provoked considerable attention in Britain. Indeed, Morley himself recognised that Chirol's book was itself a sign that the 'deficiency of interest in India were being repaired'. The following decade more than bore out Morley's prognosis, as Indian coverage attained a depth and range not previously witnessed. Underlying this shift was an on-going communication revolution which generated as many questions as opportunities for the development of British rule in India. *Reporting the Raj* focuses upon the interaction of communications and the forms of imperial organisation and practice in Britain *vis-à-vis* India and investigates the reactions of politicians and administrators to the growth of the press and the widening of channels of information in the late nineteenth and early twentieth centuries. This was an important factor changing the nature and practice of British rule and the extent and potency of the nationalist challenge. Governments seeking to shape perceptions of their Indian policy and govern in conditions of increasing transparency were forced to develop more systematic approaches to imperial control and news management through the media in Britain.

Notes

1   Cited in D. M. Chapman-Huston (ed.), *Subjects of the Day* (1915), p. 10.
2   J. S. Mills, *Press and Communications of the Empire* (1924), p. 109; J. A. Spender, *Life, Journalism and Politics* (1927) I, p. 224.
3   Cited in M. Bromley and T. O'Malley (eds), *A Journalism Reader* (1997), p. 62.
4   R. J. Deibert, *Parchment, Printing, and Hypermedia* (New York, 1997), p. ix.; see C. Marvin, *When old Technologies were New* (New York, 1987); E. Eisenstein, *Printing Press as an Agent of Change* (Cambridge, 1979); D. Crowley and P. Heyer (eds), *Communication in History: Technology, Culture, and Society* (New York, 1991); P. Heyer, *Communications and History* (New Haven CT, 1988).
5   K. W. Deutsch, *The Nerves of Government* (1963).
6   D. R. Headrick, *Tools of Empire: Technology and European Imperialism in the Nineteenth Century* (1981) and *Tentacles of Progress: Technology Transfer in the Age of Imperialism, 1850–1940* (Oxford, 1988).
7   M. McLuhan, *The Gutenberg Galaxy* (Toronto, 1962), *Understanding Media: The Extensions of Man* (New York, 1967 edn), *The Medium is the Message* (1967). Works influenced by Innis include E. Havelock, *Preface to Plato* (Cambridge MA, 1963), J. Goody (ed.), *Literacy and Traditional Societies* (Cambridge, 1968).
8   H. A. Innis, *Empire and Communication* (Toronto, 1986 edn), p. 5.
9   H. A. Innis, *The Bias of Communication* (Toronto, 1995 edn), p. 33.
10 Innis, *Empire and Communication*, p. 4.
11 *Ibid.*, p. 169.
12 P. Davidson, *Propaganda and the American Revolution, 1763–1783* (Chapel Hill NC, 1941), p. 157; P. M. Taylor, *Munitions of the Mind* (Manchester, 1995), pp. 133–44.
13 B. Anderson, *Imagined Communities: Reflections on the Origin and Spread of Nationalism* (1983), pp. 35–44, 133–4.
14 N. and J. MacKenzie (eds), *The Diary of Beatrice Webb* (1983) II, p. 118.
15 R. H. MacDonald, *Language of Empire* (Manchester, 1994), p. 2.
16 G. S. Messinger, *British Propaganda and the State in the First World War* (Manchester, 1992), p. 13.
17 J. O. Baylen, 'Politics and the new journalism', in J. H. Wiener (ed.), *Papers for the Millions* (Westport CT, 1988), pp. 110–11.
18 Gwynne to Bathurst, 27 July 1911, 1990/1/2162, Glenesk-Bathurst Papers, Leeds University (hereafter G-B).
19 J. St Loe Strachey, *Adventure of Living* (1922), p. 298.
20 J. M. MacKenzie, *Propaganda and Empire* (Manchester, 1984), pp. 6–7; J. M. MacKenzie (ed.), *Popular Imperialism and the Military, 1850–1950* (Manchester, 1992); D. Lowry (ed.), *The South African War Reappraised* (2000); D. Omissi and A. S. Thompson (eds), *The Impact of the South African War* (Basingstoke, 2002).
21 J. D. Startt, *Journalists for Empire* (Westport CT, 1991), p. 214; A. S. Thompson, *Imperial Britain* (Harlow, 2000), pp. 61–80.
22 Startt, *Journalists for Empire*, pp. 3–4.

23 J. M. MacKenzie (ed.), *Imperialism and Popular Culture* (Manchester, 1986), pp. 10–11.
24 *Ibid.*, p. 2.
25 K. Castle, *Britannia's Children* (Manchester, 1994), p. 4.
26 S. Koss, *Rise and Fall of the Political Press in Britain* (1990 edn), pp. 21–3, 424; A. J. Lee, *The Origins of the Popular Press in England, 1855–1914* (1976), p. 76; J. G. Tunstall, *Media in Britain* (1983), p. 76.
27 S. Inwood, 'Role of the Press in English Politics during the First World War', Oxford University D.Phil. thesis (1971), p. 393.
28 C. Kaul. 'The press', in B. Brivati, A. Seldon and J. Buxton (eds), *Contemporary History Handbook* (Manchester, 1996), pp. 298–310.
29 P. M. Taylor, *Projection of Britain: British Overseas Publicity and Propaganda, 1919–1939* (Cambridge, 1981), p. 4; J. Gould and W. L. Kolb (eds), *A Dictionary of the Social Sciences* (1964), p. 547.
30 Viceroy to Secretary of State, 5 May 1921, Montagu Collection MSS Eur D523/14, (hereafter MC/no.).
31 E. Katz, in T. Glasser and C. T. Shannon (eds), *Public Opinion and the Communication of Consent* (New York, 1995), p. xxiii.
32 The economic dimension of empire is not examined here, nor does Ireland form part of this work except in so far as the press drew parallels between the Indian and Irish situations.
33 Lee, *Origins*, p. 182.
34 R. Cole, *Propaganda in Twentieth Century War and Politics* (1996), p. 6; J. B. Black, *Organising the Propaganda Instrument* (1975), p. 1.
35 H. D. Lasswell, 'Theory of political propaganda', in B. Berelson and M. Janowitz (eds), *Reader in Public Opinion and Communication* (1953 edn), pp. 178, 180; J. Hargrave, *Words win Wars* (1940).
36 R. S. Lambert, *Propaganda* (1938), p. 45; F. C. Bartlett, *Political Propaganda* (Cambridge, 1942), p. 134.
37 R. Cockett, *Twilight of Truth* (1989); S. Ross, *World War Two Propaganda* (New York, 1993); B. Morris, *Roots of Appeasement* (1991).
38 Lasswell, 'Theory of political propaganda', p. 178.
39 Lord Burnham, cited in Mills, *Press and Communication*, p. xiv.
40 S. A. Husain, 'Organisation and Administration of the India Office, 1910–24', London University Ph.D. thesis (1978), p. 322.
41 Z. Steiner, *Foreign Office and Foreign Policy, 1898–1914* (Cambridge, 1969).
42 P. Taylor, 'Publicity and diplomacy' in D. Dilks (ed.), *Retreat from Power* (1981) I, pp. 48–9.
43 *Ibid.*, pp. 55–6, 62.
44 *Ibid.*, pp. 49–50.
45 N. Pronay and D. W. Spring (eds), *Propaganda, Politics and Film, 1918–45* (1982), p. 18.
46 P. F. Clarke, *Lancashire and the New Liberalism* (Cambridge, 1971), p. 6.
47 R. Cockett, 'Party, publicity, and the media', in A. Seldon and S. Bell (eds), *Conservative Century* (1994), p. 547. In 1910 Malcolm Fraser became the first press adviser to Conservative Central Office.
48 K. O. Morgan, *Consensus and Disunity: The Lloyd George Coalition Government, 1918–1922* (Oxford, 1979), pp. 149–50.
49 *Ibid.*, p. 155.
50 A. J. P. Taylor, *English History, 1914–1945* (1965), p. 262.
51 For the fight against these restrictions see J. Wiener, *War of the Unstamped* (New York, 1969); A. Aspinall, *Politics and the Press* (1949); P. Hollis, *The Pauper Press* (1970); for a re-evaluation see J. Curran and J. Seaton, *Power without Responsibility: The Press and Broadcasting in Britain* (1995 edn), pp. 9–47; G. Boyce, 'The fourth estate: reappraisal of a concept', in G. Boyce, J. Curran and P. Wingate (eds), *Newspaper History from the Seventeenth Century to the Present* (1978), pp. 19–40.

52 Koss, *Rise and Fall*, p. 198.
53 *Ibid.*, p. 361; Lee, *Origins*, p. 209.
54 N. Blewett, *Peers, the Parties and the People* (1972), p. 301.
55 Koss, *Rise and Fall*, pp. 360–1, 408.
56 Lee, *Origins*, p. 179.
57 J. M. McEwan, 'The national press during the First World War', *JCH*, 17: 3 (1982),
    466. The growth of the Labour Party was unaccompanied by the corresponding
    development of a Labour press.
58 M. Ostrogorski, cited in Lee, *Origins*, p. 187; F. Taylor, *Newspaper Press as a Power*
    (1898), p. 18.
59 D. Butler and D. Stokes, *Political Change in Britain* (1971); M. Linton, *Was it the
    Sun what won it?* (Oxford, 1995); M. Scammel and M. Harrop, 'The press', in D.
    Butler and D. Kavanagh (eds), *British General Election of 1997* (1997).
60 J. A. Thomas, *House of Commons, 1906–1911* (1958), pp. 22–3.
61 H. W. Havighurst, *Radical Journalist: J. W. Massingham* (1974); D. Ayerst, *Garvin
    of the* Observer (1985); J. Stubbs, 'The *Observer* and J. L. Garvin', in Boyce *et al.*,
    Newspaper History, pp. 320–38.
62 Curran and Seaton, *Power without Responsibility*, pp. 49–50
63 Cited in H. Fyfe, *Sixty Years of Fleet Street* (1949), p. 77
64 C. Seymour-Ure, 'Press and party system between the wars', in G. Peele and C.
    Cook (eds), *Politics of Reappraisal* (1975), p. 247.
65 Lee, *Origins*, p. 167; Koss, *Rise and Fall*, pp. 494–9.
66 G. Lansbury, *Miracle of Fleet Street* (1925), p. 161.
67 Koss, *Rise and Fall*, p. 421.
68 Lee, *Origins*, p. 178.
69 Curran and Seaton, *Power without Responsibility*, p. 33.
70 Lee, *Origins*, p. 134.
71 A. K. Russell, *Liberal Landslide* (1973), pp. 138–9.
72 Koss, *Rise and Fall*, p. 7.
73 Cited in F. Williams, *Dangerous Estate* (1957), p. 48.
74 Koss, *Rise and Fall*, pp. 445–7.
75 H. A. Gwynne, 'The independent newspaper', *Sell's* (1913), p. 41.
76 Williams, *Dangerous Estate*, p. 139.
77 Spender, *Life* II, p. 170.
78 Inwood, 'Press in English politics', p. 25.
79 L. J. Jennings (ed.), *Correspondence and Diaries of J. W. Croker* (1884) I, p. 170;
    Though Bagehot, editor of the *Economist*, observed that Peel was, of contempo-
    rary politicians, the most sensitive to the shifting pattern of public opinion,
    tending to change his mind on important issues only when the average man did
    so. (W. Bagehot, *Biographical Studies*, 1881, p. 7.)
80 Peel himself placed articles in the *Quarterly Review* defending his policies;
    Palmerston kept up with a range of influential editors, as did Disraeli, Gladstone,
    Milner, Joseph Chamberlain and Lloyd George.
81 D. W. Harding, 'General conceptions of the study of public opinion', *Sociological
    Review*, 29: 4 (1937), 371; D. Katz *et al.* (eds), *Public Opinion and Propaganda*
    (New York, 1954); R. E. Lane and D. O. Sears (eds), *Public Opinion* (Englewood
    Cliffs NJ, 1964).
82 A. L. Lowell, *Public Opinion in War and Peace* (Cambridge MA, 1923), pp. 104–5.
83 W. Lippman, *Public Opinion* (New York, 1997 edn), p. 224.
84 D. Waley, *British Public Opinion and the Abyssinian War, 1935–1936* (1975).
85 D. G. Boyce, 'Public opinion and historians', *History*, 63 (June 1978), p. 225.
86 K. M. Wilson, *A Study in the History and Politics of the* Morning Post, *1905–1926*
    (Lampeter, 1990), p. 2.
87 J. P. Thomas, 'British Empire and the Press, 1763–1774', Oxford University D.Phil.
    thesis (1982), pp. 233–50.
88 P. J. Marshall, ' "Cornwallis Triumphant": war in India and the British public in
    the late eighteenth century', in L. Freedman, P. Hayes and R. O'Neill (eds), *War,*

Strategy and International Politics: Essays in Honour of Sir Michael Howard (Oxford, 1992), pp. 57–74.

89 E. Palmegiano, 'The Indian Mutiny in the mid-Victorian press', *Journal of Newspaper and Periodical History*, 7 (1991), 3–11.

90 D. M. Peers, ' "Those Noble Exemplars of the True Military Tradition': constructions of the Indian army in the mid-Victorian press', *MAS*, 31: 1 (1997), 120.

91 D. Finkelstein and D. M. Peers (eds), *Negotiating India in the Nineteenth Century Media* (2000), pp. 17–18.

92 K. K. Aziz, *Britain and Muslim India* (1963), p. 205.

93 They also built upon a long-standing indigenous tradition of newsletters and information gathering. (M. H. Fisher, 'The office of Akhbar Nawis: the transition from Mughal to British forms', *MAS*, 27: 1, 1993, 45–82.)

94 P. Griffiths, *British Impact on India* (1952), p. 266; W. H. Wickwar, *Struggle for the Freedom of the Press* (1928), pp. 275–9.

95 M. Barns, *The Indian Press* (1940); J. Natarajan, *History of Indian Journalism*, Part II of Government of India Press Commission (Delhi, 1997 edn); S. Natarajan, *A History of the Press in India* (1962); P. Narain, *Press and Politics in India, 1885–1905* (Delhi, 1970); G. N. S. Raghavan, *The Press in India* (New Delhi, 1994), S. Ghosh, *Modern History of Indian Press* (Delhi, 1998).

96 N. G. Barrier, *Banned: Controversial Literature and Political Control in British India, 1907–1947* (Columbia MO, 1974), pp. 8–9, 53, 157–8, respectively.

97 C. Bayly, *Empire and Information: Intelligence Gathering and Social Communication in India, 1780–1870* (Cambridge, 1996), p. ix; also 'Knowing the country: empire and information in India', *MAS*, 27: 1 (1993), 3–43.

98 Bayly, *Empire and Information*, pp. 2, 322, 336.

99 See also J. W. Kaye, *History of the Sepoy War* (7th edn, 1875); P. J. O. Taylor (ed.), *A Companion to the Indian Mutiny* (Delhi, 1996), p. 91.

100 M. Israel, *Communications and Power: Propaganda and the Press in the Indian Nationalist Struggle, 1920–47* (Cambridge, 1994), p. 19.

101 *Ibid.*, pp. 7, 19–20, 29, 40, 44.

102 H. S. Maine, 'The Effects of Observation of India on Modern European Thought', Rede Lecture (Cambridge, 1875).

103 J. Morley, 'British democracy and Indian government', *Nineteenth Century and After*, 69 (February 1911), 189–90.

PART I

The networks of information and communication

CHAPTER TWO

Communications
and the Indian empire

The distance and difficulty of transmission, as well as the prohibitive costs involved in collection, had traditionally regulated news of the Indian empire. It was considered a great achievement when, in 1797, regular monthly communication was established between India and London via Basra and Aleppo. In 1825 the mails from Calcutta to Falmouth took nearly four months. Though the sea voyage was much reduced by the opening of an overland route from Suez to Alexandria ten years later, the time taken was still nearly seven weeks.[1] By 1852 the average time taken for mail to reach England from Bombay and Calcutta varied between thirty three and forty four days. The Suez Canal (1869), allied with the introduction of the steamship, impacted dramatically on these journey times. By 1913 the average time of travel by steamship from London to Bombay was twenty-one days and if the twenty-three- hour overland route from London to Marseilles was undertaken the sea journey time could be reduced to only fourteen days; and if the special train to Brindisi which took two days was used, then the sea voyage was further reduced to eleven days.[2]

The electric telegraph

In terms of the transmission of information and ideas the crucial breakthrough was the establishment of electric telegraph links between metropolis and periphery. As the *Observer* remarked when the Prince of Wales visited India in 1875–76, 'news of his progress came by every mail four weeks later'; during his grandson's tour in 1921 he was 'in hourly touch with the Royal Family at home'.[3] Imperial communications were irrevocably transformed by the opening of the Indo-European line in early 1865.[4] Government and imperial strategists were concerned with the telegraph route to India from the outset. The Red Sea & India Telegraph Company was formed in 1857 with a cable passing through Europe to the Red Sea, and thence to Muscat and Karachi. Although the government initially guaranteed the company's dividend, and later offered an annual subsidy of £36,000, the project failed.[5] The Government of India then decided to take the matter into its own hands. The first section, from London to Constantinople, was already complete. Turkey was planning a landline as far as Baghdad, and by agreement it was arranged that it should be continued from Baghdad to Fao at the mouth of the Shatt el Arab. A cable of 1,450 miles was then laid between Fao and Karachi by the Indo-European Telegraph Department (IETD) of the Government of India. Though the opening of the route was delayed until 1865, for the next five years this line earned over £100,000 a year for its promoters.[6] The Indian government also financed the building of a landline across Persia from Bushire to Teheran, and shortly another service was inaugurated between Teheran and Moscow, and this was connected to the earlier line. Thus there were, by the end of the 1860s, two possible routes between Western Europe and India: one via Constantinople and the other via Moscow.[7] Transmission, however, was exceedingly slow, taking on average five days.[8] Also, given the state of Anglo-Russian relations, Britain could never rely on the Moscow route, and the unreliability of the Turkish route was therefore more worrying.

The delays in messages between England and India were the subject of widespread complaint and a parliamentary select committee took evidence in 1866. Recognising the opportunity for providing a line connecting Britain and India entirely in the hands of one private company, the German firm of Werner von Siemens founded the Indo-European Telegraph Company. Commencing operations in 1870, this was an amalgam of land and sea lines, which joined up with the Indian government lines in Teheran.[9] The average speed of messages to and from India was reduced from thirty-seven hours in 1870 to eight and a half in 1871 and six in 1872.[10]

Yet it almost immediately faced a rival in the shape of the British Indian Telegraph Company, whose submarine cables connected Alexandria and Bombay via the Red Sea and Aden. In 1872 this company and five others merged to form the Eastern Telegraph Company (ETC). The ensuing competition meant prolonged losses for the Indo-European until it agreed to share profits with the ETC through a joint purse agreement in 1875.[11] The IETD soon joined this scheme, in which each partner paid its net receipts into a common fund and then drew out a sum calculated on the basis of the average revenue generated by each route.[12] The ETC route consisted entirely of submarine cables, and the company had to pay only a small royalty on landlines in Britain. The Indo-European, by contrast, was made up of

Table 2.1 Cis- and trans-India joint purse
divisions, 1901 (%)

Route	Cis- (up to) India messages	Trans- (beyond) India messages
ETC	59.8	80.3
Indo-European	22.1	12.0
IETD	18.1	7.4

Source Memo by Director-in-chief, IETD, 18 March 1901,
appendix B, enclosure 2, L/PWD/7/1390.

landlines, and dues had to be paid to the British, German, Russian and
Persian governments.[13] The IETD (with lines from Teheran to Karachi)
also had to pay a royalty to Persia but retained the whole
cable rate from Bushire to Karachi. Thus, while the ETC retained
approximately the whole charge on messages sent by their route,
the Indo-European and the IETD each retained about 90 per cent.[14]
Table 2.1 indicates the division of the joint revenue between the three
companies.

The fact that the IETD, which was part of the Government of India,
benefited from the near-monopoly position of these private companies
provoked criticism. C. H. Reynolds, late Director General of Indian
Telegraphs, defended government support for the scheme on the
grounds that, while the Indo-European and ETC were useful, there
was need for a third line which would not be vulnerable during times
of conflict. Potentially the Turkish line could supply this, but in
practice it was not well maintained and could not attract sufficient
traffic. The need to retain control over the telegraphic system was
crucial strategically. Although being part of the joint purse would
entail sharing profits, it would also provide the government with
a voice in the running of the system and act as a controlling mecha-
nism on the private companies, which would otherwise have
free rein.[15]

At the turn of the century there accordingly existed three main telegraphic routes to India: (1) the ETC (7,664 miles in length) via Aden,
Egypt and Gibraltar, (2) the Indo-European (including the IETD lines),
via the Persian Gulf, Persia, Russia and Germany (5,618 miles) and (3)
the Turkish (5,155 miles), via the Persian Gulf, Constantinople and
various European routes. The first two were the more dependable, but
the Turkish route, though slow and prone to disturbances, was the
most direct. In 1899–1900 the mean speed of transmission between

Britain and Calcutta via the ETC was 117 minutes, via the Indo-European seventy-four minutes, and via Turkey was thirty-five hours.[16]

Cost of news and information

In general the expense of the telegraphic connection curtailed its press use to the largest of the metropolitan dailies. Commercial bodies and merchants devised various ways of reducing expenses, such as clubbing together or 'packing' and the use of code words, yet there was a limit to which newspapers could similarly reduce costs. However, the turn of the century saw the beginning of a period of rapid reduction in telegraph and press rates. Several factors contributed to bring this about: official pressure, British as well as international; the advantages of drawing more subscribers; the extension of the network beyond India, making it attractive to the Australasian and South East Asian markets; and the increasing demand for foreign news in Britain with the expansion of the cheap popular press.

The telegraph companies were, however, reluctant to lower Indian tariffs, arguing that demand was relatively inelastic. In 1865 the tariff for sending a message from England to India was 5s per word.[17] As the technology became consolidated the rate declined; from 1871 to 1886 it averaged 4s 6d per word and in 1886 was reduced to 4s per word.[18] But as charges to other parts of the world fell further, concern was increasingly expressed at the rates levied on Indian messages. Indeed, telegraph rates probably rose in relative terms, since this was a period of generally falling prices – from the early 1870s to the mid-1890s average prices fell in Britain by around 35 per cent, whereas telegraph rates fell by only 20 per cent.

In June 1899 the Indian government sent a dispatch to the Secretary of State, Lord George Hamilton, asking for a 50 per cent reduction in rates.[19] It drew attention to the fact that the rate between Australia and Europe was only 4s 9d per word, and that in 1897 the rates between other countries in the Far East and Europe were considerably reduced, whereas the Indian rate remained at 4s.[20] Hitherto the companies had resisted further decreases in the tariff on the ground that the reduction of 1886 had not been followed by 'a marked increase of traffic'.[21] To this the Government of India replied that the 'stationary character' of the traffic was because the tariff remained prohibitively high. Referring to the 'striking' results of the reduction of the Australasian tariff in 1891, it claimed that although the Australasian governments had agreed to pay the companies half the sum by which their receipts might fall short of those in 1889, since 1894–95 the

[34]

colonies had had 'nothing to pay' under the guarantee. The Indian Tele-graph Department (ITD) had itself reduced the rate charged on all trans-Indian messages and the initial loss of revenue had been 'more than recouped' by the increased receipts on such messages. Hamilton was therefore persuaded to offer a similar guarantee in the Indian case, noting its importance for both Indo-British relations and the British mercantile community.[22] However, the Treasury refused on the grounds that subsidies were not favoured by Parliament.[23]

Consequently the situation in early 1900 was such that no reduc-tion seemed possible unless, as Curzon contended, the various European states through whose lands the network passed agreed to further concessions.[24] In that same year, under the chairmanship of Lord Balfour of Burleigh, an interdepartmental committee was appointed to investigate the relations between private cable compa-nies and imperial and colonial governments.[25] Sir Edward Sassoon, spokesman of the Imperial Telegraph Committee of the Commons, complained that the ETC and its associates had become 'an oppressive monopoly' whose tariffs were 'abnormal', 'arbitrary' and 'capricious' in relation to comparative distances traversed.[26] Sassoon blamed the Government of India for the 'radically wrong' state of affairs where it was 'apparently inert and enmeshed' in agreements and consequently unable to reduce rates. A telegram could be sent from London to Afghanistan by means of the Russian landlines for $5\frac{1}{2}d$ per word. If, to this, the $2\frac{1}{2}d$ per word levied throughout India for ordinary telegrams were added, the total would be 8d per word. Yet the amount actually charged by the ETC was 4s. Sassoon alleged that the ITD encouraged the private companies to make excessive profits on Indian business in order to subsidise their transmission to areas beyond India like Australia, and called for a reduction in the Indian tariff of at least 75 per cent.[27] These issues of monopoly and high tariffs were repeat-edly brought before Parliament during 1900–2 and attracted wider press comment, but no reforms were forthcoming.[28]

Meanwhile the India Office launched a series of negotiations with European states, including Turkey, as well as with private companies, the Government of India, the Foreign Office and the Treasury.[29] It was finally agreed in 1902 that the rate from Europe to India and Burma would be 2s 6d and Ceylon 2s 7d per word.[30] The government pledged that, for a ten-year period, it would make up one-third of any defi-ciency in the companies' yearly revenue compared to an assumed stan-dard of £360,000, subject to a yearly maximum of £44,000.[31] Further, stating that the traditional policy of Britain was 'to encourage "free trade" in cables' and that it should be departed from only where 'strong reasons of national interests exist',[32] the interdepartmental committee

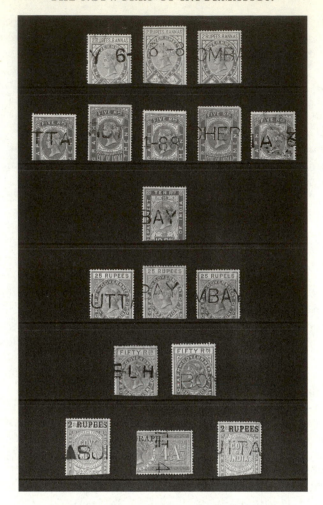

1   Government of India telegraph stamps

recommended the termination of the joint purse agreement, and it was decided that the cis-Indian section of the agreement would have a termination clause added such that any partner would be able to end its association from November 1907 upon two and a half years' notice.[33] At the same time the press rate was reduced and fixed at 1s a word. Hamilton explained to the Commons, 'This is not in exact proportion to the reduction for the rate of ordinary messages, but the shilling rate appears to be a reasonable one, and I am not prepared to press the Companies for any further reduction at present.'[34]

Imperial press conferences and the expansion of news services

The issue of high rates for press telegraphic communications figured prominently at the first Imperial Press Conference in London in 1909. The conference was the idea of the journalist Harry Brittain, later Conservative MP for Acton, and attracted support from prominent politicians, including Asquith, Balfour, Curzon, Cromer, Grey, Haldane, Morley and Rosebery. The conference represented, claimed Robert Donald, erstwhile editor of the *Chronicle*, 'a landmark in Empire history'.[35] The importance of communication systems for the promotion of imperial solidarity was emphasised[36] and there was widespread support for rate reductions, owing to the 'paramount importance' of cheapening and improving the telegraph links between the various parts of the empire.[37] An outcome of the conference was the formation of the Empire Press Union (EPU), which established branches worldwide, including India. The EPU worked to facilitate access to official and parliamentary news for overseas journalists and lobbied vigorously to reduce press costs.[38]

The conference also highlighted particular problems affecting the flow of information to and from the subcontinent. The seven delegates from India, Burma and Ceylon, out of a total of fifty-four overseas guests, included Everard Digby of the *Indian News*, Surendranath Banerjee of the *Bengalee*, Stanley Reed of the *Times of India*, G. M. Chesney from the *Pioneer*, A. E. Lawson of the *Madras Mail*, F. Crosbie Roles representing the *Times of Ceylon* and J. Stuart of the *Rangoon Gazette*.[39] Reed, Banerjee and Roles all put forward spirited arguments in favour of cheaper press telegraphic facilities. Reed argued that the conditions under which India was 'kept in telegraphic touch with the outer world can only be described as grotesque'.[40] The press rate to India was the same as that charged to Australia, which was double the distance. The price ratio between press and private cablegrams to India was one-half higher than in any other part of the British Empire. By systematic coding the charge for private cablegrams had been reduced to just over 2*d* per word, but even with the 'most conservative computation' the cost of every word of news was between 9*d* and 10*d*. Consequently press telegrams were generally 'so short that we see overseas affairs as through a glass darkly'.

> In every other part of the world news is considered of so much public importance that it is entitled to a specially cheap rate . . . [but] the picture of India, represented in large sections of the English Press, sometimes cannot be recognised as the land we live in . . . that is not only an enormous inconvenience, but a serious Imperial menace . . . May I ask

how you are going to guide the [British] democracy on the affairs of India at one shilling a word?[41]

Banerjee, the only Indian in the delegation, argued that times were critical for India, with the spread of political violence and the inauguration of the Morley–Minto reforms. It was therefore of great importance that the 'truth' regarding India should be accurately conveyed to the British: 'If we had cheap cablegrams, the false, misleading telegrams regarding Indian affairs would not be sent to this country. They would be wired back for confirmation and correction.'[42]

The conference undoubtedly played a leading role in maintaining pressure on the authorities in keeping this issue to the fore. A Cable and Imperial News Service Committee was set up under the presidency of Lord Burnham which kept 'hammering away' at government departments and companies, with 'encouraging results'.[43] A rate revision took place in July 1909, when the India Office authorised a reduction from 12d to 9d per word.[44] A year later more thoroughgoing organisational reform was undertaken. At that time over 500,000 words were transmitted to India, South Africa and Australia per annum, and it was estimated that about half the news sent to each place was general to all. It was consequently suggested that arrangements should be made for a common Imperial News Service.[45] Reuters was considered the only agency able to provide such a service, and the ETC made arrangements with the company for placing 150,000 words (per annum) of general and imperial news at Aden, from where it could be distributed to India, Australia, South Africa and other places. The rate from Aden to India on the retransmitted messages would be reduced to 2d per word. At the time Reuters supplied Indian newspapers with about 128,000 words of news per annum, of which 117,000 was sent to Bombay and 11,000 direct to Calcutta. It was suggested that, of this total, 58,500 should continue to be sent from London to Bombay and 11,000 to Calcutta at the ordinary press rate of 9d per word, and that, in lieu of the rest of the Bombay news, the 150,000 words available at Aden would be retransmitted to Bombay at the low rate of 2d per word, thereby increasing news for India from 128,000 to 219,500 words per annum.[46] The effect of these changes on actual news flows as projected by the ETC is shown in Table 2.2.

The extended news service became operational from July 1910. However, the new total for India (as in Table 2.2) was lower, to take into account the proportion of news that was commercial and encoded. The latter continued at 2s per word. Reuters proved effective, and the quality – 'especially the way of giving us fuller details of important Parliamentary debates affecting India' – was also thought to have

Table 2.2   Particulars of proposed news service, in words, 1910

	Present	Proposed Direct	Aden to	Total each place
India	128,000	64,000	150,000	214,000
South Africa	146,666	73,333	150,000	223,333
Australia	266,666	133,333	150,000	283,333
Grand totals	541,332	270,666	450,000	720,666

Source   Hibberdine to H. A. Kirk, IETD 9 July 1910, L/PWD/7/1551.

improved. However, officials suggested that Reuters should reduce general sporting news, like the lengthy football results every Sunday, which was felt to be of little interest to 'anyone outside the circle of Dundee Scotsmen in the Calcutta Jute Mills'.[47] The company received a higher subsidy from the Government of India, the new monthly sum being increased to Rs 2,600, which included one-third of the transmission costs to Aden. However, India Office concern to see further reductions in the cost of press telegrams and an increased news service to the subcontinent resulted in a further reduction, to 4*d*, in October 1912, which remained into the immediate post-war years.[48] A new press service was also introduced whereby deferred telegrams in plain language could be sent at half price.[49]

The issue of telegraph rates to India nevertheless continued to provoke concern, as witnessed in Resolution XIV of the Imperial War Conference in 1918, which stated that it was in the 'highest interests' of the empire that the rates for telegraphic communications between Britain, the dominions and India should be 'further materially reduced as soon as practicable'.[50] While, on the one hand, the war disrupted routes and caused damage to the telegraph networks, on the other it resulted in record profits for the ETC. The casualty lists of India, Australia and New Zealand, 'every initial counting as a word', represented substantial revenue. The cables were 'choked with official matter at 1*s* 6*d* a word'.[51] Special arrangements were also made to provide an outward Imperial News Service. This was practically confined to the official communiqués of the Allies and was transmitted by the ETC immediately and in precedence over every other traffic and consequently reached India with only minimal delay. Effort was made to introduce a similar service for important foreign news, but the London papers were 'unwilling to accept a news message in common' and preferred messages from their correspondents.[52]

Table 2.3 Cable rates to India, per word, 1908 and 1923

1908		1923		
Ordinary	Press	Ordinary	Deferred	Press
2s 0d	1s 0d	1s 8d	0s 10d	0s 4d

Source Compiled from Mills, *Press and Communications of the Empire* (1924), p. 81.

The second Imperial Press Conference, delayed by the war, eventually convened in Ottawa during 1920.[53] Again press cable rates and imperial unity were issues that received considerable attention, and a resolution was passed proposing plans for obtaining 'better, cheaper, and quicker facilities' for the distribution of news within the empire.[54] 'If we are desperately in earnest about Empire unity,' argued Donald, 'a penny per word cable rate is the best way of advancing it.'[55] Whilst acknowledging the penny rate as 'a fine ideal', Roderick Jones, Managing Director of Reuters, did not commit himself to a cut in the charges levied by his company. The enormous increase especially in government traffic – in some departments the officials had 'got into the habit of sending letters by cable instead of sending dispatches' – meant that pressure on cables was set to increase.[56]

Reuters: networks of information, monopoly and influence

Reuters was the main telegraph news agency within India.[57] Founded in London in 1851 by Julius Reuter, a German Jew who later became a British subject, Reuters rapidly became the leading international news agency. Its name became 'the trade-mark for semi-official foreign news all over the world'.[58] In a company history Read has stated that India was the 'most profitable' part of the empire, constituting 'a great market' for political and commercial news.[59] The initial Reuters telegram datelined Calcutta was sent in 1858, and by 1864 the Government of India had arranged to be furnished with regular Reuters telegrams. Reuters first office was established at Bombay in 1866, and within two years there were offices in Calcutta, Karachi, Madras, Colombo and Point de Galle.

Reuters drew the greater part of its revenue from commercial intelligence and business telegrams, which in turn financed its path-

Table 2.4 Salaries of Reuters branch office staff, India, 1900–7 (£)

City	1900	1901	1902	1903	1904	1905	1906	1907
Bombay	1,133	1,173	1,244	1,190	1,398	1,260	1,286	1,023
Calcutta	552	648	660	586	808	817	840	790
Colombo	500	280	280	310	350	318	465	429
Madras	239	276	318	319	366	346	479	300
Rangoon	75	75	80	80	517	476	454	376
Simla			600	650	600	600	600	792
Total salaries for India	2,499	2,452	3,182	3,135	4,039[a]	3,817[a]	4,124	3,710
% of world	22	17	22	21	22	21	21	20

Note   [a] Excluding salaries in 1905–6 for Karachi and Kanpur.

Source   Compiled from Wages/Salaries File 1888–1908, RA.

breaking ventures in news reporting and provided the basis of the agency's prestige. By 1898 the total revenue derived from Indian business was £11,500, increasing to £18,400 in 1908 and £35,200 in 1918. These figures represented 8.1 per cent, 9.4 per cent and 13.2 per cent of Reuters total income respectively.[60] The 1910 annual aeport noted that there was a

> growing demand for news, more especially on the part of India . . . We, for our part, have done our share, and the service, for instance, which we made to India, regarding the General Election, has been admitted on all hands to have eclipsed anything previously attempted in that direction.[61]

Further, the company's service from India had also been 'greatly in evidence'.[62] Table 2.4, which indicates the amount spent on the salaries of branch office staff in India, provides a means of measuring the scale of its operation. It is evident that, in terms of branch offices, India received about one-fifth of Reuters total worldwide outlay. Reuters was also sensitive to major political events and increased the number of correspondents at crisis centres. Table 2.5 shows how the political crisis of the early 1920s saw as many as a quarter of the agency's total correspondents employed in the subcontinent.

These years also witnessed burgeoning demand for telegraphic facilities from the public, press and government in India, and the internal telegraph network expanded rapidly. Though successful trials of electric transmission on the river Hooghly were undertaken in the 1830s, construction of telegraph lines began in earnest during the 1850s.

Table 2.5   Reuters correspondents in India and worldwide, 1915–25

	No. of correspondents		India as % of world total
Year	India	Worldwide	
1915	12	66	18
1916	13	70	19
1917	13	71	18
1919	16	74	22
1921	17	70	24
1923	14	72	19
1925	12	74	16

Source   Compiled from LN 325 Databook, RA.

During the Mutiny W. H. Russell, the *Times* war correspondent sent to cover the events, remarked that 'Never since its discovery has the electric telegraph played so important and daring a role as it now does in India; without it the Commander-in-Chief would lose the effect of half his force. It has served him better than his right arm.'[63] By 1865 India had some 14,500 miles of government and 3,000 miles of railway-owned telegraph lines.[64] By 1906 64,730 miles of open lines and 243,840 miles of wire were in operation, the number of paid messages exceeding 10 million per year.[65] The total line and wire mileage continued to grow steadily and in 1921–22 consisted of approximately 92,000 miles of line and cable carrying 412,000 miles of wire.[66] The internal network served to extend the potential reach of Reuters, while in 1908 the Associated Press of India (API) was formed in Madras as a domestic news agency. A leading spirit behind the API was the journalist K. C. Roy, who was employed by Reuters in 1908 to help organise the internal service.[67] From 1907 a rival Indian News Agency was run by Everard Cotes, formerly the Indian correspondent of the *Mail*, but this was taken over in 1910 by Reuters with the formation of the Eastern News Agency, which also absorbed the API. Thus Reuters also became the predominant domestic news agency in India.

The types of correspondent and their terms of engagement varied. Appointees from Britain were paid in sterling, and their salaries compared favourably with those at the head office. For example, H. Speirs, who transferred from Glasgow to Calcutta in 1904, saw his salary rise from £40 to £200 per annum.[68] Some were permanent Reuters men, others were journalists working for Anglo-Indian newspapers and paid a fixed stipend. There were, in addition, local stringers employed whenever need arose to supplement existing services or arrange cover in remote parts. The core spheres of operation included major cities like Allahabad, Bombay, Calcutta, Colombo, Delhi, Karachi, Peshawar and Simla, staffed by senior correspondents, and a periphery with fewer established staff.

What were the major areas of Reuters coverage? Political developments of all kinds received significant attention, and wars were a Reuters speciality. In the North West Frontier campaign of 1898 Reuters special correspondent gave such extensive coverage that 'nearly all the papers relied solely upon our service'.[69] Ceremonial occasions like the Delhi durbars of 1903 and 1911 were lavishly covered, as were tours by the Prince of Wales in 1905–06 and 1921–22. But Reuters always had an eye for an 'exclusive', thus noting in 1913 how

> our greatest success in the department of news was with the account of the attempt on the life of the Viceroy [Lord Hardinge] with which we were absolutely alone for many hours, the Government receiving the intelligence first through our medium.[70]

Special advice was tendered to correspondents reporting from the East. Stressing the 'great difference in the points of view' taken by the British and the 'Orientals', it advised its correspondents to bear in mind not only the importance of the event or issue, but also 'its acceptability, as a newspaper item to the public at Home'. Included were directives on 'Murders and Outrages' that stressed that these could generally be ignored unless 'Europeans are concerned either directly or indirectly. The murder of even an obscure missionary should always be chronicled'.[71] Similarly, under 'Riots and Popular Disturbances' correspondents were instructed to ignore any 'local affair', excepting if the disturbance could 'fairly be characterised "a sign of the times"'.[72]

Anglo-Indian newspapers began subscribing to Reuters from the 1860s, and they were joined from the 1890s by some Indian-run papers.[73] By 1906 their numbers had risen to twenty-two (including Burma and Ceylon), each paying a monthly fee of Rs 600.[74] The INC also made arrangements with Reuters to cover, for example, the proceedings of its annual meetings.[75] Most London papers had contracts with the company by the end of the nineteenth century, at which date Reuters service consisted of two main categories. First, there was the General Service, covering world news, chronicled in brief telegrams for a fixed annual subscription.[76] In 1906 there were thirty-four London newspapers on its books, with subscriptions ranging from £1,600 for the major dailies to £100–£400 for the smaller evening and weekly papers. Owing, however, to the continued growth of the press and

THIS AGREEMENT
REQUIRES AN
EMBOSSED 6D.
STAMP.

LONDON MORNING NEWSPAPER AGREEMENT.

An Agreement made this 2nd day of *June*, 1899, between

REUTER'S TELEGRAM COMPANY, LIMITED, of No. 24, Old Jewry,

in the City of London, hereinafter called the Company, of the one part;

and *J. H. Lingard Esqr.*

of *3 Harmsworth Buildings E.C.*

on behalf of the Proprietors of the *Daily Mail*

Newspaper, of the other part.

Witnesseth and it is hereby mutually agreed as follows, that is to say:—

1.   The Company shall supply to the said *J. H. Lingard*

solely for the use of the *Daily Mail* Newspaper,

a copy of every telegram supplied by the Company, in its general service, to the other

daily London Newspapers, and shall deliver such copies at the printing office of the

Daily Mail Newspaper, at the same time, so far as

circumstances will permit, as like copies are delivered at the offices of the other London

Newspapers without preference or priority.

2   Reuters agreement with the *Daily Mail*, 1899

demand for news, Reuters decided to introduce a supplementary Special press service of 'lengthy telegrams on occasions of great importance or of exceptional interest', for an additional payment per word published.[77] Unfortunately the Reuters archives do not enumerate the amount spent by individual papers specifically on Indian news coverage.

From 1870 onwards the world market for news was carved up into spheres of interest by European news agencies, including the French Havas (1835), the German Wolff (1849) and Reuters.[78] These major European agencies were based in *imperial* capitals, and their expansion outside Europe was linked with the territorial colonialism of the late nineteenth century. Reuters enjoyed a monopoly in news gathering from British territories around the globe and saw itself as an empire company, conscious of the necessity of maintaining the favour of the imperial government. The preamble to Reuters contract with the India Office spoke of it

being desirous of establishing more intimate relations . . . particularly with a view to ensure as great accuracy as possible in its intelligence and furthermore wishing to allow the India Office to avail itself of its various channels of information . . . and to communicate . . . all news received by it concerning or having any bearing on India.[79]

In return for £500 per year the agency undertook to have its representative

attend periodically or when required at the India Office and at the Government Offices in India to receive communications, denials, rectifications of mis-statements etc. appearing in the British or Indian Press, and other matters which it might be desired to make public both here and in India.[80]

Any special telegraphic service required by the India Office would have to be paid for separately. The government in India had a separate contract which, in 1906, involved paying Rs 1,200 per month for the ordinary outward service and Rs 600 per month for the extended service.[81] (This was increased to Rs 2,600 from 1910, as mentioned earlier.) From August 1922 the Reuters Government Service was entirely separated from the Press Service and consisted of an extended summary of 500 words per day from Bombay, with a provision to incorporate additional sections of interesting news when necessary.[82]

Reuters news service did not escape criticism from the press or in Parliament. The *Guardian* and *India*, for example, claimed that Reuters correspondents were often inaccurate in their portrayal of events, embroidering fact with fiction. From Ministers and officials came a similar charge, though in this case referring to excessive coverage of 'trivia' and a pro-nationalist bias. Reuters was always vigorous in defence. Certainly, as its contract with the INC suggests, it treated that organisation as simply another subscriber. A special correspondent was sent to the INC meeting at Allahabad in 1910, for 'Late events in India tend to impart special interest to this gathering . . . and to emphasise the need of an independent and impartial record of the discussions'.[83]

Though Reuters stressed that it was a private company, independent of government, and placed great emphasis upon the objectivity of its news coverage, it is questionable whether it always maintained this impartiality. On occasions it both suppressed and distorted information. It was frequently used by the India Office to telegraph additional words of a meeting or a speech, which it thought desirable to publicise in India, or to counteract articles in the London press. This relationship was to develop rapidly, especially under Edward Buck, the company's chief representative, who was appointed correspondent with the Government of India in 1897 and became 'the friend, confidant and unofficial counsellor' of successive Viceroys.[84] A letter from Buck to James Dunlop-Smith, private secretary of Lord Minto, is revealing in this context. Writing in 1907 in connection with increasing concern in England about the rise of sedition in the subcontinent, Buck assured Dunlop-Smith of his 'absolute readiness . . . to assist the Viceroy in every possible manner'. Reuters, he claimed, had in the past 'generally proved a useful friend' and Buck himself had been 'careful to arrange that any wires sent Home should certainly not be of a nature to embarrass the Government'.

> But in telling you candidly that, while maintaining my full right of independence, I am more than willing to help you, you on your part *must* help me and treat me with entire confidence. You need not be afraid that it will be abused.

He reminded Dunlop-Smith that during the viceroyalties of Lord Elgin and Lord Curzon he had received 'a private subsidy' through the PSV for extending Reuters service on important occasions:

> I do not . . . suggest that this subsidy be renewed . . . But I do think that the moment is one when Government could make much more use of Reuter than they now do. Here am I always ready to send a friendly message, if those concerned will when the moment arises . . . compose one, or help me to frame one myself . . . In the event of any message being of such length that I cannot feel justified in sending it at the Company's cost, it might easily be paid for by private arrangement. I think that we might both be much more useful to each other than we now are, and if

you would care to have for private information copies of messages which go Home from Reuter, or would like to have some other system introduced whereby the Secretary of State could have our messages forwarded to him, I am quite ready to talk the matter over.[85]

These words illustrate how the ascendancy of Reuters in reporting Indian news created the danger that distorted coverage, deliberate or otherwise, would appear unchallenged in the London papers. Priority was given to Reuters for receiving major official communiqués. In return, Reuters routinely gave distorted and inadequate coverage of politically sensitive events, for example its treatment of the Labour leader Keir Hardie's visit to India in 1907. His pro-Indian speeches were causing considerable alarm to the British authorities and, in an attempt to precipitate his departure, Reuters aided the government by painting a false portrait of him as inciting armed rebellion in India, reports which greatly harmed Hardie's standing with parts of British public opinion.[86] As Hardie himself remarked, 'The lie goes round the world while truth is putting on her boots.' By contrast the campaigning journalist Henry Nevinson, in India at the same time as Hardie, found his activities and pronouncements deliberately ignored, as Buck admitted to the Viceroy.[87] Nevertheless, the close Reuters relationship with the Indian government and the India Office continued throughout the twentieth century. When, after the Great War, the government appointed a committee to advise on publicity and propaganda in New Delhi, its non-official members were journalists representing Reuters (Mr Kingston) and the Eastern News Agency (Mr Roy).[88] As the Reuters secretary assured the India Office information officer, 'We are at all times anxious to give effect to the wishes of the India Office, even though they entail extra costs and labour.'[89]

However, as this relationship between the British government and Reuters strengthened under the pressures of conflict, the agency's integrity began to be questioned. The company's official historian has argued that in neither the Boer War nor the Great War did Reuters 'knowingly circulate false news', but he admits that during the former it misled the public by the suppression of news.[90] In London Roderick Jones became head of the Department of Propaganda at the Ministry of Information. Reuters also started a special Agence Reuter to transmit Allied propaganda. The service was financed by the British government, which paid transmission costs at the rate of £120,000 per annum.[91] Beaverbrook, as the first Minister of Information, acknowledged that one of his tasks in ensuring successful propaganda was 'assuming control of Reuters, and other news agencies, so that good news was disseminated abroad instead of gloom and apprehension'.[92]

3 Edward Buck and Roderick Jones, Maiden's Hotel, Delhi, 1924

It was difficult to reconcile Reuters reputation as a private impartial enterprise with its patriotic commitment to the war effort. Increasing opposition was voiced in public and Parliament, and Jones ultimately bowed to pressure and resigned his government post.[93]

Read argues that, in Britain, Reuters was not thought 'contradictory' in claiming independence, notwithstanding its reputation as a 'national and imperial institution' with obligations to the government.[94] However, this was not the basis for a successful policy. The perception of its pro-imperial bias convinced many that it was heavily subsidised by the administration. As Read acknowledges, this was manifested most graphically in its coverage of colonial conflicts, where

> the 'natives' did not recognise that Reuter war correspondents were non-combatants and neutral. Nor, in fact, were they. Whereas in conflicts between 'civilised' states Reuters tried not to take sides, in colonial wars its correspondents had no doubt that the British side was 'right'.[95]

It is difficult to avoid the conclusion that Reuters, imbued as it was with a self-professed patriotism, and conscious of the importance of empire to its success, tended to reflect the British point of view.[96] In India, throughout most of the nineteenth century, Reuters was 'essentially part of the British scheme of things'. Only gradually did it adapt to the growth of Indian nationalism.[97]

Conclusion

From the mid-nineteenth century an expanding system of imperial communications was made possible by the electric telegraph. It was generally perceived that the 'annihilation of space and time' by wires, rails and the influence of steam gave an immediate reality to events on the imperial periphery.[98] Britain owned or had an interest in 80 per cent of all submarine cables before the First World War. The French Telegraph Act (1900) claimed that 'England owes her influence in the world perhaps more to her cable communications than to her navy. She controls the news, and makes it serve her policy and commerce in a marvellous manner.'[99] The British government was conscious of the strategic importance of the telegraph system – the epitome of strategic cables was the 'All Red Route', a cable passing only through British territories, which by 1911 connected the far-flung colonies and dominions with the metropole.

From the 1860s the telegraph and the steamship were 'a commentary on the fact that the Indian Empire could no longer live in relative isolation'.[100] By the early twentieth century telegraphs were received in London within a few hours, with the result that even the smallest detail of Indian administration could, if it chose, be decided upon by the India Office and transmitted to the remotest corner of the sub-continent. George Orwell, who served in the imperial police in Burma, reflected on the changed position of the colonial administrator:

> The thing that killed them was the telegraph. In a narrowing world, more and more governed from Whitehall, there was every year less room for individual initiative . . . By 1920 nearly every inch of the colonial empire was in the grip of Whitehall. Well-meaning, over-civilised men, in dark suits and black felt hats, with neatly rolled umbrellas crooked over the left forearm, were imposing their constipated view of life in Malaya and Nigeria, Mombassa and Mandalay.[101]

Yet the new technologies did not act uniformly to enhance the authority of metropolitan administrators, for the shifting parameters of news reporting and transmission had important implications for official attempts to control the flow of information and influence its interpretation.

In general, changes in the technology of news collection and transmission, and in particular the extension of the telegraph system, and the advent of international news agencies, made possible a radical shift in the quantity and form of news coverage of the subcontinent. The heightened expectations of their readership ensured that all major British newspapers sought to exploit these opportunities. For the first time, the gathering of Indian intelligence was carried out by an agency that acted as a purveyor – not direct consumer – of news to clients like the press. Reuters dominance of the Indian news market and its symbiotic relationship with the government had a seminal influence on the structure and character of news flows between metropolis and periphery.

The emergence of Reuters also had several important effects on contemporary journalism. The outlay which had been necessary for a paper like *The Times* in establishing and maintaining a large foreign staff in India was circumvented. In this news agencies were a great leveller, promoting, especially, the ability of the cheap daily press to extend its coverage of the subcontinent. There developed some conformity in news and information, which was of political significance for the appreciation of subcontinental affairs and government policies. Reuters played an important agenda-setting function – telling readers not what to think but what to think about – and thus inevitably influencing the judgements which the press and the political public in Britain and India made about the relative importance of different kinds of news. The development of telegraphic journalism also forced newspapers to reconsider the nature of their coverage. With agencies seeking to supply factual reports, Fleet Street came to emphasise the distinctive commentary and perspective upon events that their Indian correspondents provided.

Notes

1 J. Morris, *Pax Britannica* (1968), pp. 52–60; E. A. Benians, 'Finance, trade and communications, 1870–1895', in E. A. Benians, J. Butler and C. E. Carrington (eds), *Cambridge History of the British Empire* (1959) III, pp. 201–4.
2 B. S. Finn, *Submarine Telegraphy* (1973), p. 10; Headrick, *Tools*, pp. 129–39; *Murray's Handbook* (1913), p. xxxvii.
3 *Observer*, 23 July 1922.
4 J. Merrett, *Three Miles Deep* (1958), pp. 92, 97; M. MacDonagh, 'Wires and the newspapers', *Sells*(1906), p. 35; C. Bright, *Submarine Telegraphy* (1908), p. 76.
5 H. L. Hoskins, *British Routes to India* (1966), pp. 374–96.
6 J. Ahvenainen, *Far Eastern Telegraphs* (Helsinki, 1981), p. 101; Hoskins, *British Routes*, p. 389.
7 Morris, *Pax Britannica*, p. 57; Benians, 'Imperial finance', pp. 200–1.
8 Memo on IETD and Narrative of Events to October 1914, L/PWD/7/1895.
9 F. J. Brown, *Cable and Wireless Communications of the World* (1927), p. 3; Headrick, *Tools*, p. 160.
10 Memo on the IETD and Narrative of Events to October 1914, L/PWD/7/1895.
11 Ahvenainen, *Far Eastern*, p. 17.
12 For copy of agreement see Secretary of State to Viceroy, 15 February 1901, Enclosure 37, L/PWD/7/1408.
13 Brown, Cable, p. 24.
14 House of Commons Interdepartmental Committee on Cable Rates, 1900, L/PWD/7/1390.
15 Note by Reynolds, 11 March 1901, for the Interdepartmental Committee on Telegraphs, L/PWD/7/1390.
16 Memo by Director-in-Chief, IETD, 18 March 1901, Appendix B, 4, L/PWD/7/1390.
17 Memo on the IETD and Narrative of Events to October 1914, L/PWD/7/1895.
18 Memo, Director-in-Chief, IETD, for Interdepartmental Cables Committee, 18 March 1901, L/PWD/7/1390.
19 *Ibid.*, Appendix B, 3.
20 Memo, Reduction of Telegraphic Rate between Europe and India, Enclosure 29, L/PWD/7/1408.
21 *Ibid.*, Viceroy to Secretary of State, 1 June 1899, cited in Secretary of State to Governor General, 15 February 1901.
22 India Office to Treasury, 1 November 1899, Memo on Reduction of Rate to India, Enclosure 1, L/PWD/7/1408.
23 *Ibid.*,Treasury to India Office, 5 February 1900, Enclosure 2.
24 *Ibid.*, Viceroy to Secretary of State, 1 June 1899, cited in Secretary of State to Viceroy, 15 February 1901.
25 *Ibid.*
26 E. A. Sassoon, 'Imperial telegraphic communication', *JSA*, 6 (June 1900), 591–600.
27 *Ibid.*, pp. 596–8; for British inland press rates see J. Kieve, *Electric Telegraph* (Newton Abbot, 1973), pp. 289–90.
28 L/PWD/7/1413 and L/PWD/7/1421; Sassoon's letter to the *Times*, 14 November 1900, *Morning Post*, 15 November 1900. C. Bright, the engineer of several submarine cable networks to India, was another prominent critic; see 'Imperial telegraphs', *Quarterly Review*, April 1903; 'Imperial telegraphy at a popular tariff', *Fortnightly Review*, March 1909.
29 L/PWD/7/1409–17.
30 Secretary of State to Viceroy, 21 March 1902, L/PWD/7/1891.

31   23 May 1905, L/PWD/7/1411; Memo on Reduction of Telegraphic Rate between Europe and India, Enclosures 16, 29 L/PWD/7/1408.
32   Cited in Brown, *Cables*, pp. 116, 134–5.
33   Secretary of State to Viceroy, 21 March 1902, Enclosure 1, L/PWD/7/1891.
34   Secretary of State to Sassoon, 25 February 1902, Enclosure 42, L/PWD/7/1891; also Director-in-Chief, Indo-European, to Thompson, 21 July 1902, L/PWD/7/1413.
35   R. Donald, *Imperial Press Conference in Canada* (1920), p. 5; C. Kaul, 'Imperial communications, Fleet Street and the Indian empire, *c.* 1850s–1920s', in M. Bromley and T. O'Malley (eds), *A Journalism Reader* (1997), pp. 58–86.
36   C. Woodhead, *Press and Empire* (Durban, 1909), p. 11; *Whitaker's* (1910), pp. 692–3.
37   *Ibid.*
38   See Donald, *Press Conference*, pp. 162–3, 190–2, 251–3.
39   Also Canada (fifteen), West Indies (one), Australia (fourteen), New Zealand (six) and South Africa (eleven).
40   S. Reed, *The India I Knew* (1957), pp. 40–3; T. H. Hardman, *A Parliament of the Press* (1909), pp. 40–1.
41   *Ibid.*, pp. 140–1.
42   *Ibid.*, p. 151.
43   Donald, *Press Conference*, p. 122.
44   Minute, 12 March 1912, Press Rules and Rates, Appendix B, L/PWD/7/1573.
45   Reuters Special Press Agency and Imperial News Messages, 28 February 1910, L/PWD/7/1551.
46   *Ibid.*, 23 March 1910, p. 4.
47   Home Poll B 61, May 1911, p. 9.
48   Memo on IETD and Narrative of Events to October 1914, L/PWD/7/1895; cited in R. W. Desmond, *Press and World Affairs* (New York, 1937), p. 114.
49   Secretary of State to Governor General in Council, 15 March, 2 August, 27 September and 1 October 1912, Press Rules and Rates, L/PWD/7/1573; Secretary of State to Viceroy, 28 November, 19 December 1913, Reduction of Rates 1909–1918, L/PWD/7/1545.
50   Cited in Secretary of State to Viceroy, 23 August 1918; Secretary of State to Viceroy, 23 March 1917; Government of India Department of Commerce and Industry to Secretary of State and Viceroy, 10 November 1916, Reduction of Rates 1909–1918, L/PWD/7/1545.
51   Donald, *Press Conference*, p. 166.
52   Note on Press Telegrams, 12 September 1918, L/PWD/7/1573.
53   Donald, *Press Conference*, p. 2. Indian representatives included J. P. Collins (*Civil and Military Gazette*), J. O'Brien Saunders (*Englishman*) and F. Crosbie Roles (*Times of Ceylon*).
54   Donald, *Press Conference*, p. 38. Though there was a heightened awareness of the potential of the wireless, it was not considered as threatening the cable networks; see Brown, *Cable*, pp. 73–104. In Britain wireless was put under government control in 1904. By 1911 Whitehall had decided to create an imperial wireless system primarily for strategic reasons, with stations in Cyprus, Aden, Bombay, the Straits Settlements and Australia.
55   Donald, *Press Conference*, p. 167.
56   *Ibid.*, pp. 169–70.
57   Competitors included Exchange Telegraph (1872) and Central News (1863), but their operations were small and intermittent.
58   G. B. Dibblee, *The Newspaper* (1913), p. 79.
59   D. Read, *The Power of News* (1992), p. 83.
60   Compiled from *ibid.*, p. 83.
61   Chairman's speech, Annual Report 1910, Reuters Archives (hereafter RA).
62   Annual Report 1908, RA.
63   Cited in B. L. Grover, *A New Look at Modern Indian History* (Delhi, 1997), p. 269.
64   Hoskins, *British Routes*, pp. 374, 386.

65 Report of the Indian Telegraph Committee, 1906–1907 (Calcutta, 1907), pp. i, 123.
66 L. F. Rushbrook Williams, *Statement Exhibiting the Moral and Material Progress and Condition of India, 1922–1923* (No. 58, Calcutta, 1923), p. 188.
67 Contract Book 1909, LN 293 883309, p. 32, RA.
68 Contract Book 1906, LN 293 883309, RA.
69 Chairman's address, Annual Report 1898, RA.
70 Annual Report 1913, RA.
71 General Service Suggestions to Correspondents, March 1906, p. 3, RA.
72 *Ibid.*, pp. 3–4; D. Read, 'War news from Reuters: Victorian and Edwardian reporting', *Despatches* (autumn 1993), p. 81.
73 Copies of Contracts I, Box 317, 1/8818001, RA.
74 India, Ceylon, Contract Book 1906, LN 293, 883309, pp. 18–19, RA.
75 Digby to Bradshaw, 24 November 1891; Bradshaw's reply, 25 November 1891, Copies of Contracts, Box 318 1/8818002, RA.
76 General Instructions for the Guidance of Correspondents, August 1897, LN17 863813.
77 Contract Book 1906, RA.
78 American news agencies are excluded.
79 Copy of Contract III, 12 August 1897, LN 391 1/8818003, RA.
80 *Ibid.*
81 Contract Book 1906, pp. 18–19, RA.
82 Special Traffic Routine Circular 17, Calcutta, 19 July 1922, P&T, L/PWD/7/1551.
83 *Ibid.*, pp. 63–5, 88–9.
84 R. Jones, *A Life in Reuters* (1951), p. 283; Read, *Power*, p. 83.
85 Buck to Dunlop-Smith, 20 December 1907, MSS Eur F166/13, Dunlop-Smith Collection (hereafter D-S/no.)
86 C. Benn, *Keir Hardie* (1992), p. 231; E. Hughes, *Keir Hardie* (1956), pp. 148–53; J Keir Hardie, *India: Impressions and Suggestions* (1909), pp. 112–14.
87 Buck to Dunlop-Smith, 20 December 1907, D-S /13.
88 Reuter Service Bulletin, June 1921, p. 19, RA.
89 Murray to MacGregor, 25 July 1931, File 99B, L/I/1/264, Information Department, (hereafter L/I/no).
90 Read, 'War news', pp. 83–4.
91 O. Boyd-Barrett, *The International News Agencies* (1980), p. 223.
92 Lord Beaverbrook, *Men and Power* (1956), p. 269.
93 Reuter Service Bulletin, October 1917, p. 5, September 1918, pp. 2, 10, RA.
94 Read, *Power*, p. 64.
95 Read, 'War news', pp. 74, 78.
96 For examples of Reuters biased reporting involving Gandhi (1896) and the Muslim League (1906), see Raghavan, *Press*, pp. 64–7.
97 G. Storey, *Reuter's Century, 1851–1951* (1951), pp. 123–4.
98 This phraseology was in common use; see J. Henniker-Heaton, 'One hundred reasons for penny-a-word cable messages', *Sells*(1910), p. 534; Morris, *Pax Britannica*, p. 54.
99 Cited in P. M. Kennedy, 'Imperial cable communications and strategy, 1870–1914', *Eng.*H.R., 86 (1971), 748.
100 D. Williams, *India Office, 1858–1869* (Hoshiarpur, 1983), p. 480.
101 G. Orwell, *England, Your England* (1953), pp. 216–17.

CHAPTER THREE

Fleet Street and the Raj

This chapter describes the newspaper networks that sustained and influenced reporting of the subcontinent in London and how the editorial stance of individual papers coloured their coverage. These issues are investigated by means of in-depth reference to a selection of political dailies, including the quality *Times*, the *Morning Post* and the important provincial newspaper the *Manchester Guardian*, as well as the largest mass-circulation popular paper, the *Daily Mail*. Also considered for detailed study is the journal *Round Table* and some specialist papers devoted specifically to Indian news. Tables 3.1 and 3.2 provide summary details and circulation figures of the dailies, weeklies and reviews consulted. These papers represent a cross-section of the political press in the character of their journalism, their political affiliations, the scale of their Indian operations and the nature (and number) of the audience they addressed.

The quality press included the most important London papers, and, while their circulation was not large, their readership included policy makers in Westminster and Downing Street, and they carried significant weight with politicians. *The Times* and *Manchester Guardian* had a stronger and more consistent interest in India than other papers. The former provided an expression of the informed Conservative perspective, whereas the latter provided a similar role for the Liberals. However, in practice their Indian coverage differed, as Gannon has similarly observed of their reporting of Germany in the 1930s, more in matters of context and tone than in content.[1] A range of other quality papers, including the liberal *Chronicle*, *Daily News* and *Gazette* and weeklies like the *Nation* as well as conservative publications like the *Telegraph* and the weekly *Spectator* and *Observer*, provide competing frames of reference. The radical working-class press is represented by the quality Labour *Herald* and popular papers like the weekly *Reynolds's* and the evening daily *Star*. There was also a

Table 3.1 The London press

Newspaper (founded) Price Time	Editor	Proprietor	Politics
	Dailies		
Daily Chronicle (1855) ½d–1d Morning	W. Fisher 1899 R. Donald 1902 E. Perris 1918	E. Lloyd 1987 D. Lloyd George 1918	Liberal
Daily Express (1900) ½d–1d Morning	A. Pearson 1900 R. Blumenfeld 1902	A. Pearson 1900 London Express Newspaper 1951 Beaverbrook 1916	Independent/ Conservative
Daily Herald (1912) 1d–2d Morning	R. Kenny 1912 C. Lapworth 1913 G. Lansbury 1913 R. Ryan 1922	Daily Herald Printing & Publishing Society	Labour
Daily Mail (1896) ½d–1d Morning	T. Marlowe 1899	Northcliffe Associated Newspapers	Independent/ Conservative
Daily News (and Leader from 1912) (1846) ½d–1d Morning	E. Cook 1896 R. Lehmann 1901 A. Gardiner 1902 S. Hodgson 1920	Daily News 1901 Amalgamated Morning Leader 1912	Liberal
Daily Telegraph 1855 1d–2d Morning	J. le Sage 1885	Burnham family	Conservative
Manchester Guardian (1821) 1d–2d Morning	C. P. Scott 1872	Manchester Guardian & Evening News	Liberal
Morning Post (1772) 1d–2d Morning	J. Dunn 1897 S. Wilkinson 1905 F. Ware 1905 H. Gwynne 1911	A. Borthwick 1876 Lady Bathurst 1908	Conservative
Star (1888) ½d–1d Evening	E. Parke 1891 J. Douglas 1908 W. Pope 1920	Star Newspaper Co.	Liberal

Table 3.1 *Continued*

Newspaper (founded) Price Time	Editor	Proprietor	Politics
The Times (1788) 1 *d*–3 *d* Morning	G. E. Buckle 1884 G. Dawson 1912 H. Steed 1919 G. Dawson 1923	Walters 1785 Northcliffe 1908 J. Astor and J. Walter 1922	Independent/ Conservative
Westminster Gazette (1893) 1 *d*–2 *d* Evening	J. Spender J. Hobman 1921–8	G. Newnes 1893 Liberal syndicate 1908 A. Pearson 1915	Liberal

Weeklies

Nation (1907) 9 *d* Saturday	H. W. Massingham 1907	Joseph Rowntree Trust	Liberal/ Independent
New Statesman (1913) 6 *d*	C. Sharp 1913	Statesman Publishing Co.	Fabian/ Independent
Observer (1971) 1 *d*–2 *d* Sunday	F. Beer 1894 A. Harrison 1905 J. Garvin 1908	F. Beer 1905 Northcliffe 1905 W. Astor 1911	Unionist/ Conservative
Reynolds's (1850) 1 *d*–2 *d* Sunday	W. Thompson 1894 H. Dalziel 1907 J. Crawley 1920	J. Dicks 1879 H. Dalziel 1907	Democratic
Spectator (1822) 6 *d*–9 *d* Saturday	J. St Loe Strachey 1897	J. St Loe Strachey 1898	Conservative/ Unionist

Reviews

Contemporary Review (1866) 2 *s* 6 *d* Monthly			
Fortnightly Review (1865) 2 *s* 6 *d* Monthly			
National Review (1883) 2 *s* 6 *d* Monthly			Conservative

Table 3.1 *Continued*

Newspaper (founded) Price Time	Editor	Proprietor	Politics
Nineteenth Century (and After) (1877) 2s 6d Monthly			
Quarterly Review (1806) 6d			
Review of Reviews (1890) 6d Monthly			
Round Table (1910) 6d Quarterly			
Saturday Review (1855) 6d Weekly			Conservative

Notes   The political classifications in the last column are those ascribed at the time and since. Whilst many declared political allegiance, others stated their position as officially 'Independent', e.g. *The Times.*

Sources   Butler, *British Political Facts* (1980), *Mitchell's, Sell's, Whitaker's Almanack.*

process of exchange between the quality and the popular press, which allowed their ideas to attract a broader response.

The so-called 'new journalism' that emerged during the late nineteenth century was a term used to describe the altered visual aspect of newspapers – their relative brightness of appearance, as well as the content and style of reporting, with entertaining and easily assimilable information.[2] With a marked reduction in parliamentary coverage and briefer notices of political speeches, newspapers gave more space to non-political matter. The *Mail* gave the first and fullest expression to the 'new journalism', selling nearly a million copies a day by 1900. The market exploited by 'new journalism' centred upon the lower middle and artisan classes, who were assumed to look to the press to entertain them and whose numbers were expanding rapidly under the stimulus of economic development.[3] Commercialism was thus another key feature of the 'new journalism'. The financial structure of the paper was transformed. From being private or family properties like *The Times*, valued, as the first Royal Commission noted, 'for the prestige and the political and social influence their possession con-

Table 3.2 Circulation figures, daily and weekly press, 1910–21 (000)

Newspaper	1910	Wartime	1921
Daily Chronicle	400	400	660
Daily Express	400–25	400–600	579
Daily Herald	50–250		
Daily Mail	800–900	950–1,172	1,533
Daily News	250–320	550–900	300
Daily Telegraph	230	180–200	180
Manchester Guardian	35–42		
Morning Post	60	80–150	50
Star	327–330	500	
The Times	45	150–84	113
Westminster Gazette	20–7		
Nation	5–7		
New Statesman	5–7		
Observer	20[a]–60[b]	135–75	
Reynolds's	600		
Spectator	18–22		

Notes   [a] 1908. [b] 1911.

Sources   Figures in this period are tentative and have been compiled from Blewett (1965), T. B. Browne, *Advertiser's ABC* (1910), Butler (1980), Inwood (1971), McEwen (1982), Read (1972), Richards (1994), *Sell's* (1910), Seymour-Ure (1975), *The Times History* (1952), W. B. Thomas (1928) and Wadsworth (1955).

ferred rather than as a source of dividends', newspaper production became an industry and there was a corresponding concentration of ownership. By 1910 only three proprietors controlled two-thirds of national morning and four-fifths of evening papers.[4] The formation of a popular image of empire owed much to its representation in the popular press. The mass-circulation popular papers sought out the human interest in imperial stories, and in so doing made such news accessible to a much wider audience: the empire, their readers were reminded, was 'kith and kin'. Northcliffe spoke of the 'great responsibility' of pressmen towards their readership, for they were 'looking at life through a peephole for all those people'. He was not unaware that 'there was more than one public. There were millions on whom he could play with ease and there were the thousands who read *The Times.*'[5]

In 1904 W. T. Stead published a perceptive analysis of the London daily press, dividing it into four hierarchical ranks, from the quality political dailies like *The Times* to the entertainment and picture-led popular papers like the *Daily Mirror* that were 'as much without pretence to influence as without serious capacity for it'.[6] However, it is important to stress that for much of the period under review 'new' and 'old' journalism existed side by side. Many of the quality dailies borrowed from the 'new journalism'; similarly the *Telegraph*, for instance, was a pioneer of the bright penny daily when it first appeared in 1855 and the mass-circulation dailies of the Edwardian period built on its foundations – as well as owing much to the sensationalist Sunday press which had existed since the 1840s.[7]

During the nineteenth and early twentieth centuries the political reviews were one of the most significant media for the transmission of opinion. They featured substantial essays on India and provided a platform for detailed exposition of views and debate, supplementing the daily press. While generally professing political impartiality, some had discernible agendas. Contributors also possessed similarities in terms of background and profession: more often than not they were the educated elite of administrators, politicians, ex-servicemen, academics and writers. Despite distinctive individual attributes, editors of the quality daily and weekly press saw their role as part of the wider world of metropolitan political journalism. Spender, long-serving editor of the *Gazette*, said that the paper was 'very deliberately an "organ of opinion"'. It was seeking to convert and persuade. 'To catch this kind of reader,' wrote Spender, 'it was necessary to abjure... popular appeal and to write for him and him alone. The appeal, therefore, was deliberately to the few.' By the standards of the popular press their circulation was insignificant. Yet their editors commanded respect and influence precisely because they appealed to a select audience of politically instructed readers, parliamentarians as well as other journalists who were influenced by their views. 'There could have been no better audience for the purpose of what is now called propaganda.'[8]

Prior to the mid-nineteenth century *The Times* was the only daily with an extensive system of foreign correspondents in the subcontinent, spending over £10,000 a year on this service.[9] However, with the Crown establishing suzerainty over India in 1858, increasing space was accorded to Britain's largest imperial possession in the London press. This process received a fillip from a combination of factors, including the removal of government taxes and financial constraints on newspapers by the 1860s, the continuing expansion and diversification of the metropolitan press, with the adoption of more popular formats for mass appeal; the increasing access to overseas news due to improved communication technologies and the development of news agencies; and the rising number of kith and kin, including significant numbers of women, setting up home in the Raj. There was an enormous increase in the British market for news, and the empire, reaching its apogee, offered exciting opportunities for attention-grabbing stories.

Thus by the late nineteenth century several major London dailies had a small core of salaried staff – in the 1880s *The Times* had been joined by the *Standard*, *Daily News* and *Telegraph* with correspondents at Calcutta – supplemented, when necessary, with additional reporters, including journalists of the burgeoning Anglo-Indian press. Such papers provided natural points of contact for Fleet Street. Amongst these journalists we find a mix of the professional and amateur, full-time and *ad hoc*. On the one hand, it was said to be possible for a resourceful individual to combine planting, racing and journalism. A colourful example is Lionel James, son of 'an old Bengal gunner'. After working as an indigo planter, he engaged with J. O'B. Saunders, proprietor of the *Englishman* (Calcutta) – himself a former indigo planter – to serve as a correspondent and to duplicate messages for the *Times of India* (Bombay) and Reuters. Thus it was that 'knowing nothing of the art and craft of the complete War Correspondent the bankrupt indigo planter was transformed . . . into the solvent journalist'.[10] H. E. A. Cotton (son of Sir Henry J. S. Cotton, the liberal ICS who became President of the INC in 1904) reported for the *Daily News* whilst practising in the Calcutta High Court.

Yet journalism in India also derived from that in England and was conducted along similarly professional lines. The literary staff on the *Times of India* in 1883 was drawn largely from England, including the editor, sub-editor, chief reporter and four local reporters. The menage of the *Bombay Gazette* was similar. S. K. Ratcliffe, a former editor of the London *Echo*, was made editor of the Calcutta radical daily the *Statesman* (formerly *The Friend of India*) in 1903. J. A. Jones of the *Liverpool Post* joined the paper in 1905 and became its editor (1913–24). Alfred Watson, who edited the paper from 1925 to 1932, had worked for more than twenty years on the *Gazette*. In 1906 Benjamin Guy Horniman, previously employed on the *Guardian*, took charge of the *Statesman*'s news layout. His editorial services were acquired by the *Bombay Chronicle* in 1913.

Besides journalists based in India, there were special correspondents who moved between metropolis and periphery. Henry Newman replaced Rudyard Kipling on the *Civil and Military Gazette* (Lahore) and often worked on 'specials' for newspapers in Calcutta, and for Reuters – for instance during the Third Afghan War.[11] For royal visits and durbars, major Fleet Street figures such as Garvin, Gwynne, Spender, Sidney Low and Herbert Russell journeyed to India. Metropolitan papers often collaborated to cover a particular story. The *Chronicle, Nation, Guardian* and *Glasgow Herald* combined to send Henry Nevinson on a six-month tour in 1907–08. Northcliffe often shared men and resources between the *Mail* and *The Times*. Old India hands – civilian and military – as well as a range of professional writers, students and visiting politicians also contributed to the press. Thus Spender thanked Harcourt Butler, Governor of the United Provinces, for his letters, which were 'always most welcome and a running thread of some knowledge about India which is most useful to a London editor'.[12]

The late nineteenth and early twentieth centuries also saw an increased interchange of news and information between Fleet Street and the Indian press, the latter also serving to amplify the views of the former within the subcontinent. The number of Indian papers with London offices grew rapidly, from eight in 1901 to forty-seven in 1914, reaching sixty-three in 1921. Though predominantly representing Anglo-Indian papers, after 1910 there were an increasing number of Indian-run papers as well. William Digby, the radical publicist and Anglo-Indian journalist, acted as the London correspondent of the *Hindu* (Madras) and *Amrita Bazaar Patrika* (Calcutta). The *Civil and Military Gazette* and the *Times of India* prepared special overseas editions. In 1886 the journal *English Opinion on India* was established in Poona to provide an anthology of British press reports for the use of indigenous papers. Together these provided a rich source of copy and comment. Thus Fleet Street tapped a range of sources, within both India and Britain, in forming its coverage of the subcontinent (see Appendix 1).

Dailies

The Times

The Times was the most influential British newspaper on India, with the largest financial outlay and a host of specialist leader writers, including D. D. Braham, Valentine Chirol, J. W. Flanagan, Lovat Fraser and Edward Grigg. It ran regular specials on the subcontinent and India also received substantial coverage in its Empire Day numbers, started in 1910. In 1909 the Foreign Department consisted of four men, Chirol, Braham, Fraser and Grigg, and any one of them was, noted the Manager Moberly Bell, 'continually in direct relations' with the Foreign Office, India Office and Colonial Office.[13] The close reciprocal relations between the paper and the India Office were both formal and informal.

4 Valentine Chirol, *The Times*   **5** Lovat Fraser, *The Times*

This was well illustrated by the case of Valentine Chirol (foreign editor 1899–1911), a long-standing and experienced journalist who was one of the best-informed authorities on the subcontinent. He had close official contacts and was frequently consulted by Viceroys and Secretaries of State, many of whom were close personal friends. He served on the Royal (Islington) Commission on Public Services, was knighted for his services, and wrote several influential books, continuing to serve the paper after retirement. In 1921, when an Information Officer was first appointed at the India Office, a *Times* man, Owen Lloyd–Evans, was selected for the post.

During the 1890s there were two main *Times* correspondents – Howard Hensman in Simla and James MacGregor in Calcutta – with the Foreign Manager, Mackenzie Wallace, co-ordinating coverage in London.[14] Fraser and Stanley Reed, successive editors of the *Times of India*, were prominent recruits from the Anglo-Indian press to strengthen this news team. Fraser relinquished his editorship in 1907, and worked as a special correspondent for *The Times*, based in London, till 1922. Reed, although never working directly for *The Times*, was its chief liaison officer in India. F. H. Brown also served an apprenticeship in India before joining the staff of *The Times* in 1902.[15] Woolacott of the *Pioneer* (Allahabad) and his successor, Edwin Haward, were similarly recruited to act as *Times* correspondents. During August 1918, in an attempt to increase the cable service, Reed was instructed to cable, weekly, 500–700 words of general Indian news for publication on Mondays. The object was 'to make Indian news a regular and special feature of the paper'.[16] *The Times* also sent more special correspondents to India than any other newspaper. James visited India for three months in 1907. For the Delhi durbar *The Times* dispatched Fraser and Grigg. The 'disturbed' situation in 1920 called for 'a special investigation and so far as we can help to improve an ugly situation'. Chirol was selected to send a series of articles which would be 'helpful to the British public in explaining the real position, and, so far as possible, also to troubled India'.[17]

Special correspondents received acknowledgement but for the most part reports were anonymous. Although the policy of the paper was formulated at Printing House Square, correspondents were not expected to simply expound the official line. As an editorial note to Grigg stated:

> The Times is not a department of the Foreign Office and correspondents are not supposed to 'hold' a certain 'language' like diplomatists in conformity with a preconceived policy in London. The policy of the paper . . . is expounded in its leading articles and not in the reports of its correspondents, which deal with matters of fact. A correspondent's whole value to the paper lies in telling the truth as he knows it; special qualifications, long experience and intimate knowledge of a subject become worthless if he has to 'write up' a certain view – almost anyone can do that.[18]

However, as Wallace explained to MacGregor, while the 'impressions' of overseas reporters would 'always receive attentive consideration',[19] the ultimate decision rested with the editor, who interpreted the policy of the paper.[20] Even an influential correspondent, such as Chirol, suffered rebuke if he transgressed the official line too far. G. E. Buckle telegraphed Chirol in Bombay with reference to the Curzon–Kitchener military controversy, 'Through confidence your judgement published greater portion telegram but grave misgivings strongly feel unwise reopen heated controversy beginning Royal tour likely hamper Minto.'[21] In determining the paper's line, advice from senior Indian correspondents was, of course, important. H. MacGregor thanked Reed for his notes, which were 'extremely valuable, and especially helpful in correcting the more or less academic views of those of us whose knowledge of India was gained by reading rather than by personal experience'.[22] The paper had also to temper its line in accordance with the domestic situation, especially if it represented a response to a particularly delicate issue likely to inflame sentiment. Long, writing to Reed in February 1921 in the wake of disturbances in Rae Bareli, noted that:

> we have to balance the pros and cons of a situation like that in India at the moment as carefully as we can. Often our decisions are liable to seem unintelligent to you on the spot; whereas they are due to causes which seem insuperable to us here . . . I think that unless things become really desperate it is better for *The Times* to err on the side of moderation.[23]

Developments from the 1850s and 1860s had progressively undermined the paper's supremacy. The repeal of onerous press taxes and the rapid growth of a penny press saw *The Times* offering enhanced foreign news coverage to justify its 3*d* price. Yet this, in turn, was seriously affected by the growth of the telegraph network and the much greater cost of cable messages, which increased the financial burden of overseas coverage. This development coincided with a general decline in the paper's resources. Additionally it had to deal with a powerful rival in the shape of Reuters. As its official history remarks, 'the effect of the telegraphic agencies in generally levelling-up the standard in foreign correspondence hit *The Times* as it hit no other paper'.[24] Thus by the 1890s much of the advantage which *The Times* possessed was significantly diminished. This general rivalry in foreign reporting made itself felt in India. Hensman was warned in 1892 'to keep a sharp eye on' Reuters agent in Simla, for 'he runs you very close'.[25] With Reuters matching the paper in hard news reporting, *The Times* sought to differentiate itself by the quality of its analysis. As Bell wrote:

> Reuters agent has one business, to pick up facts . . . and to wire them at the earliest moment . . . A Times correspondent has a great deal more to do, [his] duty being to comment on news rather than to give it: it is only natural that in the mere getting of facts Reuters should forestall him.[26]

The reputation of *The Times* for foreign news coverage increasingly failed to be reflected in sales, and the need for economy was pressing. Wallace and Bell were cautious managers. Telegraphic costs were a major part of expenses and the management urged its correspondents to be 'more concise'. In 1891 MacGregor had transmitted 49,505 words at a cost of £2,480. The following year, Wallace informed him, it would be 'desirable to diminish' the telegraph expenses from India and Burma by 'about one-fourth' though if 'any *important* events should unexpectedly occur, we must be kept fully informed, whatever the *neces-*

Table 3.3   Telegraph expenditure from India:
The Times, 1897–1906 (£)

Year	Amount	Year	Amount
1897	4,785	1902	446
1898	2,584	1903	850
1899	1,817	1904	1,186
1900	2,194	1905	755
1901	1,570	1906	407

Source   Bell to Fraser, 2 December 1908, MLB/50.

sary expense may be'.[27] *The Times* had a contract with the ETC by which it was bound to pay for a minimum number of words annually (during the 1890s around 40,000). When, as in 1895, the amount telegraphed fell short of this the paper had 'some dissertations transmitted to make up the amount'.[28] The telegraph companies occupied a strong bargaining position and newspapers had to pay the whole fee even when little of interest was deemed by the press to be happening in India.

With the exception of 1904, the totals for the early twentieth century were always under £1,000. Whereas an average of 300 words had been sent each day in 1897, by 1906 it was twenty-six.[29] Bell explained the economics of Indian coverage in 1908:

To begin with the telegraph rate of 1s a word is very high as compared with America at 5d. Taking a column at 1200 words it is £60 from India as against £25 from the U.S.A. It would seem to me that even in ordinary circumstances a column a week would not be too much to give to our greatest dependency but that which would only cost £1300 a year from Canada would cost £6120 from India ... If a Sunday line could be arranged for at a very much reduced rate I don't think that there need be an objection on the ground of space. Monday is the one day we have no Parliament and we might very well allow an extra 4 columns to Imperial and Foreign in place of it ... I have just looked up our agreement with the Indo-European. I find that the press rate being then 1s 4d a word we had a preferential rate of 1s on condition that we guaranteed £3000/– a year ... When the press rate was reduced to 1s they declined to give us any further reduction and of course the guarantee was no longer given. I don't know whether there is any way in which we could get some reduction upon a guarantee ... Failing any such arrangement I can only say that the quantity we can send by cable must depend upon circumstances which it is quite impossible to estimate. Judging by the state of things as it is today I should not think 1000 words a week excessive.[30]

[65]

Another major expense was the correspondents stationed in India, and here again *The Times* sought to economise. Wallace asked Hensman in the 1890s whether it was cost-effective to have a correspondent at Calcutta when the government moved to its summer capital in Simla.[31] Upon the reorganisation of the Indian network in 1908–09, Reed was put in charge of all telegraph expenses from Bombay. Hensman, who had earlier sent telegrams direct to London, was paid £200 per annum and had to work under Reed.[32] He was subsequently dismissed, then reappointed in 1914 on a lower annual retaining fee of £100. Reed received £25 per month.[33] The responsibility for co-ordination in London rested primarily with Fraser, who was given '*carte blanche* to name correspondents'.[34] All messages to and from India were to pass through the hands of Reed,[35] utilising the whole foreign news service of the *Times of India*, who was to be assisted by Hensman in Simla, Edwin Long for the United Provinces, and Vivian Gabriel in Peshawar.[36] Interestingly, Gabriel was in fact Secretary to the Government of the North West Frontier Province. To avoid falling foul of official regulations, Lovat Fraser arranged for *The Times's* nominal correspondent in the area to be Gabriel's clerk, Jackson P. Fernandez – a subterfuge that was sanctioned by the Chief Commissioner, Sir G. Roos-Kepell.[37] The possibilities of co-operation between Anglo-Indian and London papers were well exemplified by this case. According to Reed, the system worked overall to the advantage of *The Times*. 'It secures a very wide service of Indian news on which to draw and it secures also I think a very great economy and accuracy in the cable service.'[38] The centre in Bombay continued to advise the London office privately as well as through its correspondents in India.[39] *The Times* also operated an exchange system with Anglo-Indian newspapers, including the *Englishman, Indian Spectator* and *Madras Weekly Mail*.

Besides salaried correspondents, there were other writers who received a retaining fee and a fixed amount per telegram published – usually 10s. For any mail matter published, payment was made at the rate of £3 a column.[40] The costs for special correspondents varied. The visit of James in 1907 cost the paper £200.[41] Fraser and Grigg were paid £200 each and presented with court suits when they covered the coronation durbar. Their additional expenses constituted a 'very high' sum, only grudgingly accepted by the management. For the special investigation undertaken by Chirol in 1920 it was agreed that he should receive travelling expenses, a living allowance of £2 a day, £4 4s for each column published and an honorarium of £250.[42]

During Dawson's editorship India occupied a special position in *The*

Times' coverage of imperial issues.[43] Dawson's concern with empire and the Raj was constant and acute. Within India the paper's prestige was unparalleled. According to Reed, it was:

> the only English newspaper which is read in India with respect; it is the only English newspaper which influences opinion here, and which has honestly sought to guide the British public on Indian questions.[44]

Yet in addition to being an influential organ of opinion among the decision-making elite, *The Times* was a business under increasing financial pressure. When Northcliffe became proprietor in 1908 his immediate concern was to restore commercial viability. Cuts in finance and space produced consternation amongst staff, prompting Chirol to complain about:

> the difficulty of reconciling the exigencies of space under the new dispensation with the full and serious treatment of foreign politics which was one of the best features of the old, is, I fear, increasing every day with a growing tendency to consider what the general public wants in news than what the relatively small class of readers who nevertheless constitute the backbone of *The Times* and give it its prestige expect to find in the paper.[45]

This change in perspective was reflected in the nature of the copy Chirol was expected to provide in 1920. His dispatches, noted the new editor, W. Steed, were to appeal more to the generally interested reader than to those with a special knowledge of India:

> The idea is that he should write . . . a number of articles on 'India Today' from the point of view of an expert who goes to India with the definite intention of trying to make Indian conditions and Indian problems interesting and comprehensible to the general reader. There would be as much 'impression' as erudition in the articles. I think, and Lord Northcliffe agrees, that on these conditions the articles ought to be a very valuable feature next winter.[46]

This need to attract general, as well as specialist, readers was the essential dilemma faced by the paper. However much it prided itself upon the quality of its reporting and its contribution to contemporary debates, *The Times* remained financially vulnerable. Hugh MacGregor was forced to write to Reed in 1920 that, after a decade of concentration chiefly on political news:

> You will be doing a great service if you can induce our men in India to replace politics as far as possible by a variety of subjects. Newspaper conditions here are becoming rather critical, in that the public are strongly reacting against political matter . . . This is regrettable . . . but has to be recognised by journalists as businessmen whose newspaper prosperity

depends at least on a minimum circulation, and so the public must be humoured for a little.[47]

Morning Post

The arch-Conservative *Morning Post* was considered by many to be the organ of the leisured classes. Its proprietor, Algernon Borthwick (later Lord Glenesk), was an MP who had close ties with Disraeli and Randolph Churchill and was involved in the establishment of the Primrose League. Nevertheless, Borthwick consistently proclaimed the paper's independence, maintaining that it was 'the first condition of influence'.[48] His daughter, Lady Lillian Bathurst, succeeded him in 1908 and associated with politicians such as Chamberlain, Milner and Bonar Law. However, the bigger influence on the paper was the dynamic and forthright personality of H. A. Gwynne. A former Reuters correspondent in South Africa during the Boer wars, Gwynne was driven by a series of obsessions, and he had no qualms about allowing them to determine his paper's reporting. His imperialist and anti-Zionist views were to have powerful repercussions on the paper's treatment of India.

The *Morning Post*'s foreign news coverage under Glenesk reflected his predilection for aristocratic government and monarchy. Colonial reporting was strongly imperialist in tone, and Glenesk was said to know 'a very great deal about India'.[49] Unfortunately, little can be gleaned from surviving records as to the paper's outlay on Indian news and it is likely that its standard Reuters contract (£1,600 p.a.) was supplemented increasingly through private sources. With its penchant for war reporting, the *Morning Post* had well known military correspondents. Winston Churchill wrote occasionally while serving with the Tirah Expeditionary Force on the North West Frontier in 1897.[50] Prior to 1914, Spenser Wilkinson (Chichele Professor of Military History at Oxford 1909–23) was the paper's chief leader writer, military correspondent, and a specialist on India. Ian Colvin, who joined the staff as a chief leader writer in 1909, had earlier worked for the *Pioneer* at its London office and in 1900 returned to work in Allahabad for three years. He was a staunch Conservative and achieved notoriety for his defence of General Dyer, subsequently writing a fulsome biography of the disgraced soldier.

W. Pilcher, who also wrote for the *Statesman*, seems to have been the paper's chief contact in India during the 1910s and 1920s. Special correspondents were occasionally despatched to cover important events, but financial constraints restricted such opportunities. In 1905 the manager, Edward Peacock, expressed concern that Glenesk was not in favour of sending a journalist to cover the Prince of Wales's visit.

Battersby is most anxious to go, and the cost would be about £450, exclusive of any telegraphing charges . . . The only consideration that would make it worth our while to send a special man is that every other important paper will be specially represented, and we ought not to be the only exception. To a certain extent this might be met by an arrangement which I think could be made at comparatively little cost under which the 'Times of India' man would also represent us, thus enabling us to publish an occasional letter or telegram 'From our special correspondent'.[51]

The paper spent only £50 in covering the Delhi durbar and there was concern that such amounts were 'considerably exceeded' by other newspapers and 'we cannot afford to be without the news'.[52]

Yet foreign news often boosted sales. Kipling's poetry, which was first published by the *Morning Post*, guaranteed increased sales throughout the years 1907–16.[53] Kipling was a friend of Lady Bathurst, and had recommended Gwynne for the editorship.[54] The issue that earned the paper its greatest publicity was the Dyer Fund campaign of 1920, the creation of Gwynne, who pursued it with a zeal approaching fanaticism. The fund was a 'splendid thing for the paper', maintained Peacock, and it 'came just at the psychological moment when people were filled with indignation and wanted an opportunity of expressing their sympathy with a man who had been treated with gross injustice. Our action will bind our present readers to us and will bring us many new adherents.'[55] An extreme Conservative paper like the *Morning Post* was bound to oppose Indian constitutional reform. This was certainly the case under Gwynne, who enjoyed the backing of Bathurst, who approved the denunciation of the Montagu–Chelmsford Report, prompting Gwynne to acknowledge, 'I am glad you liked our leader on India. A few years ago such proposals would never have been allowed.'[56]

Manchester Guardian

Under Charles Prestwich Scott, editor and proprietor from 1872, the *Guardian* was the one of the few provincial papers to acquire a national reputation. David Ayerst, a journalist on the paper in the 1920s and its official biographer, recalled that its 'detachment' from London made it 'compulsive reading' for professional politicians.[57] Dibblee went even further, claiming that the *Guardian* was the only non-metropolitan paper 'whose editorial conduct has caused it to be . . . a newspaper of universal range and influence'.[58] Scott had close links with Liberal politicians, who valued his advocacy and support, including the Secretaries of State Morley and Montagu – who were also personal friends. Morley often wrote praising Scott for his editorial stance: 'I don't like to thank you but I may and will say that they give

Table 3.4 *Manchester Guardian* leaders on India, 1905–22

Year	No.	%
1905	24	1.9
1906	25	2.0
1907	32	2.6
1908	39	3.1
1909	33	2.6
1910	31	2.5
1911	42	3.4
1912	54	4.3
1913	23	1.8
1914	15	1.2
1915	15	1.2
1916	21	1.7
1917	26	2.1
1918	8	0.6
1919	36	2.9
1920	23	1.8
1921	20	1.6
1922	24	1.9

Source Compiled from *Manchester Guardian* Index, Central Library, Manchester.

us new courage.'[59] Support for the Liberal Party did not, however, preclude criticism of particular policies. For instance, the paper attacked Morley for the measures against freedom of the press and speech in India enacted during 1907–08.

Though the *Guardian* had 'a line of its own on Indian affairs', Ayerst contended that the paper too often offered its readers only editorial opinions insufficiently supported by facts. Consequently, unless they took other papers as well, they were 'not really free to make up their own minds'.[60] Ayerst fails, however, to do full justice to the diversity and quantity of information that the paper conveyed. As Table 3.4 makes clear, editorial attention was significant. Account must also be taken of the numerous reports of political, social and economic events, Reuters telegrams, interviews, parliamentary coverage, and the space devoted to Indian activities in Britain and abroad.

The general practice of the paper with regard to foreign news reporting was outlined by Scott:

Table 3.5 Vaughan Nash in India: statement of expenses, February–June 1900

	£	s	d
Outfit and carry equipment	63	19	11
Passage–return	103	14	10
Railway fares and transport	49	18	8
Hotels, etc.	24	19	3
Miscellaneous expenses	29	17	11
Services, 112 days	112	0	0
Telegraphing	26	0	0
Grand total	410	10	7

Source Compiled from A/N4/3, MGA.

We prefer that our correspondents should as far as possible be movable and to rely rather on special correspondents as occasion arises than upon resident men . . . .The system of local correspondents is quite useful . . . But I don't believe in keeping a good man tied down to a particular place, and think that much better results can be obtained by moving men about to whatever point at the time is most interesting.[61]

This was the system preferred in covering the subcontinent. Unfortunately, there are no extant figures indicating the amount specifically spent on gathering news and it is Ayerst's contention that, notwithstanding the importance of the Lancashire trade, the *Guardian* never had a consistently in-depth Indian service – except on certain special occasions, such as Vaughan Nash's investigation into the famine of 1900. This is understandable in the case of a provincial paper with limited resources. However, it did have a regular account with Reuters and the IETD, and Scott was aware of the possibilities of improving the service, admitting in 1902 that there was 'no doubt room for a more complete treatment of Indian subjects'.[62] The cost of sending a special correspondent to India can be gauged from the amounts spent on Nash's trip (Table 3.5).

In addition to substantial expenses, considerable forward planning was essential. Prior to his departure, Scott furnished Nash with letters of introduction to the Viceroy, the India Office gave him 'some good letters' to the chief famine officials, and he was debriefed by Lord Napier of Magdala, William Wedderburn and Florence Nightingale.[63] Conventionally no correspondent could join or write for the paper unless his political sympathies were broadly Liberal. Thus H. E. A.

Cotton was eminently suitable, given his familial connections and having edited *India* for several years.[64] Cotton in turn was 'very proud of having been permitted to contribute to the *Guardian* which is the only independent newspaper nowadays'.[65] Hewart, a principal writer for the paper, had also worked for *India*.[66] Additional opportunities for gathering Indian news were made possible by such contacts. For instance, Hewart recommended S. H. Swinny, who had written 'a good deal' about India in the *Positivist Review* and *India* and would be attending the next INC meeting.[67] Other prominent contributors included Digby, Wedderburn, Horniman, C. F. Andrews, B. C. Pal, S. K. Ratcliffe and Roper Lethbridge.[68] Scott himself maintained contact with influential Indians visiting Britain like M. K. Gandhi and Rabindranath Tagore and was Vice-president of the India Information Centre in London (1928).[69]

Under Scott political and economic issues received substantial coverage. Advising Nevinson, prior to his trip in 1907, to study the extent and causes of political unrest, plague and the machinery for its suppression, and the Swadeshi movement, Scott also urged him to 'go deeper and touch on some of the more fundamental questions . . . such as the increasing alienation of the native . . . the economic condition of the cultivator'.[70] Scott supported Montagu's constitutional reforms and was in close touch with Lionel Curtis, a leading member of the Round Table organisation who had initially advocated the principle of dyarchy. Scott's personal reflections on the 'solution of the tremendous problem' of Indian government were expressed to Rabindranath Tagore:

> It is the glory of this country . . . to have set out clearly & honestly as the true aim of policy Indian self government in the full sense. But the way is hard . . . and we go forward rather blindly . . . I approach the whole matter from the point of view of the active politician, & I turn for my remedies to publicity & to a more instructed opinion. That is why I want . . . assistance . . . and have repeatedly sent the ablest men I could find to study the Indian problem on the spot.[71]

The prestige of the paper was founded ultimately upon its editorial judgement, not on the quantity of facts furnished. Thus on the *Guardian*'s jubilee in 1920 Cotton congratulated Scott for his 'unswerving championship' of India:

> You were our staunchest friend when it was unpopular to advocate constitutional reform for India: you are still our friend now that the victory has been won and it only remains to make good. I know that I am voicing the sentiments of every responsible Indian who believes in progress on sane and settled lines when I offer you our most hearty and sincere thanks.[72]

Daily Mail

The *Mail*, according to Northcliffe, stood for 'the power, the supremacy and the greatness of the British Empire . . . the *Mail* is the embodiment and mouthpiece of the imperial idea'.[73] Besides being keen to exploit the potentialities for circulation that empire afforded Northcliffe's personal enthusiasm for the imperial idea, epitomised by the 'Empire first and parish after' policy, was responsible for innovative and interesting approaches to overseas coverage. 'We have not,' he declared, 'enough authoritative foreign or empire news in the paper . . . We do not get sufficiently in touch with big men visiting London from our great overseas Dominions . . . Dig them out. They have wonderful news stories to tell, and are most interesting and refreshing personalities.'[74] A chief factor for its success was the major investment in electric communications which meant that, by its second anniversary, Northcliffe could claim that the 'average cost of telegrams to any issue of the paper was greater than that expended by any rival in the U.K.'[75]

In November 1904 an *Overseas Daily Mail* edition was launched to meet the perceived need for 'a newspaper connection between the Old Country and the scattered hundreds of thousands of Britons in the four corners of the world . . . who were bearing the White Man's burden across the seas'. It would contain 'one hundred columns of matter', being a concise summary of the principal domestic and foreign news, leading articles and essays which would have appeared in the *Mail* as well as a weekly review by a leading author. The interests of 'the ladies abroad' would not be overlooked, and a special feature calculated to appeal to those living 'in far away Indian bungalows and Backwood settlements' was to be on 'What is Being Worn at Home'.[76] 'I have given orders,' noted Northcliffe, 'that although the newspaper cannot absolutely be non-political, it is to report each week equally speeches of ten leading men, and there will be a quotation from the *Times*.'[77] Writing to St Loe Strachey, Northcliffe announced that the 'project has been an overwhelming success', and while he could not 'see the chance of making much money out of it, I do think it will effect some good from the Imperial standpoint'.[78] Its long-serving editor, John Evelyn Wrench, admitted that he had consistently tried to give the journal 'a definitely Imperial tone'.[79] According to Wilson, the wide circulation of the *Overseas Daily Mail* edition ensured that Northcliffe's name carried 'weight throughout the Empire'.[80]

Yet the coverage accorded by the paper to Britain's largest imperial possession is an under-explored subject. The *Mail* had a separate Imperial and Foreign news page, though such news could also be scattered across its pages. In the absence of surviving records, it is impossible to ascertain the exact number of *Mail* correspondents stationed in the subcontinent or the financial outlay of the paper on India. It utilised the services of news agencies, including Central News, Dalziel, Indo-European and Reuters. By 1900 the paper had correspondents in Bombay, Calcutta, Colombo and Simla, some of whom, like Everard Cotes, were permanent, while others were engaged on short-term contracts or in conjunction with other newspapers. Old India hands and servicemen were encouraged to contribute. The *Times of India* acted as a co-ordinating office for the *Mail*, and its news network was no doubt strengthened after Northcliffe's take over of *The Times*. Special reporters like William Maxwell and Valentia Steer were sent to cover imperial pageants. Interviews and first-hand accounts were regular features. The assistant editor and chief leader writer, H. W. Wilson, contributed substantially to the opinion columns. The *Mail* even claimed to have inspired halfpenny journalism in the East in the shape of the *Indian Daily News*, edited by Everard Digby, with Cotes serving on its board.

The *Mail* usually carried several Indian news items each day. Many concerned personal tragedies and crises, reflecting a general belief that its readers were 'more interested in people than principles'.[81] Northcliffe did not attach sanctity to political coverage: 'We must not let politics dominate the paper, but we must get the *news* in politics.'[82] Relatively few editorials were devoted to India; the percentage of Indian leaders between 1909 and 1922 varied between none at all in 1915, 0.2 per cent in 1913, 1916 and 1920, and 1.9 per cent in 1909.[83] The human interest factor was ever-present, and the personal dimensions of empire were fully exploited. Always on the lookout for a scoop, the *Mail* was quick to despatch a reporter to Southampton to meet General Dyer in May 1920. With a photograph of the general, 'burnt red by 35 years' service' in India, the *Mail* informed its readers that he was 'thick-set and fairly tall, with greying hair and kindly blue eyes'. Dyer's 'first words' on landing were: 'It was my duty – my horrible, dirty duty.'[84]

Emphasis was laid on the presentation and conciseness of news stories. Leading articles were usually three short paragraphs in length, and made use of pithy and often provocative headings, such as 'Shall we give up India?', 'Montagu's mistakes', 'Gandhi's failure', 'Indian situation – cult of treason'. In matters of presentation Northcliffe was greatly influenced by the techniques evolved by Joseph Pulitzer in New York. Through its typefaces and layout the *Mail* intended to impress the reader, and Northcliffe, as Wrench remarked, 'saw life largely in headlines'.[85] For example, the report of 24 December 1912 on the assassination attempt on Hardinge employed six headers, each varying in size and boldness: 'Attempt to murder Indian Viceroy – Bomb from a roof – Lord Hardinge's six wounds – Outrage at state procession – Explosion on back of an elephant – Attendant killed'. Even for less dramatic reports, several headers introduced the topic and summed up its main features.

In terms of content the *Mail* provided coverage of variety and depth. In the years leading up to World War I crimes and 'outrages' received regular treatment. This may be attributable to the increase in political extremism in India from the turn of the century, but it also reflected Northcliffe's near-obsession with crime reporting: 'They are the sort of dramatic news that the public always affects to criticise but is always in the greatest hurry to read.'[86] From the official statistics for 1902 its readers were informed that over 23,000 criminals had been whipped and that there were 23,000 fatal snakebites per annum![87] The potential of the exotic East was also exploited in features, for instance recounting the peculiarities of the Amir of Afghanistan's 'Appearance, amusements, tastes and wives', or his prowess on the cricket pitch, where 'it is not etiquette, certainly not good policy, to get the Amir out too quickly, nor to send him "tricky" balls difficult to hit to the boundary'.[88] The Indian caste system, the practice of *sati* and the religious customs of the Brahmins were among the other topics that arrested its attention.

In addition to this underlying continuum in its coverage, certain key issues were treated in greater detail. War was the *Mail*'s forte, and imperial conflicts were covered with great attention to individual heroism and military detail. The North West Frontier campaigns in the 1890s, the march on Lhasa in 1903 and the Third Afghan War in 1919 all provided ample opportunity for dramatic reporting.[89] The heroism of the British race was reflected in the gallantry displayed in these fighting fields, where it earned the right to rule through superiority in arms. Referring to the Chitral expedition (1897), it argued that Britain 'must win. Eastern folk, like the Boers, have no delicate appreciation of a generous enemy, and unless we administer a very severe punishment, and prove our superiority beyond doubt, we shall be troubled by the tribes for all time with expeditions *adlib*.'[90] The Mutiny occupied a sacred place, with the *Mail* proclaiming on its fiftieth anniversary, 'In the whole history of Great Britain there is probably no record which has a deeper hold upon our hearts than the stirring story' of 1857.[91]

Yet social and humanitarian issues were not overlooked. The plague outbreak and catastrophic famine during 1896–97 affected a population of over 30 million. The *Mail* handled the tragedy with sensitivity, according due weight to the economic and political implications of the famine, and in the scale of its coverage may be ranked alongside such stalwarts of the quality press as the *Guardian* and *The Times*. In hard-hitting editorials it contended that, while there was rapidly increasing distress in India, England was 'holding back from the task of giving help to the starving natives'. It accused government of procrastination in setting up relief, being 'little concerned with the probable death of a few hundreds or thousands of insignificant black men in remote country districts'.[92]

> The fact is that English people do not yet realise the sufferings of the people of India. We are so lamentably unacquainted with the normal conditions under which the masses in India live from day to day that it is in a measure not surprising that we have hitherto remained inert and passive spectators of the dismal tragedy.[93]

In urging public action the *Mail* stressed how 'it falls to us to defend our Empire from the spectral armies of Famine . . . Our weapon is good honest British money, and to every Englishmen who has at heart the greatness of our Empire . . . can serve England right and well and loyally to-day by helping India in her hour of bitter need.'[94] In the jubilee year of Queen Victoria's reign, the paper argued, the Famine Fund would be a fitting memorial: 'We want to make our Queen a present; let us present her with a garland of human lives.' This would also serve to further bind the empire together.[95] Such spirited fund raising undoubtedly contributed to a public contribution of over £170,000 by the end of January 1897. The explicit emotionalism of such language was a new departure, prefiguring newspaper coverage of subsequent humanitarian crises throughout the twentieth century. Yet, along with evocative descriptions of the horrors of famine, the opportunity was taken to counterpoise the religious superstitions of the East with the rational medical methods of the West. Thus, for instance, the coverage of 'Prayer and plague' in Bombay noted how '50,000 Mahommedans petition Allah' for relief.[96] The 'fanaticism' of Muslims, the *Mail* claimed, was responsible in many instances for obstructing official sanitary and inoculation programmes. Similarly Spenser Sarle, an Anglo-Indian contributor, noted how vaccination was resented by 'an intensely conservative and fatalistic race like the Hindoos, who regard as impious any attempt to check the ravages of smallpox which does not take the form of an offering to the goddess Kali, the tutelary deity of that disease'.[97]

Another preoccupation of the *Mail*'s coverage was monarchy, which invested the East with glamour. By the end of the nineteenth century great royal occasions were also imperial ones, providing the *Mail* with the pomp and pageantry well suited to its conceptions ofpublic interest. On the occasion of the Prince of Wales's tour in 1905 the *Mail*'s special correspondent, William Maxwell, enthused about India's great welcome to 'Our Rajah': 'No lustre of wealth and ornament which the loyalty of India can furnish was wanting.'[98] When he returned as king for the Delhi durbar, Maxwell was again at hand to cover the occasion and the royal 'boons' that the emperor bestowed, including shifting the capital from Calcutta to Delhi, a city which had 'a sacredness; its soil is holy ground, fragrant with the memories of the immortal dead who served the Empire in the dark hours of the Mutiny'.[99]

The *Mail* favoured a strong and united empire. Early in its lifetime it had earned a reputation as a jingoist organ from its bellicose reporting of the Boer Wars. Yet its coverage of India reflects a more thoughtful and considered position. On many occasions it was relatively liberal in its stance, and certainly far removed from others on the extreme right wing of the political spectrum such as the *Morning Post, National Review* and *Saturday Review*. The Indian empire was undoubtedly the jewel in Britain's crown, a sacred and glorious trust that needed to be nurtured. The role of the Viceroy was critical and required respect. On the occasion of the military controversy that led to Curzon's resignation in 1905, the *Mail* strongly supported him against Kitchener and maintained the supremacy of civilian over military rule as the appropriate basis for governance. It advocated greater parliamentary interest, noting in 1897 how 'insulting' it was for the Commons to postpone its annual discussion of 'our great Indian empire to the extreme and lifeless end – to the very dregs of the session'.[100]

The paper insisted upon the necessity of suppressing political terrorism, the reality of which was brought closer to home in 1909 when Curzon Wylie of the India Office staff was assassinated while addressing a meeting of Indian students in London.[101] This did not, however, imply tolerance of brutal measures, and the paper supported the government's criticism of Dyer. The loyalty of India during the First World War brought forth much praise, such support from members of a different race demonstrating the 'spiritual existence' of the British Empire.[102] The arrival of Indian troops on European soil in October 1914 was welcomed and their fortunes were avidly followed. Though always advocating the deployment of 'the strong hand', the *Mail* realised that the war marked the dawn of 'a new age' which would embrace the Indian empire. The resulting alteration in the aspirations of Indians had to be dealt with in that spirit of sympathy and justice which were the hallmark of British, as opposed to German, government.[103]

The hand of Northcliffe was evident in the *Mail*'s coverage. Exceptionally among newspaper proprietors, he travelled twice to India. On the first trip, undertaken as a recuperative tour only a few months after the launch of the *Mail*, he was accompanied by his wife and Reginald Nicolson, his private secretary, who had himself previously worked on the Indian railways. Travelling extensively, especially in the plague and famine areas of western India, Northcliffe assumed the mantel of a roving special correspondent. His six articles, entitled 'Hard truths from India', appeared in February 1897. Assisted by T. J. Bennett, proprietor of the *Times of India*, they reveal his familiarity with contemporary literature, while his sketches of the plague and famine districts testified to his zeal as a reporter. India, he observed, was suffering an average of 1,500 to 2,000 weekly fatalities. This calamity had till recently been 'minimised to a ridiculous, nay criminal degree. The fact is that the commercial community in Bombay has been trying for months to persuade itself that the plague is no plague.' Among the factors making it difficult to ascertain the truth was the belief that it was 'largely used as a political cry' by Indians; that many 'native merchants welcome the special fund, not because of its help to the poor, but for the sake of their own market manipulations'.[104] Another article portrayed graphically his visit to 'A starvation camp': 'The spectres, the gaunt, shrivelled old men and women, the babes, who seem all head and staring eyes, are in camps called poorhouses. May I never go through such experiences as I have encountered in these awful settlements.'[105] Northcliffe was critical of Britons who argued that everything was a gross exaggeration. 'The horrors depicted in the illustrated journals are rare,' Northcliffe observed, 'but not so rare as the average Anglo-Indian pent up in his office all day, and at his club and dinner-party in the evening, might consider.'[106]

Northcliffe referred to Bombay as 'The City of Fear' and subjected the city's municipal authorities and their 'conspiracy of silence' to unrelenting attack. He also criticised the Secretary of State, George Hamilton, who was quoted in the British press referring to 'sensational cable messages', for 'trying to minimise the real state of affairs in this fearfully afflicted community'. 'I have not seen any exaggerated plague reports,' wrote Northcliffe. 'None such have yet reached India. But they must be monumentally mendacious if they exceed the truth about Bombay.' In quoting the Director General of the Indian Medical Service, who estimated that 300,000 people had fled Bombay, Northcliffe challenged Hamilton 'to deny that that is a sensational statement, or say that it is misleading?'[107]

Yet the famine relief measures that had been introduced were praised and Northcliffe highlighted British strength in the face of adversity: 'The calm confidence of our people has been most gratifying.'[108] 'With more railways, canals, roads, with the steady progress of legislation for the masses, famine will continue to be less and less frequent.'[109] This was heroism of a different magnitude from that displayed on the field of battle, yet both served to confirm and consolidate the superiority of the British as empire builders. He revisited the subcontinent in 1921–22 as part of his world tour, which according to Tom Clarke, editor of the *Mail*, did much to 'reinspire' Northcliffe as the 'apostle of a world order based on the fabric of a more closely integrated British Empire'.[110]

Biographers and historians have minimised the significance of these tours. Noting the expressions of distaste in Northcliffe's diary during 1921–22, Pound and Harmsworth conclude that 'He did not like India.'[111] Covering vast distances, and not in the best of health, he not surprisingly found travel to be 'tiring, and very dusty'.[112] 'Excepting the hills, it is a wearisome country,' he remarked. 'What do we want India for? Prestige? Perhaps. Cash? We certainly don't get any from it. The thousands of able men from home here could do far better almost anywhere else.'[113] Northcliffe disliked INC extremists and the English-educated Babus: 'These people have got swelled heads.'[114] Nevertheless, he continued to admire the spirit of service that underlay the Raj. 'Lord!' he remarked. 'How much British blood we have lost in India, and how unselfishly.' Yet he saw that the British way of life was passing.

> Now we have the swaggering, boastful, whisky-and-soda drinking, horn-spectacled and fountain-pen-wearing Babu, who likes to think that, because he has the imitative and blotting-paper mind that enables him to pass examinations, he is the equal of the Anglo-Saxon, and, *knowing* his own inferiority, is bitter and dangerous.[115]

Northcliffe's diary certainly reflects many prejudices and an overt anti-INC bias. Yet the extent of his involvement with Indian issues, and the consequences it had for their coverage in the *Mail*, is not in doubt. Whereas plague and famine confronted Northcliffe on his first tour, the non-co-operation movement greeted him on his second. To both he responded actively by contributing lengthy articles and giving interviews, resulting in their heightened coverage in Fleet Street.[116]

Thus the links between the *Mail* and India were closer than many would anticipate. However, it remained the case that India itself was often viewed in superficial terms. The eye of the *Mail* was caught by the extremes of opulence and poverty, the fantastical religious beliefs, the crimes and incidents that provided reliably arresting copy. Although there was an awareness of deeper issues, as manifested in coverage of famine and plague, here, too, language and imagery were highly coloured. Overall the conception of India was dominated by the imperial connection. The *Mail* was confident of the benefits of British rule and optimistic for the future. In Kiplingesque fashion, India was seen as the White Man's Burden – a sphere of duty, sacrifice and the heroic shedding of blood. The inherent paternalism of this position was evident in its critical line during the famine, when the framework of government duty appeared to have broken down. In general the paper assumed British rule was a necessary condition for Indian progress, reflecting which it welcomed the steady, but slow, moves to extending political rights to Indians and criticised heavyhanded displays of military force. In this the 'new journalism' as represented by the *Mail* and the 'old' journalism of the quality press were at one.

Others

Turning to other quality dailies, A. G. Gardiner of the *Daily News* and Robert Donald of the *Chronicle* were conspicuous as editors zealously striving for the Liberal cause. 'The allies of politicians, they defended policies and safeguarded secrets, which was a small price to pay for the confidences they enjoyed.'[117] On average the *Chronicle* paid the subcontinent less attention than the *Daily News* or *Guardian*. The *Daily News* was acknowledged as the official paper of the Liberal Party, and Gardiner had close links with Indian Secretaries of State. The *Herald*, notes McKibbin, possessed 'one indispensable quality – it was the only paper Labour had'.[118] Founded by George Lansbury in 1911, it was launched as 'a genuinely left-wing' national daily in 1912,[119] survived as a weekly during the war, and was taken over by the TUC and the Labour Party in 1922. 'Its loss of independence,' acknowledged Lansbury, 'was dictated by poverty.'[120] The *Herald* was an openly propagandistic organ and emphasised politics to the exclusion of most other news. Lansbury identified India, Ireland and Egypt as countries in which Britain was holding the population down by force.[121] He played a leading role in publicising the Indian cause further through his presidency of the Home Rule for India League, which concentrated primarily on the publication of pamphlets and books – such as Lajpat Rai's *Young India* and Keir Hardie's *India*. It often undertook counter-propaganda to discount the activities of opposition groups. Further, largely through his influence, visiting Indian politicians found Labour platforms across the country from which to reach British audiences – these meetings and speeches in turn being given prominent coverage in the *Herald*. Lansbury fairly deserved his reputation as one of the 'most stalwart champions' of the Indian cause and the 'fountainhead from which the others draw inspiration'.[122]

The *Telegraph*, which came close to presenting the 'official' Conservative viewpoint, remained in the family of James Moses Levy (from its foundation as the first penny daily in 1855), whose son assumed the name of Lawson and became Lord Burnham. Like his father, Burnham was a prominent political figure in Fleet Street and its chief imperial spokesman through the chairmanship in 1920 and 1925 of the EPU. He was also a member of the Indian Statutory Commission 1927–30. The *Telegraph* had a large circulation amongst middle-income groups owing in part to its price, and also, according to Burnham, to the proliferation of wars, which were covered by the *Telegraph* with 'brilliant correspondents' and extensive expenditure on organisation and cables. Though competition from the *Mail* meant that the paper lost its ascendancy in terms of circulation, as a quality journal it commanded respect from a politically informed readership. From the beginning, the *Telegraph* attempted to make its foreign news service second to none, though till the outbreak of the Great War its regular representation abroad was confined to the main European capitals and New York. Of the special correspondents covering India, Perceval Landon played a leading role. For over twenty years till his death in 1927 Landon covered a wide range of news stories for the paper: 'The East was his province and he wrote of it with rare knowledge and understanding.'[123] He also wrote *Lhasa* (1905) and the *Story of the Indian Mutiny* (1907).

Perhaps the most politically prominent of the metropolitan evening newspapers was the *Gazette*, a clubland paper with 'matchstick circulations'.[124] Spender was the doyen of political journalists, and the paper was run as a mouthpiece of the Asquith/Grey wing of the Liberal Party, relying heavily on party donations. Spender recalled that it was 'never in my mind that the *Westminster* could be anything but a . . . serious political paper, expounding Liberal ideas'.[125] Like most evening papers, the *Gazette* relied mainly on telegraph agencies for overseas news. In the interpretation of Indian events Spender played a leading part. His front-page editorials, 'elegantly phrased and couched in modulated tones, commanded a respectful hearing from the enlightened few'.[126] Spender had a wide knowledge of the subcontinent, reinforced by two visits. The first, in 1911, resulted in a book, *The Indian Scene*, while his reflections on his second visit in 1925–26 are discussed in *The Changing East* (1926) and *Life, Journalism and Politics* (1927). Spender had a long-standing friendship with Morley, to whom he was first sent for advice as a young journalist in 1886. Among the evening papers, Liberalism could also count on varying degrees of support from the halfpenny *Star*, which was aimed at a mass readership, and in its layout and style espoused tenets of the 'new journalism'. However it was the 'radical social concerns and lively reporting' of events that made the *Star* 'so significant'.[127] This stance was reflected in Indian coverage, which was dramatic and pithy. David Low's scathing cartoons on the Amritsar massacre, for instance, generated a strong reaction.[128]

Among the major popular dailies, we find the Conservative *Express* founded as a rival to the *Mail*. Under the control of two North Americans, Beaverbrook and the editor, R. D. Blumenfeld, its focus on India was similar to that of the *Mail*. It invariably gave front-page coverage – an exception to the rule for the press of the time – to significant Indian issues. Though with a relatively smaller financial outlay, it tried to compensate by speedy coverage, and often scored over the rest of Fleet Street – for instance, in December 1919, when reporting on the Hunter Committee hearings. Beaverbrook claimed that he ran his papers in the first instance for propaganda, and appropriately enough he went on to become Britain's first Minister of Information. As a friend of Montagu and many of the key political players, his proximity to the decision-making elite meant that the *Express* was in a position to have its voice heard both in government circles as well as among the wider readership.

Political reviews and periodicals

Round Table

Founded in 1910 as a 'Quarterly Review of the politics of the British Empire', the distinctiveness of the *Round Table* arose from its exclusive concentration upon imperial issues. Widespread dissemination of information was seen as a key to public education that, in turn, would promote imperial cohesion.[129] It had, as its precursor, the small monthly magazine *The State*, edited by Philip Kerr and financed by the Closer Union Movement in South Africa, with articles written by members of Milner's kindergarten. Its founders were members of the eponymous organisation, established for the purpose of regular and comprehensive study of imperial affairs from the perspective of the empire as a whole, though with an emphasis on the dominions.[130] Its members included academics, journalists, politicians and imperial administrators such as Kerr (later Lord Lothian), Curtis, Reginald Coupland, R. H. Brand, William Marris and Zimmern. Kerr, the first editor, remarked that the fundamental basis of the enterprise had been the conviction that 'the institution of a quarterly review conducted on democratic lines . . . was the best means' of working for imperial solidarity.[131] This co-operative dimension was underpinned by the practice of printing articles anonymously, which allowed the *Round Table* to present a collective voice, as well as provide a platform for officials to express their opinions on policy issues. Intimate connections with government were considered essential, for imperial correspondents had to have 'trustworthy, complete' and, importantly, ' "inside" information'.[132]

Being a journal by specialists for specialists, it was intended, wrote Curtis, not 'so much for the average reader, as for those who write for the average readers'.[133] However, initial Round Table idealism was soon tempered by commercial realities. Within a year advertising consultants were called in to help capture the wider circulation essential for the journal's survival.[134] By 1918 a publicity circular proclaimed that the *Round Table* had not only 'won an established and influential position' but, with sales of around 10,500, represented the 'largest and most widely distributed' circulation of any political quarterly in the empire.[135] In London the *Round Table* was subscribed to by all major papers, while the association of such prominent *Times* men as Dawson, Chirol, Grigg and Fraser assisted in carrying its opinions to a wider public.

The *Round Table* featured thirty-one articles on Indian issues during 1910–22, averaging two a year for the first four years, one a year in 1914–17, two in 1918 and then a consistent four articles per annum. A combination of quarterly surveys, review articles and opinion pieces characterised this coverage. The surveys ranged over subjects from education, administration and religion to Afghanistan, the princely states, foreign policy and economics. Political issues predominated overall, and from 1917 to 1922 Indian constitutional reform was high on the agenda.[136] Besides regular synopses written by Round Table discussion groups – either in India or in London – there were special focus articles by experts. William Marris was the dominant contributor before the war, L. F. Rushbrook Williams from 1917 onwards. Marris was a distinguished ICS officer who, whilst serving as Joint Secretary in the Home Department in New Delhi, had drafted the Montagu–Chelmsford report, which formed the basis of the subsequent Constitutional Act, 1919. Rushbrook Williams had left All Souls College, Oxford, for a history professorship at Allahabad University. He was seconded to play a prominent role in the formalisation of Government of India central publicity during and after the war. Once the journal was felt to be discussing politically sensitive policy issues, such as the future constitutional and political basis of imperial governance, the Government of India felt it inappropriate for an official to be formally associated with the journal.[137] Marris renounced his membership in 1917, though he continued to be privately and unofficially influential in its workings.

The impact of the war put considerable strain on both the organisation and the journal. The *Round Table* was constrained by the principles of the parent organisation, and its official connections, as well as the critical political climate developing in the subcontinent. The journal was subject to stringent editorial controls, ensuring that its line was in sympathy with general Round Table doctrine. Whereas previously individuals were approached to write somewhat theoretically about politics, the war imposed limits upon the sphere of practical politics, notably in the form of the demands of propaganda and morale.[138] Problems of constitutional reform, political agitation, ICS conservatism and personal distrust all militated against any critique of official policy. While there was, during the war, an agreed need for Indian articles to inform the British public, there were divergences as to the degree to which contributors should be free to espouse policy and opinion. While touring India in 1916–17 Curtis was urged to establish an editorial board which would supply the *Round Table* with a 'sympathetic yet impartial, and well informed' quarterly account of Indian affairs. The committee should, in the opinion of Kerr, not be totally official: 'I think it is very important that there should be on it at least one Indian who is in touch with the main currents of Indian thought . . . I doubt if you will find an Indian who could write the sort of article we require, but his criticism of the draft and his suggestions as to the matters of importance which might be recorded would be invaluable.'[139] Despite attempts by Curtis to arrange for suitable articles putting forward the Indian point of view, this proved hard to accomplish.[140] In 1917 the differing perspectives of official and non-official members of the organisation came to a head over an article, 'The genesis of the situation in India', by Williams. Marris, who questioned Williams's credentials, conveyed Home Department concern:

> He has not been long in India and like Curtis has seen only one side of Indian life; his training is an academic training; and he has for some time lived very much under Curtis's compelling and magnetic influence.[141]

Marris's criticism of the finished piece was relentless, even though he admitted to having read it only once and to having 'forgotten the mitigating passages'.[142] Marris argued that well intentioned attempts to influence judgement without sufficient knowledge or experience were 'dangerous'. He objected to Williams's treatment of self-government as a settled issue: for many, and especially the British in India, it was by no means considered certain or attainable. The 'best service' the journal could do to Indian politics was 'to let them alone'.[143]

Curtis had indeed developed a close working relationship with Rushbrook Williams – who had contributed the historical sections to his book *Dyarchy* – and was strongly opposed to Marris's attempt to curtail debate. 'I do not think that the *RT* will rise to its opportunity if it waits to influence public opinion till a crisis is passed.' At home misinformation and misguided views would remain unchallenged and only official opinion receive any coverage, while in India there would be grave disappointment:

> If you are not prepared to publish articles which treat the administration and the nationalist movement alike in the same spirit of detachment you had better make up your minds to be silent on Indian affairs altogether. You cannot guide public opinion unless you are prepared to look for errors in past navigation and correct the course thereby.[144]

Marris's reaction to Williams was, according to Curtis, typical of the service mentality – while the ICS were a fine administrative corps, they were unaccustomed to 'a weighty judicial criticism'. Ultimately the editorial committee decided to carry the article, exercising the editor's right 'of refashioning articles . . . as much as he chooses' to bring them into accord with *Round Table* policy. In this case the revision by Chirol, Coupland, Kerr and Zimmern went beyond 'excising' and 'softening' passages: 'Much of the article has been rewritten and large new passages inserted.'[145] The result was a group rather than individual effort. Another article by Williams on the reception of the Montagu–Chelmsford report in India was similarly revised. Though the case for including the opinions of Indians themselves in the *Round Table* had been made previously, it was finally realised in a December 1920 article, 'India through Indian eyes'. In prefacing the piece, the editor, though dissociating the quarterly from the views expressed on non-co-operation, remarked, 'but for that very reason they are of greater value than any views that we ourselves might express, for they help to throw light upon the Indian point of view, which, in the present complex situation, is perhaps the main factor'.[146] Thus the delicacy of the political situation in India and the general conservatism of Round Table members dictated the cautious attitude of the review. In reacting to the changing conditions thrown up by the war the organisation and journal were constrained by the preponderating position of the more traditional civil service viewpoint. Further, there were differences in perspective, personality, and objectives within the *Round Table*, as highlighted in the equivocal relationship that existed between Curtis and the Moot.

Others

Other reviews and weeklies, though having similar approaches to Indian coverage, exhibited their own particularities. Most reviews claimed political neutrality, the two prominent exceptions being the Conservative *Saturday Review* and *National Review*. Spender referred to the former as 'that organ of stern and unbending toryism'.[147] The Earl of Hardwicke, who secured an interest in the journal in 1898, was Under Secretary of State for India 1900–02 and 1903–04. The *National Review* was owned and edited by Leopold Maxse, a supporter of Joseph Chamberlain.[148] His anti–Semitic views were to colour coverage of India during Montagu's tenure.

The *New Statesman* was a Fabian organ founded by Sidney and Beatrice Webb in 1913. The Webbs had visited India in 1911 where they attended the annual session of the INC. They and their fellow Fabians have frequently been described as social imperialists, who believed the colonies would be in need of British guidance for a considerable time. This was reflected in the *New Statesman*'s coverage of India, for, while frequently critical of official measures and supporting greater constitutional reform, it did not call for complete British withdrawal. H. W. Massingham was 'the last of the great Radical Liberal editors',[149] and under his editorship the *Nation*'s position on India was more radical than the mainstream Liberal press and it had a galaxy of Liberal intellectuals on its staff, including L. T. Hobhouse, Nevinson and Henry Brailsford, who wrote on India.

Amongst the weeklies, the two most influential were the *Spectator* and the *Observer*. Maxse's close journalistic ally was St Loe Strachey, the proprietor and editor of the *Spectator*. Its readership consisted largely of the educated middle class and the policy-making elite, and it was widely read in service clubs and cantonments within the subcontinent.[150] Strachey, who dominated its pages, described himself as a 'strong democratic Imperialist'. His uncles, Sir John and Sir Richard Strachey, were long-serving Indian administrators and had sat on the India Council in London.[151] Strachey's high-level political contacts included Curzon, Morley, Crewe and Austen Chamberlain, who supplied him with classified information, as did leading politicians in India. Whilst never visiting India himself, Strachey was a voracious reader and was well informed. Thus he wrote to Chirol, 'I have long wanted to say how intensely interested I have been by the "Indian Unrest" articles in the *Times*. On several occasions I have made notes about them for the *Spectator*.'[152]

Meredith Townsend and John Buchan predominated as leader writers on India prior to 1910. Later the assistant editor, J. B. Atkins, and Harold Cox were prominent contributors. Cox had spent two years in India teaching in Aligarh. Townsend, Strachey's predecessor, had spent his formative journalistic years in the subcontinent. His uncle, John Clark Marshman, was a well known British publisher, journalist and historian working in India, who felt keenly the need 'to move public opinion in England and India', and founded *The Friend of India* in 1835.[153] Townsend commenced working for the paper in 1848, becoming its editor in 1852 and owner in 1853. Returning to England, Townsend purchased the *Spectator* in 1860. He specialised in foreign politics and in 1901 a collection of his articles was published as *Asia and Europe*, a work which Strachey felt had a great impact on public opinion in Britain.[154] Townsend's last piece, 'The unrest of Asia', appeared in 1908. All articles in the *Spectator* were anonymous, and an interesting characteristic was the significant place occupied by its correspondence columns, where many authoritative voices found expression – including a substantial number writing from India.

Forceful comment on India was also to be found in the pages of the *Observer*, the oldest Sunday newspaper in England, which had been transformed into 'a major political force' by the Unionist J. L. Garvin.[155] The paper appealed to the educated reader, and political discussion in its pages was informed with a wider historical and literary perspective. Garvin wished to give his readers 'what they don't want', pursuing the objectives of characterful reporting and a full treatment of important subjects untainted by the trivialisation of the mass commercial press. His powerful editorials were read even by those who disagreed with his opinions, and were considered masterpieces of 'studied argumentation'.[156] Garvin spent three months in India during 1903 representing the *Telegraph*, and had a maxim that 'the East changed one for ever'. According to his daughter, 'India never left him.' He had many Indian friends and 'felt keenly and impartially the weight of opposed Indian causes'.[157] At the popular end of the weekly market we find *Reynolds's News* (or *Reynolds's*) founded by the Chartist George Reynolds. His paper was initially in the *Northern Star* tradition of class-conscious radicalism, and had close links with the working-class movement. However, given that it was primarily an organ of entertainment, Liberal causes took a back seat in its pages.

The specialist press

The Overland Mail, Homeward Mail *and* Indiaman
There were published in London, from the mid-nineteenth century, newspapers which specialised in the coverage of Indian news, as well as British news relating to the subcontinent. The more important of these included the *Homeward Mail* (1857) and the *Overland Mail*

(1855) which were amalgamated in 1914 with a new publication, the *Indiaman*. The *Homeward* was a compendium of news and information from India, China and the Far East, while the *Overland* had been set up as a newspaper for despatch to India and the Eastern Settlements. Both were founded by J. W. Kaye, the noted historian of the Mutiny, who sold his interest to Henry Seymour King, head of a firm of bankers with offices in Calcutta and London. The editor of both papers till 1910 was King's brother-in-law, E. Jenkins, who was born in Bangalore and sat in the Commons as a Conservative.[158]

The *Overland* saw itself as occupying a 'unique' position in British journalism 'as an organ and defender' of the Indian services, civil and military.[159] It devoted extensive space to military affairs and to reports of parliamentary debates and questions devoted to India, Central Asia and the Far East. The texts of Ministerial answers to Indian questions were furnished daily by the India Office. Though expensive at 6*d*, these journals provided value for money. The *Homeward* consisted of around thirty pages of detailed information covering virtually all important political, economic and social events in India, notable British news, significant aspects of Anglo-Indian life, provincial news, government communiqués and commercial intelligence. Therefore it supplied Fleet Street with a valuable source of detailed Indian information. In the subcontinent too such papers had a ready market, forming, for the Anglo-Indian press, a reliable channel of news to supplement Reuters, and were the staple of reading rooms in the clubs and barracks.

At the time of their amalgamation into the *Indiaman* the leading article reassured patrons that the 'old traditions' would be maintained because Seymour King – 'that staunch friend of the Indian Services' – would be closely connected with the new management.[160] The man overseeing the foundation of the *Indiaman*, however, was George Berney Allen, who came from a family of press proprietors in India. His father, Sir George Allen, established the *Pioneer* and the *Civil and Military Gazette*, both significant Anglo-Indian newspapers, as well as the firm of Cooper Allen at Kanpur. In 1911 Allen started the weekly paper the *Near East* and in May 1914 floated the *Indiaman* as a weekly devoted to Indian affairs 'from the point of view of the imperial interests of England'.[161] The flood of letters congratulating the *Indiaman* on its launch reveal the support the publication enjoyed from ex-servicemen and officials in Britain, as well as being warmly promoted by Hardinge, who was a close personal friend of Allen. Chirol, who became a director of the enterprise, argued that 'in view of the extraordinary feebleness of the Anglo-Indian press in India, I think his new venture . . . may serve a very useful purpose from the view of public policy'. The policy of the *Indiaman* would be 'essentially moderate and by no means unfriendly to the people of India, whilst mindful of the paramount importance of maintaining absolutely intact the supremacy of the British Raj'.[162] It published more letters to the editor than its predecessors and more political comment. The editor explained that:

> We have an intense desire to bring home to our countrymen the real facts of the great Indian continent, and to make them realise the splendid qualities of the peoples of India ... Our policy ... is the good governance of India and the promotion of good feeling between the British and the Indians.[163]

'If India,' said another editorial, 'is the brightest jewel in the British Crown, it is absurd to deal with the Empire's news service as though India did not exist.'[164] Despite an auspicious start, the war years proved financially taxing, with few advertisements, staff shortages and spiralling costs. The paper folded in 1917 following Allen's sudden death.

India

The newly established INC, realising the need to appeal to the British with a continuous organ of informed opinion and news, decided to publish the journal *India*, run by its British Committee. Started as a monthly in 1890, it became a weekly in 1898 and continued in existence till 1921. *India* was a confessedly propagandist journal, published with a view to 'placing before the British public the Indian view of Indian questions'.[165] It was distributed free to parliamentarians, political clubs and the British press and paid for by a substantial number of Indian subscribers. In the 1890s it had a circulation of 10,000 copies, reduced to 7,000 by 1907. Its editors were William Digby (1890–92), Morse Stephens (1893), Gordon Hewart (1893–1905), Professor J. Muirhead (1905–06), H. E. A. Cotton (1906–19) and H. S. L. Polak (1919–20).[166] Besides long-time members like the Liberal MP G. B. Clark, J. M. Parikh and H. V. Rutherford, new recruits from the Labour Party included the MPs Josiah Wedgwood and Ben Spoor, as well as Fenner Brockway and Horniman.[167] *India* was not a paying proposition and had to be subsidised increasingly from INC funds, especially during the war, and through private donations from Indian businessmen as well as Liberal and Labour organisations in Britain. An open rift occurred between the British Committee and the INC with the latter's split into the moderate and the extremist factions. B. G. Tilak reorganised the British Committee in 1919 and INC funding, so crucial to the survival of *India*, was substantially reduced.

Parikh, Vice-chairman of the British Committee, admitted in its last issue that *India* had 'a limited scope and consequent limited utility'.

Being a propagandist journal, it had to be tailored to suit the require-ments of general readers in Britain as well as the more informed critical readership in India and Indian propagandists in Britain. It was perhaps inevitable that a paper having 'so complex a clientele should have failed to make itself universally popular'.[168] However, within its limitations, *India* was moderately successful in presenting the INC point of view within the three spheres identified as crucial – Parlia-ment, press and the public – and held in England 'a watching brief' on behalf of the INC.[169] Its editors frequently wrote for other journals like the *Contemporary Review* and *New Statesman*, and successfully extended the reach of nationalist propaganda. One of the potential threats posed by *India* was the influence it was perceived to exert on political opinion *within* India. Successive Viceroys, Curzon, Minto and Hardinge, held it responsible for sending 'distorted' news to the sub-continent. Hamilton wrote to Curzon, 'I note that *India* frequently starts lies here that are reproduced in detail by the Congress paper, in fact nearly all information about India is derived from this poisonous little rag.'[170] Hardinge welcomed ventures such as the *Indiaman* partly as a counterweight to the 'evil influences' of *India*.[171]

Conclusion

The background to the pattern of Fleet Street coverage of India was the information revolution of the late nineteenth and early twentieth centuries. Economic and technical developments had led to a bigger press that reached more people more cheaply than ever before, and had changed the character of the press. There was now greater diversity in the range and forms of news reporting. In terms of social strata there was a wider variety of readership, from *The Times*, whose circulation 'did not extend widely below Olympus',[172] to the mass-circulation *Mail* and *Reynolds's*, appealing primarily to the lower middle and working classes. Journalism as information, journalism as influence and advo-cacy, and journalism as entertainment – all found on the vast canvas that was the Indian empire enough to engage and report.

The revolution in communications, inaugurated by telegraphic news and the advent of the commercialised popular press, in turn stim-ulated and sustained the appetite for foreign and imperial news. Like Reuters, the British press exploited the enormous advantage it enjoyed as the press of empire. As part of this process more information was made available on India than ever before. The growth of the press networks within the subcontinent and their increasing presence in London further consolidated links with the metropole. Yet column space devoted to India was subject to the competing claims of domestic and European news. The expense of utilising new communication technologies was a potential barrier but such costs declined over the course of the twentieth century – between 1908 and 1923 the standard press rate for India fell by 67 per cent – and made more efficient news collection possible. A system of select permanent salaried correspondents forming the core of the news services, supplemented with additional, often temporary, reporters, was the one favoured by most major dailies. The proprietor of the *Telegraph* in the 1950s recollected 'the old days when the jam was provided by a very small and select band of staff men and the bread and butter supplied by Reuters'.[173] Several specialist journals devoted exclusively to the subcontinent added an interesting nuance to the public face of India in the metropolis.

However, the quality and depth of coverage were not a direct function of the quantity of news featured by individual papers. The political press revealed its attitudes and policies through its editorial comment, its selection of staff and the events it chose to cover. This agenda-setting role was heightened by the monopoly position the press occupied as the largest and most pervasive medium of communication. This service was not value-free, and journalism was, as it is today, guided by rules of selection. Fleet Street editors and leader writers were passionate and dominant individuals whose belief in the persuasive and seminal role of the press *vis-à-vis* public opinion and their personal advocacy of empire carried significant political weight and impacted upon Indian administrators. Individuals could play diverse roles in different settings, moving between the worlds of journalism and politics and often across continents. They and the papers they represented thus possessed widespread resources to act as a conduit of discussion. The worlds of Fleet Street, Anglo-India and the governing elite in India and Britain coalesced to an unprecedented degree and the consequent networks of information, opinion and influence, impacted one upon the other.

Notes

1 F. R. Gannon, 'The British Press and Germany, 1936–1939', Oxford University D.Phil. thesis (1968), p. 17.
2 Fyfe, *Fleet Street*, p. 10.
3 Williams, *Dangerous Estate*, p. 126. As Read and Seymour-Ure have emphasised, it is a myth to see the popular daily press as catering primarily for a new working-class audience taught to read as a result of the 1870 Education Act. (D. Read, *Edwardian England*, 1972, p. 58; Seymour-Ure, 'Press and party system', pp. 246–9.) Victorian working men had read halfpenny local evening papers and penny Sundays and continued to do so. (V. Berridge, 'Popular Sunday papers and mid-Victorian society', in Boyce *et al.*, *Newspaper History*, pp. 247–64.) In 1896 itself *Lloyd's Weekly News* was the first paper to achieve a million sale.

4   Lee, *Origins*, p. 293; these included Northcliffe, Cadbury and Pearson.
5   A. P. Ryan, *Lord Northcliffe* (1953), p. 113.
6   W. T. Stead, 'His Majesty's Public Councillors', *Review of Reviews*, 30 (1904), 593–606; the *Mail* and *Express* were placed on the third rung; J. O. Baylen, 'A contemporary estimate of the London daily press in the early twentieth century', in Bromley and O'Malley, *Journalism Reader*, pp. 91–101; Koss, *Rise and Fall*, pp. 439–40.
7   According to Williams the *Daily Mail* 'continued the revolution the *Daily Telegraph* left unfinished' (*Dangerous Estate*, p. 126); J. H. Wiener, 'How new was the new journalism?' in Wiener, *Papers for the Millions*, pp. 47–72.
8   J. Spender, *Life* II, p. 134.
9   *History of* The Times (1939) II, pp. 76–9, 80–3, 310–15.
10 L. James, *High Pressure* (1929), p. 3.
11 H. Newman, *Indian Peepshow* (1937), p. 2, and A *Roving Commission* (1937), pp. 220, 280.
12 Spender to Butler, 25 September 1921, MSS Eur F116/46, Harcourt Butler Collection (hereafter HBC/no.).
13 *History of The Times, 1912–1948* (1952) IV, pp. 1, 17.
14 Foreign Manager's Letter Book 1 (hereafter FMLB/no.), *Times* Archives (TA).
15 Assistant editor, *Bombay Gazette*; editor, *Indian Daily Telegraph*.
16 W. S. Scott to Reed, 5 August 1918, Scott Correspondence, TA.
17 MacGregor to Reed, 5 August 1920, MacGregor Correspondence, TA.
18 1 May 1912, E. W. M Grigg Correspondence, TA (hereafter Grigg).
19 Wallace to MacGregor, 6 July 1892, 10 July 1893, FMLB/1.
20 Wallace to Chirol, 27 June 1892, *ibid.*; Grigg to Chirol, 27 July 1911, Grigg.
21 Buckle to Chirol, 8/9 November 1905, Manager's Letter Book 41, TA (hereafter MLB/no).
22 MacGregor to Reed, 22 June 1920, MacGregor Correspondence.
23 B. K. Long to Reed, 3 February 1921, Long Correspondence, TA.
24 *History of* The Times III (1947), p. 787.
25 Wallace to Hensman, 23 September 1892, FMLB/1.
26 E. H. C. Moberly Bell, *Life and Letters of C. F. Moberly Bell* (1927), pp. 166–7.
27 Wallace to MacGregor, 23 August 1892, FMLB/1.
28 Wallace to Hensman, 22 July 1896, FMLB/3.
29 Wallace to Hensman, 16 April 1896, FMLB/3.
30 Bell to Fraser, 2 December 1908, MLB/50.
31 Wallace to Hensman, 22 July 1896, FMB/3.
32 Bell to Fraser, 12 March 1909, MLB/51.
33 Bell to Reed, 24 December 1908; 3 February 1909, MLB/50, 51.
34 Bell to Fraser, 20 June 1908, MLB/48.
35 Bell to Hensman, 3 November 1908, MLB/50.
36 Bell to Fraser, 6 April 1909, MLB/52.
37 Fraser to Bell, 18 March 1909, Fraser Correspondence, TA.
38 *Ibid.*
39 Reed to Dawson, 28 March 1923, MSS D69, fol. 96, Dawson Papers.
40 Assistant Manager to Hensman, 24 June 1914, Hensman Managerial File, TA.
41 Bell to James, 23 May 1907, MLB/45.
42 Chirol Managerial File, TA.
43 Geoffrey Robinson changed his name to Dawson in 1917.
44 Reed to Dawson, 2 March 1919, MSS D68 fol. 170, Dawson Papers.
45 Chirol to Steed, 14 December 1910, Chirol Papers, TA (hereafter CHP).
46 Steed to W. Smith, 9 August 1920, Chirol Managerial File.
47 MacGregor to Reed, 19 May 1920, MacGregor Correspondence.
48 Cited in W. Hindle, *Morning Post, 1772–1937* (1937), p. 217.
49 Dunlop-Smith to Viceroy, 28 June 1908, D-S/9.
50 R. Lucas, *Lord Glenesk and the* Morning Post (1910), pp. 367–8.
51 Peacock to Glenesk, 10 August 1905, 1990/1/1474, G-B.

52 Peacock to Bathurst, 12 February 1912, 1990/1/4226, G-B.
53 Peacock to Borthwick, 24 December 1907, 1900/1/1500; 27 February 1908, 1900/1/1502; 8 October 1908, 1990/1/1515, G-B.
54 Kipling to Bathurst, 15 June 1911, 1990/1/3363, G-B.
55 Peacock to Bathurst, 13 July 1920, 1900/1/4600, G-B.
56 Cited in K. Wilson (ed.), *The Rasp of War* (1988), p. 293.
57 Interviewed by author, 13 November 1991.
58 Dibblee, *Newspaper*, p. 207.
59 Secretary of State to Scott, 9 May 1908, 128/29, *Manchester Guardian* Archives (hereafter MGA).
60 Ayerst, *Guardian*, pp. 134, 575.
61 Scott to Reeves, 21 January 1920, 335/134, MGA.
62 Scott to Hewart, 26 November 1902, A/H52/6, MGA.
63 Nash to Scott, 18 February 1900, A/N4/2a, MGA.
64 Hobhouse to Scott, 12 October 1920, A/C86/3, MGA.
65 Cotton to Scott, 20 May 1922, A/C86/5, MGA.
66 Hewart to Scott, 5 December 1902, 124/117, MGA.
67 *Ibid.*, 23 November 1902, 124/113, MGA.
68 Andrews: missionary, educationalist, associate of Gandhi; Pal: author, journalist, radical nationalist.
69 Scott to E. T. Scott, 12 October 1931, 336/251; Scott to Tagore, 22 September 1926, 336/183, MGA.
70 Scott to Nevinson, 9 September 1907, A/N12/5, MGA.
71 Scott to Tagore, 22 September 1926, 336/183; Curtis to Scott, 25 June 1918, 335/34; Secretary of State to Scott, 2 July 1918, 335/36, MGA.
72 Cotton to Scott, 4 May 1920, 135/164, MGA.
73 Quoted in R. M. Wilson, *Lord Northcliffe* (1927), p. 120.
74 *Ibid.*, p. 202.
75 Cited in Ryan, *Northcliffe*, pp. 77, 89.
76 *Daily Mail*, 9 November 1904.
77 Northcliffe to Strachey, 22 November 1904, Strachey Papers, S/11/4/15.
78 Northcliffe to Strachey, 18 November 1904, *ibid*.
79 J. E. Wrench, *Uphill* (1934), p. 241.
80 Wilson, *Northcliffe*, p. 169.
81 F. Williams, *The Right to Know* (1969), p. 77.
82 Cited in T. Clarke, *My Northcliffe Diary* (1931), p. 197.
83 Compiled from *Daily Mail* Index 1909–22.
84 *Daily Mail*, 4 May 1920.
85 J. E Wrench, *Struggle, 1914–1920* (1935), p. 311
86 Clarke, *Northcliffe*, p. 199.
87 *Daily Mail*, 10 November 1904.
88 *Daily Mail*, 5 May 1908.
89 *Daily Mail*, 16 August, 20, 22 November 1897; January and February 1898, 7 September 1899; 11, 18 May 1908.
90 *Daily Mail*, 22 November 1897.
91 *Daily Mail*, 16 May 1908.
92 *Daily Mail*, 6 January 1897.
93 *Daily Mail*, 7 January 1897.
94 *Daily Mail*, 9 January 1897.
95 *Daily Mail*, 12 January 1897.
96 *Daily Mail*, 4 January 1897.
97 *Daily Mail*, 26 August 1897.
98 *Daily Mail*, 8 November 1905.
99 *Daily Mail*, 13 December 1911.
100 *Daily Mail*, 6 August 1897.
101 *Daily Mail*, 10 September 1914, 31 January, 21 August 1919.
102 *Daily Mail*, 10 September 1914.

103   *Daily Mail*, 21 August 1917.
104   *Daily Mail*, 9 February 1897.
105   *Daily Mail*, 16 February 1897.
106   *Ibid.*
107   *Daily Mail*, 24 February 1897.
108   *Daily Mail*, 8, 24 February 1897.
109   *Daily Mail*, 23 February 1897.
110   Cited in Jones, *Reuters*, p. 245.
111   R. Pound and G. Harmsworth, *Northcliffe* (1959), p. 821; P. Ferris, *House of Northcliffe* (1971), p. 247; S. J. Taylor gives three lines to Northcliffe's first trip and none to the second, *The Great Outsiders* (1996), p. 46. J. Lee Thompson devotes a little more space to these episodes (*Northcliffe*, 2000).
112   Lord Northcliffe, *My Journey round the World* (1923), p. 232.
113   *Ibid.*, p. 237.
114   *Ibid.*, p. 250.
115   *Ibid.*, pp. 235, 244.
116   *Daily Mail*, 25 January, 9 March 1922.
117   Koss, *Rise and Fall*, p. 448.
118   McKibbin, *Labour Party*, p. 222. *Daily Citizen* folded in 1915.
119   J. Curran, 'Press as agency', in Boyce *et al.*, *Newspaper History*, p. 70.
120   Cited in H. Richards, 'Ragged man of Fleet Street', *Contemporary Record*, 8: 2 (1994), 244.
121   R. Postgate, *Life of George Lansbury* (1951), p. 190.
122   Weekly Report of Director, Central Intelligence, Simla, 26 October 1918, p. 2, Home Poll, Deposit 10, 1918.
123   Lord Burnham, *Peterborough Court* (1955), pp. 96–7, 58–9, 102–3.
124   Spender, *Life* II, p. 134.
125   Spender, *Life* I pp. 62–3.
126   Koss, *Rise and Fall*, p. 448.
127   J. Goodbody, 'The *Star*', in Wiener, *Papers for the Millions*, p. 145.
128   C. Seymour-Ure and J. Schoff, *David Low* (1985), p. 164.
129   See c808, fol. 121, Round Table Papers (hereafter RT).
130   Undated typed memo, c844, fols 159–164, RT.
131   Kerr to A. Whitworth, 17 June 1915, c791, fols 112–113, RT.
132   Undated typed manuscript, c844, fols 163–164, RT.
133   L. Curtis, *Dyarchy* (1920), p. 74.
134   7 November 1911, c844, RT.
135   R. H. Brand to Bob, 4 January 1918, c845, fol. 213; c845, fol. 234, RT.
136   A. C. May, 'The *Round Table*, 1910–1966', Oxford University D.Phil. thesis (1995), Appendix F.
137   Home Poll, A, 137–42, June 1917.
138   4 June 1915, c809, fols 6–47, RT.
139   Kerr to Curtis, 28 October 1916, c809, fols 174–175, RT.
140   Curtis to Coupland, 30 March 1917, c810, fol. 29, RT.
141   Marris to Coupland, 1 October 1917, c810, fol. 180, RT.
142   *Ibid.*, 6 October 1917, c810, fol. 188, RT.
143   *Ibid.*, 1 October 1917, c810, fols 180, 185, RT.
144   Curtis to Coupland, 29 September 1917, c810, fol 176, RT.
145   Coupland to Curtis, 20 November 1917, c810, fol. 206, RT.
146   *Round Table* March 1921.
147   J. A. Spender, *New Lamps and Ancient Lights* (1940), p. 107.
148   Koss, *Rise and Fall*, p. 456.
149   H. L. Smith, 'H. W. Massingham', in Baylen *et al.*, *Biographical Dictionary*, p. 573.
150   W. B. Thomas, *The Story of the Spectator* (1928), p. 102.
151   Strachey, *Adventure*, p. 298; Startt, *Journalists for Empire*, pp. 18–19, 206–7.
152   Strachey to Chirol, 3 August 1910, S/4/9/11, SP.
153   George Smith, *Twelve Indian Statesmen* (1897), p. 239.

154 Strachey, *Adventure*, pp. 219–49.
155 J. D. Symons, *Press and its Story* (1914), p. 250.
156 J. D. Startt, 'Good journalism in the era of the new journalism', in Wiener, *Papers for the Millions*, p. 284.
157 K. Garvin, *Garvin* (1948), pp. 42–4.
158 *Homeward Mail*, 11 June 1910.
159 *Overland Mail* 14 July 1905.
160 *Indiaman*, 15 May 1914.
161 *Indiaman*, Obituary, 21 June 1917.
162 Chirol to Hardinge, 15 April 1914, Vol. II, 93, Hardinge Papers, CUL (hereafter HP).
163 *Indiaman*, 15 May 1914.
164 *Indiaman*, 11 December 1914.
165 H. E. A. Cotton to E. T. Cook, 15 February 1916, Home Poll, Deposit 28, May 1916, p. 6.
166 Stephens: lecturer in Indian history, Cambridge; Polak: close associate of Gandhi in South Africa.
167 Brockway (1888–1988), journalist, socialist campaigner and parliamentarian.
168 *India*, 14 January 1921.
169 Report of the British Committee, 1916–1917, p. 1, A. Besant Papers, Nehru Memorial Library.
170 Cited in A. P. Kaminsky, *The India Office, 1880–1910* (1986), p. 169; Narain, *Press*, p. 263.
171 Viceroy to Sir George Birdwood, 14 April 1914, 93, II, HP.
172 *Ibid.*, p. 97.
173 Burnham, *Peterborough Court*, p. 59.

PART II

Information management
and imperial control

CHAPTER FOUR

Empire and news management:
India and the London press,
c. 1880–1914

Although the government had, prior to the First World War, no systematic approach to the dissemination of information or the management of press opinion concerning India, there had nevertheless
developed an unofficial system of informal communication, usually
based upon personal contacts. It was conducted at the highest levels,
with the Secretary of State (and Viceroy) taking a direct interest in
courting editors, proprietors and special correspondents. Included in
this process were the confidential release of documents, private correspondence on policy measures and social meetings (see Appendix 2).
Such interaction was *ad hoc* and therefore depended upon the weight
particular Secretaries of State, Viceroys or officials happened to attach
to the matter, which in turn reflected the circumstances of their period
in office, their personal predilections and the state of party controversy. The following pages survey these influences and trace some of
the leading themes of the government–press relationship from the late
nineteenth century to the outbreak of war.

The India Office was 'a miniature imperial government' operating
independently of the English civil service until after the war. It acted
as a nerve centre, monitoring reports, synthesising information and
circulating memoranda to the Indian government, and its permanent
staff were important players in the process of informal diplomacy with
the press. Several factors motivated India Office attempts to shape the
reporting of India in the metropolis. Most directly the press provided
an immense and ready-made vehicle for the distribution of information and was the most effective medium to publicise a certain line in
government policy or to promote (or harm) individual careers. By con-
fiding in prominent journalists officials sought to clarify their position
and secure sympathetic coverage of their policies. A more institu-
tionally specific dimension to the process arose from the occasional
need of the India Office to use newspapers to garner support for its

point of view in cases of differences of opinion with the government in India.

Such considerations were linked with concern at the impact of reporting on domestic opinion. Most Britons derived the bulk of their knowledge about the empire from the print media. MPs, too, could form their opinion about the competence or otherwise of the Secretary of State (or Viceroy) from newspapers and journals. The influence of the quality papers on the decision-making elite, as well as the popular press on more general readers, helped to create the climate of opinion within which Parliament and government functioned. Though parliamentary and press opinion were distinct, they were interdependent, and the ultimate arbiters of the fate of the empire, the 'real government' of India, was the House of Commons.[1] The basic goal of the India Office was, in this respect, to maintain a consensus of political opinion, to avoid India becoming a subject of party controversy and thus create a passive environment within which imperial policy could be formulated. A potentially disruptive arena was the periodic Commons debate, where, as Morley noted, 'it is not quite so simple a thing as it may look to defend personal government in any assembly which lives upon government by popular majority'.[2] Officials never took the threat of parliamentary interference lightly. Ironically, it was precisely a general want of knowledge at home that enhanced the impact of opinions expressed in the press.

Linked with, and partly explaining, the importance of the above factors was the changing political configuration in Britain from the turn of the century. More radical political principles were emerging and parties were themselves undergoing change. The composition of the Commons was altering, and extension of the franchise had an impact upon the nature of electioneering, further enhancing government sensitivity to press opinion. The rise of the Labour Party, with a more radical – though not entirely consistent – approach to imperial questions, resulted in a growing body of left-wing MPs willing to challenge the Liberal Party position on India and pioneer a more aggressively pro-Indian stance in Parliament after 1905.

Secretaries of State often had little prior knowledge of the subcontinent and were first and foremost British politicians. Apart from Crewe, who briefly visited India for the 1911 durbar, no incumbent prior to 1917 was personally acquainted with the country over which he ruled. They functioned within the domestic political context, and had to respond, at least in part, to the domestic news agenda – which the press did much to set. Further, India Office concern to monitor and influence coverage was partly a reaction to the greater attempts made by Indian groups to cultivate British opinion, a process epitomised by the formation of the British Committee of the INC. The number of Indian students in British universities rose from around 650 in 1907 to 1,300 in 1917 and nearly 2,000 by the early 1920s, with London University providing the main centre of radicalism.[3] In 1907 India House was taken over by a revolutionary group led by V. D. Savarkar. Indian militants found sympathisers amongst radical MPs like H. M. Hyndman, founder of the Social Democratic Federation, Rutherford, and Hardie and Lansbury of the Independent Labour Party.[4] Parliamentary lethargy with respect to India was notorious, but was more frequently tested as the century progressed. Cumpston notes how, in 1906, membership of Parliament's India committee had reached over 190.[5] However, concurrent with such activity came the realisation that the preoccupations of Parliament meant that if Indians sought reform they needed to conduct intensive publicity work among the British electorate. *India* was directed towards public education and political proselytisation. Such developments prompted the Viceroy, Lord Minto, to caution against 'the natural sympathies' of the British people being 'misled by the misrepresentations of eloquent speakers' visiting England.[6] The India Office had, therefore, to counter the negative impressions of the character of British rule that were being projected at home.

Finally, India Office concern with pressure-group activity in London reflected to a significant degree its potentially disturbing impact within the subcontinent. The statements of the Secretary of State, parliamentary debates and the opinions of political parties were all eagerly scrutinised in India, particularly after the Liberal landslide in 1906. The potential base for political activity in India was expanding fast, with the circulation of vernacular papers rising from 299,000 in 1885 to 817,000 in 1905. There was also a mushrooming of English-language journals. In 1905 1,359 newspapers and journals, including the Anglo-Indian press, reached an estimated 2 million subscribers.[7] Cotton observed how the Indian press was emerging as 'a kind of constitutional opposition . . . The whole of its influence is in the direction of nationalisation.'[8] Officials were aware that the influential journals were also those which were 'not permeable to a reasoned exposition' of the government case. Their acceptance of official information was 'limited to the extent which they deemed they could use it as a text for criticism and misrepresentation'.[9] Papers causing increasing concern included *New India* and *Justice* (Madras), the *Bombay Chronicle*, *Amrita Bazar Patrika* (Calcutta), *Mahratta* and *Kesari* (Poona).[10] Gandhi was prominent amongst those harnessing the potential of the medium. While in South Africa he edited *Indian Opinion*, and subsequently maintained that 'the newspaper press is a great power' and

Satyagraha 'would probably have been impossible without *Indian Opinion*'.[11] *Young India* in English, and the Gujerati *Navajivan*, were similarly to serve as vehicles of his ideas in India. This growth of the press as an organ of opposition enhanced the impact of Fleet Street, as the attitudes it expressed were taken up and exaggerated in the cause of nationalist agitation.

Government information control and the press: a peripheral perspective

In the field of information control, the Indian government exploited significant structural advantages over Fleet Street. It was itself the main source of information on India and was in a position to influence news at this primary stage. As Dewey has remarked of the ICS, 'their monopoly of information meant that they could skew it in any way they chose. They took up issues that mattered to them; they tailored their reports to their recommendations; they retreated into the demi-official world if they thought their actions might be censured.'[12] The close relationship with Reuters meant that the government was also able to shape the news actually reported by the company from India. The API representative, K. C. Roy, also shared official confidences. The Viceroy, introducing him to Austen Chamberlain, stressed that Roy was in 'very close touch' with the government and had 'always been found ready to help when his assistance has been asked for'. He was also *'persona grata* with most of the men who figure prominently in Indian politics today'.[13]

Finally, the government sought to develop a similarly symbiotic relationship with the Anglo-Indian press. There were two major channels of influence between it and Fleet Street. First, metropolitan journalists read and utilised reports carried by the Anglo-Indian press. Critics complained that this practice of filtering news to London 'brewed in the offices' of the Anglo-Indian newspapers meant that news came from men 'who were local in their outlook and had already taken up positions in their own papers'.[14] With a few exceptions, like the *Times of India*, *Statesman* and *Indian Daily News*, these papers were indeed unsympathetic to the growth of Indian political aspirations.[15] Second, as discussed earlier, journalists on these papers often doubled as correspondents for Fleet Street. As Reed noted to Braham at the *Times* office, senior government members were 'quite willing to talk very freely to me about what is going on in India . . . I will make a point of always sending on to you such information as I get.'[16]

The Anglo-Indian papers were the 'unofficial apostles of western influence and all the more effective for being unofficial'.[17] By their means news from Britain as well as Indian news could be conveyed to the remotest regions. Amongst the most favoured were the so-called 'standard media of government advertisements' – the *Advocate*, the *Civil and Military Gazette*, the (Indian) *Daily Express*, *Englishman*, *Madras Mail*, *Pioneer*, *Statesman* and *Times of India*.[18] An editor's room had been set up in Calcutta during the 1850s under Lord Dalhousie for 'respectable newspapers' to access select official documents. Various direct channels for feeding the press along similar lines were experimented with during subsequent decades. It was under the Conservative Lord Lytton that a centralisation of such activities took place with the establishment of the first government press bureau in March 1877. The first Press Commissioner in 1878 was Roper Lethbridge, a distinguished civil servant who had edited the *Calcutta Review* (1871–78). His brief was a combination of prevention and publicity: 'to prevent the Press publishing mischievous falsehoods by issuing to the Press wholesome truths, and by explaining the views and intentions of the government'.[19] Yet, at the same time, vernacular journals came under surveillance following the Vernacular Press Act of 1878, aimed at suppressing opposition.

Owing to the large numbers of newspapers, the extensive nature of the country, and the delicate balance between press demands and departmental secrecy, the speed and efficiency of news transmission were undermined by the complexities of this system. In addition to practical difficulties, ideological differences surfaced with the arrival of the Liberal Lord Ripon as Viceroy. Ripon was convinced that the spheres of government and press should be clearly demarcated and that 'anything even indirectly in the nature of an attempt to "manage" the press is mischievous, and can only end in failure and discredit'.[20] When Ripon abolished the Vernacular Press Act in 1881, the press commissionership also came to an end. Not until the viceroyalty of Curzon were official press bureaus briefly re-established at Simla and Calcutta.[21] However, it was not merely the reaction of Indian opinion that concerned government. There was also the response of the non-official British community to be considered – of the potency of which Ripon was to be reminded in 1883, when his proposal to remove racial disqualification from the judiciary provoked a storm of protest from Anglo-India and its press (a process in which London papers played an active part).[22] As Henry Cotton noted, 'It is not every Viceroy in India who is able to resist the pressure brought to bear on him by his own countrymen. It requires the assurance of a strong moral support from home – support not from the English government only, but from the English people.'[23]

Official news management and the London press: a metropolitan focus

Having first sought to shape the Indian news available in Britain through its control over telegraphs, news agencies, the Indian press, and indeed news itself, the government also sought to influence the way in which the London press utilised this information and the opinions it expressed on the subcontinent.

The government had informal arrangements for feeding information to Fleet Street reporters in India. For instance, James Macgregor, correspondent of *The Times*, received confidential information from the private secretary of the Viceroy, Lord Lansdowne (1888–94), as well as from Henry Babington-Smith, private secretary to his successor, Lord Elgin. In return Babington-Smith requested copies of all Macgregor's telegrams to England. Government–Fleet Street links were displayed most dramatically when men moved between the two worlds, noticeably in the case of *The Times*. Even under the East India Company, when officials were forbidden to write for the press, Cecil Beadon, the Home Secretary, acted as the paper's Calcutta correspondent in 1856–57.[24] In the 1890s Mackenzie Wallace took charge of its foreign desk, based in London, having earlier served as private secretary to the Viceroy, Lord Dufferin (1884–88).[25] From the 1870s Owen Tudor Burne, private secretary to Viceroys Mayo and Lytton, urged the value of cultivating the press and wrote 'a good deal' for *The Times*, being on close terms with its editors, Thadeus Delane and Thomas Chenery. He carried such convictions with him to the India Office when he became head of the Political and Secret Department.[26] Procedurally, the India Office departments were responsible to the Permanent Under Secretary of State, and Kaminsky draws attention to the power exercised by Sir Arthur Godley, later Lord Kilbracken (1883–1909). Godley ruled that staff were 'not at liberty to write to any newspaper', either under their own name or anonymously, 'on any subject connected directly or indirectly with India, or to write articles or read papers, or furnish information in any shape or form to the public' without prior permission from the Under Secretary or department head.[27] When Godley came across an official acting as a sub-editor of *The Times* he demanded his resignation.

Curzon (1898–1905) took a keen interest in the conduct of newspapers in London as well as in India. He was sensitive to public opinion, and believed that press opinion, owing to its 'cumulative weight, as an expression of public opinion, cannot be ignored'.[28] While not suggesting that such opinion was 'to be kowtowed to', it was nevertheless a mistake to deny its existence, given its spectacular advance in the previous fifteen years. He was convinced that any Viceroy who acted as Lytton did in muzzling the vernacular press was 'no longer a possibility'.[29] His interest in publicity was evident most spectacularly in the pomp and ceremony attending his staging of the Delhi durbar. There were two press camps – one Indian and the other European – and Curzon visited both, as well as engaging the well known artist, Mortimer Menpes, to capture the spectacle on canvas, and the firm of Bourne & Shepherd to provide a photographic record.

Curzon favoured cheaper telegraphic rates, kept copious press cuttings, and wrote frequently to journalists, censuring their remarks, proffering information and clarifying his own position.[30] Amongst his contacts in London were prominent pressmen such as Chirol, Fraser, Strachey, Low and Northcliffe. Fraser admired Curzon and published a glowing account of his viceroyalty in 1911. The relationship with Reuters was developed through subsidies, and the private secretary to the Viceroy, Walter Lawrence, was central to the informal connections between the government and the press. Like Mackenzie Wallace before him, Lawrence went on to join *The Times*, where he was cultivated by the India Office.[31] Joining the Council of India in 1907, he played a useful role in India Office publicity during the First World War. Curzon's awareness of the potential impact in Britain of press coverage of India is revealed in his assessment of the motives behind one of the mass protests held in Calcutta against his decision to partition Bengal in 1905. The meeting's object, he cynically observed, was

> not to produce an impression in India . . . but to enable the Calcutta correspondent of the London *Daily News* [Babu Surendranath Banerji] to send a telegram to that receptive organ that all India is boiling over with rage at the insults inflicted upon her by a Tory Viceroy, and so to bring pressure to bear upon a Radical government (which they think will be in power in a few months' time) to recall the offending and offensive autocrat.[32]

Ironically, Curzon's viceroyalty did indeed end amid a furious campaign involving leading London papers and allegations of press manipulation by the India Office.

His successor, the Earl of Minto, was faced with a resurgence of political unrest, which induced greater concern with press reporting. To curb the Indian press he introduced the Newspapers (Incitement to Offences) Act of 1908 and the Press Act, 1910, both of which added to the panoply of sanctions embodied in successive Official Secrets Acts since the late nineteenth century.[33] Yet simultaneous with this repressive strategy were endeavours to court the London press. Visiting journalists were offered government hospitality. Lionel James, covering the unrest in 1907 for *The Times*, was 'ably and frankly assisted' by the Viceroy, the Commander-in-chief and numerous heads of departments and officials.[34] When Fraser and Chirol toured India in 1908–9, Minto took pains to ensure a successful visit. He was fortunate in having as his private secretary James Dunlop-Smith, whose felicitous dealings with journalists were no doubt partly traceable to the fact that his father had been a *Times* correspondent in India during the 1860s and had edited two Anglo-Indian papers.[35] Dunlop-Smith sought to explain the Viceroy's policies to Fleet Street. 'I have spoken very freely with the *Times* men,' he wrote to Minto in 1910 when on a visit to London. He found Maxse of the *National Review* 'much more favourably inclined' to Minto's administration than two years previous. Dunlop-Smith lunched with Garvin, and had a 'wrangle' with Fraser over an article: 'even then it did not satisfy me, but he went off. Then he sent me the proof and I returned it with suggestions.' To Spenser Wilkinson, who wrote for the *Morning Post*, Dunlop-Smith proposed to give facts for a forthcoming article. For Wilson different tactics were necessary: 'He is just the sort of man to find in the *Daily Mail* office . . . frankly opportunist, and seems to care little for facts, so I had to tackle him on different lines from those I have usually adopted here.' While not 'proud' of his methods, Dunlop-Smith was convinced that 'one has to suit one's weapons to the work in hand'.[36]

One of Minto's overriding concerns was with the impact of British political opinion, including the influence of the press, on the subcontinent. As we have noted, the Indian government was concerned at the coverage accorded to Keir Hardie's 1907 tour of India, and tried to censor Hardie's messages home via Reuters – Minto fearing that the 'puny group' which Hardie may 'succeed in bringing into action' in the Commons would be mistaken by the INC as representative of 'a strong force of British opinion'.[37] Nevinson, who was visiting at the same time, contends that Hardie's statements were 'misrepresented' by correspondents to the English papers as 'seditious speeches'.[38] Similarly, in appealing to Morley to censor and screen London publications such as *India* and *Labour Leader*, Minto argued, 'We do not fear criticism, but we are . . . entitled to complain of baseless misrepresentations, which, although probably accepted at their face value at home, when read in India are bound to convey a false impression.'[39] The difficulties of the Indian government were increased because it was both problematic and embarrassing to be seen to be prosecuting British papers.

Minto's successor, Lord Hardinge (1910–16), worked to a similar formula – control and suspicion of the Indian-run press combined with diplomatic overtures and manipulation of the British counterpart. He had an influential contact in Chirol, who kept him informed on the climate of opinion in Ministerial circles and acted as a conduit of information to Fleet Street.[40] Since the durbar Chirol had been 'besieged by all sorts of people asking me for "interviews" or . . . for my own personal opinion'. While refusing the former he had 'given freely' of the latter and 'I think not without good results'.[41] He was regularly supplied with confidential reports, for instance on the vernacular press and on the rise of the Muslim League, and, during the Great War, was commissioned by the Foreign Office to write articles reassuring Indian Muslims of British good faith towards the future of the Turkish Caliphate.[42] Hardinge assured Chirol, 'You may absolutely count on my providing you with the fullest information you may require, and I feel confident that even after my departure, the Government of India will give you all you ask.'[43]

Hardinge also corresponded with other journalists, sometimes taking issue with them, as for example with Fraser in connection with his articles in the *National Review* criticising the revocation of the partition of Bengal: 'I mention this . . . in no controversial spirit . . . as I do not resent . . . other people holding opinion different to my own. I am sure you will accept my above statement in the same friendly spirit as I make it.'[44] A particular concern was with the impact of *India* in England and of negative impressions being created of Indian governance. One official claimed in 1910, for example, that *India* was responsible for 'the wholesale demoralisation to which the large body of Indian students in England are exposed'.[45] Given the role of educated opinion in governing India, it was crucial to cultivate the support of the Indian elite who journeyed to Britain to complete their education. Hardinge also encouraged G. B. Allen to start a newspaper in London (as discussed in Chapter 3) articulating the government viewpoint, noting that 'what is wanted more than anything else is greater freedom for the Viceroy and more independence of Whitehall . . . Any assistance from [your paper] on those lines will be very useful.'[46] Allen's *Indiaman* duly obliged, proclaiming in its opening editorial, 'we shall watch with jealous vigilance any tendency to subordinate India to British interests, any inclination to embarrass or belittle the Government of India'.[47] Like Minto, the diplomacy characterising the Viceroy's dealings with Fleet Street was not extended to Indian-run papers. Hardinge supported the retention of the Press Act, and explained to Crewe that the latter was: 'absolutely different from the press in Europe. We have taught the Indians much, but we have not taught them journalism, and I am quite convinced in my own opinion that the flames of sedition are fanned by the press'.[48]

Meanwhile, in London, the Liberal Secretaries of State Morley (1905–10) and Crewe (1910–15) recognised the need to maintain a harmonious relationship with Fleet Street. In general Morley agreed with Minto upon the desirability of monitoring and controlling opinion in Britain, owing to its potential repercussions both within India and in Britain.[49] Morley had impeccable journalistic credentials – having edited the *Fortnightly Review* (1867–82), *Morning Star* (1869) and *Pall Mall Gazette* (1880–83) – and his period in office saw deliberate, though intermittent, efforts to manage the powerful group of London pressmen. He invited them to the India Office for official briefings, dined with them at clubs and entertained the privileged few at his home in Wimbledon. Confidential material was circulated to influential editors. Only a fortnight after assuming office Morley wrote to Strachey, a warm supporter of Curzon in his dispute with Kitchener. Morley was broadly in sympathy with Curzon's position and 'laid the blame squarely' on St John Brodrick, the Secretary of State.[50]

> The Spectator has taken . . . so strenuous a part in the Indian controversy, that I venture to write you a line . . . frankly, and in *strict confidence*. As you are the protagonist in the press, I like you to understand the line on which I expect to get round any difficulties, for your private information.[51]

Spender was another confidant. 'I used often to go home from my visits to the India Office', he reminisced, 'with bundles of papers and memoranda given me for 'evening meditation', and sometimes I was invited to make comments or suggestions'.[52]

Increasing political unrest, together with the impending Morley – Minto constitutional reforms, enhanced Morley's sensitivity to press opinion. On one occasion he reacted to Liberal press criticism of 'repression ruining the chances of reforms' by inviting the two Liberal editors involved to his offices, where he 'dealt with them as faithfully as ever I could, and they departed sadder and wiser men'. On another occasion, Morley met the *Mail*'s editor and 'treated him with a judicious mixture of frowns and smiles, scolding and bowings, that seem to have been fruitful' – the paper indeed being redolent of praise for Morley the following day.[53] Chirol's opposition to some aspects of the reforms worried him: 'This is bad news for me, for active unfriendliness and opposition from *The Times* will make a vast deal of difference here.'[54] On the whole, however, Chirol admired Morley and to some extent owed his knighthood to supporting the India Office policies. In 1910 he dedicated his influential book *Indian Unrest* to the

Secretary of State.[55] Similarly, on the occasion of Lovat Fraser's visit in 1909, Morley advised Minto: 'Pray be sure to put good arguments in the head of Lovat Fraser . . . I look to you to bring [him] into a good frame of mind.'[56]

Crewe was sensitive to the opinions of the press, taking, for instance, an active part in the first Imperial Press Conference. He felt that the presence of British and foreign journalists at the Delhi durbar would be helpful and used his personal quota of invitations to accommodate them.[57] He took a keen interest in their comfort, persuading Hardinge to inspect accommodation facilities at the press camp, believing it was 'bad policy not to treat the Press generously'.[58] Spender went out for the durbar 'burdened with the secrets' of the King's proclamation, on which 'I had written articles and left them behind me in sealed envelopes for publication on the appropriate dates'.[59] Such a breach of security was indicative of the press – politics nexus, especially given the official secrecy surrounding this episode and the contents of the King's speech – even Governors were left in the dark by the India Office. Further, Crewe only reluctantly shared Hardinge's belief in the necessity of continuing with stringent press controls, his own opinions having been worked on by Indian deputations urging a revision of the Press Act. It was difficult to deny the possibility, he argued, that 'persuasion as a first step to avoid mistaken and hasty persecutions of editors could yield positive results . . . On the face of it I should always maintain that, as our Government in India must be arbitrary in essence . . . the more cases in which it can also be paternal, the better.'[60]

The press–politics nexus under pressure

On the whole, the informal partnership between British policy makers and the national press functioned smoothly. Yet there were occasional clashes of both personality and principle, these being further complicated by the nature of the relationship between the India Office and the government in India. Inherent tensions between the two were exacerbated by the revolution in the speed and nature of imperial communications.

In general the Minto – Morley partnership was sensitive to the London press and its possible influence, both within domestic politics and indirectly through its impact on Indian politics and Indian-run newspapers. Interestingly, however, both the Conservative Viceroy and the Liberal Secretary of State found themselves criticised by their own party papers. Minto, for instance, believed that *The Times* had 'intrigue[d]' against him, his complaints stemming largely from the attitude of Chirol, a strong Curzonite.[61] He maintained that *The Times*, along with *The Times of India* (which had been 'inspired from home'), promoted perceptions of Calcutta's inability to control unrest, and that this cry of weak government impaired his status.[62] 'A great newspaper like *The Times* has no business to be Curzonian in a partisan sense. That it has been so is beyond doubt, and it consequently has been personally opposed to me.'[63] For all his journalistic connections, Morley did not enjoy a wholly docile press and from time to time encountered criticism, including from the *Manchester Guardian*. When, for example, the paper attacked the measures against the freedom of the press in India, Morley wrote in strong terms to Scott:

> If men write seditious articles, they will be punished. *Be sure* . . . Why don't you look at the Indian problem as a whole? Here am I striving might and main to introduce reforms in the giant system of bureaucracies: with immense forces against us . . . And here I am quibbled at, and quarrelled with, because I punish open wrongdoers . . . Your people have never judged the magnitude of the case.[64]

Nevinson, an acquaintance since their days of joint opposition to the Boer War, journeyed to India in 1907–8. Morley had given him 'some excellent advice' and suggested that 'it might be useful' if Minto showed him 'some trifle of civility'.[65] However, Nevinson's articles were very critical of officialdom, as was his subsequent book, *New Spirit in India*, which contained photographs and accounts of starvation and floods, as well as descriptions of racial hostility towards educated Indians, and unsurprisingly found himself *persona non grata* at the India Office.[66]

Underlying differences in personality and political perspective were compounded by the fact that Viceroys and Secretaries of State addressed, in general, different publics. Minto was faced, in the first instance, with the task of controlling increasing political unrest, and he pushed for strong sanctions. This policy Morley (like Crewe), supported with reluctance. Not only was he predisposed against controls on press freedom, but he reminded the Viceroy of the susceptibilities of the British: 'one of the secrets . . . of British freedom and power – as to the virtues of an unfettered press'.[67] He himself was answerable directly to Parliament: 'press prosecutions and editorial imprisonments are delicate things with a strongly Liberal House of Commons in front of one'.[68] Morley conveyed his displeasure at punitive press sanctions, arguing that Minto's attitude had 'embarrassed' the government and that the Viceroy 'should always remember the British Public'.[69] While he did not 'disregard' British opinion, Minto argued in

6 'The Indian Secretary Bird. Mr Morley puts his foot on sedition in India',
Punch, 5 June 1907

turn that the welfare of India 'must be my first thought, even
though I feel that the procedure necessary here is not distinctly in
accordance with British views'.[70] That Morley allowed himself to
be overruled in this case can be attributed to his cautious liberalism, his wish to minimise disruption in Britain by a debate over

[111]

Indian policy, and his fear of the impact of British opinion on the subcontinent.

Besides issues of personality, principle and practical politics, the great improvements in communications with the subcontinent enhanced the ability of Westminster to intervene in Indian governance. Possibilities of contention between the home and Indian governments were accordingly increased and in respect of disagreements both sides sought support from Fleet Street.

Ripon's tenure witnessed the clearest demonstration of the potentially disruptive power of the press in the late nineteenth century. During the year-long anti-Ilbert Bill campaign the press (in conjunction with the platform) was successfully utilised to extend and redefine the sphere of public debate and the mechanics of popular pressure to influence more directly the initiatives of government. The Bill, introduced in February 1883, aimed to extend the right of qualified Indian magistrates to try Europeans in criminal cases at all levels of the judiciary, thus removing a racial anomaly. Macaulay's so-called Black Act had accorded this right in civil cases in the 1830s and had managed to overcome minor opposition. However, by the 1880s criticism was mounted on an unprecedented scale. The Bill upset the non-official British community in India, and Anglo-Indian journalists, with support from Conservative sections of Fleet Street, joined ranks to co-ordinate and spread the disaffection, which as the year progressed even raised the spectre of a 'White Mutiny'. Ripon and Ilbert were accorded only wavering support by Parliament, the Cabinet and the India Office. This created a political vacuum in London, which was successfully exploited by the press. The small Anglo-Indian community (approximately 35,000) was able to amplify its voice through its access to the pages of Fleet Street. For the same reason, Fleet Street could strengthen its demands by claiming to speak on behalf of a beleaguered expatriate community.

The opening salvo was touched off in London by *The Times*, whose Calcutta correspondent, James Macgregor, began the attack with a cable published on 5 February 1883, just three days after the introduction of the Bill, forecasting its intense unpopularity. *The Times* praised the Europeans in India as 'the best, and, indeed, the only hope of animation and movement which may extend to the entire mass . . . a *corps d'élite*, whose opinions must be considered'.[71] The *Telegraph* and the *St James Gazette* urged the home government to check the 'breathless benevolence' of Ripon.[72] Repercussions of such coverage began to reach India. The *Times of India* published a telegram on 7 February from its London correspondent, summarising the *Times* article and stating that London papers 'generally condemn' Ilbert's Bill.

This dispatch, in turn, was telegraphed around India and reprinted the next day in the *Englishman*, *Statesman*, *Madras Mail* and *Pioneer*.

The London Liberal press responded to *The Times*, and the Conservative papers in general, by deploring the 'exaggerated declarations that the Empire is endangered if we act on the principle that native magistrates can be trusted to administer justice, when Europeans are involved'.[73] The *Pall Mall Gazette* accused MacGregor for being 'just what a correspondent ought not to be – a warm partisan'.[74] The *Daily News* urged Gladstone to support his appointee: 'There never was a time, not even during the Indian Mutiny, when it was of greater importance that the position taken up by a Viceroy should be sustained by England.'[75] Unfortunately, the capacity of the pro-Bill press to influence events was undermined by dissension within the Liberal administration. The Liberal tradition was complex, and even contradictory. Most British Liberals in 1883 were far less dogmatic than their Conservative contemporaries. Lords Kimberley, Northbrook[76] and Hartington defended the Bill on grounds of administrative convenience, precedent and innocuousness, but they avoided countering Conservative doctrines and ideals with their own. On the conclusion of the crisis in December 1883 Gladstone congratulated Ripon and 'rejoice[d] that another great forward step [had] been made in the business of governing India'.[77] However, the concessions, which in effect substituted a European British majority jury for a European British judge at the district level, undermined the very principle that the Bill was aiming to establish, and sealed Ripon's fate.

Another graphic example, two decades later, was the dispute between Curzon and his Commander-in-chief, Lord Kitchener, over the need for army reorganisation, a disagreement that escalated into an issue of the supremacy of civil over military rule. This controversy illustrates the ability of the India Office to exert considerable influence on the press in an attempt to colour metropolitan opinion. The exploitation of Fleet Street by St John Brodrick (1903–5), Arthur Balfour and Kitchener played a significant role in determining the outcome of the controversy and indicates the strength of personal connections between leading government figures and those editors and correspondents who shaped Indian coverage. Kitchener and Brodrick's common War Office background contributed to this end, as well as the growing animosity between the Secretary of State and Curzon.

Fleet Street was divided, though significantly the majority of Liberal papers supported the Conservative Viceroy. The pages of *The Times* formed one of the principal arenas in the publicity battle. Buckle, the editor, supported Kitchener, while Bell, the manager, was on the

Viceroy's side, as were Chirol and Fraser.[78] The military correspondent Charles Repington had been on Kitchener's staff in Egypt and was an 'enthusiastic conspirator'. He also enjoyed the backing of Brodrick, who, it was rumoured, 'effectively threatened to cut off all official information to *The Times*'.[79] Brodrick organised, along with Godley and to a lesser extent Balfour, a propaganda campaign to discredit Curzon, and attempts to 'square Buckle' were made in order to 'prevent a silly line' being taken by the paper.[80] 'I am sorry to think that I was inevitably more or less mixed up in it,' Godley was to admit later.[81] Gwynne, then editor of the *Standard*, also supported Kitchener, based on their association forged in South Africa.

Brodrick believed that Curzon was 'manipulating the newspapers' and exploiting the *Times of India* through Fraser, and that there were 'suspicious leakages' of cypher telegrams from India. He alleged that 'one important agency' had been 'subsidized out of public funds for the privilege of editing their telegrams' and this explained the 'indignation telegraphed from India at Kitchener's proceedings'.[82] The reference was, of course, to Reuters. But there existed another side to the case. The press in India abounded with criticisms of the home government, yet Reuters extracts took the opposite position. Buck had heard from Baron de Reuter that there had been 'no choice, on account of the Cabinet's pressure'.[83]

With Balfour and the Cabinet supporting Kitchener, the Viceroy eventually felt obliged to resign. His supporters in London were bitter at what they considered the unfair treatment he had received from the press and accused government sources of fermenting and distorting opinion.[84] 'One of the things that has disgusted me most,' commented Strachey, 'is the way in which the Press here has worked against you.'[85] Chirol regretted his inability to prevail at Printing House Square: 'my judgement', he wrote, 'has always been allowed to carry considerable weight with regard to the policy of [*The Times*] . . . This is the first time that my influence has gone for nothing.'[86] *The Times* had gone 'deplorably wrong', Buckle had been pressurised, and, 'you know the way in which wires are pulled by Cabinet Ministers and their spokesmen'.[87] Fraser was more forthright in his criticism of Kitchener: 'Of all his acts, I think the campaign in the press, the persistent lobbying at home through his own subordinates, and the compact . . . with Repington, were the most despicable.'[88] Defending the *Mail* against Curzon's charge of 'hostility', Northcliffe explained that his editor's main problem was that 'he could not get facts. He was obliged to rely on the India Office for his information and although he was most cautious in using it, he knows that they mislead him and every other newspaper'.[89] A dejected Curzon complained that in

England 'public opinion . . . captured in advance by a press campaign' organised by Kitchener, had been 'consistently misled from the start'.[90]

Curzon viewed the controversy as part of a general tendency for the India Office to manipulate press opinion against the Viceroy. During an earlier disagreement with Brodrick, Curzon made clear his displeasure at such proceedings:

> is the Secretary of State . . . to be at liberty to write privately to newspapers at home and solicit their support for his own action as opposed to that of the Government of India and its agents . . . and in fact to invite the London Press to join with him in censuring the Government of India and their representatives, of whom he is, by virtue of his office, the accredited spokesman and champion? Is he really to manufacture, in his own interests, a Press opposition against the Government of India and the Viceroy?[91]

This episode involved the publication of a Blue Book on Francis Younghusband's Tibetan campaign, edited in a fashion to throw poor light upon Younghusband and the government in India, an action compounded by Brodrick's decision to send copies to some Fleet Street editors 'accompanied by a letter drawing their attention to passages indicating the soundness of his own policy and the disobedience of Younghusband'.[92] In 1905 Curzon's weakness in the London campaign was also partly because he allowed Kitchener a head start and did not use the press as much as he could have, believing his case was unanswerable. Hamilton later recalled that Kitchener 'so manipulated public opinion and the press that Curzon's case was almost unknown and certainly not seriously studied, though it had behind it a phalanx of the best military and administrative opinion'.[93]

Conclusion

Thus from the late nineteenth century successive Secretaries of State (and Viceroys) attempted to influence perceptions of Indian policy in Britain through the national press. Such endeavours were dependent on the personal initiatives of those in charge, as well as being affected by the relationship between the India Office and the government in India. Complicating the situation further were the differences in the publics addressed. As Dunlop-Smith observed to Morley, 'all that could be seen out of the windows of the India Office was the British Public walking about in a peaceful green park. But the Viceroy is in the midst of the Indian Public and of the British Public in India' as well as having to worry about the public at home.[94] Yet this attempt to manage news by the India Office was not conducted in an explicit or formal way. As was true of many areas of national life, influence was exerted by informal contacts between leading decision takers, with two methods being chiefly used to manage newspaper reporting: first, the selective disclosure of information; second, personal contact with leading journalists. As Taylor notes similarly of the Foreign Office, this is 'a twilight area' where intelligence was divulged privately and in an informal context of a social function or over dinner at a London club. While the rising prominence of press and public opinion was increasingly acknowledged, there was little attempt to integrate its management into the business of imperial governance. Throughout Fleet Street correspondents, editors and proprietors maintained a robustly critical approach to official policy. And occasionally an issue was transformed into a controversy with the help of the press and some controversies had the capacity to transcend this limited world of informal control and restructure the terms and outcomes of debate. Further, the press was also better placed to influence debate and decisions on Indian issues when domestic political controversy was especially pronounced.

Notes

1   A. Godley to Viceroy, 8 January 1904, Kilbracken collection MSS Eur F102/53–9.
2   Cited in M. N. Das, *India under Morley and Minto* (1964), p. 72.
3   A. K. Singh, *Indian Students in Britain* (1963), p. 21.
4   E. C. Moulton, 'Early Congress and the British radical connection', in D. A. Low (ed.), *Indian National Congress Centenary Hindsights* (1988), pp. 22–53.
5   M. Cumpston, 'Some early Indian nationalists and their allies in the British Parliament, 1851–1906', *EngHR*, 76: 299 (1961), 297.
6   Cited in Das, *Morley*, p. 82.
7   S. Sarkar, *Modern India* (1995), p. 96, Barrier, *Banned*, p. 9.
8   H. J. S. Cotton, *New India* (1907 edn), pp. 6–7.
9   Home Poll, A 281–7, November 1919, pp. 13, 15.
10   Home Poll, Deposit 20, November 1918.
11   M. K. Gandhi, *Autobiography* (1927), pp. 239, 395.
12   C. Dewey, *Anglo-Indian Attitudes: The Mind of the Indian Civil Service* (1993), p. 5.
13   Viceroy to Chamberlain, 4 February 1918, MSS Eur E264/15, Chelmsford Collection (hereafter CC/no).
14   Curtis to Viceroy, 24 May 1918, CC/15.
15   H. W. Nevinson, *New Spirit in India* (1908), pp. 15–17, 206–32; Cotton, *New India*, pp. 46–76. Forthcoming biography by A.V. John.
16   Reed to Braham, 22 August 1913, Braham Papers, TA.
17   P. Spear, in V. Smith (ed.), *Oxford History of India* (1991 edn), p. 723.
18   Home Poll, 188/IV, 1922, p. 1.
19   Foreign-General A, no. 43, August 1882, p. 7, NAI.
20   *Ibid.*, pp. 11–12.
21   Barns, *Indian Press*, pp. 289–93.
22   C. Kaul, 'England and India: the Ilbert Bill, 1883: a case study of the metropolitan press', *IESHR*, 30: 4 (1993), 413–36.
23   H. J. S. Cotton, *New India* (1907 edn), p. 204.

24 *History of* The Times (1939) II, p. 309.
25 Bell, *Life and Letters*, p. 154.
26 O. T. Burne, *Memories* (1907), p. 205.
27 Lord Kilbracken, *Reminiscences* (1931), pp. 160, 18, 29.
28 Viceroy to J. S. Sandars, 5 July 1905, CurC/164.
29 Viceroy to Godley, 27 January 1904, Kilbracken collection.
30 See Viceroy – Secretary of State correspondence, L/PWD/7/1408, L/PWD/7/1390, L/PWD/7/1891.
31 W. R. Lawrence, *The India we Served* (1929), pp. 254–5.
32 Viceroy to Godley, 2 March 1905, CurC/164.
33 Natarajan, *Press*, pp. 357–65; Barrier, *Banned*, pp. 16–65.
34 L. James, *Times of Stress* (1929), p. 103.
35 *Calcutta Review* and *Friend of India*.
36 Dunlop-Smith to Viceroy, 20 April, 27 May, 28 June 1910, D-S/9.
37 Cited in Das, *Morley*, p. 72.
38 Nevinson, *New Spirit*, p. 25.
39 Viceroy to Secretary of State, 14 July 1910, Home Poll, A 55, pp. 6–7.
40 Chirol to Viceroy, 19 October 1914; also 21, 30 October, 30 November 1914, Vol. II, 93, HP.
41 Chirol to Viceroy, 21 December 1911, Vol. 1, 92, HP.
42 Chirol to Viceroy, 22 May 1914, Viceroy to Chirol, 24 September 1914, Vol. II, 93, HP.
43 Viceroy to Chirol, 24 June 1915, Vol. III, 94, HP.
44 Viceroy to Fraser, 12 May 1912, Vol. I, 92, HP.
45 Note by C. R. Cleveland, 20 June 1910, Home Poll, A 55, July 1910, p. 2.
46 Viceroy to Allen, 8/16 February 1915, Vol. II, 93, HP.
47 *Indiaman* 15 May 1914.
48 Viceroy to Secretary of State, 15 January 1914, Vol. IV, 120, HP.
49 Secretary of State to Viceroy, 28 May 1908, MSS Eur D57/3, Morley Papers (hereafter MorC/no.).
50 S. Koss, *Morley at the India Office* (1969), p. 92.
51 Secretary of State to Strachey, 26 December 1905, S/10/14/2, SP.
52 Spender, *Life* I, p. 147, II, p. 102; Secretary of State to Spender, 5 November 1910, BL, Add. MS 46392 (Spender Papers), fol. 51.
53 Secretary of State to Viceroy, 24 December 1908, 11 July 1907, cited in Mary, Countess of Minto, *India, Minto and Morley* (1934), pp. 310–11.
54 Cited in Das, *Morley*, p. 77.
55 V. Chirol, *Fifty Years in a Changing World* (1927), p. 239; A. T. Embree, 'Pledged to India: the liberal experiment, 1885–1909', in J. M. W. Bean (ed.), *Political Culture of Modern Britain* (1987), pp. 48–9.
56 Secretary of State to Viceroy, 13 January, 4 February 1909, cited in Minto, *India*, pp. 311, 313.
57 Viceroy to Secretary of State, 3 May 1911; Secretary of State to Viceroy, 28 April, 10 July, 8, 14, 30 September, 2 October, 8 November 1911, 95, HP.
58 Secretary of State to Viceroy, 15 October 1911, 95, HP.
59 Spender, *Life* II, p. 102.
60 Secretary of State to Viceroy, 6 March 1914, Vol. IV, 120, HP.
61 See Viceroy to Dunlop-Smith, 24 March, 6 April, 30 May, 25 August 1910, D-S/19.
62 Viceroy to Secretary of State, 3 September 1906, cited in Minto, *India*, p. 310.
63 Viceroy to Secretary of State, 4 February 1909, *ibid.*, p. 312.
64 Secretary of State to Scott, 30 October 1908, 128/39, MGA; S. R. Wasti, *Lord Minto and the Indian Nationalist Movement* (1964), p. 116.
65 Secretary of State to Viceroy, 3 October 1907, cited in Minto, *India*, p. 311.
66 Journals of H. W. Nevinson, 18 March 1908, MS Eng misc. e.614/4, Bodl.
67 Cited in Das, *Morley*, p. 127.
68 *Ibid.*, p. 126.
69 Cited in M. Gilbert, *Servant of India* (1966), p. 156.

70 *Ibid.*
71 *Times*, 22 December 1883.
72 *Daily Telegraph*, 7 February 1883.
73 *Pall Mall Gazette*, 10 February 1883.
74 *Ibid.*; also 26 February; *Echo*, 6 August 1883.
75 *Daily News*, 25 June 1883; *Pall Mall Gazette*, 24 July 1883.
76 Viceroy 1872–76, 1880, Indian adviser to Cabinet, First Lord of the Admiralty.
77 Gladstone to Viceroy, 18 January 1884, H. C. G. Matthew (ed.), *Gladstone Diaries* (Oxford, 1990) XI, p. 101.
78 Bell, *Life and Letters*, pp. 231–2.
79 D. Gilmour, *Curzon* (1995), pp. 298–9.
80 *Ibid.*, p. 338.
81 Kilbracken, *Reminiscences*, p. 182.
82 Earl of Midleton, *Records and Reactions* (1939), pp. 189, 193–206.
83 D. Dilks, *Curzon* (1970) II, pp. 226, 331.
84 Chirol to E. Barrow, 2 October 1906, Barrow Collection, MSS Eur E420/20; Strachey to Curzon, 19 October 1905, CurC/183.
85 Strachey to Curzon, 19 October 1905, CurC/183.
86 Chirol to Curzon, 14 September 1905, CurC/183.
87 *Ibid.*, 3 August 1905, CurC/183.
88 Fraser memo, February 1908, CurC/411.
89 Northcliffe to Curzon, 3 October 1905, CurC/183; cf. Curzon to Northcliffe, 3 August 1905, BL, Add. MS 62153 (Northcliffe Papers), fol. 132.
90 Viceroy to A. Lyall, 15 August 1905, CurC/183.
91 Viceroy to Secretary of State, 21 February 1905, CurC/164.
92 Gilmour, *Curzon*, p. 316.
93 G. Hamilton, *Parliamentary Reminiscences and Reflections* (1922), p. 305.
94 Cited in Gilbert, *Servant of India*, p. 156.

CHAPTER FIVE

War and government publicity

Of course, it is a huge gamble to denude India as we have done, but it is not a matter of choice but of sheer necessity . . . So we have got to throw every trained man we have into this appalling melting pot, whether white, brown or black. Of course we shall have to pay pretty heavily afterwards from the political point of view, but this is not the moment when we can even think about ulterior consequences.[1]

Valentine Chirol's observations, made when significant numbers of Indian troops were fighting in France at the start of the First World War, highlight the dilemma facing Britain. It was imperative to win the war. But one price of victory was the accumulation of political demands whose settlement, while it could be legitimately delayed, could not be permanently avoided. If the causes of the war had little to do with India, its conduct and outcome certainly did. Yet even before these 'ulterior consequences' had to be faced, positive measures were required to ensure that the military potential of the Indian empire could be mobilised. This meant, first, that India volunteered in sufficient numbers to sustain the war effort; and, second, that domestic conditions in India must be kept sufficiently tranquil to permit the 'denuding' of the country's armed forces. In the securing of these conditions coercion and persuasion would each play a vital part.

These concerns were not confined to the subcontinent. Public opinion played a crucial part in all the theatres of war. Waged in the context of a mass media, it was a 'total' war fought simultaneously on military, economic and ideological fronts. These years witnessed the birth of official propaganda in Britain. The government discerned the importance of sustaining public enthusiasm, winning the sympathy of neutral nations and subverting enemy morale. Central to this process was the press. By the end of the war 'a great historical divide' had been passed in the spheres of government opinion manipulation and propaganda.[2] Therefore, to appreciate India Office war publicity waged

[119]

through the press, it is necessary to situate these efforts within the context of the momentous developments in London – in the media, in official departments, and in the changed relationship more generally between Fleet Street and Downing Street.

Official propaganda and Fleet Street

The war impacted on the government–press relations in two distinct and different ways. First, at an official level, the press became subject to an organised process of propaganda and censorship. Second, and unofficially, the press became a forum in which political controversy could be played out.

Government efforts at war propaganda were 'an impressive exercise in improvisation' on several interrelated levels.[3] There was structural and organisational change, with the establishment of a Press Bureau, a War Propaganda Bureau and finally a separate Department and later Ministry of Information in 1918. Individual departments of state were forced to adopt a more proactive approach towards journalists. Yet at the same time the war gave an unofficial impetus to political journalism as animosities went underground at Westminster, only to surface in Fleet Street.[4] Foremost amongst the Liberal government's critics in the early stages of the conflict were the papers of Northcliffe and Rothermere, who doubted Asquith's ability to lead the nation. The storm of criticism they helped to create, centering on the so-called Shell scandal and Admiralty crises, compelled Asquith to form a coalition government with the Conservatives in May 1915.[5] In the context of the more fluid political conditions created by the Coalition government, and amid the unprecedented strains of conflict, the government was uncertain of the public reaction to policy decisions. Traditional party labels were in abeyance, with a Liberal–Conservative coalition confronted by shifting patterns of Labour, Liberal and independent Conservative opposition. Politicians nervously looked to the popular and quality press alike for an insight into the attitudes of democracy. Despite newsprint restrictions and the practical constraints imposed by the war, both popular and quality newspapers witnessed a boom in circulation. The total sales of all eleven London dailies were around 4.5 million, of which the Harmsworth brothers accounted for nearly half. The *Mail* was averaging sales of around a million a day by 1918, with the *Express* selling approximately 600,000 copies, while every evening 500,000 people bought the *Star*. The *Times* soared to an all-time high of over 150,000, aided by the reduction of its price to 1*d* in early 1914. The *Morning Post* was averaging an unprecedented 100,000, the *Daily News* half that number. The

7   'India For The King!' *Punch*, 9 September 1914

Herald achieved sales as high as 250,000. While the *Telegraph* suffered as a result of competition from the rejuvenated *Times*, it was still averaging 180,000 by 1918. This growth in circulation increased the ability of newspapers to speak for the people, especially as there were no general elections during the war. The idea of the press as a significant extra-parliamentary power in the political system with the capacity to influence policy decisions was taken more seriously than ever before.

In these circumstances, Asquith's failure to attach sufficient weight to the role of the press in the war effort proved a costly mistake. Even Scott and Donald found him unapproachable. 'He took no pains,' wrote Donald, 'either personally or through his secretaries, to keep in touch with newspapers which were his supporters. They had to support him in the dark.'[6] Unlike Asquith, Lloyd George fully recognised the role the press must play in a total war. He cultivated the press as Minister of Munitions, and was able to count on the support of several newspapermen in his intrigues to displace Asquith.[7] Michael MacDonagh, a journalist on *The Times*, noted the difference, 'Lloyd George's way – accessible, genial, helpful to journalists, so different from the aloofness and cold eyes of Grey and Asquith'.[8] Upon becoming Prime Minister Lloyd George moved quickly to centralise the propaganda machine. A new Department of Information was set up in 1917, and a year later Lloyd George made his friend Lord Beaverbrook Britain's first Minister of Information with a seat in the Cabinet. Beaverbrook's appointment marked the culmination, not only of his own rising influence, but of the evolution of official propaganda organisation. However, there remained much that was *ad hoc* in official initiatives. As Beaverbrook recalled, 'There was no blueprint to work on. No experience to guide the new staff. There was no office, no staff.'[9] Rothermere joined the government as Air Minister, while Northcliffe was appointed Director of Enemy Propaganda. At the Paris peace conference Lloyd George chose Lord Riddell, a close friend, and proprietor of the *News of the World*, to be the official representative of the British press. The worlds of Fleet Street and Downing Street thus coalesced to an unprecedented degree.

For Lloyd George more was involved than simply wartime expediency. In breaking with the bulk of the Liberal Party it was essential for him to continue to court newspaper owners and editors, since he had no political party to call upon for steady support.[10] A key weapon in his armoury was the honours system. Within four years, nearly fifty proprietors and editors had become Privy Counsellors, peers, baronets or knights. He lavished high office on newspapermen: at one time six of Fleet Street's families had members in his government. Thus he sought to secure Fleet Street as an alternative power base. The election campaign of December 1918 saw Lloyd George supported by a galaxy of pressmen, including Lords Rothermere, Beaverbrook, Dalziel and Riddell. The Prime Minister's machinations seemed to confirm allegations that he had 'perverted' political journalism. In the Commons criticism was spearheaded by Austen Chamberlain, who argued that the presence of newspaper proprietors in the administration threatened the demarcation between press and government and was repugnant to the traditions of British public life.[11] However, the very narrowness of Lloyd George's personal power base, resting on the support of a handful of ambitious press personalities, rendered it precarious. For example, although brought into government, Northcliffe, with growing signs of megalomania, felt slighted by the rising prominence of Beaverbrook and Riddell, and after being excluded from the Versailles peace negotiations remorselessly attacked Lloyd George via his papers. Whatever their affinities, newspapermen had their own agendas and Lloyd George, in his preparedness to engage personally with them, took risks which later politicians endeavoured to avoid.

India Office press publicity

India occupied a strategic place in the imperial war effort, and was, accordingly, subject to similar pressures making for the formalisation of government propaganda. Though informal and *ad hoc* methods of government influence on the press, as discussed in the previous chapter, continued after 1914, with the exigencies of war issues of imperial publicity and propaganda received a new impetus and the case for a more consistent approach to the management of Indian news appeared strong. India was subject to general wartime censorship. But official intervention was not confined to the supply of information. Britain's need to counter German propaganda was pressing in the dependent empire, if only to ensure its continued support for the war effort. As Barrier notes, 'From one perspective, the British were pitted against German and Indian opponents in a struggle for the minds of the population'.[12]

Censorship and suppression of news

A crucial dimension to news manipulation and propaganda was the weapon of censorship. Telegraph censorship was instituted within India in August 1914 and a detailed list of English and vernacular newspapers suitable to receive official advertisements and for consumption by Indian troops was prepared in every province. Messages from India were censored by the Press Bureau in London, and news sent to the subcontinent was at the mercy of the Indian chief censor.[13] Lansbury's *Herald* and Hyndman's *Justice*, with their support of the Russian revolution, open attacks on the Raj and generally radical tone, were strictly proscribed from export.[14] These restrictions continued even after the end of hostilities, owing to official concern that such papers were being extensively utilised by nationalist propaganda, with deleterious effects on public opinion. *India* was carefully monitored – for example, an article in its 4 February 1916 issue on 'The right to bear arms' was criticised, for it was felt that it 'might produce disaffection within the Army'.[15] The paper's editor, Cotton, protested, to no avail, that a longer version of the same article had appeared in the *Bombay Chronicle* on 29 December 1915, and that from the commencement of hostilities 'our journal . . . has loyally co-operated' in the war.[16]

London was the lynchpin in official attempts to stop subversive anti-British literature, including newspapers and pamphlets, being disseminated by *émigré* radical groups in Europe and the United States, and sent to sympathisers within Britain like Indian students and liberal academics.[17] The Defence of the Realm Act, 1917, was utilised to prohibit the import of such 'seditious' publications. A mounting concern with US opinion was evident from 1913. The Indian Information Centre in New York was the nucleus of British attempts at reaching the American public through articles in newspapers, the distribution of pamphlets and sponsorship of public lectures. In this connection the American journalist de Witt Mackenzie of the Associated Press was paid by the India Office to tour India.[18] Yet this did not prevent accusations of 'a grave breach of neutrality' by the United States in allowing the German embassy in Washington to support the activities of Indian revolutionaries.[19] This so-called 'German–Indian conspiracy', with German consular funding for the production and dissemination of 'seditious literature', including newspapers like *Ghadr* – produced by the eponymous organisation of Indian revolutionaries lead by Har Dayal, with bases in San Francisco, Washington, New York, New Jersey, Idaho and Seattle – was of continuing concern.[20]

Similar concern was evident over the practice of British newspapers reproducing German communiqués which then found their way to the subcontinent. For instance, an article entitled 'War through German spectacles' was published in English newspapers, where it might provoke amusement or derision. However, in India such articles had potentially damaging consequences, the readers, it was believed, often failing to appreciate the propaganda implicit in such news. 'We cannot exclude English papers very well,' noted R. H. Craddock, an official in the Home Department, 'and we cannot therefore prevent these German versions reaching India. The mischief is done in their reproduction in newspapers in India, and especially in those vernacular prints that circulate among the people whose knowledge of European affairs is of the vaguest.' The oral transmission of such news to the masses could result in even wider distortion. Yet there was no easy way to deal with this problem. 'Can we punish an Indian editor for printing matter which has already appeared in the London *Times*?'[21]

A wider problem was the impact of British press articles critical of the government in India.

> We find letters or articles in certain English newspapers supposed to be reputable, which constitute gross contempt of the Indian Courts, or are highly defamatory of the Indian Government. By the time they come to our notice, it is too late to stop their entry, and it is highly inconsistent to deal with such matters in India under the Press Act, and to ignore the same matter in the case of English newspapers. It ends, therefore, in our doing nothing, for if we prohibited all future entries of such newspapers, we should raise a storm in England.[22]

Even before the war the government in Delhi had requested Morley to cable early intelligence about objectionable material, so as to prohibit entry. However, Morley was against such measures, aware that any prohibition could provoke inconvenient parliamentary questions.[23] Under conditions of war such conflicts of interest between the India Office and the Indian government appeared even more intractable and highlight the continuing difficulties in operating an imperial system from a London centre subject to domestic political pressures.

Supply of news and official press publicity

In addition to attempts at suppression and censorship, the India Office was aware of the desirability of a steady flow of favourable news. A daily telegram was compiled by the India Office for publication in the Indian press, with the achievements of Indian troops in France in the early stages of the war proving a popular item in such despatches. On resignation from his short-lived directorship of the Press Bureau, the Conservative MP (and later Secretary of State for India) F. E. Smith was sent to join these troops as a representative of the Indian press, furnishing it with articles from October 1914 until late spring 1915. Smith made much of the heroism of this vanguard of the imperial forces that suffered devastating casualties in opposing major German offensives. In private he was critical, however, of the extent of news manipulation regarding Indian troops, claiming that their exploits were showcased at the expense of minimising their casualties, and an inaccurate image was conveyed in Fleet Street. Writing to his wife, he noted how 'all these things in the papers about the Indian troops are lies . . . We got yesterday's *Times*. The optimism and the buck nearly made us all sick.'[24]

There was heightened sensitivity in official circles as to the kinds of stories reported and the tone of press telegrams. The maintenance of morale was critical, given the intense demands being placed on the Indian Army. India was depleted of troops at a time when, politically, she was more stirred than ever before. It was a calculated risk, which needed the utmost diplomacy and political posturing to succeed. As Hardinge explained to Crewe:

> the present moment is extremely critical, and I think that, if I can engage the pride and sympathy of India by stories of her troops at the front, the disloyal elements out here will find themselves at a discount, and the risk we are running of denuding India of troops will be minimised.[25]

Positive publicity was thus a central element in wartime policy. 'If, when announcing casualties amongst Indian troops . . . we could publish connected news of their welfare and doings in those theatres . . . it would be of great assistance to us.'[26] To diminish the risk of disaffection and increase recruitment it was essential to focus on the exploits of Indian troops, to highlight the special dietary and religious facilities and the provision for care of the wounded. The decision to house them in the Brighton Pavilion offered obvious opportunities for favourable publicity which were not missed. Brighton Corporation, for instance provided the convalescents with an illustrated pamphlet in English and several Indian languages, 20,000 of which were also circulated in India.[27] When the King visited the troops and awarded medals for gallantry, the event was widely covered by the media.

The effect of the war on India preoccupied Chelmsford, who wrote regularly to London editors giving details of the subcontinent's contribution. Dawson, responding to one such communiqué, avowed to 'take care at the first convenient opportunity that something further shall be said in *The Times* to put people right about the scope and character of India's wonderful effort. Your details are very impressive.'[28] A sensitive issue was the disastrous defeat of the Allied – chiefly Indian – forces in Mesopotamia and the culpability of the Government of India – an issue that generated considerable press outcry.[29] Unable to respond publicly to criticism, Chelmsford privately communicated his views to the press, emphasising to Dawson: 'You will of course regard this letter as absolutely confidential, but I felt that our long friendship entitled me to write to you fully and frankly on the matter.'[30]

Combating German press propaganda and guiding the British and neutral press were linked imperatives. The India Office was concerned with the supply of newspapers to the front.[31] It employed pictorial paper propaganda by means of publications like the trilingual *Al-Hakikat* 'to advertise British naval and military strength and friendship for Islam'.[32] 'It is intended,' noted Frank Lucas at the India Office, 'as a counterblast to a German illustrated paper of the same kind and though that paper doubtless does not find its way into India, ours ought to be useful in creating an impression favourable to the Allies.'[33] The costs of its production and distribution to Indian troops were borne jointly by the Treasury and the India Office, the work of compilation being shared with the Foreign and War Offices, with the *Illustrated London News* undertaking the photogravure process at a charge of £560 for 100,000 copies. Edited by Lieutenant Edward E. Leary, the exact specifications of the fortnightly *Al-Hakikat* were considered crucial: 'in view of the importance of our not appearing to the reader to produce an inferior article to that produced by the Germans, the paper should consist of eight pages of the same size as the German propagandist paper *Welt in Bild* (which also circulates in the Middle East), namely 23 in. × 16 in.'.[34]

Within India the government undertook to distribute thousands of copies of *Al-Hakikat* to select press representatives and other official and non-official organisations, as well as arranging for it to be sold cheap through private booksellers like Wheeler & Co. and the publishers Thacker & Spink. Within a few months nearly 40,000 had been distributed, and provincial government demand continued to rise. Buck, Hensman and Cotes, the three main press advisers, were roped in to help with advertisement. Thus Cotes, for instance, confirmed he had 'sent a paragraph about it to principal Calcutta, Bombay, Madras, Rangoon, Allahabad, Lahore and Karachi newspapers, and have written to *Times of India* and *Statesman* in case they can reproduce any of the pictures in their illustrated editions'.[35] This venture was taken over by the Eastern Propaganda division in 1917 (part of the Department of Information in London), with the remit of disseminating propaganda in the East generally, but particularly amongst Muslims.[36] E. E. Long, its Deputy Controller, had extensive experience in the subcontinent, having edited the *Rangoon Times* and *Indian Daily Telegraph*, in addition to acting as an Indian correspondent for *The Times*, *Standard* and *Express*.[37]

In October 1914 the Secretary of State authorised the publication by G. B. Allen of *Akhbar-i-Jung*, a weekly paper in Urdu for 'native' troops of the Indian expeditionary forces on the subcontinent. The prime cost of production was met by the India Office up to a maximum of £50 per month.[38] The offices of the *Indiaman* were utilised, with its staff offering their services for free. The editor was an ex-colonel of the Indian Army, and the paper contained censored accounts of the war as well as general Indian news.[39] The idea originated with Walter Lawrence, who persuaded the authorities to have a Gurumukhi edition as well, for it would be 'greatly appreciated' by the Sikhs who formed a significant percentage of the force.[40] The paper first appeared in

December 1914, with Allen commenting to the Viceroy on 'the tactful way in which we have avoided showing Turkey as an enemy country!'[41] With an abundance of photographs, it was – according to officials – warmly received, with immediate demands for more frequent issues in other languages and for use in other theatres of conflict like Egypt. By May 1915 its circulation was 8,000, which meant 32,000 leaflets weekly, as it was produced four times a week. General Sir James Willcocks, commanding officer of the Indian Army in France, sent Allen 'special communiqués from the front giving names of Indian soldiers that have done well'.[42] This was a marked concession, as British papers were not allowed to mention names.

In the autumn of 1915 Allen conducted surveys amongst the Indian forces to gauge their response and elicit suggestions for improvement. He noted that troops were 'exceedingly critical' of official reports, comparing it unfavourably with news gathered from the French population. Accuracy was therefore crucial, and the 'optimistic generalities in which we have often indulged so far do not satisfy them and merely make them inclined to be suspicious of unfavourable news having been suppressed'. Soldiers also evinced a great interest in 'crops, weather, prices and general health', details of promotion and the actions of their comrades on other fronts. Allen maintained that such demands ought to be met in the *Akhbar-i-Jung* and other official sources.[43] Another of his publications, the *Near East*, was distributed free within India before the war with the help of a government subsidy (1,000 copies per issue) 'in order to disseminate accurate news regarding the actual position of affairs in the Near East'.[44] It was deemed important to encourage Allen, who was, as Butler noted, 'always ready to help Government as far as he can'.[45] Therefore it was decided to continue with the subsidy when war broke out, at an estimated cost of £1,500 for two years to be borne by imperial revenues.[46]

In addition to *Al Hakikat* and *Akhbar-i-Jung*, two new government papers published in London, the *Jangi Akbar* and *Satya Vani*, were printed in several languages and sold cheap. Said to be 'immensely popular', the Viceroy claimed they were 'of considerable value in stimulating interest' in the war.[47] Concern with the loyalty of Muslim troops prompted the Indian government to confine distribution of *Akhbar-i-Jung* to units stationed in France, preferring to supply the other forces with its own military paper, *Fauj-i-Akhbar*, 'As we are not at all sure,' the Viceroy noted, 'that proposed paper can be relied on to avoid expressions about Turkey which, though they appear harmless in England, might be harmful among Mahommedan troops'.[48]

Propaganda activities in London were broadened in scope by the establishment of the Ministry of Information. The Ministry started the first Overseas Press Centre, where journalists could meet for briefings and send cables.[49] Kipling worked as an informal adviser and 'wrote profusely' to Beaverbrook about 'ways to conduct propaganda'.[50] Beaverbrook also invited editors of Indian newspapers to visit Britain and the western front to report directly from the theatres of conflict.[51] All expenses for the trip in 1918 was undertaken by the Ministry, and Edwin Montagu wanted editors of 'the highest standing and repute'.[52] After protracted negotiations five were chosen, the selection procedure highlighting the underlying judgements on the nature of the Indian press and the propaganda imperatives of war. Representing the 'Mohammedan' vernacular press of the Punjab was Mahlub Alam, editor of the *Paisa Akhbar*. The vernacular press of Bengal was represented by Hemendra Prasad Ghosh, editor of the *Danaik Basumati* – 'This paper takes a special interest in war and Home Rule matters, is influential and well conducted, and the editor visited Mesopotamia with a similar party.' The 'moderate' vernacular press of Bombay was represented by Gopal Krishna Deodhar, editor of the *Dnyan Prakash*, and that of Madras by S. Kasturiranga Aiyar, editor of the *Hindu*. The latter 'deals with political and social subjects. Its tone has been sometimes objectionable and generally anti-government, but there has been an improvement recently.' And, finally, representing European papers in Bengal was J. A. Sandbrook, editor of the *Englishman* – a newspaper 'not always in sympathy with Indian aspirations'.[53] This selection was not altogether to the government's satisfaction, hampered as it was by the paucity of European editors as well as Indian journalists from better-known papers who preferred to remain in India for the duration of the war. Thus both Aiyar and Ghosh were 'anti-government' – Ghosh 'a registered suspect' and Aiyar 'a supporter of Mrs Besant'.[54] A suggestion by the India Office for them to visit the United States on the return journey to observe their American war efforts was vetoed by the Indian government, more concerned at the harm these journalists might do if they had access to the US press and public opinion.

The Ministry of Information also operated through the India Office and was responsive to the increasing demands of the Viceroy, especially with the establishment of the Central Publicity Bureau in Simla in 1918, with 'the great' Stanley Reed acting as vice-chairman and 'in de facto control'. It supplied literature, pamphlets, posters, films, lantern slides, photographs and cuttings from British and foreign journals to India.[55] The India Office despatched thousands of pamphlets as a means of 'instructing public opinion', such as *Why we are at War* by the Oxford Faculty of Modern History and *Great Britain and the European Crisis*, a Foreign Office compilation. These were intended for 'men of some education, not for the masses, but the more widely they are read and studied the better'.[56] The government realised that, despite the desirability of disseminating what it considered correct information regarding the conflict, 'Nothing we can do will stop rumours in a country like India, and the ill-disposed will merely cavil at official statements.'[57] However, it strove to effect this as far as possible. One aspect of this took the shape of direct subsidies to vernacular newspapers, such as *Jagad Vritta* in Bombay, which received Rs 15,000 a year for a circulation of 6,000. This was seen as providing a 'counterpoise' to the 'malicious writings' in the *Kesari* and could do 'much good by supplying correct news of the war in a readable form'.[58]

Reuters and government publicity

The war provided Reuters with the most extensive platform yet to demonstrate its imperial credentials, since no other agency had the staff or infrastructure to assure the simultaneous publication of news all over the empire. It was engaged to disseminate government publicity via a special war service paid for by a grant from the Foreign Office and later the Ministry of Information. The subsidy of Reuters services to foreign countries rose from about £3,000 to £15,000 a month 'in order that messages might be sent which had more of a propagandist than a news value commercially speaking'.[59] Reuters was also utilised by New Delhi to transmit worldwide telegrams describing India's war record. Buck argued for more official use of Reuters for 'keeping India, her loyalty, enthusiasm, and assistance constantly before the world's eye' and urged the Indian government to 'assist me in sending to London a series of useful messages regarding India and everything which she is doing. I will arrange that these are given the widest publication possible in England, in Australia, Canada, South Africa, and America.'[60] Germany's 'highly lying press campaign . . . should be met and refuted as far as possible'.[61] Such news could also be publicised within India through the Indian News Agency.

Though the government had to pay Reuters a subsidy to cover the extra transmission costs, Buck hastened to emphasise his patriotic motives: 'I have brought forward the idea entirely in Imperial interests and also for the benefit which, I believe, will accrue to India.'[62] The Indian government was immediately responsive to the potentialities of this scheme, though, as an official noted, 'anything like a daily shower is not contemplated'.[63] In the event, periodic telegrams were carefully drafted in the Home Office and the Viceroy personally amended each message before transmission. The following extracts illustrate such assiduous telegraphic publicity.[64]

War has united Hindus and Muhammadans in one great body determined to lay down their lives for Empire and to sacrifice everything for ultimate victory of England. It has welded together creeds and classes in common bond of sympathy unheard of in Indian History, and as in time of king's Darbar has evolved warmest expressions of loyalty and devotion to Sovereign and Crown, from the Maharaja to the poorest peasant. The small section of seditionists about whose activities much was heard prior to the war has receded into the background. Meanwhile, Moslem messages of disgust at manner in which Germany has duped & misled Turkey into disastrous war, and at lies which she is spreading throughout East continue streaming into Lord Hardinge from parts of the country. [7 November 1914]

Prominent Moslem gentlemen are writing freely to press expressing unflinching loyalty to Emperor under whose benign rule they enjoy perfect religious freedom and urging all Mahomedans assist Mighty British Empire. [12 November 1914]

Systematic manner in which Germany continues spread false reports regarding Indian affairs receives little serious attention here . . . Countless assurances from Mahomedan bodies through length India continued reach Viceroy regarding loyalty Crown. [24 November 1914]

War news continues to absorb entire interest all communities India and whole country engaged furthering schemes of every kind for assisting towards ultimate victory. Practically every English woman India working for comfort troops . . . Recruitment for Native Army continues extraordinary manner, fighting races having their martial instincts considerably whetted by accounts of Indian feats at front. In consequent number applications received at Headquarters Commander Chief been obliged forbid officers forwarding requests for permission proceed on service. [27 November 1914]

All great Native States have now expressed regret to Viceroy that Turkey joined Germany in fighting England under whose benign rule Moslem enjoyed perfect religious freedom. All Ruling Princes continue take keenest interest war. They have now subscribed about 190,000 sterling to the Prince of Wales Relief fund and Indian Relief Fund, and 800,000 sterling to expenses of war. This includes 400,000 from Nizam Hyderabad & 300,000 from the Maharaja of Mysore. [4 December 1914]

Reports which Government of India receive regularly from all Provinces since war indicate internal situation continues satisfactory . . . Wild rumours still circulate in bazaars ranging from reports that King Emperor has been captured by Zeppelin to another that he is hiding in the fort at Bombay disguised as an Indian. Or again that the German Emperor had appointed German judges to sit with English ones. Absurdity of such statements should defeat their circulation but every effort being made to reassure the credulous both in British India and by Rulers of Native

States. Items of German war news reproduced in English papers lend themselves to misrepresentation by evilly disposed persons and it would help situation here if origin and falsity of such items conspicuously exposed. [15 December 1914]

The break of the monsoon affords a convenient opportunity of briefly reviewing situation in India in recent months. This continues to be satisfactory. Returned emigrants of the Ghadr Party have attempted to create trouble in the Punjab but various leaders have been arrested and are now under trial while convictions have been secured in several cases. The enactment of the Defence of India Act has had a steadying effect and the situation is well in hand . . . Prices still rule high by the action taken by government to reduce them has relieved the pressure and favourable rains should expedite a fall . . . As the war continues the wild rumours that marked its commencement, though they have not disappeared, are noticeably fewer, and general confidence in the ultimate success of the Allies prevails. The stream of liberal assistance in one form and another to the armies in the field is unchecked. [6 June 1915]

Conclusion

The war years heightened the sensitivity of Britain's ruling elite to the power of publicity. 'Propaganda and news became important and public morale mattered.'[65] Fleet Street provided the chief medium by which government could address the people, while retaining at the same time a certain freedom to criticise official initiatives. The press, concluded E. T. Cook, erstwhile editor of the *Daily News* and head of press censorship, 'might with advantage have been more closely associated than it was with the business of propaganda; but, even as things were, it did more than all the other agencies combined to make or mar the work'.[66] Operating within the context of British wartime initiatives, India Office efforts formed part of a larger propaganda offensive, but they were directed simultaneously at a specific feature of the problem – imperial support for the war and the security of the empire. Because the press was regarded as mirroring British opinion, strained relations between the India Office and Fleet Street could distort perceptions of official policy within the subcontinent. The Street's coverage of the condition of India and the contribution of its troops to the war effort had the potential to impact upon attitudes within India itself.

Notwithstanding these broad trends, the differing attitudes of the leading figures towards press and publicity made a crucial difference. While Chamberlain took an interest in censorship and propaganda as part of the war effort and had contacts with leading journalists like Garvin, who was also his father's biographer, he remained disdainful of the formalisation of the government – press nexus. Ironically, the public and press outcry in Britain at the Mesopotamia debacle contributed to his resignation in the summer of 1917. Montagu presented a striking contrast in attitude and temperament. He firmly believed in the power of publicity and paid assiduous attention to the conduct of information management at the India Office, developing the arts of press diplomacy and informal persuasion practised in varying degrees by his predecessors. However, he also sought to embody these activities within a formal institutional framework. It is to a study of these themes of Montagu's Secretaryship that we turn in the following chapter.

Notes

1 Chirol to Butler, 19 November 1914, HBC/ 37–8.
2 Messinger, *British Propaganda*, p. 2.
3 M. L. Sandars and P. M. Taylor, *British Propaganda during the First World War* (1982), p. 1.
4 Koss, *Rise and Fall*, pp. 712–13; Pound and Harmsworth, *Northcliffe*, pp. 461–81.
5 S. Koss, 'The destruction of Britain's last Liberal government', *JMH*, 40: 2 (1968), 257–77; J. M. McEwan, 'The press and the fall of Asquith', *HJ*, 21: 4 (1978), 863–83.
6 H. A. Taylor, *Robert Donald* (1934), p. 123.
7 D. McCormick, *Masks of Merlin* (1964), p. 92.
8 M. MacDonagh, *In London during the Great War* (1935), p. 157; T. Clarke, *My Lloyd George Diary* (1939), p. 12.
9 Lord Beaverbrook, *Men and Power* (1956), p. 267.
10 K. O. Morgan, 'Lloyd George's premiership: a study in "Prime Ministerial government"' *HJ*, 13: 1 (1970), 130–57.
11 Hansard, 5th series, 19 February 1918, 103, 654–8, and 11 March 1918, 104, 73–9.
12 Barrier, *Banned*, p. 72.
13 Secretary of State to Viceroy, 24 November 1915, Vol. III, 103, HP; Secretary of State to Viceroy, 22 September 1914, Vol. I, 101, HP.
14 Home Poll, A, March 1921, 324–31.
15 Cook to Cotton, 14 February 1916, Home Poll, Deposit 28, May 1916, p. 5.
16 *Ibid.*, p. 7.
17 See Home Poll, Deposit 12, December 1915; A 201, February 1916; Deposit 16, May 1916; Deposit 20, November 1917.
18 Home Poll, Deposit 16, October 1916, pp. 2–7.
19 Home Poll, Deposit 43, October 1915, p. 6.
20 Home Poll, Deposit 30, December 1916.
21 Home Poll, A 61, December 1914, pp. 1–2.
22 Note, Craddock, 27 February 1915, Home Poll A, July 1915, no. 254, p. 5.
23 *Ibid.*
24 Earl of Birkenhead, *The Life of F. E. Smith* (1965), pp. 266–7.
25 Viceroy to Secretary of State, 4 November 1914, Vol. II, 102, HP.
26 Viceroy to Secretary of State, 25 November 1914, Vol. II, 102, HP.
27 Secretary of State to Viceroy, 23 October 1915, Lawrence to Viceroy, 3 November 1915, Viceroy to Lawrence, 25 November 1915, Vol. III, 103, HP.
28 Dawson to Viceroy, 5 November 1918, CC/15.
29 D. Goold, 'Lord Hardinge and the Mesopotamia expedition and inquiry, 1914–1917', *HJ*, 19: 4 (1976), 943.
30 Viceroy to Dawson, 23 February 1917; also 8, 17 September 1918, CC/15.

31 Secretary of State to Viceroy, 7 December 1914, Vol. II, 102, HP.
32 Secretary of State to Viceroy, 19 January 1916, Home Poll, A 500–690, April 1917, p. 52.
33 *Ibid.*, p. 18.
34 *Ibid.*, p. 79.
35 *Ibid.*, pp. 22–3.
36 For Government of India concern see: L/P&S/10/518 and 519, 1914, Political and Secret Department, (hereafter L/P&S/no.); cf. Viceroy to Secretary of State, 9 November 1914, Viceroy to Willingdon, 16 November 1914, Vol. II, 102, HP.
37 Long memo, 7 March 1921, L/P&J/6/1730. After the Armistice his department was taken over by the Foreign Office and Long was in charge of the eastern section of its News Department till 1921.
38 Thomas Holderness to Allen, 16 October 1914, Vol. II, 93, HP.
39 Secretary of State to Viceroy, 23 November 1914, Vol. II, 102, HP.
40 Lawrence to Viceroy, 5 July 1915, Vol. III, 103, HP.
41 Allen to Viceroy, 17 December 1914, Vol. II, 93, HP.
42 Allen to Viceroy, 19 May 1915, Vol. III, 94, HP.
43 Allen's memo, 9 October 1915, encl. Allen to Viceroy, 14 October 1915, Vol. III, 94, HP.
44 Home Poll A, May 1915, 184–217, p. 1.
45 *Ibid.*, p. 8.
46 *Ibid.*, Memo, H. Wheeler, 17 December 1914, p. 15.
47 Viceroy to Secretary of State, 17 June 1918, CC/9. Circulation: *Jangi Akbar*, 63,000; *Satya Vani*, 40,700. Memo by Long, 22 October 1920, L/P&S/10/581.
48 Viceroy to Secretary of State, 25 November 1914, Vol. II, 102, HP.
49 Chisholm and Davie, *Beaverbrook*, p. 159.
50 P. Buitenhuis, *The Great War of Words* (Vancouver, 1987), pp. 136, 156; C. Carrington, *Rudyard Kipling* (1986), p. 512.
51 Secretary of State to Viceroy, 11 June 1918, CC/9; Beaverbrook, *Men and Power*, p. 268.
52 Secretary of State to Viceroy, 11 June 1918, Home Poll, A 107–55, August 1918, p. 1.
53 *Ibid.*, p. 20.
54 *Ibid.*
55 Viceroy to Secretary of State, 8, 17 June, 22 July 1918, CC/9.
56 Home Poll B, May 1915, 420–6.
57 Home Poll A, January 1915, 98–102, p. 1.
58 Home Poll A, September 1916, 46–8, p. 2.
59 S. Gaselee, Foreign Office, to C. H. Kisch, 18 December 1918, Home Poll B, 311–14, August 1919.
60 Buck, note, 5 November 1914, Home Poll A, 230–1, November 1914, p. 1.
61 *Ibid.*, Buck to DuBoulay, 12 November 1914, p. 2.
62 *Ibid.*, Buck to H. Wheeler, 15 November 1914, p. 4.
63 *Ibid.*, H. Wheeler, note, 17 November 1914.
64 H. Wheeler to Buck, 6 July 1915, Home Poll, Deposit 10, July 1915, p. 2.
65 M. Ogilvy-Webb, *The Government Explains* (1965), p. 50.
66 Cook, *Press in War*, p. 9.

CHAPTER SIX

Edwin Montagu, publicity and news management at the India Office, 1917–22

Under the impact of war the formal management of Indian news received a great impetus. The censorship and propaganda activities of the India Office mirrored the general propaganda offensive necessitated by war. More problematic was the government's need to direct reporting in London of the political repercussions of the war within India and of its own reform policies. Grave concern existed in official circles about the impact of hostilities upon Indian opinion and the growing demands for political change. Critical was the need to silence rising nationalist clamour and reward India's war effort with a positive portrayal of British goodwill and the granting of reforms. In 1920–22 this problem was made still more urgent by the non-co-operation movement initiated by Gandhi. In the words of Chirol, 'It is assuredly no mere figure of speech to say that India is actually at the parting of the ways – either towards renewed and fortified faith in the British connection or towards a convulsive period of estrangement and revolt.'[1] In responding to these difficulties the government had to give greater attention than hitherto to the domestic coverage of Indian affairs. One effect of the conflict had been to raise the visibility of India in Britain, with the press devoting significantly more attention to the problems and future of the subcontinent. What is more, political and economic disorientation following the war rendered public response to imperial issues more uncertain. There existed the possibility that some item of news would generate a strong domestic reaction, imperilling official policy. And all the while the London press possessed, through its influence in India, the capacity to directly affect opinions and events.

All this occurred against a background characterised by two features. The first was the potentially greater availability of information. At the turn of the century limited public interest, in conjunction with high telegraph rates, ensured that few newspapers could justify comprehensive coverage of Indian affairs. However, sustained pressure

[135]

from a variety of sources, at home and in the empire, initiated a process of rate reduction. By 1913 the Indian press rate had fallen to only 4*d* per word. With an integrated Anglo-Indian communication network now becoming a reality the British government recognised that Fleet Street would have to be included in any policy directed towards the problems of India. But this highlighted an essential ambivalence: the London press was a free press at the heart of an imperial system of coercion. British newspapers were perceived to enjoy great influence, in India as well as at home, yet they were not amenable to those measures conventionally employed by the government to maintain order within India. Second, the Coalition government completed the consolidation of the press as an indispensable feature of party politics. Lloyd George went to unprecedented lengths to secure newspaper support, and the India Office, headed by a Liberal, who was, says Keynes, drawn to the Prime Minister as a moth to a flame, could not fail to be affected by the new environment.[2]

Underlying principles of Montagu's governance: 'argument, persuasion, explanation'[3]

Edwin Montagu, the 'idealistically Liberal'[4] Jewish MP, had a long-standing interest in Indian affairs and was especially sensitive to the implications of this situation. He had long felt that inflexibility and deficiency of political vision had combined to produce a 'lack of imagination' in the approach to Indian government.[5] He had wanted to succeed Hardinge as Viceroy but his pleas to Lloyd George – 'I have no other ambition save to go to India'[6] – fell on deaf ears. His interest in India found unexpected fulfilment, however, when, following the resignation in July 1917 of Chamberlain, Lloyd George felt compelled to offer him the India Office. Montagu was the last Liberal and the only Jew to become Secretary of State. He sought to build upon the 'new angle of vision' that Asquith had called for in Indian affairs at the outbreak of war. For him this did not mean only political and administrative reform. He was alert to the potential power of the press and believed that publicity and public accountability would have to assume a central place in the future governance of India.[7] During the Montagu–Chelmsford administration attempts to influence newspaper reporting were more thoroughgoing than ever before.

Montagu, the son of the Liberal MP and millionaire banker Samuel Montagu, Baron Swaythling, initially gained political recognition while a student at Cambridge, where he was President of the Liberal Club. He was adopted as the candidate for West Cambridgeshire (Chesterton) constituency, and elected to Parliament in 1906. He held the seat till 1918, representing the combined county of Cambridgeshire from 1918 until his defeat in the election of 1922. Montagu rose to prominence under the wing of Asquith, beginning a close political and personal partnership that was to last until the end of Asquith's premiership, acting as his parliamentary private secretary. Montagu's official connection with India began in early 1910, when he was appointed Under Secretary of State at the India Office, serving under Lords Morley and Crewe till February 1914.

His maiden Indian budget speech in July 1910 was a *tour de force* and marked him out for a considerable political future. From the start he displayed enormous aptitude for hard work, marked gifts of oratory, and political astuteness, yet these abilities were combined with combativeness, lack of tact and a striking degree of self-doubt and nervous anxiety. Montagu was on the radical wing of the Liberal Party and, according to Keynes, the fact that he was a Jew 'equipped, nevertheless, with the intellectual technique and atmosphere of the West, drew him naturally to the political problems of India, and allowed an instinctive, mutual sympathy between him and its peoples'.[8] In 1912 he left on a fact-finding tour of the subcontinent – the first Under Secretary to do so – being keen to establish a personal understanding of the land, its people and its problems. The visit cemented a growing passion for the Indian empire.

Applying his Liberal perspective to the question of Indian administration, Montagu favoured constitutional reform, the development of self-governing institutions and the appeasement of moderate Indians. While acknowledging that demands for increasing political participation emanated from a small section of the educated intelligentsia, the fact remained that it was the British themselves who had brought this educated opinion into existence and it was important to respond to the challenging nationalist climate in a constructive manner in order to avoid major conflagration, for 'the amount of yeast necessary to leaven a loaf is very small'. The leaven of English thought, the emphasis on individual judgement and the questioning of authority were working to stir the Indian mind. It would not be prudent to embark on a policy of reaction: 'The mighty mass of India is moving in response to our own stimulus and to try and force it back into a condition of sleep, which would now be an unwilling sleep, and which could only be achieved, if it could be achieved, by repression, would be a calamity-producing blunder.'[9] From Montagu's Liberal perspective this stirring – the gathering strength of public opinion and political dissatisfaction – was to be welcomed and differences of opinion in so diverse a country as India were inevitable. What was needed was to channel these energies into productive avenues away from violence.

India must be regarded as 'a progressive country' and the opinion of the educated minority should not be dismissed as untypical: government had to cultivate this opinion and work with it, instead of alienating it by a policy of reaction, repression and racial prejudice. This applied equally to the treatment of the 'increasing army' of Indian students in Britain, who would be the future administrators of India, thus sowing seeds of unrest.

Traditional British administrators, filled with what he called an 'antediluvian imperialism', could not see 'beyond domination and subjection, beyond governor and governed, who hate the word "progress", and will accuse me of encouraging unrest. I bow submissively in anticipation.' The war marked the opening of a new 'psychological moment' in Indian history. The resulting alteration in the aspirations of Indians had to be dealt with in that spirit of sympathy and justice which was the hallmark of British, as opposed to German, government. 'Opportunities lost in India cannot be recovered except at great cost.'[10]

The India Office occupied an important place in this process, as it represented parliamentary control over the Indian government – its duty being to oversee the interests of the 'voiceless' people of India, to act as their 'trustees', since they had no control over their government.[11] However, apart from controlling the Government of India in the interests of the governed, Parliament, in Montagu's opinion, needed to go further. Its duties 'must take the form of a gradual delegation' to Indians 'of the power of criticism and control of their own government'.[12] While reluctantly admitting to the need for the censorship of opinion when law and order were threatened, in general Montagu was against repressive measures that curbed freedom of expression.[13] He was increasingly uncomfortable with issues of police brutality, for instance, and supported Hardinge's attempts to minimise torture. While accepting the necessity for some control of the press, he did not concur with Chelmsford that the Indian Press Act was 'always wisely worked' and in principle favoured 'legal processes for executive action which may be arbitrary'.[14] Such a stance was evident in his opposition to the Rowlatt Acts and general scepticism about the declaring of martial law during 1919. He took the occasion of the Commons debate on General Dyer to denounce 'obsolete' ordinances 'infringing the principles of liberty'.[15] He stressed that he had 'never acquiesced in satisfaction at the present panoply of repressive legislation' and urged its speedy revision.[16] Montagu was similarly against the continuance of press restrictions after martial law had been lifted and was keen to implement a press amnesty in December 1919 when the King ratified the Constitutional Act.

In the creation of a Liberal political culture it was recognised that a responsible, informed press would play a central part and Montagu's opposition to censorship reflected a belief in more open government with greater dissemination of information expanding the avenues for public discussion of official initiatives. Significantly for Montagu a government, even an imperial one, could not govern without explanation and needed to promote its policies through active publicity. This contrasted with the ideal of Pax Britannica and notions of inherent superiority which still pervaded the civil service mentality.[17] It was necessary to ensure that 'the theory of government by prestige was not carried to excessive lengths' in India.[18] A vibrant public debate was not only inevitable in India but also desirable. Montagu saw the necessity of bringing into being an active political culture within the subcontinent, including the Indian government itself, which would adapt to and engage with the new communications environment. Denied the chance to be Viceroy, he had to operate indirectly and at a distance. However, London was at the heart of the imperial system and the London press occupied an important place in forming public perceptions of Indian governance and many of Montagu's personal initiatives were thus directed towards securing positive coverage in Fleet Street.

He took every opportunity to press his views upon a more sceptical Viceroy and official bureaucracy in India. 'Have you ever considered one aspect of the new angle of vision on Indian affairs?' he noted in one of his first major communiqués. 'Is it not necessary that those who are concerned with the Government of India in India should learn to a greater degree than ever the methods of political life?'[19]

> the feeding of the newspapers, the answering of enquiries, the touch between the Government and those who would support it – all this wants doing . . . It would be so splendid if political methods rather than coercive ones were successful in downing the opponents of the British government.[20]

Indian political opinion 'produced by a long series of statesmen' from Macaulay onwards was now impossible to ignore, though traditional methods of imperial rule proceeded on the assumption that it did not exist.[21] Agitation showed otherwise. It would be better, therefore to recognise this phenomenon and work with it on Western models.[22] Political reform was one element central to the development of an Indian political culture, and measures were already under way, but the other necessary element – publicity and propaganda – could be introduced and utilised more effectively. For example, in connection with the plans for introducing paper currency, Montagu wondered whether the government had taken any steps 'to prepare public opinion' – to explain the reasons for its adoption, to inform Indian opinion about the situation worldwide, and thus 'to create a demand' for paper currency.[23] On the other hand, Montagu noted that the Islington Commission report on public services (1917) was widely regarded by Indians as 'unsatisfactory, disappointing, illiberal'. The government ought to have responded by creating 'a counter-opinion' by 'advertising' the report's more positive recommendations. Such official action would be possible only if 'propaganda were one of the weapons' of the government. He acknowledged that this could be difficult in India, where such practices had 'never been attempted before', but was convinced that 'sooner or later this sort of method which the British government uses will have to be employed in India in a nascent form at any rate'.[24]

Additional to the need for a positive presentation of government policy was the rebuttal of its critics. Post-war conditions provided ample opportunity for Indian politicians to attack the government and, it was held, misrepresent its policies. As Secretary of State, Montagu was in the firing line within Britain and sought to adopt means to secure his position and defend his policies (as we shall examine later). In India, too, 'Trusting good work to tell its own story' was no longer sufficient. 'Counter-propaganda' was essential, especially since prosecutions under the Indian penal code were difficult in view of Montagu's own preference for a free press.[25] Montagu defined propaganda as the 'organised effort to create opinion in favour of the actions or policy' of the government, and believed that the Raj had a 'duty' to use such means to counteract:

> the persistent repetition . . . of specious half-truths designed to mislead the ignorant in India and to attract sympathy in other countries . . . In its intercourse with newspaper correspondents it is clearly legitimate for the publicity department to suggest a line of argument which it would be helpful for a newspaper – if so disposed – to adopt.[26]

In a major dispatch on publicity Montagu outlined the main elements of government management of information: to provide adequate facilities for the press to obtain news; correct misstatements of fact by communiqués; and the conduct of propaganda itself. In Western countries the platform and the press provided opportunities for the ventilation and influencing of opinion and there was generally no need for government publicity. However, these conditions were lacking in India and would therefore have to be created by official initiative.[27] Sympathising with Lord Ronaldshay, Governor of Bengal, who was confronted with persistent anti-government propaganda during the troubled summer of 1921, Montagu set out the imperatives which he believed should guide government action. He identified, firstly, 'publicity work pure and simple'. Government had 'to state the facts and contradict the lies', and ensure that the facts reached the intended audience. Next, there was the problematic issue of propaganda. Officials had:

> got to say, not only what the government is doing, but why. It is not always easy even in this country with an age-long Parliament and a Press with at any rate a strong tradition of responsibility. It is much harder in India, where the Councils are new-born and the Press has still to be rescued from the stage of perpetual opposition, and it is even harder because in India it is to the government that men look for the first start ... it is easy enough for me to state it, but Good Lord! it is you who have to solve it, and I am acutely conscious that my theories won't give you a solution; still they may just possibly help with defining the issues.[28]

Information management and imperial control in practice

Montagu's 'new angle of vision' was thus characterised by a fresh approach to the presentation of constitutional proposals and the need to promote positive images of official actions. It entailed also a new responsiveness by the Raj to opinion in India as well as at home. His engagement was evidenced by his decision, in late 1917, to tour India in order 'to demonstrate that a new era had opened' and solicit especially non-official opinion at first hand.[29] In addition to drawing up reform proposals with the Viceroy, Montagu conversed with many journalists and other interested parties. He believed in the efficacy of personal contact and discussion, observing:

> It may be necessary to talk about the weather or to go to lunch with somebody with a view to getting at what he really wants or thinks. The stereotyped reading of documents and the acknowledgement of them is not good enough.[30]

He accordingly urged upon the Government of India the need for an active programme to publicise the reforms. No scheme, however good, could 'stand on its own', particularly with the extremists opposing it. Civil servants were 'unaccustomed to political warfare' and would need to be 'coaxed and persuaded to do it ... I would beg of you never to lose an opportunity of seeing how you can best organise a strong fighting force in favour of our scheme.'[31]

Upon returning to England, Montagu applied himself in a similarly concerted fashion to securing a favourable response from Fleet Street. For Montagu reform and publicity were complements; the former, to be effective, had to operate in tandem with the latter. To this end he deployed his extensive contacts in Fleet Street. As he boasted to Chelmsford, 'I believe that I have more knowledge of the London Press than almost any other British Minister, the Prime Minister always excepted, and I never lose an opportunity of trying to keep them on our side.'[32] From his days as Under Secretary, Montagu had sought to cultivate good relations with the press and corresponded with editors like Scott, Gardiner and Blumenfeld, giving the latter, for instance, advance details of the 'boons' announced at the durbar in 1911.[33] With Crewe in India, Montagu had complete responsibility for managing the London press. Other press confidantes included Beaverbrook, Dawson and Garvin, as well as India specialists like Chirol, Fraser, Cotton, Bennett and Brown. He met these men to communicate ideas and proposals as well as provide confidential information. Writing to Beaverbrook during the crisis weeks in February 1922 he concluded, 'This information is for yourself alone. Please tear this up, & don't worry to answer even by telephone. I will keep you informed.[34] He recommended Brown, who was on the staff of the *Times of India* and *The Times*, for a CIE because he was 'extremely useful to us', not as a 'tame propagandist pressman' but as an 'honest and capable journalist who can, and does, instruct a fairly wide public in common sense about Indian questions. I should regard him as our chief liaison with the press in this country, and he does the work remarkably well.'[35] He socialised with journalists in London and at his country house, Breccles, in Norfolk, writing to his wife, Venetia, 'I took Blum[enfeld] to lunch . . . He always amuses me very much. He is full of knowledge which he claims to have obtained and always explains how independent he really is of Max [Aitken], prefacing every remark by eulogies of the latter coupled with cautions and warnings.'[36]

Montagu's recognition of the necessity for a new approach to Indian governance and the presentation of official initiatives, especially in the context of the reform proposals, found in the Round Table and its journal an influential ally. Curtis, in particular, proved a powerful advocate of constitutional change. The idea of dyarchy advocated by the Montagu–Chelmsford reforms had first been set forth in his work, while he had influential contacts in the world of imperial journalism. As discussed in Chapter 4, the *Round Table*, while not a government publication, was nevertheless influenced by its strong official connections. In terms of both objectives and character there are striking similarities between the Indian tours of Montagu and Curtis – indeed, Montagu's delegation included his private secretary, C. H. Kisch, Sir William Duke and Malcolm Seton, all of whom had been members of the Indian Moot. As with Montagu, there was a prominent visionary element in Curtis's politics – he was known to his fellow Round Tablers as 'the Prophet'. Arriving in the subcontinent in 1916, he sought to create confidence in British intentions and attempted to collect 'opinions, information and material', describing himself as 'a sort of super-journalist . . . ng people with first-hand knowledge'.[37] He criticised the government for having failed adequately to realise that 'we have now reached a stage in India when our only safety lies in guiding opinion instead of sitting on it'.[38]

Turning his gaze to Britain, Curtis was exercised, like Montagu, over the problem of creating a supply of trustworthy information about India:

> Really the greatest need of the moment is some first-class correspondent in India who can devote his whole time to the subject, travel all about India. He should be a man who can keep in touch with everyone including the government but who will be sufficiently independent to keep out of everyone's pocket.[39]

It was especially necessary to guide the British public on India, since the '*final* authority' on India was the British electorate – 'a British election might easily turn on the question of self-government in India'. He conceived of the *Round Table*'s task as bringing home the distinctiveness of Indian conditions and problems.[40] Indian articles, he believed, stood on a different footing from those relating to the dominions. While the latter merely informed the British public, which was not required to take decisions with regard to them, with India 'the power and duty of deciding policy rests with England and the public there know and hear much less about India than about Ireland'. Yet what was said about India in the *Round Table* 'may have much more effect for good or evil' than what was said about Ireland. Affairs in India were critical and:

> no one can select facts for an article without reference to that crisis or without the purpose, conscious or unconscious, of moulding opinion. A writer is likely to do much less harm if the motive is conscious . . . Articles without any didactic purpose are worthless, unreadable, and indeed impossible to write.[41]

Curtis was naturally keen to promote his own proposals and arranged for the republication in London in May 1918 of his *Letters to the People of India on Responsible Government*, hoping, as he observed to Chelmsford, that they 'may do something to mould opinion in the right direction'.[42] The book indeed generated much press interest, and helped prepare the ground for the official report when it appeared in July. As Lavin has noted, Montagu returned to England to find that the

'Cabinet, the India Office and the political nation had been accustomed to the idea of dyarchy'. [43]

Within the metropolis, the Round Table contacts fed into other networks of influence which Montagu could utilise to promote reform. Important contacts existed between the Round Table and *The Times*. Both Grigg and Dawson worked for *The Times* and were editors of the *Round Table*. Kerr and Grigg also served as private secretaries to Lloyd George.[44] Among the Liberal–Labour world of Fleet Street Scott, Massingham and Gardiner were natural allies, and Montagu relied on their editorial backing.[45] He also conferred regularly with the British Committee of the INC, including Cotton, editor of *India*, whose pages provided him a sympathetic platform. Cotton additionally offered to contribute articles to other publications, as he confided in Gardiner at the *Daily News*:

> You may perhaps like to know that I am in touch with Montagu on the matter of his Indian reform proposals. He tells me that publication may be expected in three weeks' time: and I think he would be glad, if I could, with your permission, give him what help I can in your columns. Have you any objection to my sending you an article or two when the occasion arises? [46]

Cotton was subsequently appointed to the India Office advisory committee on the reforms.

Efforts to smooth the path of reform bore fruit, and the report was accorded a generally positive reception. By working with Fleet Street the Secretary of State had been able to generate a wider consensus for reform, encompassing, in addition to traditional Liberal support, significant sections of Unionist opinion. Dawson, whose backing was crucial, was full of praise, noting to Harcourt Butler how the report had enjoyed:

> a very good reception in this country . . . practically the whole Press has taken the same line. From my own experience moreover, I doubt whether it is true to suggest that they have been 'nobbled' by Montagu and his friends. My impression is that, though Montagu has no doubt been very accessible and has worked hard to meet his colleagues, the general lines of his scheme do appeal to reasonable Englishmen.[47]

As Chelmsford remarked to Montagu, *The Times* 'certainly 'did you handsome', and I think the Liberal papers generally . . . you must be encouraged by response which it has received'.[48] Lord Cromer similarly approved of the publicity measures adopted by Montagu:

> there is a far larger section of the public than one imagines that takes an abiding interest in Indian affairs . . . The primary purpose aimed at in

publicity on the project of the Chelmsford–Montagu Reforms has certainly been achieved, in that they are being subjected to a wide public criticism, and in this I venture to think that tactics adopted were wise.[49]

On those occasions when Montagu was subject to press opposition he sought to respond with informed persuasion – believing in the power of 'reasoned answer to criticism'.[50] Despite, for instance, the backing given to Montagu by the *Express* over the reforms or the negotiations with Turkish delegations in early 1921,[51] neither Beaverbrook nor Blumenfeld guaranteed consistently favourable coverage. Montagu was much perturbed, for example, at what he regarded as distorted reports sent by Sir Percival Phillips, the *Express* special correspondent during the Prince of Wales' tour, which portrayed in dramatic terms the activities of nationalist protestors. 'British public opinion,' noted Chirol, was getting 'distinctly puzzled and alarmed' at the conflicting reports which 'represent one day the Prince's visit as an immense success and the next day India as on the verge of a revolution'.[52] Montagu complained to Beaverbrook, who suggested that 'if you feel you must give the *E[xpress]* a castigation I suggest you address yourself direct to Blum'.[53] On another occasion Montagu wrote directly to Blumenfeld, contending that for several months the *Express* had taken 'an alarmist view', based on information which appeared to be 'not wholly in accordance with the information in other newspapers let alone Government information'. While not wanting 'to question the policy' of the paper, he wondered if Blumenfeld would 'lunch with me, when I should like an opportunity of discussing the matter'.[54]

Montagu appreciated the need for delicacy in government–press relations, cautioning Chelmsford that:

> one must walk very warily, and you can never expect to get a paper that has taken one line to recede from that line immediately simply because of information obtained from a government Office. The most that they will do is this. If they have been wrong they will wait for an opportunity which seems to them convenient to let themselves down.[55]

Thus Montagu was worried by reports in the Indian press that *The Times* was 'under our influence'. While the paper was one of their 'most cordial' supporters, the suggestion that 'we can make the *Times* do anything we want is quite idiotic'. He was concerned that if Indian newspapers persisted in such accusations *The Times* might 'be prompted to attack us in order to show its independence'.[56]

Domestic factors affected the balance of reporting too. For instance, Dawson's departure from *The Times* after falling out with Northcliffe was a heavy blow. Montagu urgently telegraphed the Viceroy from the Paris peace conference upon hearing the news, promising to seek an interview with the new incumbent. In the event *The Times*, under Steed, though not openly hostile, adopted a more critical and less focused line on India. In another example of personalities and disagreements influencing coverage, it was believed at the India Office that the treatment in *The Times* of Indian affairs during 1919 was distorted by the estrangement between Lloyd George and Northcliffe, who was bent on destabilising the Coalition. Sir Thomas Holderness, Chief Under Secretary of State, contended that attacks on the Indian government were 'in accordance with this general policy . . . I am also told that there is no central editorial authority at Printing House Square, and that the several leader writers can go their own ways and run their own hobbies, subject to edicts which from time to time Northcliffe sends down from the sick room.'[57]

Furthermore, in the case of Montagu personal factors crucially affected Fleet Street's response to Indian events. Montagu was a Jew, and to editors like Gwynne of the *Morning Post*, Strachey of the *Spectator* and Maxse of the *National Review* this was anathema. Behind the political objections of these papers lurked a racial dislike and distrust of Montagu. One would have to go back to the attacks upon the Catholic Viceroy Ripon during the Ilbert Bill controversy to find a comparable degree of animosity. Anti–Semitism was an undermining factor – in fact Levine goes so far as to argue that it dogged and undermined Montagu's entire political career, as well as his social and private life.[58] Conservative critics often portrayed Montagu as unreliable, disreputable and corrupt on the grounds of his religion. In 1913, during his tenure as Under Secretary, Montagu had to endure antisemitic taunts in Parliament and in the press in connection with the contracts awarded to his cousin, Sir Stuart Samuel, and his father's firm of Samuel Montagu & Co. to supply silver to the Indian government. Montagu had played no part in these proceedings and though cleared of all charges of corruption he was tainted by the connection. As Searle points out, the 'extreme' Unionist papers were 'not interested in justifications' and exploited the issue 'quite unscrupulously'.[59] Strachey confessed to having 'a profound distrust, and also a profound contempt' for Montagu, as for all Jews in power.[60] Responding to the Montagu–Chelmsford report, he declared himself 'intensely disgusted and annoyed at the way in which the Government are allowing a Jew in a panic in league with a weak Viceroy and a publicist like Curtis . . . to lay a mine which must ruin British power in India'.[61] Similar hostility found reflection in the *Morning Post*, most dramatically during the pro-Dyer campaign of 1920 orchestrated by Gwynne, an antisemite with an obsessive hatred of the Secretary of State. Though Montagu tried to reason with some of these journalists – inviting Strachey to his home, for instance[62] – attacks of this nature occurred throughout his term, his position being further compromised in the eyes of sections of the press when another Jew, Lord Reading, succeeded Chelmsford as Viceroy.

Montagu, however, did not lose sight of the political differences behind personal criticism. Interpreting to Chelmsford the hostility which greeted their reform proposals from a minority in Fleet Street, he noted:

> You see you and I are so much more vulnerable than any other Secretary of State and Viceroy because we have set our signatures to plans and proposals which are controversial . . . Firstly, they do not like the pronouncement of the 20 August; they dare not attack that, so they attack our scheme. Next, when beaten in the attacks on our scheme, they find it easier to attack us.[63]

Though Montagu braved these criticisms in public, his sensitive nature was deeply wounded. Beaverbrook was a friend to whom Montagu turned for reassurance and it was seemingly on his advice that Montagu was dissuaded from resigning in 1920.[64] Montagu lamented that he had not achieved 'the confidence of the public' apart from the 'wavering, flickering, fluctuating' support of some Indians. Perhaps, he mused, 'people judge nations as they do individuals, on prejudice'.[65]

In practice opposition, personal and political, served only to enhance Montagu's commitment to the careful presentation of official initiatives and the more general control of information. The various attempts by the India Office to shape the flow of information to Fleet Street and thereby colour newspaper coverage culminated in May 1921, when an Information Officer was first appointed to handle India Office relations with the British and foreign press. The spring of 1922 saw the repeal of the Indian Press Act (as well as the Rowlatt Acts and twenty-two other measures). Though abolition nominally occurred during Reading's viceroyalty, it was substantially the work of Montagu and Chelmsford.[66]

Chelmsford and the new initiatives

While India occupied the central place in Montagu's conception of reformed government within the context of an informed public opinion, he could not directly engage with Indian political communication and had to work in conjunction with Chelmsford, whose political background was more conservative and who personally did not fully share the visionary aspects of Montagu's approach. Nevertheless,

Chelmsford responded pragmatically to wartime exigencies and played an important role both in overseeing government propaganda during the conflict and in setting post-war propaganda in India on an organised basis.[67] He claimed to be motivated by the desire to establish a system to be 'kept in touch with what is being thought and said' in the country, as well as to find ways to 'set out our policy in language understood by the people'.[68] The war publicity departments in India were now utilised to publicise the reforms. Chelmsford was wary of Montagu's suggestion that the Government of India should openly stimulate discussion, maintaining that any indication of official inspiration 'leads to suspicion, and would do more harm than good'. While every opportunity was seized of 'confuting' the extremists and 'encouraging' the moderates, official propaganda had to be worked along the lines which would best suit Indian conditions.[69]

The importance of propaganda, to which Montagu drew attention, was increasingly appreciated during the tumultuous months of 1919. The Hunter committee emphasised the responsibility of the Indian press for these disturbances, which served as additional proof that the 'danger arising to Government from agitation in the press and on the platform was very great'.[70] The non-co-operation movement, encompassing the Khilafat agitation against the Treaty of Sevres, stretched almost to breaking point the government's ability to maintain law and order and oversee the introduction of reforms. During these fraught years Chelmsford was also increasingly concerned to defend the Indian government from what he saw as the 'ill-informed and biased accounts' appearing in the British and American press.[71] In 1920 a Department of Public Information (DPI) was established in New Delhi. Rushbrook Williams, who oversaw its functioning, made a seminal contribution to publicity during these years, helping both Curtis and Montagu on their respective tours as well as writing a series of successful editions of the *Statement exhibiting the Moral and Material Progress and Condition of India*.[72] The DPI included a Foreign Division to counteract anti-government propaganda in the West and to insert government comment in foreign newspapers. The importance attached to the relationship between external and internal propaganda is well illustrated by the efforts of the Indian government to obtain favourable presentation in Britain of its response to the Hunter report. Chelmsford believed the 'Home necessity' to be greater than the Indian one, for the Indian press 'will take its cue largely from the Home press, and it is by the opinion of the British public that we shall be judged'.[73]

On day-to-day issues as well, such as the criticism by *The Times* of British policy in Mesopotamia, the Viceroy was convinced that this could have a deleterious effect, especially on Muslim troops, in the light of the Khilafat question: 'Opposition in India is strengthened and risk of disaffection in Army is increased by cabled reports of hostile criticism in home press.'[74] At Chelmsford's suggestion Montagu approached Reuters, the company agreeing to 'do what they can to meet your wishes'.[75] In his attempts to obtain favourable coverage in Fleet Street, Chelmsford had a significant ally in *The Times*. '[I]f you want me to inform you on any point', he wrote to Dawson during the war, 'don't hesitate to drop me a line.'[76]

Reading and Montagu

The success of government attempts at information management and publicity was predicated upon an effective working relationship between the heads of the two respective centres of power. Compatibility of temperament and personality was as important as agreement on political priorities. Fortunately for Montagu, he enjoyed a more harmonious relationship with Reading. Both were Liberals and Jews and had been long-standing friends. They also shared similar attitudes to imperial policy and governance, and were temperamentally well suited – Reading's charm, tact and political pragmatism proving a useful counterfoil to Montagu's impetuousness and idealism.

Like Montagu, Reading shared a common liberal perspective on the importance of public opinion and the need for the government to engage with it. To this end he was a fervent believer in official publicity and had close links with the British press, forming part of the consortium which, at the behest of Lloyd George, took over the *Chronicle* in 1918. Indeed, upon his return to England Reading was to be briefly a newspaper proprietor himself.[77] His earlier legal career had brought him into contact with several prominent proprietors and editors, including Northcliffe (whom he defended in the Soap Trust case in 1907), Riddell, Burnham, Beaverbrook, Dalziel, Blumenfeld and Garvin. When his appointment as Viceroy was announced Blumenfeld wrote requesting a meeting with their special correspondent, to 'tell him something about what you hope to achieve . . . Sir Percival knows India well and am sure that if you will agree to make a statement for publication – it would go to America as well – no one could better reproduce your views.'[78] Once in India he cultivated visiting Fleet Street grandees – including Northcliffe in 1922. 'We may be able to get him interested in Indian affairs,' he wrote to Montagu, 'and I have always liked him.'[79] In the event, Reading was pleased to find Northcliffe:

undoubtedly desirous of helping in the present trying state of affairs and will give greater publicity to Indian news and situation. I never read our

English newspapers out here without wishing that they were better informed . . . But to the average Englishman India is a long way off and the picture of it to him is I fear antiquated.[80]

Montagu approved such initiatives, and promised on Northcliffe's return to 'do everything in my power to meet him and to see if we cannot establish good relations'.[81]

Reading saw that in the changed atmosphere inaugurated by the post-war political situation the Viceroy and Secretary of State would be far more exposed to public criticism. He nonetheless argued – like Montagu – that it was a price worth paying:

> The old happy calm periods when both the Secretary of State and Viceroy were comparatively immune from criticism and attack have disappeared for all time, and unpleasant though some experiences may be to you or me, I am convinced that it is to national advantage that greater interest should be manifested, both at home and here, in the management of Indian affairs . . . It is an admission in which you will readily join that both you and I have to become impervious to unfair comment.[82]

Within a month of reaching India, Reading was 'impressed' by the need for 'more extended publicity'.[83] He appreciated the need to give 'due weight' to Indian opinion in the conduct of his government. Both he and Montagu maintained the importance of 'getting into direct touch with Indians of all shades of political opinion'.[84] Similarly, in responding to the revisions of the Press Act suggested by the committee under Tej Bahadur Sapru, Reading revealed a perspective akin to Montagu's. Though conceding that government would need to keep some control over the press, Reading assured Montagu that it would be exercised by means of the judiciary and reduced to 'the minimum absolutely necessary'.[85]

Reading quickly realised that in India anti-British propaganda was conducted 'in the bazaars' and amongst the uneducated. 'We never reach the same public and cannot get their ear and are thus always at a disadvantage. The government is attacked and can make no reply.'[86] Any official rebuttal was invariably by staid communiqués, which made 'always the driest and most uninteresting reading except to the esoteric few'.[87] There were, Reading believed, two points of view, English and Indian. Though they had to address both, there was increasing difficulty in reconciling the two. To some extent this had always been the case, but vitally in the past,

> in the end the British view prevailed, if insisted upon, because Government could make it prevail. Nowadays, with the delicate and complicated constitutional machinery in motion, it becomes much more necessary not to run in conflict with Indian opinion.[88]

Montagu, however, was unwilling to accept a necessary dichotomy between Indian and British opinion. To speak of the Indian as opposed to an English point of view implied 'a racial difference of outlook'. He believed rather that the difference in atmosphere was 'an accidental rather than a fundamental difference'. They both had to contend with 'a local atmosphere', and it was incumbent upon them 'to bring our two atmospheres into some kind of harmony by absorbing them in a proper conception of India's relation to the Empire'.[89]

Origins and early development of the Information Office, 1920–22

The appointment of an India Office Information Officer in May 1921 represented an important step in the institutionalisation of news management. To some extent it formed part of a wider move by the British government, during and after the war, to organise the direction of opinion. Before 1913 some information services existed in Whitehall, but they were 'carried out patchily and piecemeal in various odd corners of government departments'.[90] By 1923, in addition to the India Office, publicity officers were employed by the Air Ministry, the Foreign, Colonial and War Offices, the General Post Office, the National Savings Committee and the the Ministry of Pensions.[91] With this period also witnessing troubles in Ireland and Egypt, and a Coalition government seeking to operate within a Conservative House of Commons, news management became still more necessary – not only to guard government policy from sections of Conservative opinion but to protect the Coalition itself from disintegration.

Within the India Office Montagu possessed a controlling initiative in the formation of publicity policy, whilst members of the Judicial and Political Department shouldered much of the increasing burden of propaganda work, prominent among them being Lord V. Lytton, Sir William Duke, Sir Malcolm Seton and J. W. Hose.[92] Discussions within the India Office over the need to place publicity on a more organised footing led to the decision to establish a regular press officer. Hose observed, in a minute drawn up in June 1919, that there existed 'strong propaganda' in Britain against the government, conducted by Tilak and his associates, Mrs Besant and the Home Rule Leagues, Saklatvala and other 'professional agitators', and carried out 'mostly in Labour papers or by addresses in leaflets to labour bodies'. There was 'equally strong propaganda' in the United States by groups such as Lajpat Rai in *Young India* and the 'Friends of Freedom for India' with their adherents in San Francisco. In this context Hose, like Montagu, believed it all the more damaging that there was 'no decent organisation to arrange publicity for Indian affairs'. An appointee, Hose continued, could work with press cuttings from American and British papers in order to provide material for 'counter-articles, – not write counter articles himself'. He would do this by offering material to all 'reasonable' publications, as well as the 'attacking papers', so that the 'full case may be before the editors . . . [and] now and then it might have some effect'. Such a person would need to work closely with the Foreign Office and the Private Secretary at the India Office, as well as with publicity officers in India.[93] A year later Hose complained at the extent of the *ad hoc* publicity work descending upon himself. Rushbrook Williams 'appeared to look upon me personally as an authority on publicity matters here, and hoped that I would always find time for his work'. There was 'no proper arrangement' for the escalating amount of information and publicity work.[94]

Nevertheless the first concrete steps towards the establishment of an Information Officer in Britain were initiated by the Government of India. In August 1920 Chelmsford wrote that:

> in view of accusations sometimes levelled against the Government of India that they are guilty of improper secrecy, and of withholding information as to the political situation in India, and as inaccurate and incomplete accounts of conditions of affairs out here are occasionally cabled to the press in the U.S., we suggest contents of our weekly telegram to you should be more freely used for purposes of publicity.[95]

Similarly Williams recommended that, for a 'proper appreciation' of Indian news, the India Office could periodically circulate a short résumé.[96] Measures outlined by Chelmsford also included the supply of articles to periodicals and newspapers, and the provision of special cables dealing with the Raj. The effective working of these publicity measures would require close relations between the central publicity branch in New Delhi and a suitable agent in London, whose responsibility it would be to:

> keep us informed of the wants of the English public, obtain information on form, style &c, of reports for public consumption as well as secure most advantageous distribution and placing of articles, news, special cables, &c, forwarded from India which would otherwise not obtain adequate notice.[97]

Such an agent could be appointed to the staff of the High Commission for India, which had been set up in 1920.

In the ensuing discussions between Montagu, Duke, Seton and Lytton all agreed that an arrangement involving Sir William Meyer's office would not be suitable. Seton 'greatly doubt[ed]' whether the High

Commission 'should do political propaganda. I am quite certain that there should not be two separate political propaganda agencies' in Britain.[98] Duke agreed, adding that he had 'no doubt' that the Secretary of State 'should not allow propaganda in this country to go out of his own hands'.[99] Montagu was himself determined on this point:

> I propose to keep publicity in the hands of the India Office. Unfortunately I am afraid that at the present moment publicity, if run from India in England, is likely to take the form of a campaign against the India Office. I am responsible for informing English opinion about events in India.[100]

Thus Montagu, although concurring with Chelmsford's general suggestions, insisted on having a controlling hand, and ensured that the first Information Officer was attached to the Judicial and Public Department of the India Office.[101] Besides working at Whitehall, the officer would inform New Delhi of the 'wants of English public' but he would not 'supplant' the High Commission 'as your agency for obtaining material needed for publicity purposes in India'.[102]

The first occupant was Owen Lloyd-Evans, a journalist with Indian experience who had been on the *Times*'s editorial staff since 1905. Lloyd-Evans's annual salary of just over £1,000 was paid from Indian revenue, the initial appointment being for a year.[103] This was extended in 1922 for a further five years, the post being felt to have 'fully justified itself'. Lloyd-Evans had established 'good relations' with the press, 'their complaints which were frequent have stopped, and the work continually grows'.[104] Among the officer's duties were 'To be accessible at all times to representatives of the Press, to supply them with information asked for if available, and if not . . . to try and obtain it for them from India. To prepare information . . . for the Press, in the form desired by each journalist or agency' and to function as a liaison officer between the India Office and the Department of Information in New Delhi[105] (see Appendix 4). An insight into the officer's work is provided by a list of personal callers (in addition to many enquiries by telephone) at the India Office on 13 December 1921 following reports of a comprehensive boycott of the Prince of Wales's visit to Allahabad. These included:

> *Times* (Brown), *Telegraph* (Rattigan) *Morning Post* (Ford), *Daily Chronicle* (Nicholson & Bateman), *Daily Despatch* (Scudamore), Press Association, Central News (Rose), Reuters (Penman & Emmett), *Glasgow Herald* (Sloan), *Yorkshire Post* (Jobson), Associated Press (Frank H King), *New York Tribune* (W B Wells) United Press of America (Turner), *Daily Mail* (Maxwell), *Daily Express* (Cathcart[?]), *Manchester Guardian* (Dore), *Evening Standard* (Colley), International News Service–Hearst (Watson)[106]

In 1926 the India Office favourably reviewed the work of the Information Officer. His personal contact with journalists was considered significant, while the growing importance of alternative forms of communication like film and wireless was held to make his task still more crucial.[107] Edwin Haward, who replaced Lloyd-Evans in 1928, had been the *Times* correspondent in Lahore from 1914 to 1920, and for the next six years at Delhi and Simla. Hugh MacGregor, another *Times* man, was the third post holder, appointed in 1930. His successor in 1937, A. H. Joyce, was the first appointee not to be drawn from the ranks of the fourth estate.

A recurring theme in the relationship between government and the media was the contribution of personal unofficial contact. It was acknowledged by the India Office that the ability of the Information Officer to discharge his duties depended upon his personal relations with journalists.[108] Joyce argued that sustaining a wide range of contacts with journalists relied 'on a personal, as distinct from a purely official relationship. They extend hospitality to me and it is obvious that, unless there is reasonable reciprocation, contacts will be weakened and reduced to a purely official basis'.[109] From 1929 the India Office supported such interaction with an entertainment allowance. Sir Arthur Hirtzel, Permanent Under Secretary of State, contended that it was 'more than ever important to prevent errors in the press or to secure their correction, and this can only be done by keeping on very friendly terms with the journalists who specialise in them'.[110] The distinctive feature of Montagu's secretaryship was to bring to the India Office new attitudes towards government publicity and image creation. To succeeding Secretaries of State fell the task of enlarging the Information Office and extending its objectives. In 1941 the Information Officer was restyled the Adviser on Publicity Questions. By the Second World War the direction of opinion was recognised to be a crucial aspect of the Adviser's role.

Conclusion

It was taken for granted by the Raj that Fleet Street, though free of government control, was amenable to official influence – an assumption that was largely justified. On the one hand, it was important for the press to maintain a friendly relationship with officials, as Moberly Bell noted: 'We certainly like our correspondents to be on good terms with the government of the State to which they are accredited, provided those terms can be maintained without loss of self-respect.'[111] On the other, all leading journalists took pride in the British achievement in India, a sentiment heightened by the patriotism of the war. Chirol summarised the position of many:

> I look upon the influence of the British Empire, taken all in all, as probably the most powerful agency for good which exists in the world at the present day, and believe me the share which the representative of the leading English newspaper in a foreign capital has in shaping the operation of that influence, is not an insignificant one, if you measure it by the standard of what any single individual can hope to do.[112]

Yet there was significant variation of opinion upon more detailed questions concerning, for instance, the future form of Indian government. With many papers lacking a strong or tested line on such matters, scope existed for administrators to alter the mind of an editor or correspondent. Further, relatively few journalists made their way to the subcontinent, and specialists on India in London were similarly small in number. The result was a comparatively limited world, staffed by a handful of influential men, whom it was not only possible, but worthwhile, for politicians to cultivate on an individual basis.

Montagu's approach to Indian administration may be characterised as constructive engagement. Where previous Secretaries of State had been hesitant or suspicious, Montagu was determined to work with the new forces shaping Britain's relationship with the subcontinent. Amongst these was the telegraph, whose revolutionary impact upon communications was fully realised after 1914. Cheaper information helped satisfy a growing interest in India stimulated by the war and post-war developments, the news being carried by a confident metropolitan press enjoying unprecedented circulations. The government found its handling of Indian affairs subject to increasingly critical scrutiny. Montagu recognised that a new set of parameters had been created, conformity with which was essential to the ultimate success of any initiative. Far from keeping journalists at a distance, it was necessary to assist them. This meant, on one level, intensifying those unofficial contacts with Fleet Street which had long taken place. But it implied also making publicity relations an explicit dimension of government. Montagu's secretaryship thus saw a widening in the channels of communication between India Office and the press. Whereas prior to the war it was the more *informal* connections between administrators and the press that predominated, during the hostilities and in the immediate post-war years these were supplemented by a range of *formal* measures.

There were several reasons why Montagu considered favourable coverage by Fleet Street of his Indian policies so crucial. Four are deserving of emphasis. Disraeli had remarked during his last speech in Parliament in 1881, in a debate on the North West Frontier, that Merv, Ghazni, Balkh and Khandahar had all been cited as the 'keys of India'. However, although such places were important, they were not crucial – 'if the great military power were there, I trust we might still be able to maintain our Empire'.

> But, my lords, the key of India is not Herat or Candahar. The key of India is London. The majesty and sovereignty, the spirit and vigour of your Parliament, the inexhaustible resources, the ingenuity and determination of your people – these are the keys of India.[113]

The India Office governed a territory thousands of miles distant whilst subject daily to the pressures of the metropolitan political process, to which the London press was central. The attitudes of British politicians, editors and the public all circumscribed the options open to Indian administrators. However misinformed about Indian affairs, Fleet Street's coverage was a political fact Montagu was unable to ignore.

Montagu was also a Liberal politician occupying an exposed and vulnerable position in a Conservative-dominated Coalition. Throughout their life the Coalition Liberals were 'never a very effective force'.[114] Previously a follower of Asquith, Montagu had taken office under Lloyd George and was henceforth treated as 'an apostate' by the Asquithians.[115] However, Montagu could not take the support of the Prime Minister for granted. Lloyd George mistrusted Montagu's political judgement and his lack of authority – both political and personal. After his emotive speech in the Commons debate on Amritsar there was 'strong resentment against him amongst Conservative backbenchers'.[116] Lacking a political power base, he saw in the press a means to bolster his position and win Cabinet approval of his policies. Newspaper reactions to his official initiatives directly affected his ministerial standing. It was, in part, from their reading of the press that fellow Cabinet members would form their judgement of his ability.

Further, the British press had the capacity to influence events in India directly. The press in India utilised it as a source of news and comment, frequently quoting from its pages, and, in the case of the Anglo-Indian press especially, shared its personnel. Just as Fleet Street had the capacity to generate an image of India in England, so too it could help form an image of England in India. Its distortions and exaggerations were potentially doubly harmful. Finally, creating a solid basis of support for the reforms entailed, in Britain, marginalising traditional opposition to constitutional change and, in India, securing the support of moderate opinion. Reforms, by themselves, would be

THE RESPONSIBLES.

MR. MONTAGU (*to Mr. GANDHI*). "IT LOOKS AS IF ONE OF US WOULD HAVE TO GO."
JOHN BULL. "WHY NOT BOTH?"

8 'The responsibles', *Punch*, 22 February 1922

unlikely to generate the necessary goodwill if accompanied by vigorous criticism in the British press. The nation should be seen to be united behind the reform process if long-term good faith were to be convincingly portrayed.

The Secretary of State was convinced that in its control of information rather than in the levers of repression a government's strength would increasingly reside. In seeking to shape newspaper coverage Montagu was working with evolving technological and political imperatives. Yet historical contingencies shaped his capacity to realise his objectives, and information management was subject to a range of pressures – political, social and personal. In order to ascertain the character and extent of the limits to the successful operation of government publicity and information management during the war and immediate post-war years we shall examine Fleet Street's response and the politics–press nexus in the context of three major issues: reform, reaction and royalty. These case studies examine official efforts to secure support from the British press and political opinion for, in turn, the implementation of the liberal vision of a self-governing India within the empire; attempts to limit and counteract the harm caused by reaction to the Punjab disturbances in 1919 – the most serious crisis to face British rule since the Mutiny; and finally the tour of the Prince of Wales, when the government sought to shore up the aura of monarchical prestige in the troubled post-war conditions of India.

Notes

1 Chirol to Viceroy, 15 March 1921, MSS Eur F118/10, Reading (Private) Collection (hereafter RpvtC/no.).
2 J. M. Keynes, *Collected Writings* X (1972), p. 42.
3 Secretary of State to Ronaldshay, 28 June 1921, MC/28.
4 R. J. Moore, *Liberalism and Indian Politics, 1872–1922* (1966), p. 119.
5 Montagu to Asquith, spring 1916, AS5/1/13(1), Montagu Papers, Trinity College (hereafter MPTrinity).
6 Montagu to Lloyd George, 20 December 1915, AS5/1/4(1), Box 20, MPTrinity.
7 Secretary of State to Viceroy, 3 August 1917, MC/1.
8 Keynes, *Collected Writings* X, p. 41.
9 30 July 1912, Hansard, 5th series, 41, 1906–07.
10 Montagu to Lloyd George, 20 December 1915, AS5/1/4(1), Box 20, MPTrinity.
11 Secretary of State to Viceroy, 3 August 1917, MC/1.
12 26 July 1911, Hansard, 5th series, 28, 1696.
13 Secretary of State to Viceroy, 1 January 1918, CC/4.
14 Secretary of State to Viceroy, 10 October 1918, MC/2.
15 Secretary of State to Viceroy, 11 August 1920, MC/4; see 8 July 1920, Hansard, 5th series, 131, 1706–11.
16 Secretary of State to Viceroy, 29 August 1919, MC/3.
17 26 July 1911, Hansard, 5th series, 28, 1697.
18 26 July 1911, Hansard, 5th series, 28, 1695.
19 Secretary of State to Viceroy, 3 August 1917, MC/1.
20 Secretary of State to Viceroy, 27 April 1918, CC/4.
21 Secretary of State to Viceroy, 21 September 1917, MC/1; Secretary of State to Chamberlain, 9 August 1917, AS4/9/7, Box 19, MPTrinity.
22 *Ibid.*; Secretary of State to Lloyd George (draft), October 1919, AS4/33, Box 15, MPTrinity.

23 Secretary of State to Viceroy, 3 August 1917, MC/1.
24 *Ibid.*
25 W. Vincent, 22 January 1920, p. 26, in Viceroy to Secretary of State, 4 February 1920, MC/10.
26 Secretary of State to Viceroy in Council, 12 May 1921, L/P&J/6/1748.
27 Secretary of State to Viceroy, 12 May 1921, L/P&J/6/1730.
28 Secretary of State to Ronaldshay, 28 June 1921, MC/28.
29 H. Tinker, 'British liberalism and India', in Bean, *Political Culture*, p. 180.
30 E. S. Montagu, *An Indian Diary* (1930), p. 8.
31 Secretary of State to Viceroy, 26 July 1918, MC/2.
32 Secretary of State to Viceroy, 15 April 1920, MC/4.
33 Montagu to Secretary of State, 12, 14 December 1911, AS2/4, Box 7, MPTrinity; Montagu to Blumenfeld, 8 December 1911, HLRO, Blumenfeld Papers, Mont. 1.
34 Secretary of State to Beaverbrook, 16 February 1922, BBK/C/246, HLRO Beaverbrook Papers (hereafter BP).
35 Secretary of State to Viceroy, 16 June 1920, MC/4. CIE: Commander of the Indian Empire.
36 27 January 1922, Montagu Papers, Gendel Private Collection.
37 Curtis, *Dyarchy*, pp. 50, 54.
38 Curtis to Coupland, 15 March 1917, c810, fol. 15; Curtis to Kerr, 28 August 1917, c810, fols 139–140, RT.
39 Curtis to F. E. Francis, 23 May 1918, c830, fol. 194, RT.
40 Curtis, *Dyarchy*, pp. 54, 82.
41 Curtis to Coupland, 29 September 1917, c810, fols 169–170, RT.
42 Curtis to Viceroy, 24 May 1918, CC/15.
43 D. Lavin, *From Empire to International Commonwealth: A Biography of Lionel Curtis* (Oxford, 1995), p. 154.
44 R. Symonds, *Oxford and Empire* (1986), pp. 62–79.
45 Secretary of State to Gardiner, 6 July 1918, I/24, Gardiner Papers.
46 Cotton to Gardiner, 17 June 1918, I/10, Gardiner Papers.
47 Dawson to Butler, 15 August 1918, HBC/50–52.
48 Chamberlain to Secretary of State, 8 July 1918, AS3/2/53, Box 10, MPTrinity.
49 Cromer to Butler, 8 October 1918, HBC/51. Cromer (1877–53): ADC to Viceroy 1915–16; Chief of Staff, Duke of Connaught, 1920–21, Prince of Wales 1921–22.
50 Secretary of State to Viceroy, 15 July 1918, CC/9.
51 Secretary of State to Viceroy, 17 March 1921, AS4/8/51, Box 18, MPTrinity; Secretary of State to Beaverbrook, 17 March 1921, BP.
52 Chirol to Butler, 22 February 1922, HBC/37–8; cf. Secretary of State to Viceroy, 24 November 1921, MC/13.
53 Secretary of State to Beaverbrook, 17, 18 January 1922; Beaverbrook to Secretary of State, 23 January 1922, BP.
54 Secretary of State to Blumenfeld, 27 December 1921, Blumenfeld Papers, Mont. 6.
55 Secretary of State to Viceroy, 15 April 1920, MC/4.
56 Secretary of State to Viceroy, 24 November 1921, MC/13.
57 Holderness to Viceroy, 24 December 1919, CC/16.
58 Montagu to Lloyd George, 14 July 1917, AS4/3/5, Box 15, MPTrinity.
59 G. R. Searle, *Corruption in British Politics* (Oxford, 1987), pp. 209, 201–12.
60 Strachey to A. V. Dicey, 14 March 1922, S/5/8/6, SP.
61 Strachey to Salisbury, 6 September 1918, S/13/2/7, SP; Strachey to Maxse, 1 October 1918, S/10/9/22, SP.
62 The article appeared on 6 December; their meeting took place on 14 December 1919. (Memo, S/10/13/1, SP.)
63 Secretary of State to Viceroy, 24 December 1918, MC/2.
64 Beaverbrook to Secretary of State, 7 April 1920; cf. Secretary of State to Beaverbrook, 9 December 1921, BP.
65 Secretary of State to Viceroy, 1 May 1919, MC/3.

66 Chelmsford's particular motive for repeal may have been a desire to enhance the credibility of the new legislatures formed under the Reform Act, 1919. (P. G. Robb, *The Government of India and Reform, 1916–1921*, London, 1976, pp. 282–5.)

67 *Ibid.*, pp. 261–91.

68 Viceroy to Reed, 26 March 1919, CC/22.

69 *Ibid.*

70 W. Vincent, 22 January 1920, p. 26 in Viceroy to Secretary of State, 4 February 1920, MC/10.

71 Viceroy to Secretary of State, 6 February 1920, CC/12.

72 Williams to T. G. Fraser, 11 March 1974, Fraser private collection.

73 Viceroy to Secretary of State, 16 February 1920, CC/12.

74 Viceroy to Secretary of State, 24 August 1920, CC/13.

75 Secretary of State to Viceroy, 1 December 1920, CC/13.

76 Viceroy to Dawson, 8 September 1917, CC/15.

77 Reading took over United Newspapers in 1926.

78 Blumenfeld to Reading, 11 January 1921, RpvtC/5.

79 Viceroy to Secretary of State, 12 January 1922, MC/14.

80 Viceroy to Secretary of State, 26 January 1922, MC/14.

81 Secretary of State to Viceroy, 1 February 1922, MC/13.

82 Viceroy to Secretary of State, 14 July 1921, MC/14.

83 Viceroy to Secretary of State, 5 May 1921, MC/14.

84 Marquess of Reading, *Rufus Isaacs* (1945) II, p. 240.

85 Viceroy to Secretary of State, 19 May 1921, RC/10.

86 Viceroy to Secretary of State, 14 July 1921, MC/14.

87 *Ibid.*

88 Viceroy to Secretary of State, 24 November 1921, MC/14.

89 Secretary of State to Viceroy, 15 December 1921, MC/13.

90 Ogilvy-Webb, *Government Explains*, p. 49.

91 Prime Minister in Parliament, 30 July 1923, L/S&G/8/28, Services and General Department (hereafter L/S&G/no.).

92 Lytton: Under Secretary of State 1920–22; Dukes: Permanent Under Secretary of State 1919–24; Seton: Assistant Under Secretary of State 1919, Deputy Under Secretary of State 1924–33; Hose: retired ICS, at India Office 1916–26.

93 Minute by Hose, 30 June 1919, L/P&J/6/1730. Shaphurji Saklatvala (1874–1936): Parsi, socialist campaigner, later Labour and Communist MP for Battersea.

94 Minute by Hose, 20 August 1920, L/P&J/6/1730.

95 Viceroy to Secretary of State, 18 August 1920, L/P&J/6/1730.

96 Williams to Hose, 21 May 1920, L/P&J/6/1730.

97 Viceroy to Secretary of State, 19 January 1921, CC/14.

98 Seton memo, 21 January 1921, L/P&J/6/1730.

99 Dukes to Seton, 24 January 1921, L/P&J/6/1730.

100 Secretary of State to Dawson, 22 January 1921, L/P&J/6/1730.

101 The designations 'Information Officer' and 'Publicity Officer' were used interchangeably.

102 Secretary of State to Viceroy, 3 May 1921, L/P&J/6/1730.

103 Lytton to Lloyd-Evans, 10 April 1921, L/P&J/6/1730.

104 Dukes to Secretary of State, memo, March 1922; cf. note by Dukes, 20 March 1922. See related discussion, Lytton to Dukes, 27 February, 1 March 1922, Seton to Dukes, 28 February 1922, Hose to Seton, 6 March 1922, L/S&G/8/28.

105 There is a paucity of extant archival information from this initial period, partly due to the personal contact involved in such work and the destruction of papers, for example a memo with 'Destroyed' stamped on it entitled 'Mr Lloyd-Evans welcomes suggestions from India as to what should or should not be published in English press as to affairs in India'. (L/PJ/6/45, no. 7324, undated.)

106 Secretary of State to Viceroy, 14 December 1921, RC/10.

107 Ferard to Stewart, 10 November 1926; note by Hirtzel, 10 December 1926, L/S&G/8/28.

108 Memo on the Information Officer, 14 August 1937, L/S&G/8/28.
109 Joyce to Dibdin, 27 January 1939, L/S&G/8/28.
110 Hirtzel to Special Finance Committee, 19, 23 December 1929, L/S&G/8/28.
111 Bell, *Life and Letters*, p. 170.
112 Chirol to Steed, 15 June 1896, CHP.
113 Cited in W. F. Monypenny and G. E. Buckle, *Life of Benjamin Disraeli* (1929 edn) II, p. 476.
114 T. Wilson, *Downfall of the Liberal Party, 1914–1935* (1966), p. 192.
115 *Ibid.*, p. 106.
116 J. Darwin, *Britain, Egypt and the Middle East* (1981), p. 250.

PART III

Case studies, 1917–22

CHAPTER SEVEN

'Bringing India to the fore': selling Indian constitutional reform to Britain, 1917–18

The war years saw unprecedented consensus on the need for a declaration of British intent *vis-à-vis* the future governance of India. Montagu announced in the Commons on 20 August 1917 that:

> The policy of His Majesty's Government, with which the Government of India are in complete accord, is that of the increasing association of Indians in every branch of the administration, and the gradual development of self-governing institutions with a view to the progressive realisation of responsible government in India as an integral part of the British Empire.[1]

This was the first time that the goal of British policy had been officially defined, and the historic nature of the announcement was generally acknowledged. It was supported by a cross-section of political opinion in Britain, including Conservatives like Milner and Balfour. The 'imperial gatekeeper' who opened the way to parliamentary government in India by composing the declaration was, in fact, Curzon.[2] By expanding significantly upon ideas of Indian participation in administration it marked 'a real turning point in imperial policy'.[3] The final result was the Montagu–Chelmsford reforms or the Constitutional Act of 1919.

The resultant reform process – from August 1917 to the drafting of the Montagu–Chelmsford Reform Bill in the summer of 1918 (which laid down the parameters of the final Act) – provides an opportunity to examine the spectrum of opinion in Fleet Street and, in particular, to focus on the constructive effort on the part of Montagu to secure a favourable reaction from the press to his initiatives. Reform provided him with the occasion to elaborate his vision, not only of new approaches to Indian government but of the proper presentation of official policies. Anxious to build upon the declaration, Montagu recognised that what was required was not simply a comprehensive set of constitutional guidelines but measures to communicate the intent and content of the reforms to the public – in Britain and in the subcontinent. In this process Fleet Street occupied a crucial place. It was essential to convey the support of the British nation if goodwill were to be engendered in India, where political extremism was on the increase, as well as to limit potentially damaging criticism of a Coalition government dependent upon Conservative backbench support at home. It would not, in his view, be possible to launch the schemes 'without giving an opportunity . . . of public criticism' in India, since there existed 'an Indian opinion produced by a long series of statesmen from Macaulay to Morley' which it was 'now absolutely impossible to ignore'.[4] Yet it was also crucial that the scheme should not be misconceived by British opinion.

> I am particularly anxious to avoid any discussion of it in this country until we are ready with our policy. Nothing could be so fatal to our deliberations in India in my opinion as for people here to begin to discuss what might or might not be meant by responsible government and self-governing institutions[5]

The August declaration and the press

Fleet Street, noted Montagu, had been 'very favourable' to the announcement, and 'not only the Press of one Party'.[6] In the midst of intense war reporting, nearly all papers carried editorials or in-depth articles. For the *Nation* the reforms marked an 'immense advance' and would for the first time give Indians 'real, though guarded, power'. Montagu's task would be to 'invest the scheme with the appearance of a real and generous concession'. As an initial step, he would have to 'make the atmosphere as well as the scheme'.[7] The *National Review* had a detailed piece by Lovat Fraser, writing under the pseudonym 'Asiaticus'. Fraser attacked the 'Radical Press' in Britain, which had 'sedulously fostered' the impression that Montagu was to figure 'in some mysterious manner' as the 'liberator' of India and invested his forthcoming visit with 'a ridiculous solemnity'. India, too, was being 'flooded with gush' about him. With the ascendancy of the extremists and the collapse of the moderates, the 'calm atmosphere' which Montagu wished to create in India seemed 'likely to resemble the calmness of the tiger after he had swallowed the young lady of Riga'.[8]

These articles represent the two opposing poles in a press response whose chief features were compounded of a reaction to the person of the new (and first Jewish) Secretary of State, an assessment of the nature of the proposed reforms, and an analysis of Indian politics. Montagu's personality and mission attracted favourable comment

[166]

from both quality and popular papers. The *Observer* agreed with the *Chronicle* in urging even the 'most impatient friends of reform' to rest content that the Cabinet had chosen Montagu 'for its guide'.[9] The *Mail* applauded Montagu's 'very sound and businesslike decision' to visit India, while the *Gazette* hoped that all parties 'may be relied upon to give an ungrudging support to the working out of the new formula'.[10] The single discordant note among the dailies was struck by Gwynne at the *Morning Post*, who claimed that Montagu's 'rushing tactics' were causing 'profound disquiet' within Unionist circles and argued that it would be highly dangerous for the government to ignore the wishes of the party on which it relied for support.[11]

All papers agreed that the war had made a crucial difference. India's 'magnificent loyalty' had established 'firm claims on our respect', while preparedness to respond constructively was what ultimately distinguished Britain from its enemies: 'The British race has never desired to hold India with the sword but by the stronger tie of justice and sympathy. That after all is the real difference between the system of the Germans and of the British.'[12] It was acknowledged that the political situation rendered the case for such a gesture more compelling. Spender warned that no scheme would be accepted with 'pious gratitude as a gift from the gods'.[13] Most papers reiterated the need to use the reform process to strengthen the Indian moderates *vis-à-vis* the extremists. The *Mail* considered the former 'perfectly loyal' but 'if treated unsympathetically and refused any prospect of responsible government [they] might conceivably be driven to throw in their lot with the extremists'.[14] The *Guardian*'s lucid summary highlighted the importance of defining the goal of British rule to be the creation of a system comparable to the dominions.

> That goal is not near, and of necessity it will have to be approached by stages, but by accepting it as the end to be pursued a direction is given to all future reform, a standard is set up by which such reform must be tested, and a charter is given to Indian opinion.[15]

The Times's voluminous coverage applauded the declaration as 'a fresh landmark' in imperial relations, reflecting the 'matured conclusions' of the Cabinet. However, it was important not to associate the reforms too closely with one individual, for there was then 'always the risk of unnecessary prejudice'.[16] They should be regarded 'as representing an invitation extended by the British nation to the peoples of India to take a larger share in the affairs of the Empire'. To this end it was necessary for the proposals to enjoy the unanimous backing of the entire government and the British public, who were, according to *The Times*, 'the final arbiters in this grave problem'.[17]

[167]

9   Edwin S. Montagu and the India delegation, 1918

In responding to the contents of the declaration, however, the general press view was that, though the reforms proposed were a definite step ahead, they contained, as the *Mail* put it, 'nothing very revolutionary'. Further, there remained considerable ambiguity as to their implications for the future. This was hardly surprising, since the government itself was not in a position to clarify the details of the announcement. Nevertheless some papers interpreted the statement as signalling a commitment to Indian self-government. The *Express* carried a front- page report suggesting that Montagu's objectives 'foreshadowed Home Rule for India by easy stages'.[18] The *Express* was supported by the *Guardian*, which criticised the internment of Mrs Besant for agitating for Indian Home Rule as a 'strange anomaly', given that 'Home Rule for India is precisely the goal which Mr Montagu now announces as that of the Government policy'.[19]

An Indian summer of reform

Upon his return to London Montagu immediately set about projecting the case for reform. 'Things go well here,' he wrote to Chelmsford in May 1918. 'Curtis and Chirol have both promised support and I do not think there will be much difficulty in the Cabinet, but again I may be too optimistic.'[20] Writing two weeks later:

> I really do not think I can complain of the progress that I have made with our Reforms scheme, and it looks as if this week or the week after I shall get permission to publish the Report. I have already constituted

a Drafting Committee and a Propaganda Committee with a view to having everything ready when I do get the permission.[21]

In addition to support from Curtis and Chirol, the scheme had received the backing of Dawson. All three were members of the Round Table, and the organisation's journal, along with *The Times*, formed a powerful basis of support for the reforms. The Viceroy, too, urged upon these writers the necessity of a good reception and the need to carry the educated classes with them. 'I hope you have received from him our report,' he wrote to Dawson. 'To my mind it was all-important to build up our case for Reforms.'[22] By June Montagu was happy to report, 'I have got the *Times* quite easily. Chirol . . . has been bitten by Curtis with the 'two Government's' plan for the Provinces. I had him and Roberts to lunch and I think weakened him.'[23] The *Round Table* was not unanimous but Kerr, 'who has much influence with the Prime Minister', was 'strongly a supporter of our alternatives'. Significantly, Montagu added, 'I have got the *Observer*; Garvin is a person of considerable influence. I am making arrangements next week to try and get the *Daily Telegraph*.'[24]

How far was Montagu justified in his optimism concerning press coverage prior to the publication of the Montagu–Chelmsford report on 5 July? Predictably, the Liberal press strongly supported his broad objectives. In May the *Fortnightly* carried a lengthy essay by St Nihal Singh, who stressed reform as the reward earned by India's war service.[25] The *Guardian*'s voice was raised in support via a number of detailed articles. Writing on 15 June, its political correspondent predicted, with a confidence which appeared to reflect official briefing, that the scheme would be 'strictly faithful' to the August declaration. 'It will be seen, when Mr Montagu's proposals are published, that they . . . mean – by gradual development, it is true, but a development to be begun immediately – nothing less than the establishment of responsible government – and indeed Parliamentary government – for India.' Referring to 'the lost opportunities of timely action' in Ireland, it argued that the empire 'with all its power to stand strains, cannot afford itself the luxury of a second Ireland'. [26]

However, the very predictability of backing from the Liberal press meant that, for Montagu, it was the reaction of Conservative papers that was more significant. *The Times* featured in early June, as a background to the publication of the report, a series of four reviews by Chirol, who wrote of India's 'tense expectancy'. Not since the Mutiny had there been such a comprehensive inquiry and even the Morley–Minto reforms were 'in the main the outcome of an exchange of views between two statesmen whose own knowledge of India was obviously limited'.[27] The fact remained, however, that 'To political self-government the people of India have yet to be trained.'[28] In his final article, on 9 June, Chirol reiterated the continued necessity of British control during the 'stupendous change' entailed by a movement from 'autocratic' to 'democratic' forms of governance.

Montagu had earlier conveyed to Chelmsford his sense of achievement in winning support for the scheme, not just from Chirol but from Garvin, who was an influential adviser to Conservative politicians. It was accordingly significant that lengthy and positive leaders flowed from Garvin's pen in the weeks preceding and following the report's publication. A major article greeted 'The coming of a great policy'. Tracing the development of this scheme, Garvin declared, 'Our word is passed . . . both for the new ideal and the early procedure.' At present, he felt, there would be 'less danger from Indian extremism than from the weighty body of British opinion, largely official and expert, which is profoundly conservative where India is concerned, and distrustful of all genuine change in the present basis of our rule'.[29]

There were several similarities of approach in the articles by Garvin and Chirol. Garvin identified three aspects crucial to future progress: disregard for the extremists and reactionaries, education of the electorate and the maintenance of 'undiminished control' by Britain in a supervisory capacity. He was, like Chirol, convinced of Britain's role as a trustee 'for the vast inarticulate mass', relinquishing 'guardianship' only when this could be clearly shown to be no longer necessary.[30] An Anglo-Indian contributor to the *Daily News* was equally supportive of Montagu. No settlement could hope to gain universal assent, but:

> the great body of opinion, both here and in India, should rally to the support of Mr Montagu. He is the first Secretary of State who has gone to the India Office with an avowed programme of reform; and if he fails, India will have lost the best opportunity she has ever had, or is likely to have.[31]

Such positive remarks were characteristic of the London press across the political spectrum in the weeks leading up to publication of the report.

However, one discordant note had been struck which was to prove a continual source of irritation to Montagu. It arose out of the opposition of the Indo-British Association, whose chief spokesman was Lord Sydenham and which had in the *Morning Post* a strident press voice. The Association had been formed in response to Montagu's reform initiatives with the ostensible objective of protecting the interests of Britons and Indians alike in India, and had amongst its members old India hands like Sir David Yule, Sir John Hewett and Younghusband. The *Morning Post* contended that the proposals were part of a series of:

> insidious attempts to divert this country from the hard road of reality to the bogs and quagmires of political and constitutional idealism. Leagues of Nations and schemes of Federalism – in their green and glimmering depths the British dog is asked to behold the shadow of the bone he carries. Let him give up the arduous spoils of war to a 'supernational authority'; let him break up the Union and hand over Ireland to the Home Ruler; let him destroy one system of government in India in order to conciliate the agitator – all these schemes of exchanging realities for shadows are now being eagerly thrust upon a bewildered British public.[32]

The same leader vigorously attacked the stance of the *Observer*: 'That prophet of Democracy, Mr Garvin, has been allowed to take the lid off the Hebraic pot of the Montagu report, and as the reward of his support to abstract for himself a little of the meat with his three-pronged fish hook'.

Protesting at this attack, Lord Donoughmore, who had accompanied Montagu to India and was involved in drawing up the reform Bill, wrote:

> It would have been fairer to await the promised publication through presentation to Parliament before hastening to condemn these proposals before they have been seen. In any case, I feel sure that it is only a grave misapprehension . . . that leads you to impute 'stealth' to the Secretary of State on the eve of his laying his proposals openly before the country for discussion and criticism alike in England and India.[33]

In a retort, Gwynne suggested that Donoughmore should have addressed his missive at the *Observer*, which had suggested that it was 'too late either to contest the general principle . . . or to desire its indefinite adjournment'. The *Post* had merely 'protested' against this attempt to 'deny the power of veto both to Parliament and the nation', and had argued that it was 'not the time to tamper' with the Indian government. Here lay the crux of the paper's position. Gwynne's antipathy to both the reformer and his reform was to colour the *Morning Post*'s coverage in the months to come.

This interchange brought forth a spirited response from Garvin himself, who characterised the *Morning Post*'s attack as 'disingenuous raving'. 'It suggests that the *Observer*'s article was an inspired forecast of Mr Montagu's report, and it screams accordingly against some supposed sinister plot for the betrayal of British dominion in India'. Unlike the *Morning Post*'s, the *Observer*'s comments were based on 'some acquaintance with that movement and above all upon the admirable exposition' of it by Curtis. If the official report were written in the 'same constructive Imperial spirit' the *Observer* would 'rejoice'.[34]

Sydenham was meanwhile pursuing his criticisms through the letter column of *The Times*. Writing in response to Chirol's articles, he was sceptical about the expediency of transferring power through elected representative institutions. 'Have we the right to impose upon India a system still most imperfect, repugnant to all the customs and habits of thought handed down from her far-distant past, and condemned by some of her best thinkers?' Concern was expressed for the fate of the loyal princes, who would soon find their authority undermined by '"nationalist" intrigues'. Sydenham also cast himself as a champion of the masses, stating that their fate should not be trusted to 'a noisy and interested' urbanised section possessing little knowledge of the rural population.[35] The *Spectator* also featured Sydenham's views on 'The peace of India'. He conceded that Britain had not sufficiently responded to the growing political aspirations of Indians, and the result was a troubled land where unscrupulous politicians used the opportunity of war to foment unreasonable demands. The Secretary of State had perambulated the country and attempted in a few weeks to master its complex problems. This had only raised the expectations of the agitators. The majority in India had no idea about Home Rule, while in Britain 'a subsidised paper [*India*] has long been occupied in attempts to mislead public opinion'.[36] In the second essay (4 May) Sydenham argued that the medley of cultures, religions and languages of which India was constituted were held together only by the Raj. Besides providing a platform for Association publicity, the *Spectator* had a leader (almost certainly by St Loe Strachey) that argued the need for *some* change: the moot question was how it was to be accomplished. The idea of a common Indian nationality was still remote from the minds of Indians, and Strachey doubted Curtis's ability or knowledge: 'Quite frankly a perusal of his book suggests that he is looking at Indian problems with something of the attitude of a visitor from another planet.'[37]

Montagu made repeated attempts to marginalise such opposition. 'I have been busy lobbying,' he wrote to Chelmsford, 'and Chamberlain continues to assist.' Chamberlain had succeeded in getting the support of Roper Lethbridge, 'a volcano which must be approaching extinction, but every little counts'.[38] He did not feel 'sanguine' about the support of Hewett, and Sydenham was 'I fear, hopeless'. Nevertheless, Montagu received a deputation from the Indo-British Association and persuaded them, in the course of 'a very long talk', to accept the validity of the August announcement: 'In writing to me the Committee acknowledge that the government's duty is to carry out the pronouncement of the 20th August, so there is that amount of common ground between us.'[39] Montagu also received support from the *Herald*. Lansbury complained that Anglo-Indians, led by Sydenham, were 'engaged in poisoning the minds' about British policy.[40] The Labour MP Ramsay MacDonald was critical of the government's decision to prevent a deputation of Indian Home Rulers, including Tilak, from visiting Britain while permitting members of the Anglo-Indian Association to enter and present the case against self-government. 'Can the Government suppress this agitation too, or does it mean to leave Mr Montagu to be attacked on the Right without being defended on the Left?'[41] For MacDonald, as for Montagu, creating positive impressions upon the Indian mind was essential: 'what I care most about is the effect it will have upon India'.[42]

Post-publication response

Writing to the Governor of Madras, Lord Willingdon, in early July 1918 (on the eve of its presentation to Parliament), Montagu explained how he had been 'working hard here to smooth the path of the report. I have seen politicians and journalists of all sorts and so far have nothing to complain of the general attitude.' If anything 'a certain amount of criticism here will, I think, be actually helpful in India because if Sydenham and his friends gave the report their blessing the Indian politicians would think they were getting nothing and look askance at our measures'.[43] Throughout July Montagu sent Chelmsford regular summaries of press coverage of their proposals. He was, for instance, 'disappointed' with the *Telegraph*, 'over which I took some trouble . . . But whenever a leaderwriter on Indian questions says that East is East and West is West, *etc.*, you know he is pretty hopeless!'[44] He was, further, upset at the personal attacks directed at him. 'I hate that sort of thing and it wounds me more than I can say. It would appear that our proposals are going to suffer by my connection with them.'[45] However, he noted to Willingdon that *The Times* and *Guardian* were 'very favourable', as were the *Daily News* and *Express*. However, the *Morning Post* was 'frankly hostile'.[46] In mid-July Montagu sent another account to the Viceroy, this time featuring some of the weeklies: the report had been 'bitterly attacked' in the *Spectator* and *Saturday Review* but 'cordially received' by the *New Statesman*, *India* and *Nation*.[47]

The *Morning Post* was the most unrelenting in its opposition, as was evident in a series of leaders which reflected both the criticisms directed by Gwynne against Montagu's initiative and the paper's general stance on India. Entitling its first piece 'The Great Indian

Mystery', the paper claimed that the details of the report had appeared in two sources before its publication – in Curtis's *Letters* and in the 'Apocalyptic columns' of the *Observer*. Curtis, hitherto regarded as an 'innocent and harmless' federal fanatic, had come to see Indian self-government as 'requisite to the symmetry of his scheme', and by an 'evil chance' Montagu was:

> at his wit's end for a scheme which might both justify the wild words he had addressed to Parliament and allay the fears of the right wing of the Coalition. Mr Curtis's inventive mind supplied him with just what he desired – something with an appearance both of radicalism and moderation, a plan as logically faultless as it is practically absurd. Mr Montagu embraced the proposal, embodied it is his report, and induced the unhappy Lord Chelmsford to sign it. On the way home he was haunted with doubts. How would it be received in the sober circles of Unionism? He determined, if we may venture on a vulgar phrase, to 'try it on the dog'. And so it was announced in the *Observer*.[48]

The government's policy was a betrayal of friends to placate enemies and 'For ourselves, we are bound to say we dislike and distrust both the report and its chief author'.

The *Morning Post* sustained its critique throughout July. 'The "sucking-up" policy in India' (8 July) claimed that pressure for reform emanated only from a small number of Brahmin agitators, and it was to placate such people that Montagu was embarking upon potentially dangerous constitutional changes. Far from consolidating British power amidst the trying conditions of war, he was preparing to relax it as a preliminary to relinquishing authority altogether. Further leaders witnessed the opening of the attack on new flanks. 13 July saw a comparison between the Irish situation and that which, the paper believed, was about to be unleashed in India. The government had tried to give Ireland Home Rule and failed because 'it is impossible to give Ireland Home Rule'. Similar dangers were now faced in India, and the plan was 'so similar and the coincidence of time and method so close that we cannot believe that the two conspiracies are altogether separate'. The 'real' responsibility lay with Montagu, who had 'engineered the whole conspiracy', while Chelmsford was merely 'a puppet' in his hands. Referring to Montagu's earlier stint as Under Secretary, the paper hinted that all had not been satisfactorily explained in the matter of the silver controversy involving his brother's firm. In a racist attack the leader declared that the Indian empire 'was not built by Mr Montagu or by his ancestors; it was built up by the blood and sweat of honest Englishman . . . The idea of Asiatics controlling Englishmen may be native to the mind of Mr Montagu: it is repugnant to British instincts . . . no white man of good type would accept such a situation.'[49]

Responding to the article, the Conservative MP J. D. Rees, a former member of the Governor General's Council, admitted that the choice of the word 'relax' in the report was perhaps 'unfortunate', but a careful reading showed it was intended to signify 'interference with the administration in fewer directions and details, not that such interference shall be weaker on occasions when it is required'.[50] Rees also emphasised that Montagu was carrying forward a project that had the support of the whole Cabinet, and had 'a stronger Imperialistic strain than any other Radical I know . . . But why is it all Mr Montagu? Is the Cabinet of no account? Is Lord Chelmsford a cipher? He equally organised and now signs the report.'[51]

The *Telegraph*, the other daily cited by Montagu as critical of the report, nevertheless acknowledged that 'a large devolution of powers' to Indians was 'necessary'.[52] However, like the *Morning Post* and *Spectator*, it emphasised the impossibility of speaking of India as one single community; the only principle holding the 'conglomerate mass' together was allegiance to Britain. Reminding its readers of Kipling's dictum of East and West never meeting, it argued that parliamentary government did not suit oriental communities. The *Telegraph* nevertheless concluded on a more upbeat note – possibly reflecting Montagu's efforts at persuasion:

> Granting that present circumstances require somewhat drastic changes in order to avoid discontent and promote loyalty, we have to acknowledge that, though we do not agree with it, the Montagu-Chelmsford scheme as a whole is a conscientious attempt to effect a wide-reaching reform in the government of India. It has, at any rate, the merit of recognising the necessity of preserving the ultimate and decisive authority of the British government.[53]

By stressing, like Chirol and Garvin, the fact of continued British control overall control as well as the necessity for reform, the *Telegraph*'s opposition was not so unyielding as that of others in the Conservative camp.

It is important to emphasise that such views occupied a minority position in Fleet Street. The opposition of the above-named papers was more than matched by the vociferous support amongst stalwart Liberal dailies like the *Daily News*, *Chronicle*, *Gazette* and *Guardian*, as well as the Conservative *Times*. Spender argued that the demand for self-government was:

> a product of our own making, for we have from the beginning of our rule presented ourselves to the people of India as trustees for their welfare,

whose special purpose it is to fit them ultimately to govern themselves, like other responsible communities under our flag.

He considered dyarchy an 'ingenious scheme' and provincial autonomy 'undoubtedly the wisest and safest line of advance'.[54] According to the *Chronicle*, the report's 'prompt and successful adoption might place it in the same category of achievement as Lord Durham's Report on Canada; its shelving might prove as irretrievably disastrous as George III's shelving of Pitt's proposal to emancipate the Irish Catholics'[55] Indeed, the *Daily News* went so far as to declare it 'one of the great state documents of the world', whose success or failure would 'determine the whole course of the history of India for good or evil'.[56]

In terms of column inches, the coverage of the *Guardian* and *The Times* was unsurpassed. In its leader on 6 July the *Guardian* welcomed the reforms as one of the 'boldest and most far-reaching schemes of enfranchisement ever proposed'. In the first of a series of essays entitled 'Western Institutions and the East', objectors, it was noted:

> pounce promptly upon the self-evident proposition that 'East is East . . . ', forgetting that even in the poem . . . the respect for fighting men of different race for each other proved a meeting-point . . . Why are we so dogmatically certain that we cannot also give our teaching to the East? Is the relation of a representative to his constituents or the responsibility of an Executive to a Legislature, and ultimately to an electorate, really so esoteric or so unintelligible an idea?[57]

The report faced initial difficulties, yet these pointed 'not to the impracticability of self-government' but to the maintenance of law and order during the period of evolution. The remaining five articles discussed differing aspects of the measures proposed – 'Modifications in the central government' (11 July), 'Self-government in the provinces' (15, 19 July), 'Machinery for expansion' (23 July) and 'Religion and caste' (30 July).

Similarly, *The Times* devoted several columns to the report, including an entire page on 6 July, contending that the document brought home:

> the responsibilities we have to discharge and how serious is the problem for which we have to find the right solution . . . It is in this spirit, we believe, that the British people will be most inclined to study the Report and to assent to its general conclusions[58]

The Times claimed that its letters pages reflected significant sections of British public opinion, and the reform proposals attracted a range of informed comment – thirteen letters were printed in the two weeks after publication. Sir George Forrest suggested the appointment of a parliamentary committee, while Archdale Earle, late Chief Commissioner of Assam, contended that such a measure would merely cause 'regrettable delay' and could not be expected to surpass the 'exhaustive, masterly, statesmanlike character' of the document.[59] In a letter titled 'A question of good faith' Curtis countered the arguments put forward by Sydenham, the *Morning Post* and the *Spectator*. He acknowledged that all laws depended on force, but force would 'recoil and destroy you if you seek to wield it unhinged from the primal axis of right'. That was the principle for which Britain was waging war and it was essential to keep the pledges to India.[60]

Amongst the popular papers, the *Express* praised the report's 'Sound statesmanship'. Though progress was to be 'gradual and careful', it was hoped ultimately to lead to Indian self-government within the empire.[61] The *Mail*'s leader emphasised the importance of a thorough study of the Bill's contents prior to any parliamentary discussion: 'A mock debate at the end of the session would be an insult to India.' Though critical of the document's length and verbosity, it expressed 'no spirit of hostility' to its broad purpose.[62] The *Star* anticipated that extremists on both sides would 'denounce' the scheme, and its fortunes would depend upon how it appealed to the moderates in India. To the *Star* it had been apparent since the time when Indian troops first 'fought and bled' for the empire that 'the older ("Mutiny") view of our relations would have to be revised'. While recognising the complexity of the problem,

> the real question is whether the British nation, the British Parliament, and above all the British Government, will give the Indian people what President Roosevelt called 'the square deal'. Will they adopt the Montagu scheme, and see that it is honestly carried out and not rendered inoperative by some secret drug, some poisoned dagger, in the shape of an insidious amendment?[63]

The report drew praise from the spectrum of Liberal–Labour weeklies. The *New Statesman* felt it had 'discovered a formula for one of the most baffling problems of racial and political chemistry, the problem of how to fuse the people of India with the other peoples of the British Empire in a commonwealth of free nations'.[64] The *Nation* noted that there were two propositions about India upon which 'average opinion' in Britain was agreed: that at some date Indians 'must eventually govern themselves' and that it would be 'rash to confer instantly . . . a complete measure of autonomy'. The grant of provincial self-government was not a half-way house: 'It is the actual terminus.' The *Nation* was convinced that the reforms would be successful, 'for to admit the possibility of failure would be to despair of the possibility of a Liberal Empire'. The prevailing atmosphere was 'so friendly' that, if there were obstacles, they would 'not come from British public opinion, from Parliament, or from the Press at home'. Urging prompt action, it warned, 'We dare not risk in India a repetition of the Irish failures and delays.'[65] The *Herald* described the reforms as dealing 'a severe defeat to the forces of darkness', but the 'ultimate salvation' of the provinces would lie in the character of the legislative assemblies that were established and the nature of the control vested in them.[66] *Reynolds's Newspaper* featured an article by H. E. A. Cotton, who predicted that the Bill would gain general acceptance: 'Advance is the only policy, and it could not be provided for more satisfactorily than in the Montagu–Chelmsford Report.'[67]

A lengthy essay by Garvin in the *Observer* was more forthright in welcoming the Report:

> It is invaluable for comprehensiveness of study, thoroughness of intellectual attack, for bold and steady thinking on some parts of the subject, for closest discrimination on others, and it is full of vigorous and felicitous writing . . . We wish . . . that a Blue Book so profound in its issues and vivid in its treatment could be put out in penny numbers and circulated at least amongst the more intelligent of the democracy which knows so little of India, but under penalty must be made to know more and that during the next few months.[68]

Even before the end of the nineteenth century the foundations of the old order had passed under the influence of railways, the press, education and agitation. The report was 'a great project of timely and creative statesmanship in true succession to our best achievements in harmonising Empire and liberty'.

Although also a Conservative weekly, the *Spectator*, exhibited, during July, a position on Indian self-government utterly removed from that of the *Observer*, Montagu himself observed that the former had been 'thoroughly collared by Sydenham's people, and is very hostile'.[69] The *Spectator* claimed that the day when India would be able to govern herself was 'a very long way off'. 'If we leave India we must leave it with clean hands, and not from fear or favour.'[70] This was to be Strachey's recurring maxim. The *Spectator*, like the *Morning Post*, referred to rumours that the report had been 'written by Curtis, camouflaged by Montagu, and signed by Chelmsford!' 'Long-winded' and 'confused', it represented '*Bolshevism by Order in Council*'.[71] What, asked Strachey, did the people of India want? Good government. But that was already being provided by a Pax Britannica which, if not

10 J. L. Garvin

perfect, was considerably better than anything existing previously. Was, then, the British nation to 'sacrifice the dumb millions' to the political section of the Brahmanical caste ... who may best be described, in the words of Burke, as 'the grave, demure, insidious, spring-nailed, velvet-pawed, green-eyed philosophers of Hindostan'?[72] 'We are invited,' it noted the following week, 'to believe that the clamorous few in India really must be appeased, and that the interests of the vast majority – most of them strong loyalists – may be safely ignored.'[73] All the while the British people were being exhorted to create an atmosphere favourable to the reforms, and told that resistance to the report was 'an extreme kind of mischief-making and unpatriotism ... We are in India because India cannot get on without us. If we were not indispensable to India, the miracle of our rule would be ended in an hour.'[74]

[179]

The *Saturday Review* also came out vehemently against the reforms, claiming, in somewhat extraordinary fashion, that neither Montagu nor the Viceroy 'knows anything about India from personal experience'. Although the former was 'of amiable manner and great industry, we are obliged to say that his opinion on India can be worth very little'. Its leading article, 'India in the melting pot', contended that the report exhibited two fundamental defects. Like the *Telegraph*, it warned of the dangers of forgetting the essential difference of East and West: the conditions suitable for the 'white man of the West' were at variance with those to which the 'black man of the East' was accustomed. Secondly, the proposals had put 'the cart before the horse', as there was no general demand amongst Indians for self-government.[75]

August and the parliamentary debates

At the beginning of August Montagu wrote optimistically: 'The Reforms Scheme goes better. In fact, the *Post* and Sydenham seem to me to be more and more isolated. Their opposition helps us probably with the Indians.'[76] The Bill based on the report was discussed in Parliament on 6 August. In general the Commons, noted the *Guardian*'s correspondent, 'exhibited a degree of unanimity almost too unqualified to be real'. Similarly the Lords debate offered 'the strongest encouragement' to proceed with the scheme.[77] Most papers reaffirmed their earlier support in the light of the debates. *The Times* too commented upon the 'very favourable reception' and how Sydenham's 'gloomy warnings' had made him 'a rather lonely figure'.[78] The *Express*, under Beaverbrook, remained staunchly supportive of Montagu, describing him as 'one of the most far-seeing statesmen among those who have governed India'.

> Montagu goes to his own bailiwick, so to speak, studies, examines, and dissects the problems for himself. He comes back with a plan which from his experienced point of view would give a measure of justice to India. When he has unfolded his scheme the gnats come out to bite. We are glad to note that they were in a minority in Parliament last night.[79]

The *Observer* carried an interview with Montagu by Edward Marshall on 18 August, entitled 'The new era in India . . . our aims and our hopes', which allowed Montagu to present his case directly to the reader. The columns of *The Times* were awash with official and unofficial opinions and helped to convey an image of the public impact of the reforms. One important theme to emerge concerned the nature of the communal electorates. Chirol initiated the debate with a letter referring to 'lower caste anxiety' contending that, while communal representation was 'not an ideal system', yet, given the social cleavages which existed, it might be the only feasible way to secure 'adequate representation for the lower castes'.[80] Sir Theodore Morison similarly argued that communal representation was an effective means to prevent elections from being contested solely upon a racial or communal issue, while P. C. Lyon of Oriel College, Oxford, contended that it was the inclusion of communal representation in the Morley–Minto reforms which had ensured that different communities had gained experience and 'mutual respect', making a further advance towards self-government possible.[81]

The critique in the wake of the debates came from the expected sources – with the *Telegraph* again occupying an ambiguous position. The paper reiterated that, while it was not opposed to all parts of the scheme, several aspects would have to be amended if criticisms raised by Indian and Anglo-Indian opinion were to be accommodated.[82] Sydenham's arguments attracted support in two leaders in the *Morning Post*.[83] Criticism from an opposite perspective came from the *Herald*, which, echoing views of extremist Congress leaders, felt that the report had not gone far enough to satisfy Indian aspirations. The paper warned that the 'real danger' was the 'complete ignorance of Indian feeling' on the one hand, and the 'energetic propaganda' of Sydenham and his friends on the other.[84] On 17 August the *Herald* featured the first of three essays signed 'Young India', in which the writer presented what were essentially the views of extremists like Tilak and Lajpat Rai. Subsequent pieces examined dyarchy and the powers of the Governor (24 August) and the central government (31 August). The author concluded:

> Freedom for India is yet far off . . . The minimum that would have reconciled India to-day would be a complete Home Rule. That is not granted. So India is not deceived; we hope the democracy of the world is not.[85]

The *Herald* thus provided a platform for radical Indian (and British Labour) sentiments. For instance, in a page devoted to 'Home Rule for India' the paper featured Annie Besant's critique, an article by Singh and another by a 'representative of the younger Indians resident in this country'.[86]

Parliamentary debates following the report's publication provided a focus for media discussion, and there was a subsequent lull in coverage. Montagu nevertheless endeavoured to keep Indian discussion alive in the press, and remained concerned with the availability of information. He noted that Indian news was 'very scanty' and there had been complaints regarding delays in telegrams from Bombay.[87] He reminded Chelmsford that, when he was visiting India, 'we used to receive Reuters within a day or two of their despatch' from London. But now the telegrams in *The Times* were 'even nine or ten days' in coming. He wondered whether it would be possible to 'devise some system of supplying a certain modicum of Indian news with expedition?'[88] A House of Lords debate in October provided a renewed opportunity for discussion, though Fleet Street carried only brief reports. As Dawson informed Chelmsford, the opposition was still chiefly led by Sydenham, 'who has bored everyone so much that he no longer carries even as much influence as he deserves'.[89] Montagu characteristically took a gloomier view, worried that such criticism would have 'a bad effect in India and depress those who hope that without delay they will get what we have designed for them'.[90]

Montagu's dissatisfaction with the extent of discussion in the autumn of 1918 highlights a recurrent feature of Indian coverage. Though over the first decades of the twentieth century there was increasing press interest in India, it always had to compete with domestic and European news. Whilst the war gave a tremendous fillip to Indian reportage, it was the conflagration in Europe which dominated the pages of the press. Montagu admitted at the end of September that 'People here are more than ever engrossed in the war, particularly as the day of victory seems to draw nearer'.[91] India tended to receive sustained coverage when an event of considerable significance marked it out for attention. Although the inauguration of the reforms generated much press interest, in the aftermath press coverage subsided. These general limits to Indian reporting were compounded by what Montagu perceived as indifference in official circles. 'It is so disheartening to find that lack of interest in Indian affairs, excused now because of the preoccupations of the war, but I am afraid always present, is one of our greatest obstacles.'[92] Montagu's position was made more problematic by his exclusion from the War Cabinet. This, remarked Rumbold, left Curzon 'as a sort of super Secretary of State for India: his colleagues, the House of Lords, and the Unionist party looked to him for a lead . . . Allergy to change in India discouraged him from giving high priority . . . to study of the joint report. He distrusted and disliked Montagu.'[93] However, Lloyd George took an active – if spasmodic – interest and C. P. Scott, a frequent guest of the Prime Minister, noted how, in the summer of 1918, constitutional change was often discussed in relation to both India and Ireland. During a breakfast meeting on 8 May, at which Sir S. Sinha was present, Lloyd George argued that. India 'must be regarded as 'a partner' in the Imperial Commonwealth and Englishmen must get it into their heads that Indians were not just "natives" to be governed, but members of "a more ancient and in some respects a finer civilization"'.[94] Montagu himself confirmed that Lloyd George had given an assurance that 'whatever happened he was going on with the intention of carrying our Reform policy'.[95] Lloyd George's motives may at this stage have had more to do with the imminence of a general election, which compelled him to ensure the loyalty of his Liberal colleagues. Indeed, Grigg, his biographer, observes that Lloyd George 'had no sense of urgency' about Indian reform. 'Had he visited India, as Montagu had, his vivid imagination might have grasped the country's political potential.'[96] Montagu's personality also contributed to his constant self-doubt. Thus Scott, having been warned by Garvin that Montagu was prone to 'depression' and 'timidity', encouraged him 'not to bother his head about the future, but to go right ahead and make a success of his present task and all would be well'. Nevertheless Montagu remained 'full of anxieties' about the success of his mission and his political fortune.[97]

Reuters and reform

Reuters formed an essential component in the official strategy of shaping opinion within and outside India. Yet as a commercial enterprise it could not afford to alienate its large Indian clientele. A delicate balance had to be struck. For instance, in November 1918 Reuters editor, P. W. Dickinson, wrote to the General Manager in India, A. H. Kingston, complaining that the agency had referred to the 'Indian Native Congress': 'How this serious and inexcusable mistake came to be made, it is difficult to surmise. It has become part of our political education nowadays to know that the word "native" is excluded from the lexicon so far as India is concerned'.[98] 'All Indian subjects,' he was gratified to note, 'are nowadays very carefully and fully dealt with and we know from the correspondents of the Indian papers here that we leave them practically nothing to telegraph about on their own account.'[99]

Considerable attention was given to the reporting of reform-related issues and Reuters regularly carried the views of Fleet Street, despite, on occasion, attracting criticism from the Indian press. After receiving from Kingston cuttings from the *Bombay Chronicle* and *Indian Daily News* complaining about the summary of a leading article from *The Times*, Dickinson explained:

> It is quite true that there was not much that was new or striking in it but there are seasons when it is difficult to be silent and we felt that were we to ignore a leading article from the 'Times' just when India

might be looking for comments from this side on Mr Montagu's mission, we might give an opportunity for reproof from the Indian newspapers.[100]

In another instance, Reuters learned that Montagu was to deliver an important speech at the Reform Club in Manchester on 9 October. The company requested the Press Association to arrange for 'a good report' to be telegraphed to it.[101] The editor also wrote to C. H. Kisch, Montagu's private secretary:

> I suppose there is no chance of our having Mr Montagu's speech in advance? It would save us a world of trouble and anxiety if this were possible. We have no regular reporting staff of our own, and I rather tremble to think what may happen with a casual reporter who knows nothing of Indian affairs. Are you giving the *Times* a hint? If so, we might perhaps be able to arrange something with them.[102]

Care was taken in presenting Indian opinion to the British public. The company published, for example, a telegram sent to Head Office by Surendranath Banerjee representing the views of moderate politicians who welcomed the scheme as 'a definite stage in the progressive realisation of Responsible Government'.[103] Similarly, in praising Kingston for a summary of the views of a number of Indian newspapers, Dickinson wrote, 'it arrived opportunely just as people were beginning to ask what India was saying about the proposals'.[104] Thus Dickinson felt able to claim that Reuters was:

> fully alive to its responsibilities towards India and the Indian press and likewise towards the British Government, particularly in relation to the Indian Reform Scheme. We recognise the extreme importance of accuracy in all telegrams dealing with this momentous matter and the essential need of reporting Ministerial and other speeches on the subject with all possible exactness.[105]

However, the Company's positive coverage of Indian reactions to the report in July 1918 attracted some criticism in Britain. In a spirited letter Hewett claimed that Reuters correspondent in Simla 'may have been a little precipitate in beating the big drum so violently in his cable of the 8th inst., reproduced in your issue of the 15th'. The report was published in India on Friday 5 July:

> Simla is 1,176 miles from Calcutta, 1,112 miles from Bombay, and still farther from Madras. Considering that India is not normally in a hurry it was a notable feat of Reuter's correspondent to gauge public opinion all over the continent from a distant hill station between Saturday and Monday.[106]

Hewett particularly objected to the telegram's summary of official responses to the proposals, it being reported that 'they recognize them as an honest endeavour to meet an admitted political necessity for the extension of democratic institutions'. The failure to quote specifically any such opinion, the fact that ordinary officials were scattered across the country, and that 'none could have been permitted to write to the newspapers', caused Hewett to question Reuters sources. Hewett suspected that the information was in fact supplied by the 'official hierarchy' in Simla.[107]

Hewett's criticism had undoubted force. The correspondent responsible was a Reuters veteran, Everard Cotes, and there was little reason for Head Office to doubt the soundness of his views. 'On the whole, it strikes us as being a fair statement,' remarked Dickinson, who claimed to have read the telegram 'very carefully' and believed it reflected 'opinion pretty fairly, more particularly on the point raised by Hewett. It would be impossible for any correspondent to obtain the views of Governors and Lieut. Governors because they would not be drawn to speak against the Viceroy's proposals.'[108] Dickinson nevertheless noted that Hewett was:

> certainly justified in saying that our correspondent appears to have been precipitate in forming such exact conclusions regarding the reception of the Report, considering that the message was dispatched on July 8, whereas, so far as we know, the Report itself was only published in India on July 6.

Although recognising that it would 'not to be right to blame Mr Cotes for omitting to quote views of these high personages in such a general summary', the editor was keen to take some action. 'The point which we should like him to meet is that which relates to the question of precipitancy and we shall be glad if you will bring the whole matter before him.'[109]

Reuters was also troubled by delays in cable transmission – during the spring of 1918 some messages took ten or twelve days to arrive. Though the situation had much improved by November, messages from India could still take 'twelve to twenty four hours in coming through'.[110] Such delays compounded the more serious issue of government censorship, the latter forming a matter of frequent complaint to the India Office.[111] As Dickinson argued, the 'seeming ruthlessness' of the Indian censorship 'deprives us of all certainty as to what is published there and what is not'. During the first three months of 1918, 7,000 words were deleted from their telegrams to India, a figure that increased over the next quarter to 8,568.[112] 'The total is really horrifying,' complained the editor, concerned that the India Office would form an 'incorrect notion' of Reuters service.[113] Montagu raised the subject with Chelmsford, pointing out that Reuters had been 'very helpful' and he had 'reason to believe that they feel somewhat acutely the use of the blue pencil to which their messages have been subjected'.[114] The issue was pursued by Kisch, whose letter to J. L. Maffey (private secretary to the Viceroy) indicates the importance the India Office attached to the Reuters connection, especially over the issue of reform.[115] As Kisch explained:

> The Cable Company naturally feel hurt when their messages are held up, though I have no doubt that this is often necessary from Indian point of view, but I am sure you will remember in this connection that we are asking them now to give a good service of news from this country in regard to reforms, and special care in handling Reuter's cables would no doubt he amply rewarded.[116]

Underpinning all Reuters activity was the question of finance. The company needed to reconcile its responsibilities with 'the matter of pounds, shillings and pence'. Owing to the demands of the war, but also 'very considerably to the long despatches which we have sent about Indian Reform', Reuters had cabled 'some 60,000 words over our due limit' and Dickinson explained that they did not see any chance of doing justice to the debates on constitutional reform unless assistance was given to them. He therefore requested an official letter 'emphasising the importance' to the government and the India Office of 'full and accurate reports being cabled to India' which would serve as 'a voucher for any call that we might have to make for . . . a grant in aid without which, frankly, it would be impossible for us to do justice to the extremely important political questions involved'.[117]

Press and reforms: an overview

Government activity prior to publication ensured the report fell, by and large, on receptive ground. This was recognised, not only by Montagu's supporters, but also by the more critical papers in London, which were quick to denounce the presence of official propaganda. A second factor was the general parliamentary consensus in favour of granting a 'boon' in recognition of India's wartime contribution. India had proffered a 'gift', which had to be redeemed. This consensus smoothed the path of reform, diminishing points of contention and ensuring that, where opposition remained, it was frequently personal in motivation.

The fact that the report was couched in moderate terms assisted the press in approaching it in a constructive spirit. With the war reaching its climax in 1918 the press was, in any case, preoccupied with military affairs. Indeed, it is a measure of the importance now attached to

Indian issues that Fleet Street accorded as much space as it did to the reforms. The very precariousness of the military situation in fact reinforced the pressure for national unity around government measures. Personal factors were also important. Scott at the *Guardian* had a long record of supporting Indian causes; he was, additionally, a friend of Montagu's. Friendship played a more significant role in the case of the *Express*, whose proprietor Beaverbrook was on close terms with Montagu (and even closer terms with his wife Venetia). Blumenfeld, the paper's editor, was in frequent contact with the India Office. The support of a Conservative popular daily was thus secured. Liberal editors like Spender and Massingham, who took a close interest in Indian issues, were naturally positively disposed towards the reforms.

Since the support of Liberal papers could be largely taken for granted, it was, in the context of a Coalition government, the opposition from sections of the Conservative press which was more dangerous. The two most influential Conservative papers, the *Observer* and *The Times*, were edited by the informed imperialists Garvin and Dawson. Both tempered their commitment to empire with a realistic appraisal of the Indian situation and acceptance of the need for constitutional advance. The *Observer*, recognised as 'Unionist Journal No. 1', was a source of many of that party's ideas.[118] Garvin's was not, however, a rigidly Conservative position – he had been a Liberal imperialist before moving into the Unionist camp. On domestic issues during the war he made common cause with Liberal editors like Scott, who wrote in 1915 that Garvin's papers were 'the best in London and the only ones in which independence takes a really useful form'.[119] Montagu personally cultivated Garvin and was successful in securing him as an unofficial spokesman within the Unionist camp, and in the pages of the *Observer* the reforms received unstinted approval. Detaching Garvin in this manner was crucial, since, by gaining support also from *The Times*, a consensus was created and vociferous opponents like the *Morning Post*, *Spectator* and Sydenham were marginalised.

The Times gave sustained support, with Dawson corresponding regularly with the Viceroy on 'the great subject of constitutional Reform'.[120] Dawson received a pre-publication copy of the report and *Times* staff regularly met Montagu. However, *The Times* was by no means a monolithic institution, with the experts in its foreign and imperial departments taking independent positions. Thus with respect to Curtis's proposals Dawson's advisers were 'completely at variance': Chirol 'seems to think very highly of his work in India', while Fraser 'is altogether sceptical'.[121] In November Dawson reflected upon the principles guiding the paper's coverage:

It seemed to me that the great thing during the early stages was to stick to the broad principles which lie at the back of the scheme and to make the country realise their necessity. Chirol's articles . . . made certain cautious suggestions, and later on there will be something more to be said on the minor points[122]

The personal factor: anti-Semitism, Strachey and reform

The attacks on the reforms launched by Strachey in the *Spectator* displayed a degree of personal animus that merits discussion. Chirol remonstrated with Strachey, confessing himself 'distressed & alarmed' at the line adopted by his paper.[123] Pointing out that one could not repudiate the scheme without in effect repudiating the August pronouncement, he reminded Strachey of Curzon's 'considerable share' in drafting the pronouncement – and the erstwhile Viceroy could 'surely not be suspected of any desire to promote revolutionary changes for the benefit of the Brahmin politician'. Chirol argued that:

> it would be impossible to go on indefinitely trying to govern & administer India in defiance of the views bred by the education we have ourselves given them . . . The Report . . . gives the better elements of this class the opportunity they have been agitating for of showing whether they are capable of wielding power & bearing responsibility within a circumscribed field in which they can be put to the test without imperiling, even if the experiment fails, the vital structure of our Raj.[124]

Concentrating on the personal attacks on Montagu and Curtis, Chirol felt it was 'very unfortunate' that Strachey should allow his views 'on a question of policy which would have inevitably arisen' even if Montagu had never gone to the India Office to be coloured by 'your personal distrust of the man'. Strachey's statements on the report 'would have rather gained than lost strength if it had betrayed less personal animus'. While Chirol admitted to having 'very little liking for Jews though I try not to be an antisemite. But I know him [Montagu] fairly well & I think you judge him rather harshly'. Montagu's personal attitude to Judaism, in particular, showed 'the man to have a less sordid side than you & doubtless many other people give him credit for'.[125] Reiterating support for Curtis, who had been made 'one of the villains of your piece', Chirol maintained that he knew 'no one for whose character & ability & absolute single-mindedness of purpose I have a greater respect & admiration'.[126] Like Chirol Curtis was disturbed about the 'determined effort' by the reactionaries to get the report 'shelved', in particular the *Morning Post* and the *Spectator*, where Strachey 'seems completely to have lost his balance'.[127]

11   John St Loe Strachey

Strachey's opposition reflected not only his scepticism regarding the possibility of Eastern people governing themselves (about which he remained 'absolutely impenitent',[128]) but his generally critical attitude *vis-a-vis* Lloyd George's administration, and he maintained that:

> it is no use merely to abuse Montagu, as I confess to have done, and as the *Morning Post* does so continually and, I think, so ably. After all, the people most to blame for Montagu's misdeeds are the people who keep him in office and give him the power to ruin us in India. It is the Government who are responsible. Montagu is not a curse that they have to bear because they cannot help it, but a purely voluntary piece of wickedness. They have not even the excuse that the Government would

fall if they turned him out for he has no following either in the Commons or in the country.[129]

Strachey reflected upon his *own* position when writing to Salisbury:

> I can find no words to express what I feel about the folly of Montaguism and the utterly reckless way in which the campaign for adopting the report is being conducted. Here again if the Unionist Party is going to support directly or indirectly, or not to protest against Montagu's Bolshevism in India, I cannot remain in the Party . . . From all I hear I and *The Spectator* are regarded in Ministerial circles as 'Untouchables', owing to my having criticised Lloyd George.[130]

Sydenham's articles on the 'true side' for the *Spectator*, which was 'very largely read in India and by old Anglo-Indians here', would, Strachey contended, 'at once meet with a grateful echo'.[131] Strachey's position was derived from no direct personal experience, as he admitted – 'I know nothing of India' – but he claimed that his knowledge of 'human nature and of the man in the field and the street' convinced him that 'of the two forms of knowledge the geographical is the least important'.[132]

However, Strachey's dislike of Montagu and the reforms was not motivated solely by general political considerations. Like Sydenham, Maxse and Gwynne, Strachey was an anti–Semite. As he noted in August 1918:

> I used to be very proud as a young man of not being antisemitic, but those illusions have gone. The Jew is always in a state of terror, but oddly enough at the same time always believes that if he is given scope enough he will be able to turn things to his own advantage. That is why in all revolutions Jews turn up and play almost invariably a bad part.[133]

On the issue of Indian finance, Strachey believed there was a Jewish conspiracy at the India Office, where Montagu's family was in control, a situation which was 'absolutely unpardonable'.[134] He was similarly hostile toward Hinduism:

> I do not see why we should not take off the gloves and have a really strong clear article dealing with a good many of the horrors and cruelties of native worship and tell the truth . . . about certain sections and developments of Brahmanism. . . . The British mind always imagines that people who talk philosophy and deal with abstractions are necessarily virtuous. I think it would be a very good thing to disabuse the public of the notion of the pious Hindoo.[135]

Strachey believed that a Brahmin oligarchy was stirring up political agitation in order to secure dominance, and while he could 'consent to leaving India . . . the one thing I can never consent to is holding down the victim – the unfortunate ryot and still more unfortunate "Untouchable" – while the Brahmin cuts his throat, pillages his pockets, and debauches him body and soul'.[136] The Indo-British Association and the *Spectator* co-operated in their opposition to the report through 1918. For instance, the Association's secretary, S. M. Edwardes, sought Strachey's advice on a pamphlet regarding 'little known and repulsive features of Brahmanic Hinduism'.[137] Copies of the *Spectator* were distributed by the Association within India, including the European Associations in Calcutta, Madras and Rangoon, as well as the South Indian People's Federation, Monghyr Loyalists' League and Deccan Ryots' Association. In this manner the impact of the weekly extended beyond its British readership to reach varied sections of Indian opinion.

Official analysis

Montagu was determined to secure the most favourable coverage possible for his reforms. 'Whether,' he wrote to the Viceroy, 'we are disappointed or not, I hold the opinion that it is more than desirable to take every step possible to prevent public opinion criticising on unreasonable grounds.' He felt that the difficulty, both in Britain and in India, was that their scheme was 'so moderate, so cautious, so like the elephant . . . in its steady march, that it is difficult to secure that enthusiastic assistance which is necessary to carry through a thing of this sort'.[138] The generally positive response within India testified, he believed, to the importance of personal initiative in pushing forward pro-reform publicity. For instance, it was 'more than coincidence that the report seems to have gone better in Calcutta and the Central Provinces than elsewhere. Is this not due to the attitude of Ronaldshay and Robertson?' In responding to press attack Montagu recommended that:

> Articles criticising in newspapers should, I think, be answered not in the shape of condemnatory argument, but of reasoned answer to criticism. For example, where a paper describes the scheme as a broken pledge, pledge should be set out and demonstration should be given of how the scheme fulfills it.[139]

There was consensus at the India Office that 'the reception we have received here indicates that we can possibly get what we propose, but there is no likelihood of getting more'.[140] So far as Montagu could see, criticism was:

> mainly based upon the principle of the thing, the wickedness of relaxing British control over Indian affairs, the horror of giving Asiatics

control over their own country, and so forth, and even those who criticise the details of the scheme really in the main are against the principle even when they don't say so.[141]

Sydenham and Hewett's use of the press was a constant source of irritation. They were 'typical of the old fashioned Civil Servant, of great efficiency and no soul . . . certain in his assumption of superiority, despising all alternative methods . . . and desiring above all to keep India as a crystallised fruit unchanging and unchanged'.[142] He admitted that the reforms were far from an accomplished fact: 'we are playing our fish and have got to play it with patience and with industry for many a month to come. You may rely upon me to keep a tight line. I am having great difficulties!'[143] Here Montagu was being characteristically melodramatic, as the above account of Fleet Street's response illustrates. He admitted to Lord Willingdon, Governor of Madras, that the report had 'on the whole had as favourable a reception as could be expected in the circumstances'.[144]

Chelmsford, meanwhile, declared himself 'very well satisfied with the general tone' of the Indian press response in July.[145] He urged Montagu not to be discouraged by the more negative press notices, for it would be 'out of keeping with the Oriental mind to cease asking for more than it expects to receive'. The 'storm centre' Chelmsford believed would be 'at home, and you will have to meet the main bulk of the opposition'.[146] Chelmsford was 'certain that the attitude of the English Press and the English politicians will have a powerful effect in this country in moulding public opinion',[147] and wondered if Montagu could 'make arrangements to send messages, at reasonable intervals, through Reuter, in which pronouncements of leading men and journals on the Report are embodied? In order to discharge this function satisfactorily Reuter would need assistance.' Writing to Curtis at the end of July, Chelmsford analysed the general criticism thus:

> There are apparently two schools of thought among the extremists: that represented by the *Morning Post* which depicts Montagu as the villain of the piece and the Viceroy as his unfortunate victim who signed perforce against his will and better judgement; and that of the extreme Indians, who regard the sympathetic Secretary of State as having been caught in the meshes of the cold bureaucracy and made to put forward proposals alien from his thought and habit.[148]

'Your field of work,' he added, 'seems to lie among the former, who look only at the real and substantial advance and ignore the safeguards, or treat them as illusory and a sham. It is difficult with these folks to convince them of the imperative necessity of a change of spirit towards, and of co-operation with, the Indian.'[149]

Montagu, we have argued, perceived the importance of favourable publicity and newspaper coverage to the eventual success of his reforms. He saw, also, that the issue of reform could provide a catalyst for that wider emphasis upon communication and sensitivity to opinion which formed a significant element in his 'new angle of vision'. Two further factors made support from the national press crucial to the fate of his proposals. The first was the necessity of creating a political consensus in Britain. By gaining the support of the press, that of Parliament would be reinforced and an impression conveyed of wholehearted backing from the British nation. Pockets of conservative opposition would be isolated, with little opportunity of utilising the press to focus grievances. This, in itself, would strengthen the position of the Secretary of State and his reform strategy. But, equally important, an impression of unanimity was important to convince India of the good intent of the Raj and strengthen the moderates against the extremists, who would seize upon any expression of opposition in the British press as signifying the government's bad faith. In the words of a *Guardian* correspondent writing from India in July 1918:

> The opinion of the British press is of great importance at the present juncture. If India is reassured . . . of the reform scheme being the maximum concessions possible at the moment, the moderates will probably rally round the proposals. The extremists are quite irreconcilable.[150]

Did Montagu realise his objective? Broadly speaking, yes. The media accorded an essentially positive reception to the 1917 declaration and the subsequent report and Reform Bill. General (though not complete) Fleet Street approval reinforced parliamentary support for the measure, and this impression of solidarity strengthened the position of the government in India. Montagu and the reforms overcame their first, and most formidable, hurdle in 1917–18. One contemporary wrote of the:

> untiring pains which he took personally to persuade, convince, and even to cajole doubters or opponents, both British and Indian. He resented the Olympian airs of the government of India, and consulted Indian opinion as it had never been consulted before. If the scheme went through with goodwill, or at least acquiescence, it was largely due to the pertinacity, drive and determination with which the secretary of state had previously rallied the bulk of opinion to his side.[151]

If Roberts, a close collaborator of Montagu's, might be considered a biased source, the same could not be said of one of Montagu's fiercest critics, the *Spectator*. During the present conflict, noted a leader, Britain had been introduced to the value of 'publicity in waging war'. But the negative side of the case was:

[193]

that the channels for conveying information may also be used unfairly
by those who control them for forming opinion. We do not know altogether what may have been going on in the business of popularising the
Montagu Report on Indian Reforms, but we do know that the chorus of
approval which is chanted by a large part of the Press has all the appearance of being prearranged.[152]

There was, the *Spectator* claimed, 'an enormous volume of opinion in
India against the Reforms', yet people in Britain had had no opportunity of becoming acquainted with it. The paper drew attention to the
'unusualness, if not the impropriety' of the interviews with government officials like S. P. Sinha which appeared in Fleet Street advocating the principles of the report. It bemoaned the fact that 'this kind of
one-sided controversy' had found its way into *The Times*, where
another long manifesto in praise of the scheme by Bhupendra Nath
Basu, a member of the Secretary of State's Council, had been published.[153] Sydenham pursued a similar line in the *Contemporary
Review*. There was 'no precedent for the procedure adopted', which
appeared 'manifestly irregular'.[154] The report was published 'before the
Government had considered its proposals; attempts were made in
advance to create a favourable atmosphere for its reception; Indian officials were induced publicly to support it, such action being forbidden
to British officials'. In short, an effort was being made 'to force the
hand' of government and Parliament in order to secure the passage of
'a revolutionary measure'.[155] Ironically, the very vociferousness of such
complaints testifies to the success of the official publicity measures
initiated by the Secretary of State.

It is instructive here to consider a discussion of such official tactics
which appeared in the *Statesman* (Calcutta) a liberal Anglo-Indian
paper which was often critical of the government. 'A notable
innovation,' it remarked, distinguishing discussion of the Montagu–
Chelmsford proposals from those of former projects, was 'the active
official propaganda carried on in favour of the scheme'.[156] When Morley
and Minto propounded their reforms:

> the public were left to form their own judgement on their merits, aided
> only by the debates in Parliament, in which all points of view were
> presented, and by a free discussion on the platform and in the press.
> This was the old way of legislation. But in the case of the Montagu–
> Chelmsford scheme all the arts of modern publicity have been employed.
> Sedulous care has been taken to secure what is known as a 'good
> press'.

In an astute analysis of the position of Fleet Street, the *Statesman*
continued:

The business of advance agents . . . has been well done. The *Observer* and the *New Statesman*, some time before the Report was published, came out with quite intelligent anticipations of its contents, and no higher critic would have the slightest hesitation in concluding that their predictions were based upon a disclosure of the essential features of the scheme. What indiscreet person thus revealed the secret is, of course, a mystery, but it may safely be said that he was no enemy of Mr Montagu, for the two journals prematurely initiated showed their gratitude by a judicious eulogy of the scheme as the only possible compromise between doing nothing and doing too much. With two exceptions, the London newspapers as a whole seem to have come into line, the Montagu line . . . We live in an age of advertisement, the age of the Harmsworths . . . Thus is the public in India and in England being brought to believe that the one and only cure for Indian political congestion and internal unrest is the celebrated Montagu–Chelmsford mixture, based on the prescription of the famous Mr Curtis.

The months prior to the formal passage of the Constitutional Act in December 1919 saw further discussion of details and adjustments to the overall structure of the proposals. Cotton in the *Contemporary Review* celebrated Montagu's 'driving energy, the boundless enthusiasm, the intense devotion to Liberal principles, and the deep knowledge of Indian questions'. Though being 'venomously and scurrilously attacked', he had 'weathered every storm'.[157] During 1919 the issue of reform was to become entangled with the far more contentious tragedy of Amritsar and the Hunter Commission. There occurred, nevertheless, in the years 1914–18 an almost unprecedented closing of ranks among political parties in their support for Indian reform. This political consensus ultimately carried the day. As the Conservative MP J. D. Rees remarked during the final passage of the Act, 'We are all Radicals now, the whole of us.'[158]

Notes

1 S. Char (ed.), *Readings in the Constitutional History of India* (Delhi, 1983), p. 457.
2 R. J. Moore, 'Curzon and Indian reform', *MAS*, 27: 4 (1993), 719.
3 J. M. Brown, *Modern India: Origins of an Asian Democracy* (Oxford, 1985), pp. 197–8; P. Robb, 'British Cabinet and Indian reform, 1917–1919', *JICH*, 4: 3 (1976), 331; A. Rumbold, *Watershed in India, 1914–22* (1979), p. 322; P. Woods, 'Montagu–Chelmsford reform (1919): a reassessment', *South Asia*, 17: 1 (1994), 42.
4 Secretary of State to Viceroy, 3 August, 21 September 1917, MC/1.
5 Secretary of State to Viceroy, 21 September 1917, MC/1.
6 Secretary of State to Viceroy, 6 September 1917, MC/1.
7 *Nation*, 25 August 1917.
8 *National Review*, November 1917.
9 *Daily Chronicle*, 21 August, *Observer* 26 August, *Daily News*, 21 August 1917.
10 *Westminster Gazette*, 21 August, *Manchester Guardian*, 18 August, *Daily Mail*, 21 August 1917.

11 *Morning Post*, 21 August 1917.
12 *Daily Mail*, 21 August 1917.
13 *Westminster Gazette*, 21 August 1917.
14 *Daily Mail*, 21 August 1917.
15 *Manchester Guardian*, 21 August 1917.
16 *Times*, 21 August 1917.
17 *Times*, 22 August 1917.
18 *Daily Express*, 21 August 1917.
19 *Manchester Guardian*, 22 August 1917.
20 Secretary of State to Viceroy, 16 May 1918, MC/2.
21 Secretary of State to Viceroy, 31 May 1918, MC/2.
22 Viceroy to Dawson, 17 May 1918, CC/15.
23 Secretary of State to Viceroy, 15 June 1918, MC/2.
24 *Ibid.*
25 *Fortnightly Review*, May 1918; *Daily Herald*, 18 May 1918; *Manchester Guardian*, 15 June 1918. Singh: freelance journalist.
26 *Manchester Guardian*, 1 July 1918.
27 *Times*, 6, 7 June 1918.
28 *Times*, 8 June 1918.
29 *Observer*, 16 June 1918.
30 *Ibid.*
31 *Daily News*, 28 June 1918.
32 *Morning Post*, 17 June 1918.
33 *Morning Post*, 19, 22 June 1918.
34 *Observer*, 23 June 1918.
35 *Times*, 24 June 1918.
36 *Spectator*, 27 April 1918.
37 *Spectator*, 29 June 1918.
38 Secretary of State to Viceroy, 3 July 1918, MC/2.
39 *Ibid.*
40 *Daily Herald*, 13 April 1918.
41 *Daily Herald*, 27 April 1918.
42 *Daily Herald*, 15 June 1918.
43 Secretary of State to Willingdon, 4 July 1918, MC/16.
44 Secretary of State to Viceroy, 8 July 1918, MC/2.
45 *Ibid.*
46 Secretary of State to Willingdon, 4 July 1918, MC/16.
47 Secretary of State to Viceroy, 15 July 1918, CC/9; Secretary of State to Willingdon, 26 July 1918, MC/16.
48 *Morning Post*, 5 July 1918.
49 *Morning Post*, 17, 30 July 1918.
50 *Morning Post*, 13 July 1918.
51 *Morning Post*, 10 July 1918.
52 *Daily Telegraph*, 6 July 1918.
53 *Ibid.*
54 *Westminster Gazette*, 6 July 1918.
55 *Daily Chronicle*, 6, 10 July 1918.
56 *Daily News*, 6 July 1918.
57 *Manchester Guardian*, 9 July 1918.
58 *Times*, 6,10 July 1918.
59 *Times*, 9, 11 July 1918. Forrest (1846–1926): professor, Elphinstone College.
60 *Times*, 24 July 1918.
61 *Daily Express*, 6 July 1918.
62 *Daily Mail*, 24 July 1918.
63 *Star*, 6 July 1918.
64 *New Statesman*, 13 July 1918.
65 *Nation*, 13 July 1918.

66 *Daily Herald*, 13, 20, 27 July 1918.
67 *Reynolds's News*, 14 July 1918.
68 *Observer*, 7 July 1918.
69 Secretary of State to Willingdon, 26 July 1918, MC/16.
70 *Spectator*, 13 July 1918.
71 *Ibid.*
72 *Ibid.*
73 *Spectator*, 20 July 1918.
74 *Ibid.*, also 27 July 1918.
75 *Saturday Review*, 13 July 1918.
76 Secretary of State to Viceroy, 7 August 1918, MC/2.
77 *Manchester Guardian*, 7 August 1918.
78 *Times*, 7, 19 August 1918; also *Daily Chronicle, Westminster Gazette, Daily News, Manchester Guardian*, 7 August 1918.
79 *Daily Express*, 7 August 1918.
80 *Times*, 9 August 1918.
81 *Times*, 10 August 1918. Morison (1863–1936): former professor, Mohammedan Anglo-Oriental College; Aligarh: member, Islington Commission.
82 *Daily Telegraph*, 7 August 1918.
83 *Morning Post*, 7 August 1918.
84 *Daily Herald*, 3 August 1918.
85 *Daily Herald*, 31 August 1918.
86 *Daily Herald*, 14 September 1918.
87 Secretary of State to Viceroy, 25 September 1918, MC/2.
88 *Ibid.*
89 Dawson to Viceroy, 5 November 1918, CC/15.
90 Secretary of State to Viceroy, 22 October 1918, MC/2.
91 Secretary of State to Viceroy, 25 September 1918, MC/2.
92 Secretary of State to Viceroy, 5 September 1918, MC/2.
93 Rumbold, *Watershed*, p. 121; Darwin, *Britain, Egypt*, p. 250.
94 Cited in Wilson, *Political Diaries*, p. 288. Sinha (1864–1928): 1919, Parliamentary Under Secretary of State; member, Imperial War Cabinet.
95 Secretary of State to Viceroy, 7 November 1918, MC/2.
96 J. Grigg, *Myths about the Approach to Indian Independence* (Austin TX, 1995), p. 14; J. Turner, *Lloyd George's Secretariat* (Cambridge, 1980), p. 138.
97 28 September 1918 (Wilson, *Political Diaries*, p. 307).
98 Dickinson to Kingston, 29 November 1918, Roderick Jones File, 1915–18, RA, (hereafter RJ).
99 Dickinson to Kingston, 11 September 1918, RJ.
100 Editor to Kingston, 11 July 1918, RJ.
101 W. L. Murray to H. C. Robbins, 4 October 1918, RJ.
102 Dickinson to Kisch, 4 October 1918, RJ.
103 17 July 1918, RJ.
104 Dickinson to Kingston, 22 July 1918, RJ.
105 Dickinson to Kisch, 26 November 1918, RJ.
106 *Times*, 17 July 1918.
107 *Ibid.*
108 Dickinson to Kingston, 18 July 1918, RJ.
109 *Ibid.*
110 Dickinson to Chirol, 9 November 1918, RJ.
111 *Ibid.*
112 Dickinson to Curtis, 24 June 1918, and Dickinson to Kingston, 1 October 1918, RJ.
113 Dickinson to Kisch, 1 October 1918, RJ.
114 Secretary of State to Viceroy, 22 October 1918, MC/2.
115 Kisch to Maffey, 2 October 1918, CC/15.
116 Kisch to Maffey, 13 July 1918, CC/15.

117 Dickinson to Kisch, 26 November 1918, RJ.
118 A. M. Gollin, *The* Observer *and J. L. Garvin, 1908–1914* (1960), p. 94.
119 *Ibid.*, p. 187.
120 Dawson to Viceroy, 28 January 1918, CC/15.
121 *Ibid.*
122 Dawson to Viceroy, 5 November 1918, CC/15.
123 Chirol to Strachey, 16 July 1918, S/4/9/13, SP.
124 *Ibid.*
125 Chirol to Strachey, 26 July 1918, S/4/9/13, SP.
126 *Ibid.*
127 Curtis to Viceroy, 2 September 1918, CC/15.
128 Strachey to Gorst, 24 May 1910, S/17/1/15(b), SP.
129 Strachey to Sydenham, 5 September 1920, S/13/18/7; Strachey to Morrison, 4 March 1918, S/22/2/4, SP.
130 Strachey to Salisbury, 6 September 1918, S/13/2/7, SP.
131 Strachey to Sydenham, 26 March 1918, S/13/18/4, SP.
132 Strachey to Hewett, 23 August 1918, S/22/2/12A, SP.
133 Strachey to Sydenham, 29 August 1918, S/13/18/4, SP.
134 *Ibid.*
135 Strachey to Sydenham, 12 July 1918, S/13/18/4, SP.
136 Strachey to Hewett, 23 August 1918, S/22/2/12A, SP.
137 Edwardes to Strachey, 27 July, 7 August 1918, S/22/2/11, SP.
138 Secretary of State to Viceroy, 15 July 1918, CC/9.
139 *Ibid.*
140 *Ibid.*
141 Secretary of State to Viceroy, 26 July 1918, MC/2.
142 Secretary of State to Viceroy, 10 October 1918, MC/2.
143 Secretary of State to Viceroy, 26 July 1918, MC/2.
144 Cited in Secretary of State to Viceroy, 4 July 1918, MC/16; 31 July 1918 MC/2.
145 Viceroy to Secretary of State, 10, 12 July 1918, CC/9.
146 Viceroy to Secretary of State, 13 July 1918, CC/4.
147 Viceroy to Secretary of State, 10 July 1918, CC/9.
148 Viceroy to Curtis, 26 July 1918, CC/15.
149 *Ibid.*
150 *Manchester Guardian*, 31 July 1918.
151 C. Roberts, 'Montagu', *DNB 1922–1930* (1937), p. 609.
152 *Spectator* 20 July 1918.
153 *Ibid.*
154 *Contemporary Review*, November 1918.
155 *Ibid.*
156 Viceroy to Secretary of State, 17 September 1918, enclosure B, MC/7.
157 *Contemporary Review*, December 1920.
158 Hansard, 5th series, 1919, 122, 800.

CHAPTER EIGHT

Managing the crisis? Fleet Street, government and the Jallianwallah Bagh massacre, 1919–20

Constituting the largest massacre of civilians in peacetime in the history of the British Empire, Jallianwallah Bagh marked the beginning of the end of British rule in India. While numerous studies of the massacre bear testimony to its importance, none has provided a thorough analysis of the reaction of the British press and of the government's efforts to shape the reporting of the massacre by Fleet Street.[1] These are significant omissions, since the expression of opinion in Britain is widely acknowledged to have been a decisive turning point in the alienation of Indians from the Raj. From an official perspective the months following the massacre saw an example of crisis management. In the case of reform, government had been able to provide a coherent picture of its policies, possessing discretion as to both content and presentation. In the aftermath of the massacre it was a question, less of *creating* press reactions, than of *controlling* them.

Initial Fleet Street reporting of the massacre

On 19 April London papers carried a brief India Office communiqué to the effect that: 'At Amritsar, on April 13, the mob defied the proclamation forbidding public meetings. Firing ensued, and 200 casualties occurred'. No distinction was made between the numbers killed and wounded. The news had in fact been released on the evening of 17 April, but the next day being Good Friday caused a publishing delay to Saturday, when traditional weekend lethargy contributed to the almost immediate death of the story. Since the Rowlatt *satyagraha* called by Gandhi in March, Delhi, Punjab, Bombay and other parts of the country had experienced sporadic violence and unrest. The Viceroy's declaration of a state of 'open rebellion' in the Punjab and the imposition of news censorship ensured that the portrayal of unrest in the press was based primarily on official telegrams, which referred to excesses committed but made little attempt to present an informed picture of the general situation. The circumstances of the killings were not questioned. Significantly even *India*, which might have been expected to have access to INC and indigenous sources of information, merely quoted a Reuters telegram dated Simla 14 April: 'At Amritsar the mob made another violent attack against the authorities, but the rebels were repulsed by the military, losing 200 in killed and wounded.'[2] This is not to imply that government repression in the Punjab went wholly unreported. News of government bombing in Gujranwallah, for instance, appeared in London, and was taken to indicate the extreme gravity of the situation. Yet Jallianwallah Bagh itself was largely absent from the news.

In the Punjab complete press censorship had been imposed during April and May. This 'discriminative order' was calculated, according to the *Bombay Chronicle*, 'to produce pro-Government versions of the trouble ... If the Indian press had not been gagged, we should have had more of the truth.'[3] The *Civil and Military Gazette* was employed to carry official announcements, and coverage in other Anglo-Indian papers was in the main confined to official information. Of the five with overseas editions, only the *Englishman's Overland Mail* carried a graphic, if still brief, report on 23 April (datelined Lahore, 15 April):

AMRITSAR MOB MEETING DECLINES TO DISPERSE
GENERAL GIVES ORDER TO FIRE
HEAVY CASUALTIES

An attempt to hold a proscribed meeting at Amritsar was frustrated after the arrest of some ringleaders. The General with only Indian troops and police gave the order to disperse. As the crowd refused the order to fire was given. There were heavy casualties amongst the mob, several hundreds being killed and injured. There was no further trouble.

This did not add substantially to earlier reports and failed to stir press interest, being submerged within general accounts of unrest. However except for the severity of the casualties, it was erroneous in important respects and compounded earlier misconceptions. Thus while the first message of 19 April claimed that the peaceful gathering in the Bagh was a 'rioting mob' that had come into 'collision' with the troops, this later report incorrectly suggested that the general had given the order to disperse before firing. Even at the time of Montagu's Commons speech on the disturbances on 22 May, details of the massacre were absent from Fleet Street. There was merely a reference to Montagu's statement by *The Times* that the disorders 'cost the lives of 9 Europeans and of some 400 Indians'.[4] It also carried a full-page spread on 12 May recounting the most important events between 5 and 18 April which made no reference to Jallianwallah Bagh.

General press coverage of unrest, spring and summer 1919

The occurrence of violence so soon after India's loyal support in the war caused dismay in Fleet Street. The *Guardian* summed up the sense of bafflement:

> After presenting to the world, for close upon five years, an example of loyalty which is the most extraordinary phenomenon of its kind in the annals of empire, India has broken out in violent disorder which the Viceroy does not hesitate to describe as open rebellion. To the British public the contrast is inexplicable, and so complete has been the official silence, in regard to actual or impending trouble, that when news of the disturbances began to arrive ... the British public was no less puzzled than shocked.[5]

Why, after India's magnificent display of support, and when peace terms were being drawn up, was India inflamed?

War had seen severe economic burdens imposed on India, and the *Gazette, Daily News, Guardian* and *Observer* saw this as an important contributory factor.[6] The *Observer* claimed that there had been 'far too much secrecy' about India during the war: 'the British public seems unaware that ... high prices, new taxes, political ferment, and religious excitement have brought India into a more restless state than has prevailed for twenty years'.[7] Politically, too, Indians had 'seen the British Raj shaken' and 'they know the limitations of Empire'.[8] The *Guardian* felt that the West was fighting a war in the name of liberty and self-determination and this was bound to have an impact upon an East 'in its turn absorbing a good deal of the potent doctrine and expecting its application to itself'.[9]

There was considerable discussion of the Rowlatt Acts (a result of the Sedition Committee report of Justice Rowlatt), with papers sharply divided as to its contribution to the disturbances. Rushed through between 6 February and 18 March 1919 against unanimous Indian opposition, the Acts attempted to make wartime restrictions on civil rights permanent through special courts, detention without trial, etc. The *Observer, Gazette, Daily News, Herald, Guardian, Nation* and *Chronicle* argued that, but for the Acts, the 'varied elements of disaffection could not have been united into so strong an insurgent force'.[10] The Acts were widely seen as 'an intolerable extension of coercive rule at a time when India, having given a marvellous exhibition of loyalty to the Empire during the war, is preparing for peace and for the adoption of a great scheme of constitutional reconstruction'.[11] 'We should,' wrote Spender, 'have supposed that a sagacious government would at such a moment have done its utmost to forget past quarrels and remember present benefits.'[12] The *Nation* felt that to bring the Acts into force as a response to India's war effort was 'like giving scorpions to hungry children who were promised food'.[13] *Reynolds's* was convinced that the policy of 'talking reforms but practising coercion' was chiefly responsible for the combustion of readily inflammable material.[14]

In contrast to the bulk of Fleet Street, a minority of papers, led by the *Morning Post*, saw the unrest as a direct consequence of the Montagu–Chelmsford reforms, which had deliberately set out to disturb '"the pathetic contentment of the masses"'. Rowlatt's recommendations had been distorted by Indian politicians who had 'spread about among the people all manner of lies and calumnies well calculated to inflame ignorance, to panic and outrage'. The result of that agitation was 'the murder of a number of innocent people, who have been sacrificed on the altar of constitutional reform'.[15] The *Times* and the *Mail* agreed with the *Morning Post* in arguing against attributing to the Acts the major share of blame for the unrest.[16] The *Times* contended it was a mere pretext for the 'organised hostility'. The rising was in essence 'a deliberate attempt to overturn British rule altogether'.[17] The 'tentacles of the conspiracy' extended far beyond India, and its 'secret leaders' were 'now unquestionably in touch with the Russian Bolshevist movement'.[18]

The *Herald* emphasised the comparative aspects of the case, with India taking its place alongside the demands of Egypt for the Egyptians and Irish Home Rule. Comparable parallels were drawn by other papers, including the *Chronicle*, *Daily News*, *Guardian*, *Gazette*, *New Statesman* and *Observer*. The *Guardian* saw similarities between prewar and current disorders in Egypt and India. In both, earlier agitations were confined to a small educated elite, whereas now they covered a large area and embraced almost all sections of the population. The *New Statesman*'s correspondent noted how there had 'never been this calculated display of sympathy between the two religions, this ostentatious breaking down – if only for the occasion – the barriers that separate them'.[19] This Hindu–Muslim fraternisation was considered a portentous development by both Liberal and Conservative papers,[20] and the Mutiny syndrome was often to the fore. The participation of Sikh agitators, however, marked a significant change – though precisely how far 'sedition' had permeated the Sikhs had still to be determined.[21]

Measures of response

Although papers across the political spectrum agreed that the restoration of order was imperative, there was little consensus on the
methods to be employed. The *Express* argued against 'Any kind of tem-
porising', since the 'suspicion of weakness might lead to violence
recalling the horrors of the Mutiny. We hold India by the sword, and
we are there to rule and govern for the benefit of all.'[22] In contrast the
Herald referred to 'Britain's Iron Heel in India and Egypt' and
the deployment of 'Prussian Methods where Union Jack is waning'.[23]
The *Nation* was amazed that no protest had been heard in Parliament
'against the use of aeroplanes against defenceless and unarmed
people'[24] and complained about the delays in reporting such actions.[25]

Predictably, amongst left-wing critics of the government there
was a demand for the immediate repeal of the Rowlatt Acts. The
Herald mounted a vociferous campaign. It condemned official policy
of attempting to 'repress Nationalism by alternate promises of future
good government and repressive laws of a most autocratic character'.[26]
Coercion and conciliation could never go hand in hand, and the paper
appealed to the Labour movement to:

> insist on all this pernicious legislation being withdrawn, and the people
> of India allowed the very fullest right of Free Speech, Free Press, and –
> greatest of all – the right of self-determination, on behalf of which so
> many sons of India fought and died in Europe and Asia.[27]

A large meeting in London on 7 April was addressed by Tilak and
Lansbury, as well as the Labour MPs Colonel Wedgewood and V. H.
Rutherford. The *Herald* commended a Labour motion in the
Commons to suspend the Acts.[28]

Despite the disturbances, the consensus regarding the need for
reform was broadly maintained. Discussions of the on-going process –
the committee proceedings, the visit of Indian delegates to London,
and the movement of the Bill through Parliament – occurred in almost
all papers. The Liberal *Gazette* urged the government not to repeat the
mistakes it had made in Ireland, where a golden opportunity for settlement had been missed by 'coupling the promise of Home Rule with
the threat of Conscription'.[29] Similarly the Unionist *Observer* insisted
that 'we have no right to plant another Ulster in India, nor allow sheer
fanaticism to impede a just policy'.[30] The Fabian *New Statesman*
agreed with the *Express* that 'Restoration of order, followed by a mag-
nanimous measure of reform, is the road to safety'. 'It would,' the
Express continued, be 'a bankrupt statesmanship that failed to press
forward reforms of which the urgency is nowhere questioned.'[31] The

Guardian contended that 'the physician is not deterred from treating the roots of a disease by the virulence of the symptoms'.[32] And *The Times* claimed that 'Whatever may occur now in India, spacious reforms continue to be imperatively required. Rebellion may check the introduction, but the need remains.'[33]

Government news management and control prior to December 1919

Even before the massacre criticism had been mounting in the press regarding delayed and censored news from India. A leader in *The Times* on 10 April complained that:

> Because government business chokes the cables, Press messages are often delayed for several days. The consequence is that the Nile might change its course, or India might be riven asunder by earthquakes, and no one in Great Britain outside Government Departments would have the smallest knowledge of what had happened for a week or more.

Citing the recent riots in Delhi, the public, it claimed, 'knew nothing' until *The Times* published a telegram nine days later.

> We do not know why Mr Montagu is so fearful lest any news about India should reach this country . . . Mr Montagu's whole policy in the matter of publicity is arousing, even among those anxious to support him, the most unwelcome suspicion of his methods.

The paper warned that 'we cannot have Mr Montagu bottling up information about India in time of peace'.[34] This was a notable indictment of Montagu by a paper which had been generally sympathetic to his administration. A possible explanation can be found in the fact that Wickham Steed had replaced Dawson as editor. Steed knew little about the subcontinent, being a specialist on Eastern Europe. Chelmsford had expressed concern at this development, noting that Dawson was 'a staunch supporter and I sincerely hope his departure will not mean an alteration in the Indian policy of that paper. We want all the friends we have and cannot afford to lose any of them.'[35] The editorial in *The Times* appeared to justify his concern.

Yet, while papers accused Montagu of deliberately withholding news from India, he was himself complaining about delays in his receipt of information. He was, for instance, frustrated by accusations of duplicity made by Fleet Street in connection with the Afghan War which broke out in May 1919.

> I find it very difficult to fulfil to the public satisfaction the task of news purveyor which seems to be expected of a Secretary of State in these

days . . . Unofficial messages are so delayed; I don't like to publish news which you may wish to withhold or which may prove to be unauthentic, and it has been found therefore very difficult to give an account of what is happening in Afghanistan in proper consecutive order from day to day. I have been somewhat upbraided in the papers.[36]

Following press criticism of the conduct of the campaign, Montagu held that Reuters was to blame for sending 'nothing helpful from India for home consumption and a good deal that was positively harmful'. Chelmsford assured him that the matter had been 'brought to the notice of . . . Buck, and I hope there will be an improvement. Buck's special agents employed on the frontier were not men of a good stamp. . . . Spiciness certainly came before truth.'[37]

The Amritsar massacre therefore occurred amidst a background of official as well as press concern with the flow of information from India. How soon was Montagu informed as to the *full* gravity of the situation? Chelmsford wrote to Montagu three days after the massacre, giving a general impression of the disturbances, and simply noting, 'Amritsar had a very severe lesson the other day at the hands of the Military, but it remains to be seen how far it will have been efficacious.'[38] The cables received at the India Office from the Indian Home Department provided minimal details. A telegram dated 15 April from the government in India to the India Office was received 17 April and stated: 'In parts of the districts of Amritsar and Lahore a state of open rebellion exists'. 'At Amritsar there was defiance on the 13th of a proclamation forbidding public meetings, and it was necessary to fire on the mob, 200 casualties resulting'. Another, dated 17 April, read: 'Further particulars show that 50 Sepoys faced unlawful assembly numbering 5,000. Sepoys fired with salutary effect. Casualties reported were deaths.'[39] Summaries of these and other viceregal telegrams were regularly issued to Fleet Street. Yet that the Government of India was already in possession of greater information is suggested by the evidence to the Hunter committee of J. P. Thompson, Secretary to the Government of Punjab. Asked when the government first learnt that Dyer 'had gone to the meeting and had fired at once and without warning and continued to fire for a considerable time', Thompson answered, 'I think that must have been at about 3 or 4 in the morning of the 14th.'[40]

A crucial factor underlying official reticence in the release of information to London was the stance adopted by Chelmsford and the Indian government to the unrest. A policy of repression was combined with active suppression of news within India. In Punjab martial law was enforced *de facto* from 10 April and *de jure* from 13 April. Ralph Verney, Military Member of the Viceroy's Council, who was holidaying in Ceylon, heard nothing of the details of the unrest, such news being 'absolutely censored here'.[41] Rushbrook Williams admitted in the *Moral and Material Progress Report* that 'As long as the situation remained serious, there had been a rigorous censorship on the publication of the news concerning the Punjab' and that martial law had 'been employed in a manner which certainly did not facilitate communication between the Punjab and the rest of India'.[42] Martial law was lifted only on 11 June. Besides the perceived security imperative behind the control of reporting was concern with the public image of official actions. Writing to Michael O'Dwyer, Governor of Punjab, the Viceroy recommended that publicity relating to flogging incidents 'should be avoided as far as possible', requesting him to consider 'editing Press messages', as 'References to people being cowed and sullen and so forth do more harm than good.'[43] Thompson also described how pre-publication censorship was imposed in Lahore to prevent 'exaggerated accounts' in the press.[44]

An indication of the extent to which the government was prepared to suppress reporting in India was the deportation in April of Horniman, the English editor of the *Bombay Chronicle* who had been denouncing official repression. George Lloyd, the Governor of Bombay, noted how Horniman was publishing 'very inflammatory articles' causing 'serious reaction in public feeling in favour of lawlessness'.[45] The Viceroy explained to Montagu that such 'propaganda' was likely to cause a 'recrudescence' of the recent troubles and 'foment discontent among the troops' by the free distribution of his paper.[46] Samples of Horniman's writings were sent to London, including an editorial written on 23 April, entitled 'Dangerous secrecy', which accused the government of 'exercising horrid and detestable powers of torture and terrorisation'.[47] Chelmsford's concern to protect his government's actions from misrepresentation thus impacted on the nature of news sent home. Like Montagu, he was especially alert to the effect of press reports on the attitude to reform in London.[48] Such concern was also evident with respect to the United States. The British Bureau of Information in New York was warned about 'seditious Indian propaganda', and some effort was made to publish articles in the *New York Times* explaining the official point of view.[49] Chelmsford stressed the need for 'counter-propaganda' which had been 'forcibly impressed upon us by the sympathy evoked among the American public by the persistent and malignant misrepresentation of our administration in the American Press' by Mrs Besant, the Ghadr party and men like Lajpat Rai and Hyndman. 'False ideas of our work and methods are widely disseminated, the dangers of which to the Indian Administration are self-evident.'[50]

The *Report on the Native Papers* supplied regularly to the India Office made no mention of Jallianwallah Bagh. On 21 May the Viceroy telegraphed Montagu with estimates of casualties at Delhi, Amritsar, Lahore, Ahmedabad and Calcutta, citing a figure for deaths of 'six or nine Europeans and about 400 Indians' and of wounded: 'Europeans not known and Indians about 400'.[51] During the formal statement on unrest in the Commons, on 22 May, Montagu did mention a total of 400 fatalities, but given that this figure represented the total number for disturbances lasting several months, it did not appear exceptional and failed to arouse suspicion. Whether this manner of presentation was a deliberate attempt at concealment is impossible to say with certainty, but it appears likely that Montagu's stance was disingenuous, given the extent of India Office knowledge and the fact that an inquiry had been promised.

Yet, in general, there was a marked divergence of opinion between Montagu and Chelmsford over the nature and principles underlying British rule in India which the unrest and massacre brought to the fore.[52] Reacting to Rowlatt's recommendations in autumn 1918, Montagu, while wanting to help 'stamp out rebellion and revolution', 'loath[ed]' the suggestion of preserving the Defence of India Act in peacetime to the extent Rowlatt thought necessary.[53] Now he took a strong stand against Dyer and the repressive policies of the Punjab and central governments. Dyer's crawling orders he found 'reprehensible': 'I think you should relieve him of his command at once and send him home,' Montagu suggested to the Viceroy in early June.[54] Chelmsford, however, defended the conduct of his officials and claimed that Dyer had 'saved the situation from being infinitely worse ... An error of judgement should not bring down upon him a penalty which would be all out of proportion to the offence.'[55] It was 'not a case of defending O'Dwyerism' but of 'supporting constituted authority and officials who had a very great responsibility put upon them'.[56] Reacting to Montagu's criticism of the continuing proscription of newspapers and banning of public meetings, Chelmsford argued that conditions had been 'abnormal' and:

> some restraint upon wilder newspapers, which were grossly misrepresenting position in Punjab, and attributing unworthy motives, was inevitable. Deliberate misrepresentation rather than bad arguments has been feature of Press campaign. Recent experience has shown with painful clearness immense difficulties of allowing misrepresentations to be addressed unchecked to ignorant and uncritical audiences ... but Government with its limited staff of officers ... cannot expect by defensive means alone to counteract successfully persistent and extensive campaign of misrepresentation.[57]

Montagu took the initiative in pushing for a commission on the disturbances, and the official correspondence bears witness to its importance in his eyes.[58] Yet it was the case, also, that the appointment of a commission had important political advantages. If he had unilaterally condemned Dyer or attempted to have him dismissed, Montagu would have been censured for prejudging the issue without the accused being heard. On the other hand if he had appeared to ignore or minimise the gravity of the situation, he might have jeopardised moderate Indian politicians who were crucial to the success of his reforms. 'To avoid both risks and develop a joint resolution,' writes Fein, 'what better method was there than to appoint a committee composed of official Britishers and Indians?'[59] Especially if, as Brown notes, 'he had no idea that it would reveal anything that would embarrass the government'.[60] Chelmsford agreed to an inquiry, but stressed that it would be possible only after the re-establishment of order, and Montagu felt compelled to support his Viceroy's stance in Parliament.[61] The Indian government had little cause to welcome a high-profile inquiry, and once the Hunter committee was set up it increasingly hid behind the legalism of *sub judice* to avoid commenting on the unrest.

Montagu's personal commitment to a full and open inquiry cannot be doubted. The evidence he had received confirmed him in the opinion that were it not for the inquiry 'I should have had to take serious official action'.

> Don't let us make the mistake of defending O'Dwyerism right or wrong. Nothing is so fatal to British prestige in a developing country like India than a belief that there is no redress for mistakes and that, whatever an official does, he will be backed.[62]

Montagu stressed similar ideas to Justice Hunter: 'You may find men and newspapers anxious to lead you past alleys which you should explore in order that you may be prevailed upon to "whitewash"'. The government had nothing 'to fear from searching enquiry', its object being to restore public confidence and present to the world the truth 'as to the causes of and the measures taken to cope with these occurrences'.[63] In addition, Montagu was convinced of the usefulness of making its proceedings public, as they would provide the 'best antidote' to a 'rather persistent impression' in London that 'we have accepted the Enquiry with bad grace, and once it has been forced upon us, mean to turn it to our own account'.[64] Ironically it was precisely the revelations of such proceedings that were to result in widespread press and parliamentary criticism and accusations of government censorship in December 1919.

Dénouement, *December 1919*

It was eight months later, on Saturday 13 December, that the story resurfaced in Fleet Street with the arrival of mails describing the Hunter hearings that had taken place in November. The following days saw questions raised in the Commons regarding the newspaper disclosures: Montagu was firmly in the dock.

The *Express* was the first London paper to carry the story, and since its report appeared on Saturday it led the field till Monday. Even *The Times* was caught unawares. As Northcliffe remarked to Steed, 'We were badly beaten by the *Daily Express* and *The Manchester Guardian* in connection with the Amritsar happening'.[65] For the *Express* this was arguably its greatest scoop on India.

2,000 INDIANS SHOT DOWN
A GENERAL'S TERRIBLE REMEDY TO CURB REBELLION
HIS JUSTIFICATION
'I LOOKED ON IT AS A HORRIBLE DUTY'.

There followed a report on Dyer's testimony, as well as the following words as a boxed item:

'The publication of the Amritsar shooting was due to the enterprise of one special London journal, which always seems to be the best informed on Indian affairs. They collected this particular information, I suppose, from their correspondent at Allahabad, and what they printed was copied in the other newspapers'. – Mr Montagu, Secretary of State for India, in the House of Commons, yesterday. *The London journal referred to is the 'Daily Express'.*

The story was given front-page exposure in bold headlines during the week following, supplemented with pictures of Dyer. The *Express* also featured a photograph and interview with the convalescing Miss Sherwood, 'a cultured Englishwoman who had been beaten, bludgeoned, and triumphantly left for dead on the roadside by fanatical Indian revolutionaries'.[66] Taking up the story, most papers drew attention to the virtual absence of coverage during the intervening eight months – a discrepancy further highlighted by the puzzling absence of any telegraphic news.[67] Although Dyer gave evidence on 19 November, the first press reports appeared on 13 December and were based on Indian newspapers received by mail.

There were two major strands of criticism and comment. One pointed to news censorship and suppression; the other, focusing upon Montagu's Commons statements, questioned the nature of the relationship between the Secretary of State and the Government of India. With regard to the first, Fleet Street's condemnation was universal.

[209]

The *Nation*, for instance, noted that the April telegram from Simla had merely stated that there had been 200 casualties.

> There were, in fact, about 2,000 casualties, including over 400 killed. It appears then, that Lord Chelmsford or his subordinates have concealed the facts, not merely from the British public, but even from the responsible Minister himself.

As to the continued obstruction which prevented correspondents from cabling the evidence given before the committee, Montagu could 'hardly expect us to believe that it was due to congestion of the wires. The censorship is, evidently, still at work: wires may be congested by order.'[68] The *Nation*'s critique was matched in verve by the *Herald*, which provided a record of Montagu's statements from May to November to show how the massacre had not received more than passing reference. It was clear that:

> the man responsible for the government of India is not allowed to know anything about it by the culpable officials until nearly nine months after the event, he gathers his information from a newspaper. Only one meaning can be attached to this grave confession: the military in India must have deliberately kept Mr Montagu in ignorance of their crime.[69]

The *Guardian*'s initial coverage featured its correspondent's despatch from Punjab (dated 21 November), which contended that government reports were 'totally misleading, minimising the extent of the rebellion and the extent of the casualties'.[70] The paper concluded that 'few more dreadful incidents can be found in the history of British rule in India than the story of their suppression'.[71] *The Times* noted that while it was 'vaguely known' in April that 'severe measures' were taken to quell disturbances, it was 'certainly not known that an unarmed gathering which had met in an enclosed space' was shot at, with vast numbers killed. 'The public are shocked, not only by the occurrence itself, but also because this disclosure has only been made in Great Britain nine months after the event occurred.'[72] It was necessary to enquire why Montagu and Chelmsford:

> in their public statements and in the summaries offered to the Press, never made any allusion to what happened in this Amritsar garden. Not by any means for the first time, there appears to have been studious concealment of relevant facts; but perhaps Mr Montagu was not permitted to know the whole truth, because on May 29, and again on October 30, he made statements in the House of Commons at variance with the number of casualties now acknowledged.[73]

As far as could be ascertained, Montagu 'never received any detailed account' of Dyer's action:

How comes it that a British general can inflict nearly 2,000 casualties in an unarmed mob in the Punjab, without the full facts being forwarded within a reasonable time by the Viceroy to the Secretary of State? We have examined the whole of the Viceroy' s reports as transmitted to the Press in this country for publication, and they contain very little indication of what happened at Amritsar on the day in question.[74]

The Times's remarks caused consternation in India, especially since the paper had hitherto been seen as a staunch ally of the administration. Even the diehard Morning Post, the only London daily that was strongly pro-Dyer, admitted in December that it was 'a pity that the British public was not allowed to know all that happened'.[75]

Press response to the massacre: General Dyer and British policy

In general, press coverage responded to the event itself and its perpetrator, suggested means to ameliorate the crisis and reflected on the future lines of imperial policy. Several papers, including the Gazette, Nation and Herald, compared the incident to the atrocities committed by the Germans in Belgium. The 'sincerity' of Dyer was likened to that of Prussian soldiers and Bolsheviks. For the Observer it was 'humiliating' to turn after Louvain and Odessa to Amritsar for an illustration of the 'perils that abound when the power of government passes to the hands of a military fanatic, confident in his simple dogmas and knowing no other'.[76] 'What should we say if the things done in India, Egypt and Ireland had been in Belgium under German occupation?' questioned the Herald.[77] But, noted H. N. Brailsford, 'we were not at war with India. These people were our fellow citizens, the relatives of our Sikh comrades of the great war.[78] The Nation felt the possibility of like action in Ireland and Egypt: 'There are potential imitators of this man in many a mess-room in Indian, Egypt, and Ireland . . . What was done in Punjab, in April, may be repeated in Dublin to-morrow.'[79] Dyer was almost unanimously denounced on his own testimony. The Daily News claimed that the unarmed crowd was not asked to disperse, in Dyer's words, because '"they would have come back and laughed at me and I would have made what I consider a fool of myself"'.[80] The Times noted editorially, 'On his own showing, his conduct appears to us to be indefensible, and its worst feature was that he did not stop firing when the crowd instantly began to disperse.'[81]

For the Guardian it was because Dyer's action had violated the basic norms of British rule that it was to be deplored. The 'basis' and 'spirit' of the relations between the government and Indians were predicated upon the latter being treated 'as nearly as possible as we should treat our own people'. It was because the right of Indians appeared to have been 'in almost every particular violated' at Jallianwallah that 'we so profoundly regret that most deplorable incident'.[82] The *Herald* was appalled not only by the shooting but by the callous indifference exhibited towards the wounded and the infliction of humiliating punishments.

IMPERIAL ATROCITIES
Butchery of unarmed Punjab natives at angry General's order
'HE WOULDN'T BE LAUGHED AT'

In addition to the 'slaughter', thousands of 'our Indian brethren' had been flogged, interned, deported, and on the frontier bombed from the air.[83] The public impact of the events increased still further when photographs of government repression in the Punjab began to appear in early 1920.[84]

The main response of Fleet Street was to call for justice and the continuance of reform, as evidenced in the stance of the *Observer* and *Gazette*.[85] The *Nation* argued that 'We shall show ourselves as a nation unfit to rule if we pass this thing over lightly. To condone it, to minimise it, is to court its repetition... The British Empire would not survive many Amritsar massacres.'[86] The only major discordant note was struck by the *Morning Post*, which looked upon Dyer as a man who had saved British rule from 'a danger comparable only to the Indian Mutiny'.[87] Its page-length report on 30 December emphasised the numbers of Europeans killed and the terror within the English community. Dyer, it contended, had taken all possible measures to warn the people that public meetings were forbidden: 'In defiance of these orders a great meeting 5,000 strong was held'. The general was convinced that 'if he permitted this defiance his authority was set at naught and Amritsar would be lost'. The *Morning Post* concluded this spirited defence thus: 'We do not know; but we hope at least that the British public will do no injustice – and see that no injustice is done – to its brave servants who saved the British position in Northern India at Amritsar and Lahore last spring.'

Montagu and Fleet Street

Montagu wrote at once to the Viceroy on 13 December requesting the latest details regarding the number of casualties.[88] Dyer's evidence had caused 'great public perturbation, and I have my work cut out to urge suspension of judgement until the completion of Hunter's enquiry'.[89] It was not merely the numbers killed or wounded but the nature of Dyer's defence which had 'created a very strong and a very painful impression here'.[90] Criticism of Dyer's evidence was 'universal', wrote

Montagu at the end of year, 'and does not emanate from one section of the Press or one section of the public'.[91]

As discussed earlier, the majority of Fleet Street papers accused the government of censorship. The *Nation* had an insightful piece on the gravity of Montagu's position, having given Parliament

> an account of this capital event so false that it is passed over by the Press and public opinion as if it were an ugly street riot, suppressed without undue violence...I suppose the first thought about Mr Montagu's silence was that it was a tactical one; that he thought it better to be silent till the reform Bill was through. But Mr Montagu cuts this ground away. He says that he did not know. Now that he does know, will he and Lord Chelmsford remain in office together?[92]

Similar doubts were raised by speakers in the Commons on 16 December who questioned how such news was kept from the country for a period of eight months. Lord Robert Cecil asked whether the government had exercised censorship to prevent the telegraphing of the evidence, because it had only come by mail?[93] Montagu, in defence, reiterated that he had 'not received any detailed account, nor do I expect to do so' because the government, having agreed to set up an official committee, had now to await its findings. He also denied any official censorship, noting, 'The wires are very much congested, and it may have been for that reason that none of this evidence was telegraphed.'[94]

Montagu's position was difficult, given his dependence on Indian authorities for information. Though defending the government position in the Commons, he was worried. 'I want you to know that so far as I can judge...I did not understate the case when I told the House of Commons that I appreciated the profound disturbance which must have been caused in public opinion by the evidence published.'[95] Chelmsford remonstrated that such information as was available had been sent in a series of Home Department telegrams in April, May, August and September, and it was:

> difficult to see what ground there is for suggesting that we have in any way endeavoured to hush up the incidents at Amritsar. We have not censored any telegram going home and the only inference that one can draw is that Indian affairs do not interest the papers unless they can make some spicy capital out of them.[96]

He also informed Montagu that the casualty total was 379. The fact that martial law had been *de facto* introduced at least two days before the incident made it difficult to gauge events. On 10 September the Imperial Legislative Council had discussed the issue and Chelmsford argued that there had been 'no attempt' in its proceedings to 'min-imise' the number of casualties, nor to 'avoid publicity or conceal facts'.[97] Chelmsford's concern at press reception at home was governed partly by a desire to clear his name and partly by a recognition of the impact that the reporting would have on Indian political opinion, as public reaction to Dyer's evidence had 'received considerable stimu-lus from recent references in Parliament and Home Press'. The *Times* correspondent in India noted, too, how Montagu's statements and the

> comments of the English newspapers, notably The Times, continue to be the subject of strongly worded articles in the British-edited Press . . . the Pioneer asserting that the comments of the home Press have aroused a bitter feeling of resentment among Englishmen in India.[98]

An added twist to the controversy concerning the extent of Montagu's knowledge of the massacre was provided by O'Dwyer, who claimed that he had detailed discussions with the Secretary of State while in London on 30 June and 24 July, when 'we went over all the main facts of Dyer's action at Amritsar, and the impression I then formed was that the India Office knew as much about all the material facts as I did'.[99] In a dramatic move, O'Dwyer outlined his case in a letter to *The Times*.[100]

Yet India Office records lend support to Montagu's claim that he was not kept *promptly* and *fully* informed about events in general, includ-ing the Hunter hearings. He repeatedly complained to New Delhi: 'May I ask you if serious steps cannot be taken by you to provide me with better information regarding what is going on in India? I get no news . . . You will see, if you will turn up the fortnightly telegrams which your Home Department sends me how meagre is my information as to events in India.'[101] He remonstrated again two days later: 'there is some defect in organisation which prevents my getting from you current news of important events in the way I should like to get it, and should have expected to get it'. He was perturbed at having to rely on press telegrams.[102] The initial telegrams in the summer of 1919, as examined earlier, carried the minimum of detail. Montagu himself reminded the Viceroy that 'in one of your letters you have told me that you deli-berately minimised the situation in the Punjab because you did not wish unduly to alarm public opinion at home'.[103] Similarly, Montagu received the official telegraphic report of Dyer's evidence only on 19 December – an amazing instance when mails taking a minimum of three weeks by sea arrived six days before the electric telegraph!

The exposures in the London press forced the government's hand. Montagu pleaded with Chelmsford to be sent sufficient copies of Hunter's report 'for immediate publication . . . public opinion is very much inflamed and extremely difficult to keep steady'.[104] Publication of Dyer's evidence was thus a *coup* for Fleet Street. Montagu admitted in Parliament that he derived his first knowledge of the hearings from the press, but this failed to allay suggestions of censorship and official duplicity. The manner and timing of release gave the disclosures an impact especially damaging to a publicity-conscious India Office and overshadowed coverage of the final passage of the Constitutional Act through Parliament. As the *Morning Post* remarked, 'now the British public is suddenly treated to the most lurid part of the story of suppression without any adequate description of the events which led up to it'.[105]

January–July 1920: a summer of reaction

India Office information management

Reporting of the Hunter committee hearings continued throughout the early weeks of 1920. Montagu remained perturbed. 'Hardly a newspaper,' he wrote, 'has raised a voice in whole-hearted defence of what took place.'[106] It would have to be a convincing report to reassure opinion in Britain. Chelmsford was especially concerned as Indian newspapers largely took their cue from the home press, and he believed that it was by the opinion of the British public that his government would be judged. Thus the 'extremist' press continued to give 'great prominence' to Amritsar 'reprinting *in extenso* articles appearing in English papers, e.g., *Westminster Gazette, Times, Daily News, Daily Herald, Truth* and *Star*'.[107]

In Montagu's estimation the situation required sustained government publicity, the necessity for which was 'as pressing at present as it was at any time'.[108] In general, he explained, 'You have no conception of how large a part propaganda has come to play, and I feel so strongly about its necessity in India. It should be done by negotiation, by interviews and by ever-patient explanation, by leaflet, by speeches, by newspaper.'[109] As the publication of the Hunter report approached, Chelmsford wished to send Rushbrook Williams to Britain to assist the India Office in its attempts to manage press response. It was also, Chelmsford argued:

> most important to try to induce British newspapers to establish better-informed agencies in India for the transmission of Indian news and comments thereon. The whole reputation of British rule in India in present conditions suffers from ill-informed and biased comments.[110]

Williams, who was to leave at the end of February with an advance copy of the report, would be

12   L. F. Rushbrook Williams

of great assistance in securing from British Press a fair presentation of
report and impartial treatment of such portions of it as may support
action of civil and military authorities in this country. In view of the
way in which the British Press has been stampeded on this subject by
efforts of Indian extremists, I feel strongly that unless some effort of this
kind is made on our behalf, the case of our officers is likely to go by
default, and the result would be most unfortunate. Williams has special
qualifications for the task, a vigorous pen and a considerable acquaintance in English journalistic circle.[111]

Montagu, however, doubted the expediency of the proposal. While it
was understandable that Chelmsford should be 'anxious to develop
propaganda by means of your own accredited agent which will prevent
or modify criticism of your Government's conduct and action' in
America and England, he warned the Viceroy:

do not delude yourself into thinking that the British Press has been stampeded by any Indian views on the Punjab enquiry. The view of the English Press has been formed perhaps prematurely by public accounts telegraphed from India and reports in Indian newspapers sent by mail to this country of the evidence . . . you will not be able to concert an adequate policy with me if you do not realise the profoundly disturbing effect of this evidence and if you dismiss it as the work of the Indian Extremists.[112]

Montagu was also concerned at Williams's absence from India, given that he was the Director of Publicity. The Viceroy reassured Montagu regarding the dual purpose of Williams's visit. The general object was to establish contacts with the newspaper world in America and England 'without which not only is external propaganda not possible, but internal propaganda is also beginning to be seriously handicapped'. The 'special' purpose was 'to secure with your assistance a fair presentation in the home press of our decision' on the Hunter report. He acknowledged that Dyer's evidence, by itself, had:

created a great deal of public feeling and we do not attribute it to the extremist press except that we feel that the information conveyed by that press has been directed to one side of the question only and at a time when the difficulties of the situation in April are no longer remembered. We want to publish the whole case as defined in the report of the Commission and to secure a fair presentment of all the facts.[113]

It was in this connection that Williams's deputation promised to be useful, especially if Montagu 'could associate with him some influential Pressmen at home'.[114] While Montagu claimed to appreciate Chelmsford's objectives:

I regard myself as the proper person to explain to the British Press the action on the Report which will be combined with action of His Majesty's Government and the Government of India; the pressmen are known to me and no visitor from India can know them sufficiently well. I shall of course be glad of the assistance Rushbrook Williams can give.[115]

Nevertheless, Chelmsford's persistence paid off, and after a month of negotiations Montagu finally gave his approval.[116] And Williams later reminisced about how the India Office 'found it very useful to use me . . . when they wanted to make a statement, committing nobody but myself with the sort of statement that they wanted put out'.[117]

The INC published its own report in March, prior to the appearance of Hunter's findings. Worried at the possible impact in Britain, Chelmsford hoped that Montagu could 'do something to hold it up temporarily or at least influence press to suspend judgement or moderate its comments' and offered several 'points of view' to suggest to journalists. These included arguing that Gandhi, its 'chief author', was 'primarily responsible' for the disturbances; that all the framers of the report were extremists who had already passed judgement on the events, and that non-official evidence was 'deliberately withheld' and therefore 'not subjected to cross-examination by impartial tribunal'.[118] It was:

> most important that home press should not comment without restraint on non-official report because success of such comments will be repeated to India and will as happened in December last revive and accentuate anti-government agitation which will not only threaten public tranquillity but also prevent Hunter Report from receiving fair hearing.[119]

Montagu reassured the Viceroy that, though the summary had already been issued by Reuters on 2 April, it had 'attracted very little attention. *Times* did not publish at all. *Daily News* published without comment and so far as I know only *Daily Herald* had emotional headlines.' Montagu added, 'I understand that Reuters will not make a feature of this matter in their news telegrams to India.'[120]

The Hunter report, the India Office and Parliament

The India Office finally received the Hunter report on 7 April 1920. The committee divided on racial lines, with the three Indian members signing a minority report which argued that there had been no rebellion at Amritsar and that martial law had been unnecessary. Although much more critical in its condemnation of Dyer, it also laid more blame at the door of the Indian government. The majority report characterised Dyer's conduct as 'an error of judgement', rejecting his excuse that he acted out of fear of a major insurrection. It was critical that the firing began without any warning and continued even though the crowd was unarmed. The duty of an officer under such circumstances was to maintain order and not to 'strike terror' into the populace. O'Dwyer was more or less acquitted of blame. Gandhi bitterly described it as 'page after page of thinly disguised official whitewash'.[121]

The Cabinet appointed a committee under Montagu to consider the report, and it was published on 26 May along with a resolution by the Government of India and a despatch by the Secretary of State. Montagu was 'full of apprehension' about the impact of the publication, and strenuous efforts were made to present a united front in Britain.[122] His concern was well founded. Parliament saw a series of heated debates, during which Dyer's evidence was fiercely assailed and as strongly defended, in addition to sustained questioning of Montagu by Conservative members, who accused him of misleading Parliament 'until he got his Government of India Bill through'.[123] The Commons debate on 8 July, technically on the motion to reduce the salary of the Secretary of State by £100, was intended to focus on the issues raised in the report. However, Montagu's speech became less an address on the subject of Hunter's recommendations than an emotional critique of the 'doctrine of terrorism' which, he claimed, Dyer represented. This infuriated the diehard Tory MPs, who believed that a 'Radical' Secretary of State had inflicted injustice on a gallant soldier whose action had suppressed a possible mutiny. Though the government gained a majority of 247 to 37 votes, it was to face defeat shortly afterwards when the Lords rejected the censure of Dyer by 129 to 86.

It was an altogether uncomfortable summer for Montagu, as the issues thrown up by the massacre were increasingly personalised, in Parliament as well as in the press, around the character and conduct of Dyer and Montagu. In this manner reactionary elements were able to shift attention from the defendable sphere of government policy towards more emotive comparisons between the two – providing, in the process, a focus around which broader general opposition to Montagu on the Conservative benches could form. Maffey, summarising the Commons debate to the Viceroy, explained how 'the old true-blue "service" section rallied in force, determined to make more noise than their numbers justified, not very clear or caring greatly about the facts and greatly prejudiced by "personal" considerations'. In effect, the issue became whether a British general ought 'to be downed at the bidding of a crooked Jew?'[124]

Behind these personal controversies lay irreconcilable differences on the future course of imperial governance. For Liberals like Montagu, British rule in India was part of a process leading ultimately to self-governance and the full extension of civil liberties. This process necessitated a changed approach. As he warned Chelmsford, it was no longer possible to rule India by the old methods. The Indian people 'will not stand now what they stood in 1818 or even before the war . . . I cannot help thinking that you and the local Governors are too much seeking the assistance that repression gives you for the moment, and do not think of the aftermath.'[125] Very different was the conception of important sections of Conservative opinion which, although recognising the duty of the government to further the interests of Indians, were convinced that British rule ultimately rested upon the ability and willingness to impose its will by force. 'That England,' declared the *Saturday Review*, 'has won India by the sword, and can only keep it by the sword, was once an historical platitude: by Mr Montagu and his colleagues it is regarded as a wicked paradox.'[126] It was this schism in understanding, largely – if not completely – compressed by wartime imperatives, that the debates surrounding Dyer did much to reopen.

Thus though the question before the House in July 1920 was one on which all the relevant levels of authority – the Government of India, the Secretary of State, the Commander-in-chief, the Army Council and the home government – were agreed, it nonetheless provided the occasion, as Spender observed, 'for the first definite revolt' against the government by its Unionist supporters.[127] The *Gazette* considered it a serious portent that the Tory rank and file should have 'broken away' from the government on an issue which raised 'the fundamental question whether terrorism shall be condoned as a permissible weapon of British Imperial administration'.[128]

Fleet Street and the Dyer factor, May–July 1920

The Hunter report generated significant press coverage, the majority of papers agreeing with the *Express* that 'the judgements passed on a most unfortunate soldier cannot be impugned'. Dyer had exceeded his duty and gone beyond 'an essential severity to a savage barbarity'.[129] There were, however, divisions within the ranks of those left-of-centre papers which could have been expected to be more sympathetic to the government. The *Herald* considered the Hunter report 'scandalous', and for the *Nation* it was a 'whitewashing Report', for it 'excuse[d] some of the worst examples of military tyranny, and half-censure[d] the rest'. Were it not for Montagu's speech in Parliament, in which he went beyond the committee's verdict in his condemnation of Dyer, O'Dwyer and the administration of martial law, 'we should regard the Report of the British majority of the Hunter Committee as an almost irretrievable disaster to the Empire'.[130] The *Gazette*, on the other hand, strongly protested against the *Herald*'s stance as representing neither 'honest journalism' nor 'even competent handling of a grave situation'.[131]

Parliamentary questioning, especially by the pro-Dyer Tory rebels, influenced press response. The *Spectator* renewed demands for Montagu's resignation, citing the now familiar range of factors, including his Jewishness and his connection with the silver scandal at the India Office. Montagu had not been 'candid' with the Commons: he was 'desperately anxious' to get his reform Bill through and therefore felt 'it was not wise to present the dangers of insurrection with which we are faced in India in too lurid a light'.[132] The *National Review* confessed itself relieved that Montagu's political chances 'were blighted by his demeanour' during the Dyer debates.[133] According to the *Saturday Review*, 'That a Radical Secretary of State for India and a servile Viceroy should agree in trying to break an officer for the prompt use of military force in suppressing a rebellion is quite intelligible.'[134] By these papers the result of the Lords debate was warmly welcomed. T. J. Bennett regretted that:

> we have got a mischievous Press in England poisoning the wells against the Secretary for India. I think we have seen some co-operation in that unworthy purpose in some of the questions which have been put in this House during the last few days. The great obstacles to a friendly understanding, which is profoundly to be desired, therefore come from two sides.[135]

However, most of Fleet Street remained critical of Dyer. The *Observer*, *Guardian*, *Gazette* and *Daily News* agreed that if the event went 'unmarked with that severe and unmistakable censure which serves to stamp it as the act of a man repudiated by the calm judgement of his country, then it will go down through Indian memories ... as the revelation of the real basis of British Imperial rule'.[136] The *Review of Reviews* contended that there could be 'no possible justification for the atrocious brutality' of Dyer, while the *Gazette* felt that the epithets 'UN-British' and 'inhuman' were justified and 'a man who loses his head and strikes wildly and blindly is not fit for employment and cannot be exculpated because his "conception of duty" is honestly at variance with that of his Majesty's Government'.[137]

These papers condemned the conduct of the pro-Dyer section during the Commons debate, the *Daily News* claiming it represented a case of 'TERRORISM v. GOODWILL'.[138] Linked with this was an understanding of the personal nature of the attack, which the *Guardian* contended was 'designed' for the 'destruction' of Montagu and a 'falsification of the issue'.[139] Like Montagu and Chelmsford, the Liberal press was concerned that sympathy for Dyer would have the effect of undermining the trust amongst educated Indian opinion which was essential for the success of reform. They accordingly took pains to emphasise that the voice of 'reaction' in press and Parliament was not representative of British opinion. 'We have got to see,' said *Reynolds's*, 'that in the mind of India there is a feeling of trust in British justice.'[140] Describing the Lords debate as 'a foolish act of pro-Dyerism', the *Nation* contended that 'it is Dyer, not Montagu, who must "go"'.[141] 'British democracy,' the paper added, 'spoke through Mr Montagu's voice.'[142]

However some papers which broadly welcomed the Hunter report hesitated to single out Dyer for sole criticism. The *Telegraph* and *Express* felt that, despite the Hunter recommendations, 'It would be wrong and cruel to underestimate his difficulties, unjust to withhold from him a considerable sympathy. He was the victim of a task too great for him.'[143] Dyer's conduct produced differing reactions even within the left-of-centre camp. The *Chronicle* noted that Dyer was 'a conscientious and gallant officer, who in a terrible crisis committed a terrible mistake'.[144] The *New Statesman* was equally critical of Dyer's 'inhuman' proceedings, but believed that it was unfair that he should be expected to shoulder the entire load of censure. Significant blame should also be apportioned to the civil authorities who 'panicked' and entrusted to the military the duty of maintaining order.[145]

Thus while, on the whole, both the press and Parliament supported Montagu and the recommendations of the Hunter committee, there was ambiguity and significant fracturing of opinion within both these forums of opinion. In addition to the opposition of individual papers, the press operated as a sounding board for sections of parliamentary diehard opinion, in turn reinforcing such sentiment and carrying it to a wider public. The stridency of Dyer's supporters, combined with the perceived softening of attitude in prominent newspapers like the *Telegraph*, *Express* and *Chronicle*, as well as the *Morning Post* campaign discussed below, contributed to the INC disappointment with the Hunter report and to Gandhi's loss of faith in British goodwill – which he had championed even as late as December 1919 in the annual Congress meeting, after Dyer's evidence had become public. These 'indications of a basic lack of sympathy', Beloff claims, 'did as much as the original event to prevent the development of the co-operation necessary between the government and the national movement'.[146] The arrival in India of news about such developments 'acted as a catalyst' in the hardening of opinion against the government and the decision of the INC in August 1920 to launch the non-co-operation movement.[147] As Brown remarks, 'On the tide of this controversy Gandhi launched himself as the champion of Indian self-respect.'[148]

The Morning Post *and the Dyer campaign*

The most vivid testimony to Bennett's apprehensions of a 'poisoning of the wells' against Montagu was provided by the *Morning Post*'s pro-Dyer campaign. For the newspaper the events at Amritsar, besides being a decisive imperial issue, provided the basis for a substantial and personal attack on Montagu.[149] Its leader headings capture some of the provocative tone of its writings: 'What is Truth?', 'Montagu *v.* Dyer', 'Nothing lost save honour', 'These be THY GODS, O ISRAEL'. The coverage of the Commons debate was summed up under the header 'Ordeal of General Dyer', that of the Lords debate as 'General Dyer vindicated'.[150] On 9 July it launched a 'General Dyer Fund' for 'The man who saved India', to 'relieve a gallant and despicably used soldier of a grievous embarrassment' and, more important, to 'give him, in his hour of bitterness and tribulation, an assurance that some of his fellow countrymen . . . dissociate themselves from the mean and cowardly conduct of the politicians and the time-servers'. Gwynne felt that the 'damage' caused was 'irreparable', and 'we should now concentrate on getting rid of Montagu'.[151] Dyer was a patriot persecuted for doing his duty – a 'splendid fellow' whose case amounted to a test of 'our existence as a governing force in India'.[152] Gwynne even sent telegrams to what he claimed were 'all the good Indian newspapers'– *Pioneer, Statesman, Englishman, Madras Mail* and *Civil and Military Gazette* – to publicise his cause. Writing to Dyer, he hoped that the fund would serve as a comfort:

> for the terribly unjust way in which you have been treated by the Government . . . I anticipate a very large subscription . . . though the Government tried to disgrace you, no man, it seems to me, is held in higher honour by all the decent people in England than yourself.[153]

The subscription list appearing daily for several weeks in the *Morning Post*, together with resounding letters of support, illustrated the popular sentiment which the press was able to evoke. The paper maintained that public feeling had been deeply touched and the growth of the fund revealed a 'flood-tide of emotion'.[154] Many of those most vocal had direct connections with the subcontinent, including retired officials and servicemen, and they contributed significantly to the fund.[155] Gwynne felt his belief vindicated: 'in my experience of newspapers I have never known a fund meet with such an instant response and success'.[156] The total collected was £26,317, and the *Morning Post* presented Dyer with a golden sword as 'Defender of the Empire'.[157]

Conclusion

'No one serving in India at the time,' recalled Sir Malcolm Hailey, could 'fail to remember the impression caused in India by the reaction of so large a part of the British public to the news of this unhappy incident . . . it became difficult for Indians to believe in the reality of forecasts made by the more sympathetic British thinkers regarding impending liberal reforms in India.'[158] Rushbrook Williams recollected that the 'worst feature' of the reaction to the massacre was the 'extraordinary and, to my mind, perverse support' given to Dyer by the *Morning Post*.[159] Montagu himself thought that the affair had been 'hopelessly mishandled from the public relations point of view', and that Dyer ought to have been 'muzzled'.[160] He was 'furious' at the way Dyer justified his actions: 'as the *Morning Post* hated him, he saw in their eulogy of Dyer something like a personal attack on himself. I myself thought him over-touchy; but as a Jew his status in the Cabinet was uneasy anyway.'[161] The consequences of this public relations disaster were succinctly summarised by Chirol, touring India in 1921. Analysing the factors influencing political disaffection, he gave priority to the 'one passionate sense of wrong' done in the Punjab. Indian feeling had 'gradually crystallised into hatred when Government instead of making early and frank and full atonement seemed to take refuge in delays and evasions only tardily followed by half-hearted expressions of regret for the past and assurances for the future'.[162]

The massacre of civilians at Jallianwallah Bagh constituted, in itself, a crisis for the Raj. One effect, as we have seen, was to bring to the fore criticism from both the left and the right of the government's approach to India. Montagu's unenviable task was to steer between these two extremes and carry with him the majority of parliamentary and press opinion. As he himself explained, 'We have taken a middle course which no one expected to satisfy either the extreme right or the extreme left wing. They will both make their own clamour.' But he believed there was 'a strong inclination on the part of the public' in Britain to accept the Hunter report.[163] On the whole he was successful in securing this middle ground. The majority of influential papers broadly accepted the government position, and a Commons majority was registered for the report. Horniman noted, 'The British Press, with one or two ignoble exceptions, and of all shades of opinion, has condemned ... the perpetration of a deed which has profoundly shocked, not merely the public of Great Britain, but of the whole world.'[164]

Yet this acceptance was not complete. The Commons debate had witnessed considerable rancour on the government benches, and as the *Saturday Review* remarked, 'Another such episode as the Dyer debate and the Coalition will break up.'[165] Equally important, Montagu was (perhaps inevitably) unable to carry with him his more trenchant critics at home and it was the adverse comment ultimately emerging that precipitated a more threatening level of unrest in India. To that extent the India Office failed to limit negative reaction to the event. The concerted approach to press management had been found wanting – albeit in the face of an especially severe test.

Several specific factors hindered India Office efforts to manage reporting of the crisis. First, lack of information. Montagu's commitment to greater publicity at the India Office was circumscribed by the priorities of the 'man on the spot', and when confronted with the massacre Chelmsford fell back upon the traditional policy of press restriction and suppression of information. Montagu himself was hindered by inadequate knowledge of events. He did not control the release of information from India, and was often placed on the defensive as details of Dyer's action gradually emerged. A number of sessions of the Hunter committee were held *in camera*, which contributed to the lack of early intelligence, and the report itself, though available to the Government of India in early March, took over a month to reach London. Indeed, the press occasionally seemed to have prior knowledge of events. Further, the very fact that news did not appear immediately but leaked out over months reinforced the impact of the story and gave an impression of official duplicity. This in turn compromised future India Office endeavours to secure acceptance for its interpretation of events. By seeking to combine strategies of censorship and persuasion in its dealings with the press, that trust necessary for the exercise of the latter was fractured and the story acquired a new strength. Finally, the strong feelings and personal animosities aroused by the events proved decisive and damaging. By emphasising the conduct of Dyer and Montagu the opponents of the Secretary of State were able to exploit a series of stereotypes: Dyer, the upright British soldier doing his duty to maintain imperial authority, versus Montagu, the Liberal Jew prepared to reform away the British Empire. Montagu himself contributed to this personalisation of the issues, however unintentionally, by his emotional statements in the Commons debate. Thus when Gwynne raised the case of Dyer, he succeeded in taking discussion of Indian issues beyond the limited and more manageable world of the political elite and into the unpredictable and emotive realm of prejudice and popular feeling.

Notes

1 For political reactions to the crisis see D. Sayer, 'British reaction to the Amritsar massacre, 1919–1920', *Past and Present*, 131 (1991), 130–64; amongst books marking its seventy-fifth anniversary are V. N. Datta and S. Settar (eds), *Jallianwallah Bagh Massacre* (Delhi, 2000); S. Singh *et al.* (eds), *Jallianwallah Bagh* (Patiala, 1997).

2 *India*, 27 April 1919.

3 Quoted in Bombay Native Newspaper Reports, Part I, 1919, p. 26, L/R/5/175.

4 *Times*, 23 May, *Morning Post*, 26 May 1919.

5 *Manchester Guardian*, 21 April, *Daily Telegraph*, 17 April 1919.

6 *Westminster Gazette*, 23 April, *Daily News*, 22 April, *Manchester Guardian*, 15 April, *Reynolds's News*, 20 April 1919.

7 *Observer*, 20 April 1919.

8 *Ibid.*; *Fortnightly Review*, July 1919.

9 *Manchester Guardian*, 19 April, *Fortnightly Review*, May 1919.

10 *Observer*, 20 April, *Westminster Gazette*, 23 April, *Daily Herald*, 12, 15–17 April, *Manchester Guardian*, 21 April, *Nation*, 19 April, *Daily Chronicle* 21 April 1919.

11 *Daily News*, 22 April 1919.

12 *Westminster Gazette*, 23 April 1919; *Review of Reviews*, May 1919.

13 *Nation*, 3, 13 May 1919.

14 *Reynolds's News*, 20 April 1919.

15 *Morning Post*, 17 April, also 13 May 1919; *Spectator*, 26 April, 3 May, 5 July, 30 August, 6, 20 September 1919. The phrase is from the Montagu–Chelmsford report.
16 *Morning Post, Daily Mail*, 17 April 1919.
17 *Times*, 15 April 1919.
18 *Times*, 19 April, *Morning Post*, 17 April, *Star*, 16 April, *Daily Chronicle*, 23 May, *Spectator*, 26 April 1919.
19 *New Statesman*, 26 April, *Daily Chronicle*, 21 April 1919.
20 *Westminster Gazette and Times*, 15 April, *Manchester Guardian*, 19 April, *Morning Post*, 17 April, *Reynolds's News*, 20 April, *Spectator*, 26 April, *Nation*, 19 April 1919.
21 *Times*, 19 April 1919. For references to 1857 see *Daily Chronicle*, 16 April, *Daily Express*, 22 April, *Daily Mail*, 17 April, *Nation*, 26 April, *Fortnightly Review*, July 1919.
22 *Daily Express*, 22 April, *Daily Mail*, 16 April, *Fortnightly Review*, August 1919.
23 *Daily Herald*, 27 May, 7 June 1919.
24 *Nation*, 17 May 1919.
25 *Nation*, 26 July, also 6 April, 12 July, 2, 30 August, 13 September 1919.
26 *Daily Herald*, 22, 23, 24 April 1919; *Nation*, 26 April, *Observer*, 20 April 1919.
27 *Daily Herald*, 16 April 1919; also interview with H. S. Polak, 29 March 1919.
28 *Daily Herald*, 12 April 1919.
29 *Westminster Gazette*, 23, 15 April, also 16 September 1919.
30 *Observer*, 20 April 1919.
31 *Daily Express*, 22 April; *Reynolds's News*, 27 April, *Daily Chronicle*, 16 April, 23, 31 May 1919.
32 *Manchester Guardian*, 19 April 1919.
33 *Times*, 19 April, 23 May 1919; *Observer*, 20 April 1919.
34 *Times*, 10 April 1919.
35 Viceroy to Secretary of State, 5 March 1919, MC/8.
36 Secretary of State to Viceroy, 28 May 1919, MC/3.
37 Viceroy to Secretary of State, 8 October 1919, CC/5; Viceroy to Secretary of State, 13, 26 November 1919, CC/11.
38 Viceroy to Secretary of State, 16 April 1919, MC/8.
39 Indian Riots (Printed) Collection, 31 March–20 April 1919, L/P&J/6/1583.
40 J. P. Thompson Diaries, MSS Eur F137/32, p. 55 (hereafter JPT/no).
41 Verney to his wife, 20 April 1919; also 17, 18 April 1919, MSS Eur D921, Verney Collection.
42 *Moral and Material Progress Report, 1919* (1920), p. 39.
43 Viceroy to O'Dwyer, 23 April 1919, enclosed in Viceroy to Secretary of State, 30 April 1919, L/PO/10/1, Private Office Papers (hereafter L/PO/no).
44 JPT/31, p. 44.
45 George Lloyd to Viceroy, 24 April, enclosed in Viceroy to Secretary of State, 27 April 1919, CC/10.
46 Viceroy to Secretary of State, 28 April 1919, CC/10.
47 *Ibid*.
48 Secretary of State to Viceroy, 22 April, also 1 May 1919, MC/3.
49 Foreign Office to Under Secretary of State, 12, 24 June 1919, L/P&J/6/1568.
50 Viceroy to Secretary of State, 24 November 1919, CC/11.
51 Viceroy to Secretary of State, 21 May 1919, L/PO/10/1.
52 See Secretary of State–Viceroy correspondence, 28 May, 11 June 1919, MC/3.
53 Secretary of State to Viceroy, 10 October 1919, MC/2.
54 Secretary of State to Viceroy, 5 June 1919; Secretary of State to Viceroy, 11 June 1919, L/PO/10/1. Residents were made to crawl along a street in Amritsar where Miss Sherwood had been assaulted.
55 Viceroy to Secretary of State, 11 June 1919, MC/8.
56 Viceroy to Secretary of State, 25 September 1919, MC/9.
57 Viceroy to Secretary of State, 16 September 1919, L/PO/10/1.

58 Secretary of State suggested it on 2 May 1919, Viceroy agreed on 5 May 1919.
59 H. Fein, *Imperial Crime and Punishment* (Honolulu, 1977), p. 104.
60 J. M. Brown, *Gandhi's Rise to Power: Indian Politics, 1915–1922* (Cambridge, 1972), p. 232.
61 Viceroy to Secretary of State, 23 July 1919, L/PO/10/1.
62 Secretary of State to Viceroy, 29 August 1919, MC/3.
63 Secretary of State to Hunter, 29 August 1919, CC/5; Secretary of State to Hunter, 25 August 1919, in L/PO/6/4.
64 Secretary of State to Viceroy, 31 October 1919, MC/3.
65 Northcliffe to Steed, 2 January 1920, BL Add. MS 62247 A and B (Northcliffe Papers).
66 Also *Daily Express*, 13, 15, 16, 17 December 1919.
67 *Times, Westminster Gazette*, 15 December 1919.
68 *Nation*, 20 December 1919.
69 *Daily Herald*, 17 December 1919.
70 *Manchester Guardian*, 13 December 1919.
71 *Manchester Guardian*, 17 December 1919.
72 *Times*, 15 December 1919.
73 *Times*, 16 December 1919.
74 *Times*, 17 December; *Nation* 20 December 1919.
75 *Morning Post*, 15 December 1919.
76 *Observer*, 21 December, *Westminster Gazette*, 15 December, *Nation*, 20 December 1919.
77 *Daily Herald*, 15 December 1919.
78 *Daily Herald*, 17, 15 December 1919. Brailsford (1873–1958): journalist and author, *Manchester Guardian, Nation*; editor, *New Leader* 1922–26.
79 *Nation*, 20 December 1919.
80 *Daily News*, 15 December 1919.
81 *Times*, 16 December, *Observer*, 21 December 1919.
82 *Manchester Guardian*, 15 December 1919.
83 *Daily Herald*, 15 December 1919.
84 See *Daily News*, 5 January 1920.
85 *Observer*, 7 December, *Westminster Gazette*, 15 December 1919.
86 *Nation*, 20 December 1919.
87 *Morning Post*, 15 December 1919.
88 Secretary of State to Viceroy, 13 December 1919, CC/11.
89 Secretary of State to Viceroy, 17 December 1919, MC/3.
90 Secretary of State to Viceroy, 18 December 1919, MC/3.
91 Secretary of State to Viceroy, 30 December 1919, L/PO/10/1.
92 *Nation*, 20 December, *Daily Herald*, 19 December 1919.
93 Hansard, 5th series, 1919, 123, 242. Cecil: third son of third Marquess of Salisbury.
94 *Ibid.*
95 Secretary of State to Viceroy, 18 December 1919, MC/3.
96 Viceroy to Secretary of State, 24 December 1919, MC/9.
97 Viceroy to Secretary of State, 24 December 1919, CC/11.
98 *The Times*, report dated 25 December, published 31 December 1919; cf. Secretary of State to Viceroy, 30 December 1919, CC/11.
99 O'Dwyer to Montagu, 30 December 1919, enclosed in O'Dwyer to Maffey, 31 December 1919, CC/23.
100 *The Times*, 9 February 1920. This controversy continued into the summer of 1920 with further letters from O'Dwyer, including a copy of a letter of 30 December 1919 which he claimed to have sent to Montagu, in *The Times*, 2 July 1920. The *Morning Post* took up this issue, publishing a letter from O'Dwyer in which he alleged having been denied a hearing before the Cabinet, 9 June 1920. This letter, Levine claims, 'inflamed the Conservative community' and though Montagu tried to give his side of the story (*Morning Post*, 14 June 1920) 'the damage had already been done' (*Politics, Religion*, p. 557).

101 Secretary of State to Viceroy, 12 November 1919, CC/11.
102 Secretary of State to Viceroy, 14 November 1919, MC/3; also Secretary of State to Viceroy, 11 August 1919, CC/11.
103 Secretary of State to Viceroy, 30 December 1919, L/PO/10/1.
104 Secretary of State to Viceroy, 23 December 1919, CC/11.
105 *Morning Post*, 15 December 1919.
106 Secretary of State to Viceroy, 11 February 1920, CC/12.
107 Viceroy to Secretary of State, 20 January 1920, CC/12; Fortnightly Reports – Punjab, 15 January 1920, fol. 28, 31 January 1920, fols 29–30, JPT/31.
108 Secretary of State to Viceroy, 30 December 1919, Home Poll, A, IOR Pos 8958.
109 Secretary of State to Viceroy, 24 January 1920, CC/12.
110 Viceroy to Secretary of State, 6 February 1920, CC/12.
111 *Ibid.*
112 Secretary of State to Viceroy, 10 February 1920, CC/12.
113 Viceroy to Secretary of State, 16 February 1920, in reply to Secretary of State to Viceroy, 11 February 1920, CC/12.
114 Viceroy to Secretary of State, 16 February 1920, CC/12.
115 Secretary of State to Viceroy, 18 February 1920, CC/12.
116 Secretary of State to Viceroy, 9 March 1920, CC/12.
117 Williams, T 130/2, Oral Archives (transcripts), p. 38.
118 Viceroy to Secretary of State, 6 April 1920, L/P&J/6/1678.
119 *Ibid.*
120 Secretary of State to Viceroy, 8 April 1920, also 9 April 1920, L/PJ/6/1678.
121 Cited in Sarkar, *Modern India*, p. 196.
122 Cited in S. D. Waley, *Edwin Montagu* (1964), p. 230.
123 Debates on 23 and 30 June, 8, 19, 20 and 28 July 1920.
124 Maffey to Viceroy, 10 July 1920, CC/16.
125 Secretary of State to Viceroy, 20 May; Secretary of State to Viceroy, 8 April 1920, MC/4.
126 *Saturday Review*, 5 June 1920.
127 *Westminster Gazette*, 21 July 1920.
128 *Ibid.*
129 *Daily Express*, 27 May; *Daily Telegraph*, 28 May 1920; *Contemporary Review*, 'The Hunter reports', Nihal Singh, July 1920, and 'Quo vadis in India?', Lord Meston, October 1920; *Review of Reviews*, January, July 1920; *Fortnightly Review*, 'The Hunter report and Amritsar', Stanley Rice, 1920; *Nineteenth Century*, 'Prelude to Amritsar', Rushbrook Williams, June 1920, 'Reflections on the Hunter report', General Sir O'Moore Creagh, July 1920; *Daily News, Westminster Gazette* and *Reynolds's News*, 27 May, 11 July 1920.
130 *Daily Herald*, 26 May; *Nation*, 29 May 1920.
131 *Westminster Gazette*, 27 May 1920.
132 *Spectator*, 17 July 1920.
133 *National Review*, November 1920.
134 *Saturday Review*, 10, 24 July 1920.
135 8 July 1920, Hansard, 5th series, 131, 1765–6.
136 *Manchester Guardian*, 8 January 1920; *Daily News*, 9 July 1920.
137 *Westminster Gazette*, 27 May; *New Statesman*, 17 July, *Nation*, 29 May 1920; *Review of Reviews*, July 1920.
138 *Daily News*, 9 July, also 10, 19–21 July 1920.
139 *Manchester Guardian*, 19 July, *New Statesman*, 3 July 1920.
140 *Reynolds's News*, 11, 25 July 1920; *New Statesman*, 29 May 1920.
141 *Nation*, 24 July 1920; for letters see 3 January, 5 June, 17, 24 July 1920.
142 *Nation*, 17 July, *Westminster Gazette*, 9 July 1920.
143 *Daily Telegraph, Daily Express*, 9 July 1920.
144 *Daily Chronicle*, 27 May 1920.
145 *New Statesman*, 17 July 1920.
146 M. Beloff, *Britain's Liberal Empire, 1897–1921* (1969) I, p. 309.

147 S. R. Mehrotra, *India and the Commonwealth, 1885–1929* (1965), p. 112.
148 Brown, *Gandhi's Rise*, p. 244.
149 *Morning Post*, 1, 3, 6, 8–10, 12–17, 19–22, 23 July 1920.
150 *Morning Post*, 9, 21 July 1920.
151 Gwynne to Sydenham, 21 July 1920, dep 8(b), HAG.
152 Gwynne to R. McCalmont, 31 May 1920, dep 8 (b), HAG.
153 Gwynne to Dyer, 11 July 1920, dep 8(b), HAG.
154 *Morning Post*, 13, 14 July 1920.
155 R. Furneaux, *Massacre at Amritsar* (1963), pp. 156–7; Sayer, 'British reaction', pp. 158–9. A. Draper, *The Amritsar Massacre* (1985), pp. 236–8.
156 Gwynne to Dickinson, 22 July 1920, dep 8(b), HAG.
157 Gwynne to Sydenham, 21 July 1920, dep 8(b), HAG.
158 Note, MSS Eur E220/57, p. 7, Hailey Collection. Hailey: Chief Commissioner, Delhi, 1912–18; member, Viceroy's Executive Council, 1919–24.
159 Williams, MSS Eur T130/2, pp. 30–1.
160 Williams to T. J. Fraser, 13 December 1975, Fraser private collection.
161 *Ibid*.
162 Chirol to Viceroy, 15 March 1921, RpvtC/10.
163 Secretary of State to Viceroy, 3 June 1920, MC/4.
164 B. G. Horniman, *Amritsar and our Duty to India* (1920), p. 121.
165 *Saturday Review*, 17 July 1920.

CHAPTER NINE

Ambassador of empire:
the Prince of Wales's tour,
Fleet Street and government publicity,
1921–22

There was, by the late nineteenth century, an established tradition of placing the monarchy in the context of Britain's role as an imperial power. The relationship between the Crown and India had been formally proclaimed in the aftermath of the Mutiny. Disraeli, in particular, wished to establish personal contact between the sovereign and the Indian people as a means of consolidating British authority. He encouraged the tour of the Prince of Wales in 1875–76, and as 'a pendant' to the visit was also responsible for proclaiming Victoria Empress of India at an extravagantly staged Imperial Assemblage, in Delhi, in 1877. 'It is only in the amplification of titles,' he argued in Parliament, 'that you can often touch and satisfy the imagination of nations; and that is an element which Governments must not despise.'[1] The Imperial Assemblage, Lytton believed, would appeal to the imagination of both the British and Indian masses, and 'raise the enthusiasm' of the aristocracy for empire.[2] The legacy of Lytton's effort was visible at successive durbars in 1903 to proclaim Edward VII Emperor of India, and in 1911 when George V visited India to be crowned in person. These durbars and royal tours provide striking instances of the 'invented traditions' that Cohn and Cannadine have seen as characteristic of the late Victorian and Edwardian period – when old ceremonials were staged with an expertise and appeal previously lacking and new rituals were invented. The monarchy's image, in particular, became 'splendid, public and popular', and royal ceremonies were described with 'unprecedented immediacy and vividness in a sentimental, emotional, admiring way'.[3] MacKenzie has similarly noted, 'imperialism made spectacular theatre, with the monarchy its gorgeously opulent centrepiece'.[4]

13 'Kaiser-i-Hind, 1877. The Queen proclaimed Empress of India at Delhi, January 1, 1877', *Punch*, 30 January 1901

Monarchy in the new era

While this tour can be viewed as the latest of a royal series, it never-theless presented certain distinctive features in terms of both expec-tation and timing and was by far the most complex politically. It was, of course, about tradition, hierarchy, unity, order and class, as analysed so perceptively in Cannadine's *Ornamentalism*. Yet the prince's tour did not represent only a further – and effectively final – outing for the old machinery of monarchical splendour. In significant ways it was – or at least, it was intended to be – a new departure. Its purpose was not simply to demonstrate the stability of the imperial connection, but symbolically to endorse the process of political change that had been initiated in 1917 – the 'new angle of vision' on India's future. The visit was to be less a static reaffirmation of the *status quo* than a dynamic factor in an evolving situation. When the Government of India Act received the royal assent in December 1919 it was announced that, in keeping with the new spirit it sought to embody, the Prince of Wales would visit India to inaugurate the Imperial Legislative Assembly and the Chamber of Princes. The visit would set the monarchical stamp of approval on a new India, and who better to do it than a youthful and 'modern' prince who appeared to represent the imperial unity reaffirmed by war?

Unfortunately, these expectations were never met. and from the beginning events unfolded very differently. Edward was scheduled to visit in 1920 but, exhausted by previous imperial sojourns, and close to emotional and physical collapse, he insisted that the tour should be cancelled or at least postponed.[5] The postponement also reflected political considerations, with loyalty to the Raj seemingly being tested to breaking point in the aftermath of Jallianwallah Bagh and mass non-co-operation. In the event it was the Duke of Connaught who initiated the two assemblies, landing at Madras instead of the customary Bombay owing to the threat of unrest. The India which greeted Edward when he finally reached its shores in November 1921 was far removed from that which had existed in his father's day. 'It was the India of a new era . . . confidently expect[ing] the attainment . . . of equal status' with the self-governing dominions.[6] The tour became the most politically motivated of all royal visits, representing an attempt to transform the climate of disaffection and turmoil engendered by the nationalist movement. The imperative need to present India as a stable imperial possession and to convince domestic opinion that the constitutional reforms and disaffection had not imperilled British rule became paramount for the Secretary of State. Post-war scepticism and weariness in Britain combined with an unstable and bickering Coalition increasingly critical of the Indian government's wait-and-see policy *vis-à-vis* Gandhi and the extremists. The Viceroy believed that cancellation or further postponement would create the impression that India was 'so disloyal that it was not safe for the Prince to visit'.[7] The consequence would be 'serious' and arouse 'bitter feeling' against India in Britain and in the dominions.[8]

Government publicity

Thus the royal tour was conceived primarily as a public relations event. Its organisation reflected an attempt to secure the maximum political dividend. As an explicit attempt to create goodwill and affirm the strength of the Raj and the loyalty of its subjects, negative publicity would have been destructive of its very purpose. Montagu's attention to detail was reflected in his considerations regarding the press arrangements. The Chairman of the Newspaper Proprietors' Association was invited to assist the India Office to ensure that the arrangements would be 'helpful' to the press.[9] Reading suggested that papers should be encouraged to combine to send representatives.[10] Montagu disagreed.

> It ought surely to be our endeavour to secure maximum publicity for the tour and India which can only be done by encouraging papers to send their special correspondents. If they combine, papers will publish comparatively brief accounts of visit and publicity will be a failure. Presses of the Dominions, it must be remembered, will also obtain reports of the visit from the correspondents of the London Press ... I am certain you will agree as to imperative necessity of making Press happy and contented if publicity is to be complete success.[11]

Along with one delegate of the Associated Press and Reuters (they worked in conjunction), one cinematographer and one photographer, this meant a party of thirteen or fifteen. 'But I am convinced,' Montagu concluded, 'that [the] trouble involved in extending full facilities to this number and increased expenditure will be repaid in wider publicity obtained'.[12] The Viceroy agreed on the need for 'maximum publicity', and reassured Montagu that he could 'depend upon our doing our utmost to make Press representatives happy'.[13]

In the event, the royal party was accompanied by a 'formidable phalanx' of British and Indian newspapermen.[14] Fleet Street special correspondents included Sir Harry Robinson (*The Times*), Sir Herbert Russell (Reuters), George Pilcher (*Morning Post*), Sir Percival Phillips (*Express*), Perceval Landon (*Telegraph*) and Mr Fair, a Central News photographer. Robinson's wide experience included stints in Belgium and Serbia and on the western front, and he was following in the footsteps of his illustrious predecessor W. H. Russell, who had been chosen by the Prince of Wales to chronicle his 1870s tour. Herbert Russell had a strong record as a Reuters war correspondent. Both Robinson and Russell received the KBE in 1920, as did Phillips, an American who had covered George V's tour. Landon had reported the Boer War for *The Times*, and was private secretary to the Governor of New South Wales, before journeying to India as a special correspondent for the *Mail* at Curzon's durbar. His subsequent forays to India were for the *Telegraph* and included the royal tour of 1905, a trip to India, Nepal and Persia in 1908, and the 1911 durbar. The Anglo-Indian journalists accompanying the Prince included E. Haward (*Pioneer*), D. Walker (*Times of India*), H. H. Holman (*Illustrated Times of India*), Mr U. N. Sen (as far as Calcutta) and F. R. Edwards (beyond) of the Associated Press. Indian pressmen included, amongst others, Krishnaswamy Aiyer (*New India*), R. Sharma (*New Empire*) and Habib-ur-Rahman Khan (*Fauj-i-Akbar*).[15]

Rushbrook Williams, on deputation from his directorship of the Central Bureau of Information, was given responsibility for overseeing royal publicity in general. He formed part of the Prince's entourage and was charged with producing an official history of the tour.[16] In 1905 a history had been compiled privately by Reed at the *Times of India* office. However, it was now believed, as William Vincent, the Home Member, argued, that the 'political importance' of 'a good and read-able history' was 'so great' and 'so valuable for propaganda purposes' that the government was willing to spend over Rs 20,000 and depute an officer (with stenographer and photographer) on full-time duty for the purpose.[17] Three trains were provided to transport the Prince and his retinue, including a travelling post office with telegraph facilities. At each major city the local Director of Information was to brief journalists, issue press passes and provide accommodation, transport and telegraphic facilities.[18] Meticulous planning was in evidence everywhere: Motor cars ferried journalists about town and it was 'most important that no hitch in the speedy transport of pressmen should occur through the holding up of their motorcars by police or military cordons. Nothing is more likely to affect adversely the success of the press arrangements.'[19] 'Bicycle peons' were in constant attendance at press camps and hotels to carry telegraph messages. Governors were similarly at the service of Fleet Street. George Lloyd explained how he had taken:

> infinite trouble about the journalists. I personally inspected their camp before they arrived to be sure that they were comfortable: in spite of the press of work and anxieties during the visit I gave half an hour's inter-view to each one of them at various times of the day and night explain-ing the situation, warning them of exaggeration and so on.[20]

Arrangements were made between provincial publicity bodies and Lloyd-Evans, the India Office Information Officer, for the dissemina-tion of publicity in Britain. Press publicity was strengthened by the cinematic potential afforded by the tour, and the London-based Anglo-Oriental Film Corporation was selected to produce the official film.[21]

Such personal attention to detail was a hallmark of Montagu's atti-tude to publicity. The consideration shown towards Indian journalists was again a courtesy not observed on earlier visits. Reed had impressed

upon Montagu that to have two classes of facilities for press correspondents would make it 'impossible to avoid great jealousy and
bitterness' amongst the Indians.[22] Spender personally attested to the
transformed relationship between officialdom and the Indian press
since the 1911 durbar, when he had been horrified by the racial segre-
gation of the press camps.[23]

The royal itinerary reflected government's political agenda. A
popular welcome at Bombay was essential, the city being the 'headquarters' of Gandhi's influence, and 'it is this which we have got to
knock out when the Prince comes'.[24] A visit to Aligarh University was
arranged to act as a Muslim counterweight to the conferring of an hon-
orary degree at Benares Hindu University. At Poona the Prince was to
lay the foundation stone of a memorial to the great Maratha, Shivaji.
George V had requested the cancellation of this visit, as it had
been agreed that the Prince would not participate in ceremonies of a
political nature.[25] However, Reading was vehement that, as the
Maharajas of Gwalior and Kohlapur were 'our staunchest friends', any
disregard of traditional Mahratta sentiment threatened the counter-
balance they provided to Brahmin ascendancy in the region, as well
as strengthening the voice of the local extremists opposed to the
visit.[26] 'I do not look upon this ceremony as political, it is one of
sentiments, although it will assist the Government by its effect on
the Mahrattas.'[27] The government anticipated making significant
political capital out of the visits to princely states, which it saw as a
bulwark against the political forces unleashed by Congress. Kohlapur,
for instance, was a vehement opponent of non-co-operation.[28] During
the first two decades of the twentieth century the princes emerged as
'acknowledged partners' of the Raj, 'no longer scorned but lauded
as repositories of tradition and loyalty and political wisdom'.[29] (The
Montagu–Chelmsford reforms reaffirmed this status by creating a
separate Chamber of Princes at the centre.) Edward spent almost half
his time in Indian states, where he could be assured of a splendid
welcome from rulers motivated by prestige and political expediency.
Pageantry, it was hoped, would help to drive protest from the pages of
Fleet Street.

Government counter-publicity and the press

This is not to suggest that the agitation and hartals called by Gandhi
to oppose the visit went unreported. It was ironic, as the *Guardian*
noted, that the tour which was to 'furnish the occasion for an overwhelming display of loyalism' had provided Gandhi's movement also
with 'an occasion to demonstrate its strength'.[30] The Prince recollected

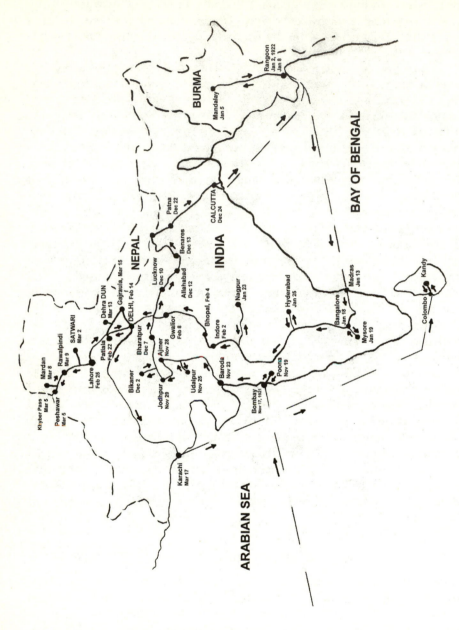

14   The Prince of Wales Tour: route and itinerary

in his memoirs how one 'unexpected effect' of the visit was to bring Gandhi 'into the open', though his attacks were 'muffled' by the 'boom of saluting guns, the hum of conversation at the garden parties, or the thunder of horses' hooves on the polo fields'.[31]

By encouraging significant numbers of British journalists to travel to India, the India Office indeed exposed itself to the possibility that unrest would secure increased coverage. Positive publicity could be obtained, but at the potential cost of negative images of the difficulties confronting British rule. Montagu attempted to head off the risk in two ways. First, as discussed earlier, he utilised his personal skills and Fleet Street contacts to limit coverage of unrest. Though able to diminish the extent of unfavourable reportage, the government could not altogether prevent the reporting of boycotts and demonstrations. Thus upon the Prince's arrival at Bombay several journalists, notwithstanding the arrangements made by Lloyd, 'broke away and filled a part of the London Press with sensational and, as I believed, misleading accounts of what had occurred'.[32] Lloyd vented his frustration at the 'ingratitude' of some correspondents who published 'such extravagant lies' about the situation, and felt that it reflected their lack of knowledge and their unwillingness to 'accept anyone else's view as regards the realities of the situation'.[33] To counter such an impression, Montagu gave the 'widest publicity' in London to official reports refuting a negative picture of the Prince's reception.[34] But he was realistic enough to appreciate that 'the British public naturally turns more eagerly to accounts of what are made to appear like disasters than to accounts like successes' and, therefore, it 'would not do merely to let the two sets of accounts come on side by side'.[35]

If controlling information was difficult, influencing its *interpretation* was less so. To this end Montagu sought to make the visit a focus of criticism of the non-co-operation movement. He encouraged newspapers to play down the extent of mass support for non-co-operation and the threat it posed. One of the key figures employed for this purpose was Lovat Fraser. George Lloyd affirmed Fraser's credentials: 'There is nothing that he does not know about India, and I know that anything he can properly do to help me personally as well as to help the Prince's tour he would gladly do if he were given the facts.'[36] Montagu had a 'very long talk' with Fraser, who was 'doing his best to help us in presenting the facts in their true perspective'.[37] Fraser was given access to detailed and confidential information, with the result evident in the weeks following as *The Times* presented a picture conforming more closely to that held by the government. Even when, during December, Allahabad produced the most complete hartal of the visit, a *Times* editorial proclaimed:

we steadily decline to believe that the organised attempts at a boycott represent the true feeling of the bulk of the people of India. They are an outcome of the tactics of terrorism and inflammatory propaganda practiced among the more ignorant sections of the population.[38]

The *Mail* correspondent provided a similar interpretation of events:

> One does not wish to minimise the present discontent in India and the difficulties of the problem, which are serious enough, but it remains that the extremists are small in numbers, and the immense mass of the people are moderate and well inclined. That mass, when it is not terrified, has shown every desire to express its loyalty, and I have nowhere been able to hear stories of the Prince's visit and personality doing other than good[39]

Montagu also took issue with Beaverbrook and Blumenfeld over what he regarded as the sensationalist reports from their special correspondent. Whereas there had been some rioting in Madras, which most papers had touched upon, Phillips's continued use of dramatic headlines seemed to him inappropriate. On 16 January whilst papers were reporting a royal success – for instance, headlines in *The Times* read, 'Greeted by happy crowds,' and the *Morning Post*, 'Brilliant reception' – Phillips's headlines proclaimed, 'Bayonet work in Madras. Leinsters scatter the Gandhist rioters. Grim scene of the royal route.' He was, Montagu contended, giving the *Express* 'a wholly wrong impression' of events. 'I cannot fathom the reason unless somebody has fussed him, but that is the truth. I am certain, and I would venture, with great respect for your paper, to suggest that the effect of his telegrams is enhanced by the choice of headlines used.' The evidence convinced Montagu that:

> I am right in deducing that Phillips is as wrong about Madras as he was about Bombay and Calcutta. It is to nobody's advantage to conceal the truth, but, in my opinion, it is very bad for our reputation abroad to allege the truth to be as unpalatable as the *DE* alleges it to be.[40]

Montagu's efforts at counterbalancing 'sensationalist misrepresentations' in Fleet Street were, however, affected by the system of news transmission between periphery and metropole. Writing to Reading regarding the Bombay visit, Montagu acknowledged that, despite his best efforts to 'supply a correct perspective' to the British public, the 'more sensational' papers had already 'got some start of us'. Reuters had sent accounts of both the Prince's welcome and the disturbances. While it was their business to 'transmit news without fear or favour', they had sent the two accounts in one message. Fleet Street 'not unnaturally connected the two, and in some instances gave the impression that the Prince had had to fight his way through molesting crowds'.[41] The India Office had done its best, and 'I believe successfully, to correct that sort of impression'; nevertheless Montagu wondered whether it would be possible

> to exercise some sort of guidance on the spot before these messages are sent? Once they are sent, we cannot very well hope to catch them up at this end, and it seems to me to be for consideration whether some means might not be found, some working arrangement with Reuters, to which they would be willing to agree, to ensure that, while news is freely sent to this country, it should be sent in a form not quite so capable of misrepresentation by the recipients.[42]

Montagu's complaints at not being supplied quickly with full intelligence continued into December. Official telegrams did not enable him to add much to the very full press messages which had been published.[43] Lloyd-Evans devised a plan to rectify this situation. At least two sets of telegrams were to be dispatched from each province by the Governor (or the Agent in the princely states), the first on the Prince's reception, the second near the end of the stay. Each province should summarise incidents of the visit and provide general impressions of the Prince's experiences, popular attitudes and any major consequences.[44]

The necessity for such measures was revealed with the near-total hartal at Allahabad on 12 December. The newspapers, Montagu noted the following day, were 'ringing with the most dramatic versions' of events, and on 14 December he reiterated that it was essential for him to 'contradict the constant flow of rumours of untoward incidents . . . [and] to deal with sensational headlines and disquieting allegations'.

> I am seriously concerned because up to the present moment I have had no official account of the proceedings at Allahabad. The press accounts, which were published in all the leading papers yesterday morning and since, point out complete success of *hartal* and boycott of visit and the public opinion is naturally excited by their accounts. Not less than 30 enquiries were made at the India Office during yesterday by responsible papers and agencies, including all the principal American Agencies, to which we could give no reply whatever based on official information respecting Allahabad.[45]

India Office staff, including Lloyd-Evans, Hose and Seton, concurred that the Secretary of State could contradict such an impression only by producing an authoritative account of what had actually occurred on each occasion.[46]

Reading was caught on the horns of a dilemma in trying to contain hartal and violent demonstrations without making martyrs of the extremists. As the *Gazette* commented, 'to inaugurate a campaign of repression while his tour was in progress would have been fatal to the fundamental purpose of the Royal visit itself'.[47] The image of a powerful Raj would be tarnished if punitive measures appeared to be the only way to secure order, yet mounting pressure was exerted by a Conservative-dominated Commons irritated at apparent official impotence. Thus repressive measures were utilised to palliate fears for the Prince's safety, with mass arrests before Allahabad and armoured patrols at Calcutta and Madras. Reading attributed great importance to the Calcutta visit, for a disagreeable reception there would 'affect the public mind' in England and in India more than in Allahabad.[48] He was therefore relieved that the Prince's welcome had been 'much above expectation' – though the gathering of a 'large mob of mill-hands parading streets and shouting' led to about 900 arrests.[49] Writing to congratulate the Governor, Lord Ronaldshay, Montagu felt the visit was achieving its purpose: 'the stabilisation of loyalty where loyalty already exists, and the conviction from firsthand knowledge that the ties between India and the reigning house are a reality'.[50] For Ronaldshay and others on the ground, however, it had been a tense affair and he admitted that the reception had been 'far better than I ever dared hope and the hartal far less effective'.[51] Ronaldshay sent detailed official telegrams to counter Fleet Street reports, which he maintained were 'a tissue of *suppressio veri and suggestio falsi*'.[52] Montagu used these telegrams to 'persuade' the *Express* into 'a better frame of mind'.[53]

Yet, in general, confrontation was avoided. This meant, for instance, that a scheduled trip to Aligarh University was cancelled owing to the threat of trouble. Where necessary popular welcomes were arranged. Phillips noted that in Lucknow, Agra, Delhi and Lahore, where the local population observed a day of mourning, the 'imposing crowds' were 'largely due to the efforts of the authorities to prevent a repetition of the dismal picture of deserted thoroughfares' at Allahabad. Between 20,000 and 50,000 villagers from outlying districts were brought by special trains to cover the gaps along the royal route made by the boycott. In some cases, such as at Lahore, these reinforcements came 'voluntarily', at others crowds were 'gathered' with the assistance of the local landlords, as in Awadh.[54] In the capital, New Delhi, Reading oversaw the orchestration of the crowds. The *Star* estimated that '20,000 Chamars' (literally shoemakers, low caste) were brought to line the routes. The *Morning Post* admitted that there had been stage management:

Special efforts were made to disperse the crowds of Delhi proper. Zemindars from the Delhi district to the number of 15,000 and from

other neighbouring districts to the number of 10,000 were invited to
come in ... They all brought with them their trusty *lathis* [wooden
stick], and woe betide the non-co-operator who obstructed their loyal
intention.[55]

Aspects of press coverage

Significant dimensions of press coverage were brought into relief by
the visit. The initial Fleet Street response demonstrated implicit faith
in this royal enterprise. For the more important side of the tour's dual
purpose was to strengthen the prestige of the ruling authority and
deepen, as the *Observer* remarked, that 'instinctive loyalty' to the
monarch which, in the East, was the 'ultimate security of social
order'.[56] This belief in the role of monarchy was predicated upon a particular construction of political reality in the Orient, where the love
of prestige and visual display was combined with personal loyalty to
an individual ruler. Tradition and instinct characterised the Indian
outlook to authority, and this made Indians 'look towards the Crown
rather than towards Governments and executive authorities'.[57] Most
papers, whether Liberal or Conservative, quality or popular, manifested striking uniformity in their interpretation of Eastern political
sentiment. Despite its 'new-fangled revolutionists and republicans'
India was, the *Telegraph* contended, essentially monarchical. 'King-
ship is the only form of government the East has really understood,
and the tradition of loyalty is deeply ingrained among its peoples.'[58]
This instinct could best be tapped by *personal* contact with the 'most
popular young man in the British Empire'.[59] For *The Times* the 'personal and friendly' association of the Prince counted for 'much more
in the East even than good government'.[60] The *Guardian* noted how
the presence of the Prince would appeal to the 'instinct of the masses
and powerfully counteract the agitation for immediate Swaraj'.[61]
Echoing such views, the *Morning Post* wrote of the 'instinct of personal loyalty' to the sovereign being the 'first natural political sentiment in the Indian breast'.[62] In the East government was 'a business
conducted not by men but by a man. Loyalty is paid to a man and not
to a committee or a council or a system.' To most Indians, therefore,
the Prince appeared as invested with all the powers of government,
and that was why his 'vigorous, sympathetic and vivid personality'
would encourage their loyalty.[63] It was believed that both the personality of the royal ambassador and the loyalty of the Indian masses
would ensure a successful visit, and render an important service in the
tense political context of contemporary India. The political dimensions were emphasised equally by, for instance, such stalwarts of the

weekly press as the *Nation* and *Observer*. According to the former, if Reading and Montagu could frame a scheme by which the Prince would go to India 'as the herald of a new and courageous purpose, the visit may count as an epoch-making event'.[64] For the *Observer* the tour offered the 'best sedative' that India could experience. Though it might be used as a 'pretext for demonstrations of subversive opinion', in its appeal to the 'deeper spirit' of India it would afford a 'new standard of measurement for the forces of militant discontent and exhibit them as dwarfed by the volume of profound and usually silent devotion'.[65] Similar arguments were voiced in the daily press – the *Guardian*, like the *Express*, acknowledged the visit to be 'an act of state' by which the Raj hoped to 'strike a blow at the growing political discontents'.[66] From the beginning, therefore, the perspective of the London press mirrored that of government.

'Our prince in fairyland': capturing the spectacle

The London papers competed with each other to present the Prince to the British public. They delighted in describing the colour and pageantry which surrounded each visit to princely India, the grandeur being captured in widespread photographic coverage, often on the back pages to ensure wider impact. Phillips observed how:

> Politics have not troubled the Prince of Wales's progress through Rajputana . . . For the past fortnight we have lived largely in the Arabian Nights, with no discordant note to mar the harmony of successive pageants. Four Maharajahs have vied with each other in reviving the splendour of medieval India.[67]

The *Mail* found it 'impossible to exaggerate the magnificence of the reception and the lavishness of the hospitality', while the Prince himself wrote that he had 'enjoyed Oriental hospitality and sport such as I imagined existed only in books'.[68] 'Our eyes were aching with the beauty and splendour of it all,' concluded one reporter.[69]

Both the popular and the quality papers also highlighted the personal exploits of Edward to convey an image of a virile prince representative of a vibrant monarchy. The glamour of big game shooting, the British world of trophies and *shikar*, had traditionally formed a background to royal progresses through the subcontinent, and the Prince was keen to emulate his father's exploits.[70] The *Star* reported such engagements under evocative captions: 'Polo Prince wins India's heart – sporting prowess better than ceremonies,' 'Two more tigers in Prince's bag,' and 'Prince's visit to Khyber Pass – wild hill men cheer.'[71] A cheetah-aided buck hunt in Udaipur (*Guardian*, *Observer*), his first tiger shoot (*Gazette*), pig sticking in Jodhpur (*Telegraph*), his triumph at the Calcutta races (*Mail*), playing polo at Bikaner (*Daily News*) – these formed only a fraction of the exploits carried by Fleet Street, all emphasising how India was impressed by the 'soldier prince who speaks Hindustani'.[72] Though government efforts at stage management were alluded to, most papers assured their readers that the government merely provided transport for those unable to travel to see the Prince and denied any forced participation. Even Phillips, who reported at length on the official management of the tour, reassured the British public: 'In no sense has the tour been a failure. I do not see how in the circumstances it could have been a greater success.'[73]

Reporting opposition

Nevertheless there was disaffection in several cities. As discussed earlier, Montagu attempted to 'manage' what he considered misleading and exaggerated accounts of opposition in Bombay, Allahabad and Calcutta. However, it is important to note that press comment on unrest largely occurred within the context of royal coverage. This had the effect of marginalising the reporting that might otherwise have been devoted to non-co-operation *per se*. It also meant that even the Liberal, and to some extent pro-Congress, papers could not condone the attacks directed at the government through the person of the Prince. The press was torn between a desire to report the royal progress in terms of imperial strength and order and the obligation to cover the disturbances which formed its backdrop.

This was demonstrated at the beginning of the tour. Bombay was the triumphant entry that the officials had planned. According to Landon in the *Telegraph*:

> Nowhere upon the surface of Bombay was there visible even a trace of that disaffection which is troubling India today. But Mr Gandhi has determined to challenge this spontaneous, whole-hearted welcome from Indians of every race, religion, caste, and colour . . . the 'First City in India' has completely and contemptuously ignored him and all his works. Nothing could have exceeded the magnificence of the welcome of the Prince.[74]

The *Guardian* agreed, noting how 'Bombay creates a record for enthusiasm'.[75] The *Mail* described 'Five miles of festal streets' and highlighted the Prince's speech: 'I want to know you and you to know me.'[76] However, occurring simultaneously in parts of the city were violent clashes between non co-operators and the police, leaving 400 injured and twenty dead (including some Europeans).[77] The *Express*'s

15 'Huge crowds greeted His Highness, the Prince of Wales, Bombay, November 1921'

correspondent spoke of 'the Bombay battle zone', 'District where no European dare go unguarded', 'Howling fanatics'. Touring the city in an armoured car, Phillips found it 'seething' with unrest; in the 'native quarters' the scene was one of 'constant rioting and attacks on Europeans'.[78] Ironically, such incidents were occasionally reported side by side with articles proclaiming the success of the tour – for instance, in the *Daily News* and *Mail*.[79] Yet in general the press played down the seriousness of the disturbances. The *Morning Post* claimed that the agitators were 'representative only of the minority'.[80] According to the *Telegraph*, the 'actual casualties and damage' had been magnified as rumour has spread',[81] while the *Mail*'s special correspondent remarked, 'I do not know what impression has been made in England by the reports, but to us here, though deplorable, the whole thing has been trivial.'[82] A *Times* editorial summing up the tour in mid-December contended, 'We have heard too much of the riotous persons who disturbed a limited area, and not enough of the moving spectacle of the Prince's triumphant departure from Bombay. We must get these episodes into a right perspective.'[83]

Allahabad witnessed the most complete boycott of the tour. All papers reported the near complete closure of the city on the day of the Prince's arrival. 'The news from India today,' wrote the *Daily News* on 12 December, 'is so grave that we abstain, until we have further information of what is actually happening, from any comment upon it.' The following day's reports were little better and the paper had a front-page spread on the 'general lifelessness of the gaily bedecked city'. This was, the *Express* noted, the 'first check to a triumphant tour'.[84] Yet, as in Bombay, the papers generally sought to downplay the significance of the unrest. The 'immense mass' of the people, said the *Mail*, were 'moderate and well inclined' and when not 'terrified' had shown 'every desire to express its loyalty'.[85] It was 'intimidation and terrorisation of the most shameless kind' that were responsible for the boycott, claimed the *Telegraph* and *Morning Post*.[86]

Calcutta was viewed as a critical stage of the tour. As discussed earlier, prior to the visit Reading authorised thousands of arrests and used armoured patrols to prevent any recurrence of the incidents that had caught the government unawares in Bombay. Once again, Fleet Street generally chose to interpret the hartal as 'a failure'. The *Daily News*, though reporting that 'thousands of extremists' had been arrested, could still write of the 'pageantry' in Calcutta and the 'wonderful welcome' for the Prince.[87] The *Chronicle* noted how 'Indians defy Gandhi', while the *Morning Post* wrote: 'Calcutta makes history' and the 'Hartal overthrown.'[88] The *Express* acknowledged that there had been 10,000 arrests prior to the visit and that there was 'half mourning' in the city, yet proclaimed in large letters: 'Terrorism beaten'.[89] The next day the paper declared: 'Natives flout Gandhi' and '7,000 attend the races with the Prince.'[90] Similar headlines appeared in the *Observer* and *Telegraph*. The *Mail* reassured its readers that the city had 'belied all forebodings' and given the Prince a 'great welcome' with shouts of 'Ki jai'.[91]

Madras witnessed events similar to Calcutta, though on a smaller scale. While not wholly neglected by Fleet Street, which noted the contrast presented by 'Triumphal arches and shuttered shops', Madras was regarded as yet another triumph for the tour. The *Daily News* and *The Times* characterised the troublemakers as 'a mob of hooligans', while the *Guardian* referred to 'some rather ugly desultory rioting on the part of the budmashes'.[92] 'Rumour,' its editorial argued:

has been killing rioters heavily in Madras since the Prince of Wales arrived here. It began with one corpse . . . the figure then jumped to six dead natives, although nobody claimed to have actually seen these. When somebody conceived the idea of pushing bruised Gandhists into the river, gossip rushed the mortality up to startling figures . . . On inquiry from the highest official sources late last night, I was informed that the known number of deaths through fighting was five . . . Seeing that Madras city has a population of more than half a million, a sense of proportion forbids characterising the outbreaks as really serious . . . The whole business has had absolutely no effect whatever. The Prince's reception has been on splendid and spacious lines, testifying to the fine loyalty of Madras outside the inevitable little minority.[93]

For the *Spectator*, Gandhi and his followers, 'having failed to boycott the Prince, stirred up a violent riot and had to be dispersed by the troops'.[94] 'The forces of sedition have utterly failed,' declared the *Telegraph*.[95] Other stops in south India like Hyderabad, Mysore and Bangalore were similarly covered. Commenting on the Delhi visit in February 1922, the *Daily News* noted the 'Prince's triumph' and how 'Gandhi's followers call off boycott'.[96] The *Mail* similarly felt the Prince had a 'splendid reception' from the 'immense crowds', and the hartal was 'completely eclipsed';[97] 'Miles of cheering natives defy the hartal,' reported the *Express*.[98]

The conjunction of the Prince's tour and the non-co-operation movement had an unanticipated benefit for the government: it caused the latter to appear, at home, in an exceedingly negative light. As the *Saturday Review* maintained, 'the Bombay rioting . . . tends to heighten the wonderful impression he is making, for did not that rioting lead to the penitence by Gandhi . . . that he had been mistaken?'[99] Even papers like the *Herald* and *Guardian*, otherwise sympathetic to aspects of the Congress programme, condemned the violent opposition to the tour. The *Herald* found itself unable to commend the opposition, despite protesting against the violence used in its suppression: that the Prince's visit 'should be made the occasion of violent hostile demonstration is deplorable and disastrous'.[100] Similarly, the *Guardian* argued that Gandhi's confession meant that 'Civil disobedience hope [was] dashed to pieces'.[101] Gandhi's 'prestige', commented the *New Statesman*, suffered 'a double blow' in Bombay: 'Half the population of the city disobeyed him by gathering to welcome the Prince with remarkable enthusiasm; while the other half, or at least another fraction, disobeyed him equally, and much more seriously, by resorting to violence.'[102] Gandhi's penance was futile, said the *Express*, as it would not bring the dead back to life, adding, 'That Gandhi should go hungry may restore to his mind the common sense driven out by a confusion of shoddy sentimentality and anti-British venom.'[103] This downplaying of the significance of the unrest, and its perceived discrediting of Congress policy, after an initial shock response from some papers, was in evidence for the remainder of the tour.

According to the *Observer*, which was guided by the first-hand experiences of Chirol, the extremists had a twofold purpose in causing unrest. First, to force the government to undertake repression which would then be denounced as a return to autocracy; second, to create in Britain 'a sense of alarm and distrust, which may turn British public opinion against the reforms'.[104] But liberal opinion in Britain was turning against Gandhi and his methods.

> It is a fact worthy of note that the *Manchester Guardian* and other organs of Liberal opinion at home are at one in recognising that nothing but unmeasured anarchy can flow from the reckless programme which Gandhi presses on his countrymen ... It will certainly strengthen Lord Reading's hand in his policy of firmness and tolerance to know that all shades of progressive opinion in England realise to the full the real and grave dangers to India and the Indian peoples with which he is coping.[105]

Herbert Russell, the Reuters correspondent, reflected that at Bombay, even amongst the extremists, there was a:

> sort of sheepishness and shamefacedness as though born of the realisation that they had not really been playing the game towards this royal visitor who, whilst manifestly wishing them nothing but good, could by no stretch of reasoning be associated with what they were pleased to regard as their grievances. Such was the magnetic triumph of the finest Ambassador the Empire has known.[106]

There was therefore some justification in George Lloyd's observation that 'we did turn a highly delicate situation into a colossal triumph for the Prince and the worst defeat for Gandhi that he has ever suffered'.[107] Thus the majority opinion within Fleet Street was that the tour was a success – a personal triumph as well as beneficial for the empire. Landon wrote in the *Chronicle* that, though Edward remained above the political conflict: 'For a passing moment he has even coloured and assuaged the surface of sedition in India. It may well be that his presence here has saved us from a catastrophe far greater than that of 1857.'[108] Likewise, for the *Saturday Review* the Prince's visit had served to 'strengthen the ties' binding India to the British Empire.[109] His 'momentous' tour, added the *Morning Post*, was 'one more link to that golden chain which binds together the Monarchy and its subjects in an unbreakable bond'.[110]

There was, nevertheless, criticism – albeit infrequent and muted. Readers of the *Guardian*, for instance, were reminded that, though the hartals had failed to interfere with the impressiveness of the Prince's reception in Calcutta, the crowds at the state entry were mainly composed of Europeans and Anglo-Indians.[111] Stronger criticism was found predominantly in right and left-wing papers and was directed chiefly towards the visit as a political gambit. The *Morning Post*, *National Review* and *Spectator* all concurred with the *Saturday Review* in deprecating 'extravagant optimism' about its anticipated benefits: 'There are limits to what can be accomplished by even so winning a representative of the Crown . . . The visit would have admirably confirmed a successful policy; it cannot be an alternative to it.'[112] From an opposite political viewpoint, the *Herald* argued that 'empires in which gross injustice is permitted and gross tyranny practised cannot be held together by "smiling" tours . . . The ghosts of Amritsar cannot be laid by smiles and speeches . . . It is statesmanship, not sentimental journeys that make real and lasting peace.'[113] *The Nation* was more scathing and argued that the scenes of government intimidation must have shocked the designers of the royal tour, who 'never intended to evoke that note within the hearing of listeners in this country'.

> Yet now we are aware, in spite of the warm efforts of the special correspondents, that if native Calcutta did not entirely desert the line of route, the crowd was thin enough to disclose the solid character of the parade of military force.[114]

Criticising the 'semi-mystical parade' of the Prince, the journal argued that the:

> ancient troubles and complicated sorrows of a continent cannot be soothed by sending a pleasant young man about in railway trains, all handshakes and jollity, and proclaiming in his graver moments that he is 'anxious to learn'.[115]

Landon felt that, despite the manner in which the Prince had acquitted himself, 'he has not been able to make a single convert from Gandhism'.[116] Similarly the *Gazette* and the *Review of Reviews*, though at first proclaiming the visit a success, had by the end of the tour adopted a more pessimistic outlook. The *Gazette* believed that to some extent the visit had acted as a spur to the non-co-operation movement. The 'magic' of the King's name was:

> a force in India which we need to use carefully lest we exhaust it altogether. To bring it into operation at the present juncture may have seemed a legitimate risk to take, but it is doubtful whether that risk has been justified by the results.[117]

Writing in March 1922, the *Review of Reviews* admitted that the tour might have 'strengthened and confirmed the loyalty of ruling princes and others who were already loyal. But apart from this it is difficult to see that it has done any good, and therefore, since prestige goes a very long way with the native, it is regrettable that it was undertaken.' Such reactions at the end of the tour bore the impact of the events of early 1922, when the increasing violence of the non-co-operators culminated in the Chauri Chaura incident in February when twenty-two policemen were burnt to death. The government responded by taking a harder line, including the arrest of Gandhi on 10 March. Yet it is important to stress that even papers critical of the longer-term benefit of the visit, like the *Gazette*, seemed compelled to acknowledge some success for the Prince. It is this muffling of criticism, the drawing of the teeth of British critics that is significant. 'Fortunately,' concluded the *Gazette*,

> there is another side to the picture. There is another India besides that to which Gandhi and his allies in the main appeal . . . in the native states among the quiet, non-political agricultural people, and among the more virile but more vociferous races, it has been more potent for good.[118]

Dénouement

The difficulties facing the planners of the tour rendered the successes achieved all the more notable. The forces for change (political reforms and Indian reaction) threatened to come into conflict with the continuity the royal visit was intended to symbolise. It was precisely because of the atmosphere of Indian disaffection that methods of political propaganda and persuasion needed to be rigorously employed. Fortunately for the government, the Prince was a figure commanding the reverence of the bulk of Fleet Street, which made attempts to ensure the positive reporting of his activities far easier. As Chirol later reflected:

> English newspapers in India and at home, loyally taking their cue from official quarters, ignored or minimised the many unpleasant episodes of the tour, and the Prince, with his inborn tact and good temper, professed to make light of them.[119]

Although there were a minority of sceptics who felt like E. M. Forster (then private secretary to the Maharaja of Dewas) that 'You can't solve real, complicated and ancient troubles by sending out a good-tempered boy,'[120] it remained the case that, in the short term, a positive and grand image of the Raj was conveyed through the British press. Government publicity stressed how, despite the 'malicious efforts' of the non-co-operators, they had – with a couple of exceptions – produced 'negligible' results and the Prince traversed India with 'unshakable

courage, determination and good humour'.[121] Reading's summary of
the political benefits highlights the official imperatives behind the
visit. He claimed that the 'tour of duty' had strengthened the position
of both the princes and the moderate nationalists, whose cultivation
had been an important feature of the Raj, and had also boosted the
morale of the British in India.[122] To maintain imperial prestige it
was necessary for India 'to stand well' with the home government,
Parliament and people and to reassure vested imperial interests and
symbolise continuity and stability.[123] India's 'attachment to the
Throne' had been demonstrated through the general popularity of the
Prince's reception, which had 'confirmed the loyalty of the masses'.[124]
These could well have been Disraeli's words over four decades earlier.

Yet behind such rhetoric lay a harder political reality for the beleaguered Montagu. Coalition Liberals were under pressure throughout
1921 from the Conservative rank and file's vendettas against particular Liberal reforming Ministers. Montagu 'they hated most of all, as
a Jew . . . who had presumed to condemn the British perpetrators' of
Jallianwallah Bagh.[125] The efforts at news management by Montagu
reflected to an important degree his weakening political position.
There were two central issues at stake: the *problems* of India and the
image of the Raj in Britain. It is unlikely that either Montagu or
Reading seriously expected the royal visit to strengthen British rule.
Their chief purpose was rather to demonstrate to the British public
that India remained, notwithstanding the agitation of the preceding
years, a fundamentally ordered and respectful society in which the
authority of the Raj continued unimpinged. Whilst little could be
expected from the tour in concrete terms, to have cancelled or even
postponed it would, as Montagu saw, have sent a disastrous message
as to the essential ungovernability of India and, by implication, dis-
credited the recent political reforms and vindicated his critics: a 'visit
twice promised cannot be twice cancelled'.[126] The symbolism of the
tour was thus crucial, and helps explain why Montagu went to such
lengths to ensure that, whatever the reality, this at least rebounded to
his credit. Indeed, having the Prince as the focus of a demonstration
of loyalty was particularly appropriate, since the Conservative politicians and journalists who had been Montagu's most trenchant critics
also had a deep attachment to the monarchy. Hence a paper like the
Morning Post, however inclined to seize upon Indian protests and non-
co-operation as evidence of the failure of Montagu's policies, felt itself
obliged to emphasise the Prince's successes and the enthusiasm of
India.

Official claims for the benefits of the tour were endorsed by contemporaries, and some later commentators have concurred. Grigg

argued that the bulk of Fleet Street had 'made it perfectly clear that the hartals and disturbances have been a passing episode . . . There is no doubt at all in the public mind here, I believe, as to the tact and understanding with which he has carried out a very difficult task, or as to the profound impression he has made upon India.'[127] Despite the Bombay riots, according to Judd, the tour was 'never again to occasion such violence' and Gandhi's boycott calls were 'largely unsuccessful'.[128] Ziegler contends that in Bombay the Prince 'achieved something close to triumph'.[129] Other historians, however, have stressed the achievements of non-co-operation; the Prince, Sarkar writes, 'was greeted with an extremely successful countrywide *hartal*' on 17 November.[130] According to Rumbold, the decision to go ahead with the visit was a serious mistake, while Woods concludes that Montagu and Reading took 'an unnecessary gamble'.[131]

In terms of its wider political repercussions it can be argued that the hostility towards the Prince created an adverse reaction in Britain. Reading's wait-and see-policy *vis-à-vis* Gandhi and the extremists fed the critics of Montagu in London. Levine contends that the hartals were not just embarrassing for the government but 'aggravated' the attacks against Montagu in Parliament and 'set the stage for the end of his political career' in 1922.[132] Woods likewise argues that Montagu, who was forced to resign on 9 March, was the 'victim of a right-wing backlash' resulting from anger at the boycott of the Prince and also from worry within the Conservative Party at the speed of developments in Egypt and Ireland.[133] To an extent this was unavoidable. The timing of the tour would always have created a bigger strain for Montagu than the Viceroy. But over this he had little control. What he could seek to influence was the portrayal of the royal visit in Britain. In this Montagu was relatively successful, as this case study has demonstrated. However, in themselves media manipulation and news management were not sufficient to prevent the visit and the reactions it evoked forming another element in the growing political tide moving against the Secretary of State.

The Prince and publicity

Edward's perceptions highlight the distinction between the official image of the tour and the realities of the political situation. For one thing, as Ziegler notes, Edward was 'quite as colour-conscious as any of the British rulers' and was reluctant to visit India, having recently returned from lengthy worldwide tours.[134] Nevertheless, he had expressed a desire not to view sights but 'to see and meet people'.[135] The obvious attempt to keep him from the very people whose loyalty

the government was lauding – 'the distant waves of the hand to mur-
murous crowds' – was thus especially irksome.[136] He complained to
Reading:

> The ostensible reason for my coming to India was to see as many of the
> natives as possible and to get as near to them as I could. At least, I
> presume it was the main reason, and I looked upon that as my duty.
> Well, I am afraid that I have not had many opportunities of doing this,
> either in British India or in the Native States.[137]

However, he observed that the Indians 'love a tamasha' (show) and was
human enough to be taken by the crowds that turned out to watch
him play polo. Judging by the applause that greeted his every shot the
Prince wondered whether:

> one might have thought it was Pandit Nehru and not the Prince of Wales
> who was on the pony. But, while I was still not so naive as to suppose
> that the India won by Clive had been saved through my exertions on the
> polo field of Allahabad, I was thereafter inclined to take with a grain of
> salt the newspaper accounts of hostile demonstrations against the British
> Raj.[138]

The 'Ambassador of Empire' nevertheless understood the official
game and was not wholly taken in by the extravagant enthusiasm on
display. The dissatisfaction of Edward at the cover-up only emphasises
the success of the government measures at presentation and publicity.
At Lucknow, for instance, he observed that the government had countered the call for non-co-operation with 'certain material induce-
ments'. 'I noticed,' wrote the Prince, 'trucks circulating through the
streets with signs printed in Urdu saying "Come and see the Prince
and have a free ride," a form of enticement that never had to be
employed when my father travelled about India.'[139] He was 'very angry'
and 'insulted' at student boycotts at the universities in Allahabad and
Lucknow, and particularly infuriated when, at Benares, the authorities
tried to ' "kid" me' by filling the empty seats with high-school boys,
Boy Scouts, and Europeans: 'I suppose they hoped I would never get to
hear of what had been done, or realise what a b.f. they had made of
me!!!'[140] Edward realised that he had not been in touch with Indian
realities; rather he had perceived India through 'an interposed layer of
British officialdom and princely autocracy'.[141] To Montagu, whom he
disliked intensely and referred to as 'that despicable man', he complained in strong terms on New Year's Day 1922:

> let me tell you at once that the newspaper accounts at home of the
> various visits, ceremonies and receptions have almost invariably been
> hopelessly exaggerated, and reading these accounts from this end I feel

that camouflage is almost invariably the dominant feature. Naturally I deplore this, as I cannot bear to think that people at home are being given a wrong impression, which they most certainly are. They think my tour is a success ... this tour is by no means the triumphal progress that it is reported to be at home by the newspapers.[142]

Thus the attempt to use the Prince to set the seal on a new constitutional India failed because of the deteriorating political situation. The loyalty that the majesty of the royal presence was intended to display was visibly crumbling in the streets. The tour became largely a media event – a triumph of the ceremonial over the substance of a politically volatile India. There was much greater reliance upon traditional forms of pageantry, largely independent of the political circumstances in which the tour was occurring. The Disraelian facade needed to be maintained at least for the duration of the visit and domestic opinion assuaged. In this enterprise the press played a crucial part and, despite occasional misgivings, Montagu's media manipulation paid dividends in the short run. Imperial politics was about prestige, image and reputation – of nations, governments and individuals. The press was ideally suited in the creation of perceptions and the mass medium for its dissemination. Yet Montagu had originally hoped for significantly more from the tour; though it appeared largely successful from the pages of the British press, it did little to reassure Conservative critics of India's stability and nothing to reinforce the reform process.

Notes

1 Moneypenny and Buckle, *Life of Disraeli*, pp. 805, 827.
2 B. S. Cohn, 'Representing authority in Victorian India', in E. J. Hobsbawm and T. O. Ranger (eds), *The Invention of Tradition* (1983), pp. 185, 188.
3 *Ibid*. D. Cannadine, 'The context, performance and meaning of ritual', p. 108.
4 MacKenzie, *Propaganda*, p. 5, also pp. 3–4, 82.
5 B. N. Ramusack, *Princes of India in the Twilight of Empire* (Cincinnati OH, 1978), p. 92.
6 L. F. Rushbrook Williams, *History of the Indian Tour of H.R.H. the Prince of Wales* (1922), p. 219, RC/34.
7 Viceroy to Secretary of State, 6, 25 October 1921, RC/3; Rumbold, *Watershed*, pp. 259–60.
8 Viceroy to Secretary of State, 3 June 1921 RC/10. In India only Willingdon urged that the prince should not come while non-co-operation continued. (Willingdon to Viceroy, 15 April, 22 August 1921, RC/23; Willingdon to Secretary of State, 23 August 1921, MC/21.)
9 S. K. Brown to Beaverbrook, 5 June 1921, BP.
10 Viceroy to Secretary of State, 29 June, 19 July 1921, RC/10.
11 Secretary of State to Viceroy, 22 July 1921, RC/10.
12 *Ibid*.
13 Viceroy to Secretary of State, 24 July 1921, RC/10.
14 L. F. Rushbrook Williams, *Inside both Indias, 1914–1938* (n.d.), p. 45.

15 Home Poll, 195, 1921, p. 18.
16 Viceroy to Secretary of State, 30 July 1921, RC/10.
17 Home Poll, 238, 1922, p. 4.
18 Viceroy to Secretary of State, 12 October 1921, RC/10; Williams, *History*, p. 3.
19 Home Poll, 195, 1921, p. 15.
20 Lloyd to Secretary of State, 25 November 1921, MC/26.
21 Secretary of State to Viceroy, 29 July, and Viceroy to Secretary of State, 5 September 1921, RC/10.
22 Secretary of State to Viceroy, 30 July 1921, RC/10.
23 Spender, *Life* II, pp. 103–7.
24 Lloyd to Secretary of State, 1 July 1921, MC/26.
25 Secretary of State to Viceroy, 24 October 1921, RC/10; 'Memorials: Shivaji Memorial at Poona', L/PO/11/18; Husain, 'Organisation and Administration of the India Office', pp. 196–9.
26 Viceroy to Secretary of State, 19, 28 October 1921, RC/10. Ramusack, *Princes of India*, p. 113.
27 Viceroy to Secretary of State, 6 November 1921, RC/10. For negotiations prior to the visit see Gwalior to Viceroy, 2 July 1920, MC/11; Patiala to Secretary of State, 16 April 1921, MC/12; Viceroy to Secretary of State, 3 June 1920, MC/10; Secretary of State to Viceroy, 20 April 1921, MC/12; Lloyd to Secretary of State, 23 September 1921, MC/26.
28 Ramusack, *Princes of India*, p. 113.
29 I. Copland, *Princes of India in the Endgame of Empire* (Cambridge, 1997), pp. 28–44.
30 *Manchester Guardian*, 16 December 1921.
31 Duke of Windsor, *A King's Story* (1951), p. 169.
32 Secretary of State to Lloyd, 15 December 1921, MC/23.
33 Lloyd to Secretary of State, 25 November 1921, MC/26.
34 All dailies, 19 November 1921.
35 Secretary of State to Lloyd, 15 December 1921, MC/23.
36 Lloyd to Secretary of State, 25 November 1921, MC/26.
37 Secretary of State to Lloyd, 15 December 1921, MC/23.
38 *Times*, 14 December 1921.
39 *Daily Mail*, 15 December 1921.
40 Secretary of State to Beaverbrook, 17 January 1922, BP.
41 Secretary of State to Viceroy, 24 November 1921, MC/13.
42 *Ibid.*
43 Secretary of State to Viceroy, 9 December 1921, RC/10.
44 Secretary of State to Viceroy, 5, 9 December 1921, L/P&J/6/1777.
45 Secretary of State to Viceroy, 14 December 1921 RC/10.
46 *Ibid.*
47 *Westminster Gazette*, 18 March 1922.
48 Viceroy to Secretary of State, 18 December 1921, RC/10.
49 Viceroy to Secretary of State, 24 December 1921, RC/10.
50 Secretary of State to Ronaldshay, 2 February 1922, MC/28.
51 Lord Zetland (Ronaldshay), *My Bengal Diary*, 25 December 1921, II, 142, MSS Eur D609/2, Zetland Collection.
52 Ronaldshay to Secretary of State, 29 December 1921, *ibid.*, D 609/4.
53 Secretary of State to Ronaldshay, 2 February 1922, MC/28.
54 *Daily Express*, 17 March 1922.
55 *Star*, 18 March, *Morning Post*, 17 February 1922.
56 *Observer*, 23 October 1921.
57 *Times*, 26 October 1921.
58 *Daily Telegraph*, 26 October 1921.
59 *Star* 26 October 1921.
60 *Times*, 26 October 1921.
61 *Manchester Guardian*, 16 December 1921.

62 *Morning Post*, 26 October, *Daily Chronicle*, 26 October, *Daily News*, 18 November, *Daily News*, 27 October, *Daily Telegraph*, 26 October, *Spectator*, 29 October, *Daily Mail*, 26 October, *Times*, 17 November 1921.

63 *Morning Post*, 18 November 1921.

64 *Nation*, 1 October 1921.

65 *Observer*, 23 October 1921.

66 *Manchester Guardian*, 16 December, *Daily Chronicle*, 26 October, *Daily Express*, 18 November 1921.

67 *Daily Express*, 28 December 1921.

68 *Daily Mail*, 1, 21 December 1921; Windsor, *King's Story*, p. 164.

69 *Daily Express*, 28 December 1921.

70 Windsor, *King's Story*, p. 167.

71 *Star*, 30 January, 13 February, 6 March 1922.

72 *Manchester Guardian*, 28 November, *Observer*, 27 November 1921, *Daily News*, *Westminster Gazette*, 12 January 1922, *Daily Telegraph*, 1 December, *Daily Mail*, 28 December, *Daily News*, 31 December 1921, *Westminster Gazette*, 2 March 1922.

73 *Daily Express*, 17 March 1922.

74 *Daily Telegraph*, 18 November 1921.

75 *Manchester Guardian*, 18 November 1921.

76 *Daily Mail*, 25 November 1921.

77 Sarkar, *Modern India*, p. 212. Higher figures are cited in e.g. S. Jackson, *Rufus Isaacs* (1936), p. 257; H. Tinker, *Viceroy Curzon to Mountbatten* (Karachi, 1997), p. 94.

78 *Daily Express*, 21, 23 November 1921.

79 'Brilliant scene' and 'Serious riot', 18 November; 'Bayonets in Bombay', 'Soldiers charge riotous mob', 'Over 200 arrests', 'Loyal Indians welcome the Prince', *ibid.*, 21 November; 'More Bombay riots' and 'The prince garlanded with flowers', *Daily Mail*, 21 November.

80 *Morning Post*, 19 November 1921.

81 *Daily Telegraph*, 21 November 1921.

82 *Daily Mail*, 25 November 1921.

83 *Times*, 14 December 1921.

84 *Daily Express*, 13 December 1921.

85 *Daily Mail*, 15 December, *Daily Herald*, 14 December 1921.

86 *Daily Telegraph*, *Morning Post*, 13 December 1921.

87 *Daily News*, 27–9 December 1921.

88 *Daily Chronicle*, 27 December, *Morning Post* 28–9 December 1921.

89 *Daily Express*, 27 December 1921.

90 *Daily Express*, 28 December 1921.

91 *Daily Mail*, 27 December 1921.

92 *Manchester Guardian* and *Daily News*, 14, 16 January, *Times*, 16 January, *Morning Post* 15 January 1922.

93 *Manchester Guardian*, 17 January 1922.

94 *Spectator*, 21 January 1922.

95 *Daily Telegraph*, 20 January 1922.

96 *Daily News*, 12 February 1922.

97 *Daily Mail*, 15–17 February 1922; *Daily Telegraph*, 18, 23 February 1922.

98 *Daily Express*, 16 February 1922; *Westminster Gazette*, 17–18, 20 February 1922.

99 *Saturday Review*, 26 November 1921.

100 *Daily Herald*, 21 November 1921; *Saturday Review*, 17, 31 December 1921.

101 *Manchester Guardian*, 21 November, also 16 December 1921.

102 *New Stateman*, 26 November 1921.

103 *Daily Express*, 21 November 1921.

104 *Observer*, 18 December 1921.

105 *Observer*, 22 January 1922; *Nation*, 18 February 1922.

106 H. Russell, *With the Prince in the East* (1922), p. 23.

107 Lloyd to Secretary of State, 25 November 1921, MC/25; Viceroy to King, 17, 20, 24 November 1921, RC/1.
108 *Daily Chronicle*, 17 March 1922; *Daily Mail*, 30 December 1921; *Review of Reviews*, December 1921.
109 *Saturday Review*, 24 June 1922.
110 *Morning Post*, 18 March 1922.
111 *Manchester Guardian*, 27 December 1921.
112 *Saturday Review*, 5 November 1921; *Morning Post*, 26 October 1921; *National Review*, February 1922.
113 *Daily Herald*, 27 October 1921.
114 *Nation*, 31 December 1921.
115 *Nation*, 28 January 1922.
116 *Daily Express*, 17 March 1922.
117 *Westminster Gazette*, 18 March 1922.
118 *Ibid.*
119 V. Chirol, *India* (1926), p. 247.
120 M. Lago and P. N. Furbank (eds), *Selected Letters of E. M. Forster* (1985), p. 17.
121 Williams, *History*, pp. 221–2, RC/34; Viceroy to Secretary of State, 22 March 1922, RC/11; Williams to E. W. M. Grigg, 23 February 1922, MS Film 1000, Grigg Papers, Bodl.; *History of* The Times (1952)IV, pp. 2, 855.
122 This was to be welcomed, given falling European recruitment to the ICS after the war. (D. C. Potter, *India's Political Administrators*, Oxford, 1986, pp. 84–5.)
123 Viceroy to George V, 23 February 1922, RC/1; Viceroy to Secretary of State, 16 February 1922, RC/4.
124 Viceroy to Secretary of State, 22 March 1922, RC/11.
125 Wilson, *Downfall of the Liberal Party*, p. 221.
126 Cited in Rumbold, *Watershed*, p. 260.
127 Grigg to Godfrey Thomas, 19 January 1922; Grigg to Thomas, 30 March 1922; to Williams, 23 March 1922; to Dudley North, 6 April 1922, MS Film 1000, Grigg Papers, Bodl; J. Grigg, 'Edward VIII', *DNB* (Oxford, 1986), p. 273.
128 D. Judd, *Lord Reading* (1982), p. 223.
129 P. Ziegler, *King Edward VIII* (1990), p. 143.
130 Sarkar, *Modern India*, p. 205; R. Kumar, *Essays in the Social History of Modern India* (Delhi, 1983), p. 258.
131 Rumbold, *Watershed*, p. 260; P. Woods, *Roots of Parliamentary Democracy in India* (Delhi, 1996), p. 151.
132 Levine, *Politics, Religion*, p. 600.
133 Woods, *Parliamentary Democracy*, p. 181.
134 Ziegler, *Edward VIII*, pp. 136–7; R. Godfrey (ed.), *Letters from a Prince* (1998).
135 Prince to Nita Verney, 23 June 1920, MSS Eur D921/3, Verney Papers.
136 Windsor, *King's Story*, p. 165.
137 Prince to Viceroy, 28 December 1921, MC/46/4.
138 Windsor, *King's Story*, p. 163.
139 *Ibid.*, p. 162.
140 Prince to Viceroy, 28 December 1921, MC/46/4.
141 Windsor, *King's Story*, p. 165.
142 Prince to Secretary of State, 1 January 1922, MC/46/3.

CHAPTER TEN

Conclusion

London was the centre, not only of the largest empire in modern history, but also of a communications network extending around the world. The 'communications environment' within which the empire operated was a factor which shaped both the evolving character of British rule in India and the extent and potency of the nationalist challenge. Developing the insights of Innis, our attempts to understand political culture and practice in the imperial context have thus acknowledged the significance of the dominant modes of communication – which in the period before 1920 meant primarily the newspaper press, the electric telegraph and news agencies. It was these 'space-biased' and portable media that created the possibility of a hegemonic informational empire bound to the metropolitan centre. And it was, in turn, the character of these media – the content of their messages, the cost of information retrieval and use, along with the institutional and economic framework of domination – that were instrumental in determining the governing strategies of the Raj. The communicational environment – both communications as a process and its technological dimensions – was integral to the functioning of the imperial political structure in London as well as in the periphery.

At the heart of Britain's imperial and communications system was Fleet Street. Despite the development of wireless telegraphy and the cinematograph, the press remained the most significant medium of communication for projecting the image of empire in the late nineteenth and early twentieth centuries. Indeed, it was itself undergoing a technological revolution affecting the speed, cost, quantity and quality of information available. Equally significant were developments intrinsic to the medium – the growth of a more vibrant national press staffed by politically prominent journalists, with greater popular appeal and mass circulations, and conducted by a new breed of assertive proprietors.

These changes would, in themselves, have brought Indian affairs into greater media prominence. What ensured that they did was the simultaneous development of a more sophisticated and self-conscious nationalist opposition within India which made skilful use of the press and platform to galvanise the masses whilst engaging in direct appeals to Parliament and the British public – thus posing an increasingly formidable challenge to British rule. The press both contributed to and reflected this confrontational environment. Empire became a contested terrain, and one of the key theatres in which the contest took place was the print media.

The developing power and influence of the press transformed the morphology of the information environment within which the government operated. It responded by trying to influence the shape of press coverage, a goal it took increasingly seriously in the first decades of the twentieth century. Traditionally the constraints of distance and time reduced the capacity of newspapers to influence Indian events and facilitated the control of reporting by the Raj. Ronald Storrs, who was involved in the dissemination of British propaganda in Egypt during the First World War, reflected upon 'the damping and blanketing effect of remoteness, whether of time or place'.[1] Indeed, the Indian government was itself the main font of subcontinental news. The arrival of the telegraph appeared to threaten this privileged access to information and forced an official response, one aspect of which was to develop a symbiotic relationship with Reuters. The company received government patronage and subsidies, and was accorded priority for major official communiqués. Reuters, in return, often delayed or distorted coverage. Fleet Street's reliance on Reuters, together with the agency's dominant position within the subcontinent, meant that its distortions had a major impact on perceptions of Indian events. Thus, despite the enhanced facilities for information transmission, structural features of the communications environment continued to provide government with opportunities for influencing the content of news transmitted to London.

But government did not only seek to influence the flow of news to London; it sought also to influence the interpretation of events and official policy by the press. Facilitating this endeavour was the fact that all leading journalists took pride in the British achievement in India, and in the empire generally. Yet, this imperialist sentiment notwithstanding, there was a spectrum of opinion on how Indian policy should evolve in response to the challenges of the new century. Importantly, many papers lacked a firm or coherent line on such matters as the necessity for reform or repression, and officials could work to alter the mind of an editor – by meeting him for a discussion, or supplying him with confidential information.

This India Office concern to manage news and comment by the national press was motivated by two main considerations: the effect of press reporting on attitudes in Britain towards the government's India policy and the influence that the London press was perceived to exert in India. This dual capacity for influence was a concern for imperial administrators which intensified over time. Prior to 1914 endeavours to shape newspaper reporting were undertaken almost exclusively through informal channels, relations between journalists and government being conducted at the highest levels, with the Secretary of State (and Viceroy) directly courting editors and proprietors. These efforts were *ad hoc*, contingent upon the weight particular Secretaries of State happened to attach to the matter. Thus, while Morley took advantage of Fleet Street contacts to cultivate newspaper opinion, Chamberlain made only minimal moves in that direction. The effectiveness of informal contacts owed much to the fact that relatively few journalists made their way to the subcontinent and there were not very many India specialists in London. The resulting small world of press experts included such influential commentators as Chirol, Fraser, Scott, Cotton, Gardiner, Strachey, Lansbury, Spender, Garvin and Dawson. These journalists were part of the critical elite of opinion formers on India, and their commentaries interpreted to a wider public the character of events in India and the nature – and degree of success – of government initiatives. Politicians and administrators inevitably considered that they were being judged by these press critics, and this formed part of a wider sense in which the Fourth Estate, and the millions of readers (and hence voters) behind it, were an element in the political process that could not be ignored.

Though the above pages have analysed and described how the nature of the coverage accorded by the quality and popular press varied in tone, style and often content, it is nevertheless both appropriate and necessary to speak of the Press as a whole, for to overemphasise the distinction between the two would hinder a complete appreciation of the press–politics nexus. Much united as well as divided the so-called quality and popular papers, and it is frequently useful to speak of a collective Press opinion on India. While the full range of issues covered by papers might vary, there were common themes in their imperial coverage. Indeed, most papers derived much of their basic information from the same source – Reuters news agency. Journalists, too, moved between quality and popular (as well as between Anglo-Indian and British) papers or contributed articles to both. Proprietors – like

Newnes and Northcliffe – could have their feet in both camps. Politicians were aware of gradations in press coverage, and might well hold personal views on individual papers and journalists. Yet they had to treat Fleet Street as a whole and could not afford to ignore certain sections. Similarly, Indian nationalists considered the range of British press coverage as indicative of the state of public opinion on India – though it was certainly true that some papers were better known and considered more influential in India than others.

The Great War did not merely intensify each of the above developments, but shifted the accepted parameters of press involvement in official propaganda in Britain, as well as government's attitudes *vis-à-vis* print and publicity. The war raised the visibility of India in London, with newspapers devoting significantly more attention to its problems and future, while domestic political and economic disorientation following the war rendered the public response to imperial policy more uncertain. These developments needed to be addressed and countered in London as well as in India, since, paradoxically, the vulnerability of the Raj coincided with the increasing confidence and reach of the national press and its ability to impact on political and public debate. Pushed on to the defensive, the government had to evolve more deliberate and systematic approaches to imperial publicity and opinion formation through the media.

The war years marked a watershed in government–press relations. They heightened awareness of the power of publicity, and formal relations between Whitehall and the press were established – despite misgivings in many quarters. Within days of the outbreak of conflict 'Governments discovered that the Press was going to play a vital part, and began to show a solicitude for editors and writers which was both new and flattering'.[2] Fleet Street responded by providing a medium for the government to address the people. Yet it retained a certain critical freedom, and performed, in important respects, the function of an opposition. The war therefore highlighted the multi-faceted role of the press as purveyor of news, critic and propagandist. This was appreciated by Lloyd George, who was convinced that propaganda and public morale could decisively affect the outcome of the conflict. Individual government departments established press offices, a separate Ministry of Information was set up, and numerous journalists and proprietors entered government service. By the end of the war information and propaganda had become accepted features of government. The logic of Coalition politics in the post-war years reinforced this process, as parties and individuals (most notably the Prime Minister himself) sought to strengthen their position by appealing to newspaper support.

The India Office shared in these wartime moves towards the formalisation of mechanisms for publicity and news management. Although part of the broader trend to greater political involvement with the press, these developments also reflected certain distinctive features of the Indian situation. To begin with, the war stretched Britain's imperial commitments to the limit and there was a need to ensure India's loyalty and maintain its flow of recruits into the armed services. In addition to control through censorship, attempts to influence through propaganda were undertaken by the India Office. Along with the Ministry of Information it distributed newspapers and pamphlets to boost the morale and recruitment of Indian troops, manipulated briefs to Fleet Street and the Indian press, and generally controlled media access to the war front.

The individual who did most to initiate and oversee the shift from informal to formal press management at the India Office during the war years, and consolidate the new regime in the immediate post-war period, was Edwin Montagu. His political philosophy encompassed an approach to imperial rule where it was hoped that public opinion, debate and co-operation would modify (and if possible replace) coercion, repression and force as the underlying principles of imperial praxis.

> The feeding of the newspapers, the answering of enquiries, the touch between the government and those who would support it, all this needs doing. It would be so splendid if political methods rather than coercive ones were successful in downing the opponents of the British government.[3]

What distinguished Montagu was not simply his belief in the necessity of cultivating a good press but the importance he attached to integrating the press management function into India Office procedure and routine. Under Montagu there was a coalescence of two trends. One, which had been set in motion prior to his appointment but which he was resolved to carry through, was the advancement of India's political development through constitutional reform. Yet Montagu saw that in the political culture of the new India that was to be brought into existence there would be a crucial role for publicity in creating a positive public image of imperial rule. 'You cannot govern without explanation,' he remarked to Chelmsford, and saw favourable publicity and newspaper coverage as essential to the success of reform.[4] Separate committees were accordingly set up to oversee reform and publicity at the India Office. This entailed not merely developing further long-standing informal contacts between the government and press, but making press relations an explicit dimension of imperial government.

Montagu's conception of liberal governance implied an informed public debate within the parameters set by the requirements of imperial governance. The state, at this stage in the development of Indian civil society, needed to nurture this process and play a role in disseminating information and actively shaping debate. But this was not merely a product of Liberal theorising. Hard political necessities pointed in the same direction. Montagu needed to bolster his political standing. As a Liberal member of a Conservative-dominated Coalition, Montagu's position became increasingly precarious after the war. Negative press reporting threatened to compromise his official initiatives and further weaken his Ministerial standing. News management acquired a new significance under these circumstances – as the conduct of the similarly placed Prime Minister demonstrated. Equally significant, Montagu considered the reaction of the British 'political public', as gauged largely through the pages of the press, to be crucial to the fate of the reforms. By gaining newspaper support, that of Parliament would be reinforced and an impression conveyed of whole-hearted backing from the British nation. Pockets of opposition would be isolated, with little opportunity of utilising the press to focus grievances. This, in itself, would strengthen the position of the Secretary of State and his policies. An impression of unanimity would assist in convincing India of the good intentions of the Raj. Because the British press was regarded as mirroring British opinion, strained relations between the India Office and Fleet Street could undermine the goodwill in India necessary for the effective operation of the new constitutional arrangements.

Thus during Montagu's tenure the press–politics nexus was transformed. Several objective factors were at work which could have pushed most Secretaries of State in this direction, such as the propaganda requirements of the war and the rise of an increasingly sophisticated nationalist movement employing new weapons of resistance – many of them intended to generate publicity. Yet Montagu's contribution was vital. As the last inheritor of the Liberal tradition of Macaulay and Ripon, Montagu welcomed the idea of promoting debate concerning the evolution of official policy in India. The reforms had sought to do this, and one of Montagu's long-standing complaints was the reluctance of the rigid hierarchy of the Government of India and the ICS to carry forward the process of public debate – its unwillingness to countenance the idea of an independent, active and informed Indian public opinion. But if Montagu was continually pushing the Government of India forward, he himself was equally under pressure domestically. Having burnt his Liberal boats in 1917, Montagu was highly vulnerable politically – as one of the few remaining Liberals in the Coalition, and one lacking any real resources of personal or political popularity or respect. Quite the reverse – Montagu's introverted and sensitive personality, combined with the currents of anti-Semitism still strong in British politics and the fact that his Indian policies, however necessary in the context of the war, were essentially anathema to many Unionists, meant that he was despised by a large section of the Conservative Party. Montagu needed allies and sought them in the fourth estate. This supplied a powerful imperative to his media management agenda. Ideology and personality combined in Montagu to accelerate the process by which the India Office responded to the challenges of the new media environment.

The consequences of press management and publicity under Montagu, as analysed in the case studies, were varied and limited by a variety of factors operating both in the metropolis and on the periphery. Censorship and war propaganda were generally effective, though in terms of recruitment the government in India utilised a variety of strong-arm tactics little short of coercion to fill its military ranks as the war dragged on. Montagu obtained press support for his reform initiatives through 1917 and 1918. The pressures of the conflict had created a remarkable degree of political consensus in Britain. There was agreement in Parliament and the Cabinet that India's war effort needed to be rewarded and the reforms, as drafted, were a joint product of Conservative and Liberal initiatives. The press had warmed to Indian gallantry in the field: *The Times* remarked how the Indian empire had 'overwhelmed the British nation by the completeness and unanimity of its enthusiastic aid'.[5] Even so, there remained the possibility that a small but vocal opposition to the reform process could coalesce around the more Conservative press. Efforts to ensure wide press support could therefore not be neglected, and there was general recognition, even among Montagu's critics, that his attempts to court the press had been successful. The *Saturday Review* complained that he appeared to have 'comatised any amount of good-natured peers and MPs; the Northcliffe press purrs approval, and every Sunday Mr Garvin indites a first or second or third Book of Montagu'.[6]

Yet the success of attempts to shape newspaper coverage could never be taken for granted. Fleet Street reacted to events and issues in ways which the India Office could not dictate. Montagu was aware of the need to 'walk very warily', and did not expect an immediate change of emphasis in a paper 'simply because of information obtained from a Government office'.[7] His efforts, for instance, to persuade Strachey of the merits of the reforms ended in failure, while his friendship with Beaverbrook did not prevent the *Express* giving dramatic coverage of opposition to the Prince of Wales in India. More important, the attempt to influence the line of an editor or journalist was likely to be successful only at the margin, when the paper had no strong or predetermined opinion on an issue, or where it was not at odds with some wider political agenda. In the face of more controversial issues, or profounder shifts in party allegiance, the personal appeals of a Secretary of State were likely to prove ineffectual.

The transitory nature of the political consensus over India and the fragility of Coalition politics were revealed even before the reforms had passed on to the statute book. Press coverage of the Amritsar massacre and its aftermath fatally damaged the press–politics nexus that Montagu had cultivated over reforms as well his own standing within the Coalition. 'Dyerarchy' appeared to have triumphed over 'Dyarchy'. Revealed was the capacity of the press to affect domestic politics, to impact on Indian opinion, to undermine the position of the Secretary of State and expose the limitations of India Office media management. By rallying to Dyer's defence Gwynne, Strachey and Maxse took discussion of Indian issues beyond the more manageable world of the political elite into the emotive realm of general popular feeling. In responding to the crisis Montagu's scope for manoeuvre was circumscribed by the actions and attitudes of the Viceroy and government in India. Censorship was imposed in the immediate aftermath of the massacre and proved effective in the short run – in the sense that the event went largely unreported in London. However, when the full story surfaced in December the reaction was all the more powerful. The exposure of government prevarication and censorship undermined the trust necessary for the exercise of media influence, and the story acquired new strength. Further, whereas over the issue of reforms a united front was conveyed, in the case of Jallianwallah Bagh the press was able to exploit the political cleavages exposed between Whitehall and New Delhi. For the Viceroy, too, the negative publicity generated in Britain was damaging, since, as he remarked to Montagu, the Indian newspapers took their lead from Fleet Street and it was by the opinion of the British public that the government of India would ultimately be judged. Dyer's action sent shock waves throughout India, the empire and the world. For a government seeking to build a consensus around reform, this was disastrous. It was hoped, however, that the unanimity with which Dyer was condemned at home would reassure Indian opinion that Britain remained committed to liberal reform. Consequently it was highly damaging when a section of the diehard Conservative opinion in Fleet Street (and in Parliament) came to Dyer's defence.

The visit of the Prince of Wales, originally planned for 1920 as the coping stone of the reform process, became far more defensive in character in the context of reaction to the Amritsar massacre and Gandhi's launch of non-co-operation. In this tense political situation the symbolism inherent in any royal tour gained added significance. The visit represented an attempt to restore consensus around a monarchical figure who, it was hoped, would appeal to the Indian masses as well as the Conservative elements in British politics and society. Pressure for the visit came from Reading, for whom it became a test of India's governability. Montagu's efforts in London were directed chiefly at circumventing bad publicity and deflecting criticism. In the short run a variety of stratagems, assisted by an essentially reverential and loyal press, created a relatively positive image of the royal progress in the pages of Fleet Street. As the *Review of Reviews* remarked at the tour's completion in March 1922: 'By clever window-dressing all its brilliant features and its apparent successes have been brought into the limelight, and all disorder and disaffection has been thrust into the background and carefully veiled.' However, the deep-rooted political problems in India, as well as within the Coalition government, could not be solved by a stage-managed royal tour. Politically Montagu's actions were undermined by Reading's reluctance to arrest Gandhi and take a harder line against the non-co-operators. With the further weakening of the Coalition and crises over Turkey, Egypt and Ireland, critics in Parliament saw the decision to expose the representative of the monarchy to hartals as further proof of Montagu's ineptitude, and an indictment of the reform process he had initiated.

Overall, the notion that Fleet Street could be reliably integrated into the politics of India was subject to limitations. Publicity and debate couldn't obscure the essentially authoritarian nature of imperial rule. The Montagu–Chelmsford reforms did not appease all sections of the INC, and the weakness of the moderate Indian support meant Montagu was unable to demonstrate sizeable political dividends. Pro-reform publicity could not overcome or disguise this fact. Press operations involved a constant process of papering over cracks within the British establishment, between London and New Delhi, as well as between individual Secretaries of State and Viceroys. Further, co-operation between the London press and government could never be taken for granted, as coverage of the Amritsar massacre illustrated. On the basis of their reading of the London press, Indian politicians received an impression of a fractured British public opinion where ideas of Indian self-government and democracy were dismissed as facile illusions. In portraying Dyer as a hero the press gave Indians, as Rushbrook Williams noted, 'a very very poor impression as to the attitude of the British people in general . . . towards India's claims for self-government and that had an extremely unfortunate effect with all shades of liberal opinion'.[8]

It is apparent that the British press was a central institution of the Raj – a defining feature of the experience of empire, in Britain as well as in India. Though by the early twentieth century the line between press and politics had become increasingly blurred, the essential energy and variety of Fleet Street meant that homogeneity was barely sustained. The press was also a dynamic factor in the Raj equation. This was partly because it quickly struck deep roots in India, but it was also due to the rapidly changing technological and communication background of the late nineteenth and early twentieth centuries. Yet the impact of the press was also a product of the personalities who made and staffed it. Despite increasing commercialisation, there was still scope for men such as Dawson, Strachey and Garvin to pursue an independent line on imperial questions. Newspaper editors and proprietors were opinionated men of forceful character and they, as much as generals, civil servants and businessmen, made the empire what it was. Not only were they to be found in imperial centres like Calcutta, Simla, Delhi and Bombay, but their reporting and writing constituted the consciousness of the Raj. They described its ceremonies and catastrophes, its triumphs and tribulations, and did much to make the empire what it was in the eyes of millions of Britons and worldwide. As such their idiosyncrasies and prejudices were vitally important – a factor politicians such as Montagu could ill afford to ignore, but which they found difficult to manage or even predict.

Nevertheless, behind the personalities and political contingencies of the first decades of the twentieth century, more fundamental forces were at work. Europe's nineteenth-century lead in communication technology permitted the creation of extensive centralised empires. However, as Innis has argued, the extension of empire on these terms also sowed the seeds of its eventual decline as the governed peoples began to catch up with the imperial powers. Imperial rule depended very largely on a monopoly of information and control over its interpretation, both factors which came under pressure owing to the inroads of the London press and the communications revolution from the late nineteenth century. The efforts of politicians like Montagu represented an attempt to come to terms with the government's weakening comparative information advantage. As a nationalist literature and press developed in India, and also as British newspaper access to Indian information increased, the government had to win the battle for the minds of its own and subject populations in order to retain hegemony. This was in two senses a transitional period, with a growth in press, public opinion and nationalism, as well as a communications revolution which at first strengthened and then undermined the traditional system of imperial control. It was Montagu's achievement that he both responded to developments and recognised the connections between them. Yet it was beyond his capacity to reverse a set of parameters that had originated in the logic of imperial rule itself. His efforts to manipulate and manage the press during these years must also be interpreted as a sign of overall imperial weakness rather than of strength. By 1917 a Liberal experiment in reforming government in the context of informed Indian debate was probably already impractical. Attitudes were too polarised, and the structures of the Raj too immutable. The terminal blow was struck by Jallianwallah Bagh – an event which fatally compromised Montagu's political and media strategy. His fraught speech during the Commons debate on Amritsar can arguably be seen as marking the end of his career and even of the Coalition government. More important, it demonstrated that Montagu himself was all too painfully aware that an epoch in Indian government had drawn to a premature close.

Notes

1 R. Storrs, *Orientations* (1937), p. 151.
2 Spender, *Life* II, p. 21.
3 Secretary of State to Viceroy, 27 April 1918, CC/4.
4 Secretary of State to Viceroy, 10 February 1920, CC/12.
5 *Times*, 10 September 1914.
6 *Saturday Review*, 10 August 1918.
7 Secretary of State to Viceroy, 15 April 1920, MC/4.
8 Williams, MSS Eur T130/2, pp. 30–1.

APPENDIX ONE

Main information flows to Fleet Street

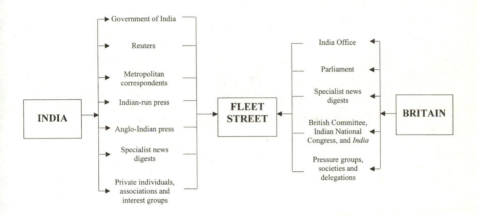

APPENDIX TWO

Politics–press:
official press management and control
prior to the First World War

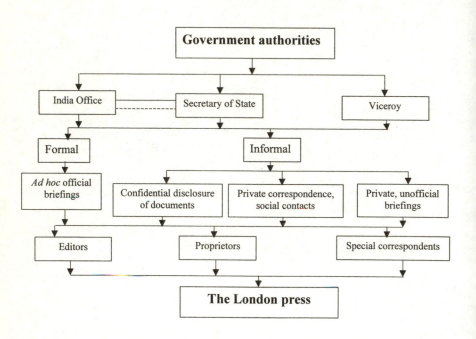

APPENDIX THREE

Official press management and control during and after the First World War

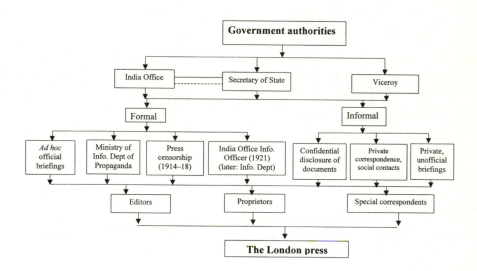

Government authorities

India Office — — — Secretary of State   Viceroy

Formal   Informal

| *Ad hoc* official briefings | Ministry of Info. Dept of Propaganda | Press censorship (1914–18) | India Office Info. Officer (1921) (later: Info. Dept) | Confidential disclosure of documents | Private correspondence, social contacts | Private, unofficial briefings |

Editors   Proprietors   Special correspondents

The London press

APPENDIX FOUR

Duties of the Publicity Officer

1 To collect from all departments in the office information which may be made public concerning India.
2 To sort, classify and prepare for publication the information so collected.
3 To issue to the Press all communiqués from the Office.
4 To be accessible at all times to representatives of the Press, to supply them with information asked for if available, and if not available to try and obtain it for them from India. To prepare information available for the Press, in the form desired by each journalist or agency.
5 To write periodically to the Director of Information, India (1) on points of news not sufficiently noted in London's correspondents' letters to Indian newspapers (2) and to obtain from them information specially required by the English Press.
6 To examine all Press cuttings, and generally to follow the current of opinion in Indian topics.
7 To keep in touch with the High Commissioner's Office both in obtaining information from it and supplying information to it and to issue communiques which the High Commission wishes to make to the Press.
8 To examine and report from the pamphlets and literature received from the Indian Publicity Department.
9 To keep in touch with the Indian Trade Commissioner.
10 To see the weekly reports from the several provinces on the Indian press, and the summary of them prepared in the India Office, and to make use of them in his work.
11 To undertake such other duties of a like nature as the Secretary-of-State may from time to time decide.
12 It is to be understood that the duties of this Officer are to be confined to the issue of information and that it will not be part of his duties to try and influence the opinions of the Press.

Source L/PWD/5/28, No. 259.

Prominent journalists and writers

Aitken, William Maxwell (Baron Beaverbrook) (1879–1964): Canadian entrepreneur and newspaper proprietor; MP (U.) 1910; owner *Express* 1916; first Minister of Information 1918; knighted 1911; peerage 1916.

Allen, George Berney (1862–1917): son of George Allen; businessman and proprietor of London journals *The Near East* and *Indiaman* 1914–17.

Allen, George William (1831–1900): businessman in India; founder *Pioneer* (Allahabad) and *Civil and Military Gazette* (Lahore); CIE 1879, KCIE 1897.

Bell (Charles) (Frederic) Moberly (1847–1911): founder *Egyptian Gazette* (1880); *Times* special correspondent in Egypt and manager 1890–1911.

Blumenfeld, Ralph David (1864–1948): American journalist *New York Herald* 1887–94; news editor *Mail* 1900–2; foreign editor and editor *Express* 1904–32.

Buck, Edward (John) (1862–1948): general manager Reuters India; Reuters representative Government of India from 1897; CBE and OBE 1918, knighted 1929; author *Simla Past and Present* (1904); retired 1933.

Buckle, George Earle (1854–1935): fellow All Souls College 1877–85; editor *The Times* 1884–1912; author with W. F. Moneypenny *Life of Benjamin Disraeli* (1914–20).

Chirol, Valentine (Ignatius) (1852–1929): clerk Foreign Office 1872–76; contributor *Levant Herald* 1880; Berlin correspondent *The Times* 1892–96; deputy director foreign department 1896–99, director 1899–1912; freelance special correspondent 1912–29; paid seventeen visits to India; member Royal Commission on Indian Public Services 1912–16; publications include *Indian Unrest* (1910); knighted 1912.

Colvin, Ian Duncan (1877–1938): journalist London office *Pioneer* and later at head office Allahabad 1900–3; assistant editor *Cape Times* 1903–7; leader writer *Morning Post* 1909–37; publications include *Life of General Dyer* (1929).

Cotton, H. E. A. (1868–1939): member Calcutta Corporation 1900–6; president Bengal legislature 1922–25; practised at Calcutta bar and special correspondent *Guardian*, Calcutta correspondent *Daily News*; India Office advisory committee on reform 1919; editor *India* 1906–19; publications include *The Century in India, 1800–1900*; CIE 1921, knighted 1925.

Cotton, Henry John Stedman (1845–1915): Bengal civil service from 1867, including chief secretary 1891–96; chief commissioner Assam 1896–1902; regular writer for London newspapers; KCSI 1902.

Cox, Harold (1859–1936): taught mathematics at Mohammedan Anglo-Oriental College, Aligarh, 1885–87; freelance correspondent *Guardian*; MP (L.) 1906–9; editor *Edinburgh Review* 1912–29.

Curtis, Lionel George (1872–1955): colonial administrator and author; worked on South African federation; joint founder of Round Table organisation and journal; prominent role in Indian constitutional reforms 1916–17; helped establish Royal Institute of International Affairs 1920–21; fellow All Souls College; CH 1949.

Dawson (Robinson) (George) Geoffrey (1874–1944): fellow All Souls College from 1898; Colonial Office South Africa 1899; editor Johannesburg *Star* 1905–10; twice editor *The Times* 1912–19, 1923–41; member Round Table organisation, editor of its journal.

Digby, William (1849–1904): merchant and journalist Ceylon 1871–76; editor *Madras Times* 1877–79; founder director Indian Political Agency 1887–92; secretary British Committee INC; editor *India* 1890–92; publications include *Famine Campaign in Southern India*; CIE 1878.

Donald, Robert (1860–1933): provincial journalist; editor *Chronicle* 1902–18; director Department of Information 1917; chairman Empire Press Union 1915–26; GBE 1924.

Fraser, Lovat (1871–1926): editor *Times of India* till 1907; editorial staff *The Times* 1907–22; chief literary adviser and contributor *Sunday Pictorial* and *Daily Mirror*; publications include *India under Curzon and After* (1912).

Gardiner, Alfred George (1865–1946): reporter *Northern Daily Telegraph* 1886; editor *Daily News* 1902–19; publications include life of Sir William Harcourt (1923).

Garvin, James Louis (1868–1947): provincial journalist; leader writer *Telegraph* 1899; editor *Outlook* 1905–6, *Pall Mall Gazette* 1912–15, *Observer* 1908–42; publications include *Life of Joseph Chamberlain* (1932–34); CH 1941.

Grigg, Edward William Macleay, first Baron Altrincham (1879–1955): secretary to editor *The Times* 1903; head Colonial Department *The Times* 1908–13; joint editor *Round Table* 1913; MP (L.) 1922–25; governor Kenya 1925–30; CVO 1919, KCVO 1920, KCMG 1928, peerage 1945.

Gwynne, Howell Arthur (1865–1950): Reuters special correspondent 1893–1904; editor *Standard* 1904–11, *Morning Post* 1911–37; CH 1938.

Harmsworth, Alfred Charles William (Viscount Northcliffe) (1865–1922): proprietor of weekly and daily newspapers; founder *Mail* 1896; proprietor *The Times* 1908–22; director British war mission to United States 1917; Director of Propaganda in Enemy Countries 1918; baronet 1903, baron 1905, viscount 1917.

Horniman, Benjamin Guy (1873–1948): journalist and author; staff *Portsmouth Evening Mail* 1894; special correspondent *Morning Leader* 1900, *Chronicle*, *Express* and *Guardian* 1903–4; *Statesman* (Calcutta) 1906–13; editor

Bombay Chronicle 1913; deported 1919; author *Amritsar and our Duty to India* (1920).

Hyndman, H. M. (1842–1921): journalist and politician; occasional contributor *Pall Mall Gazette, Fortnightly Review, Herald*; founder *Justice*; founder Social Democratic Federation; publications include *Indian Policy and English Justice* (1874).

James, Lionel (1871–1955): Anglo-Indian journalist; correspondent Reuters and *Times of India* – Chitral (1894–95), Mohmand, Malakand, Tirah (1897–98); special correspondent *The Times* covering Indian unrest 1907, Delhi durbar 1912; commanded BEF 1915–18; publications include *With the Chitral Relief Force* (1895); DSO 1918, CBE 1924.

Jones, Roderick (1877–1962): journalist in South Africa 1895; general manager Reuters South Africa 1905; general manager and managing director London 1915; director of propaganda Ministry of Information 1918; OBE 1918.

Kipling, Joseph Rudyard (1865–1936): author and journalist; correspondent *Civil and Military Gazette* (Lahore) 1882, subsequently *Pioneer* (Allahabad) till 1889; author of many books set in India; freelance contributor to London newspapers.

Landon, Perceval (1869–1927): *Times* special correspondent South African war 1899–1900, Lhasa 1903; *Mail* Delhi durbar 1903; India specialist *Telegraph* Prince of Wales's visit 1905–6, 1921–22; Persia, India, Nepal 1908; Delhi durbar 1911; publications include *Lhasa* (1905).

Lansbury, George (1859–1940): politician and journalist; MP (Lab.) 1910–12, 1922–40; founder editor *Herald* 1912; interested in Indian religions and theosophy.

Lethbridge, Roper (1840–1919): Bengal education service 1868–76; Indian political service and press commissioner Government of India 1878; editor *Calcutta Review* 1871–78; MP North Kensington; knighted KCIE.

Levy-Lawson, Harry Lawson Webster (Viscount Burnham) (1862–1933): politician and press proprietor; MP (L.) 1885–92 (U.) 1910–16; managing proprietor *Telegraph* 1903–28; chairman Newspaper Proprietors' Association; president Empire Press Union and Imperial Press Conferences 1920, 1925; member Indian Statutory Commission 1927–30; viscountcy 1919, GCMG 1927.

Low, Sidney James Mark (1857–1932): barrister, author, journalist; editor *St James's Gazette* 1888–97; literary editor *Standard* 1904–5, special correspondent Prince of Wales's Indian tour 1905–6; publications include *A Vision of India* (1906); knighted 1918.

Massingham, Henry William (1860–1924): provincial press correspondent; joined *Star* 1888, briefly editor 1890; editor *Labour World* 1891; editor *Chronicle* 1895–89; staff of *Daily News* 1901–6; editor *Nation* 1907–23.

Maxse, Leopold James (1864–1932): visited India on world tour 1886–87; editor *National Review* 1893–1932.

Nevinson, Henry Woodd (1856–1941): leader writer *Chronicle* 1897–1903, *Daily News* 1908–9, *Nation* 1907–23; Indian correspondent *Guardian* 1907–8; publications include *The New Spirit in India* (1908).

Phillips, Percival (1877–1937): American journalist 1895–1901; staff *Express* 1901–22; special correspondent *Mail* 1922–34; coronation durbar and tour 1911–12; Prince of Wales's tour 1921–22; inauguration of New Delhi 1931; KBE 1920.

Pilcher, G. (1882–1962): joined *Morning Post* 1907; private secretary to foreign editor 1909–14; its Calcutta correspondent and joint editor *Statesman* 1914–24; special correspondent North West Frontier, Sikkim, 1920, Duke of Connaught's and Prince of Wales's Indian tours 1920–22; MP (C.) 1924–29.

Reed, Stanley (1872–1969): joined *Times of India* 1897, editor 1907–23; *Chronicle* special correspondent India 1900, 1905–7; represented western India at Imperial Press Conferences 1909–30; director Government of India publicity 1914–18, vice- president Central Publicity Board, New Delhi, 1918; MP (C.) 1938–50; knighted 1916, KBE 1919.

Robinson, Harry Perry (1859–1930): American journalist and author; *Times* special correspondent worldwide and during Great War; Prince of Wales's Indian tour 1921–22; KBE 1920.

Russell, Herbert (William Henry) (1869–1944): joined *Express* 1900; Reuters war correspondent Great War and Prince of Wales's Indian tour 1921–22; publications include *With the Prince in the East* (1922); KBE 1920.

Russell, William Howard (1820–1907): *Times* journalist and war correspondent; covered Indian rebellion 1857–58, Prince of Wales's Indian tour 1876–77; publications include *My Diary in India* (1860); knighted 1895, CVO 1902.

Scott, Charles Prestwich (1846–1932): editor and proprietor (from 1905) *Guardian* 1872–1929; MP (L.) 1895–1905.

Spender, John Alfred (1862–1942): editor *Eastern Morning News*, Hull, 1886–90; staff *Pall Mall Gazette* 1892; assistant editor, then editor *Gazette* 1893, 1896–1922; publications include *The Changing East* (1926).

Strachey, John St Loe (1860–1927): freelance journalist *Saturday Review*, *Pall Mall Gazette*, *Economist*, *Standard* 1894; editor with C. L. Graves *Liberal Unionist*; editor *Cornhill Magazine* 1896–97; editor and proprietor *Spectator* 1898–1925.

Wedderburn, William (1838–1918): administrator, politician and writer; Bombay civil service 1860–87; president INC 1899, 1910; chairman British Committee INC; MP (L.) 1893–1900; succeeded his brother, the third Bart, 1882.

Wilkinson (Henry) Spenser (1853–1937): chief leader writer and specialist India correspondent *Morning Post*; first Chichele Professor of Military History and fellow All Souls College 1909–23; occasional correspondent *Post* till 1914, thereafter *Mail*.

Williams (Laurence Frederick) Rushbrook (1890–1978): fellow All Souls College 1914–21; professor of history Allahabad University 1914–25; director Central Publicity Bureau, New Delhi, during First World War, and Central Bureau of Public Information 1920–26; numerous publications; OBE 1919, CBE 1923.

Wrench (John) Evelyn (Leslie) (1882–1966): joined *Mail* 1904; editor *Overseas Daily Mail* 1904–12; founder English Speaking Union and Overseas Club 1910; editor *Spectator* 1925–32; CMG 1917, knighted 1932, KCMG 1960.

BIBLIOGRAPHY

Manuscript sources

Oriental and India Office Library and Records, British Library, London
Edmund Barrow Collection, MSS Eur E 420
Basil Blackett Collection, MSS Eur E 397
S. K. Brown Collection, MSS Eur E 253
Harcourt Butler Collection, MSS Eur F 116
Chelmsford Collection, MSS Eur E 264
H. E. A. Cotton Collection, IOR Neg 12037, Reels 1 and 2
H. J. S. Cotton Collection, IOR Neg 12037, Reels 1 and 2
Curzon Collection, MSS Eur F 111
James Dunlop-Smith Collection, MSS Eur F 166
G. K. Gokhale Collection, IOR Pos 11701, Reel 5
Hailey Collection, MSS Eur E 220
Hardinge Collection, MSS Eur E 389
Arthur Hirtzel Papers, MSS Eur D 713
Arthur Hirtzel Diaries, MSS Eur D 1090
K. M. Howgego Collection, MSS Eur C 340
Kilbracken Collection, MSS Eur F 102
Montagu Collection, MSS Eur D 523
Morley Collection, MSS Eur D 57
Reading Collection, MSS Eur E 238
Reading (Private) Collection, MSS Eur F 118
Richmond Ritchie Collection, MSS Eur C 342
Charles Roberts Collection, MSS Eur F 170
L. F. Rushbrook Williams Oral Archives, T 130/2
M. C. Seton Collection, MSS Eur E 267
J. P. Thompson Diaries, MSS Eur F 137
Ralph Verney Collection, MSS Eur D 921
Willingdon Collection, MSS Eur F 93
Fleetwood Wilson Collection, MSS Eur E 224
Zetland Collection, MSS Eur D 609

Departmental files
Information Department (L/I)
Political and Secret (L/P&S)
Private Office Papers(L/PO)
Public and Judicial (L/P&J)
Public Works Department (L/PWD)
Reports on Native Papers (L/R/5)
Services and General Department (L/S&G)

BIBLIOGRAPHY

State Proceedings (Political), Bengal and Punjab (select years)
House of Lords Record Office, London
Lord Beaverbrook Papers BBK/C/246 (Hist. Colls. 184 & 247)
R. D. Blumenfeld Papers (Hist. Coll. 185)
John St Loe Strachey Papers (Hist. Coll. 196)

British Library, London
Lord Northcliffe (Alfred Harmsworth) Papers
C. P. Scott Papers
J. A. Spender Papers

British Library of Political and Economic Science, London
A. G. Gardiner Papers
George Lansbury Collection

The Times *Archives, TNL Archives, London*
D. D. Braham papers
Geoffrey Dawson papers
R. Deakin collection
Foreign Managers' letter books
E. W. M. Grigg correspondence
Leader writers' diaries
B. K. Long collection
James MacGregor collection
Managers' letter books
Managerial files
Stanley Reed correspondence
H. W. Steed papers
The Times annotated copies
The Times obituaries
Valentine Chirol papers

Reuters Archives, Reuters Ltd, London
Annual Reports
Contract Books, 1906–26
Data books
General Service Suggestions to Correspondents
Roderick Jones File, 1915–18
Reuter Service Bulletins
Wages and Salaries File, 1888–1908

Northcliffe House, Offices of Associated Newspapers Ltd, London
Daily Mail Archives, including the *Daily Mail* Index

Offices of the Spectator, *London*
Bound files of *Spectator*
Letter Books

BIBLIOGRAPHY

Birmingham University Library
Austen Chamberlain Papers

Cambridge University Library
Crewe Collection
Hardinge Papers

Wren Library, Trinity College, Cambridge
Montagu Collection

Brotherton Library, University of Leeds
Morning Post Archives, Glenesk–Bathurst Papers

John Rylands University Library of Manchester
Manchester Guardian Archives

Central Reference Library, Manchester
Manchester Evening News Index
Manchester Guardian Index

Robinson Library, University of Newcastle upon Tyne
Walter Runciman Papers

Bodleian Library, University of Oxford
Geoffrey Dawson Papers
E. W. M. Grigg Papers
H. A. Gwynne Papers
H. H. Asquith Papers
Henry Nevinson Diaries/Journals
Round Table Papers
Selborne Papers

Nuffield College, Oxford
Raymond Postgate Papers, Cole Collection

Private collections
Edwin Montagu papers, Milton Gendel Collection, Rome
L. F. Rushbrook Williams letters, T. J. Fraser Collection, University of Ulster, Coleraine

India
A. Besant Papers, Nehru Memorial Museum and Library, Delhi
Government of India Papers, National Archives of India, Delhi: Home Political (Home Poll), series A, B and Deposit; Home Foreign
Indian Institute of Advanced Study, Simla

BIBLIOGRAPHY

Printed sources

Primary sources

Official publications
India Telegraph Department, Administrative Report, 1867–1913 (Calcutta, 1913)
Report of the Telegraph Committee 1906–07 (Calcutta, 1907)
First Royal Commission on the Press *Report* (1949)
Statement exhibiting the Moral and Material Progress and Condition of India, 1917–22, Government of India

Press files
(Bodleian Library, Oxford, and British Library Newspaper Library, Colindale)
Dailies: *Daily Chronicle, Daily Express, Daily Herald, Daily Mail, Daily News, Daily Telegraph, Manchester Guardian, Morning Post, Star, The Times, Westminster Gazette.*
Weeklies: *Nation, New Statesman, Observer, Reynolds's Weekly Newspaper, Spectator.*
Reviews: *Contemporary Review, Fortnightly Review, National Review, Nineteenth Century and After, Quarterly Review, Review of Reviews, Round Table, Saturday Review.*
Others (selected issues): *Asiatic Review, Echo, Grand Magazine, Homeward Mail, Illustrated London News, India, Indiaman, Indian Sociologist, Monthly Review, Overseas Mail, Pall Mall Gazette, Punch, St James Gazette, The Lloyd George Liberal Magazine, Truth,* overseas editions of Anglo-Indian newspapers

Oral sources interviewed
David Astor, Editor, *Observer* (1948–75), London, 1996
David Ayerst, journalist, *Manchester Guardian* (1920s, 1930s), Burford, 1991
John Linton, BBC, India (1940s, 1950s), Oxford, 1995
Iverach Macdonald, *The Times,* sub-editor (1935), Diplomatic Correspondent (1938), Assistant Editor (1948) and Foreign Editor (1952), Headington, Oxford, 1996

Secondary sources
(place of publication London unless stated otherwise)

Reference books
Baylen, J. O., and Grossman, N. J. (eds), *Biographical Dictionary of Modern British Radicals* (New York and London, 1988), III
Benn's Press Directory
Browne, T. B., *Advertiser's ABC*
Butler, D., and Sloman, A., *British Political Facts* (1980)
Dictionary of Indian Biography

BIBLIOGRAPHY

Griffiths, D. (ed.), *The Encyclopedia of the British Press, 1422–1992* (1992)
Houghton, W. E., *Wellesley Index to Victorian Periodicals* (Toronto, 1966–69)
Linton, D., and Boston, R. (eds), *The Newspaper Press in Britain* (1987)
——*The Twentieth Century Newspaper Press* (1994)
Mitchell's Press Directory
Murray's Handbook of India, Burma and Ceylon
Palmer's Index to *The Times*, 1790–1905
Sell's Dictionary of the World's Press
The Times Official Index, 1906 onwards
Willing's Press Directory

Books and pamphlets
Adas, M., *Machines as the Measure of Men* (Ithaca NY, 1989)
Agrawal, S., *Press, Public Opinion and Government in India* (Jaipur, 1970)
Ahvenainen, J., *The Far Eastern Telegraphs* (Helsinki, 1981)
Anderson, B., *Imagined Communities: Reflections on the Origin and Spread of Nationalism* (1983)
Angell, N., *The Press and the Organisation of Society* (1922)
Ashton, S. R., *British Policy towards the Indian States, 1905–1939* (1982)
Aspinall, A., *Politics and the Press* (1949)
Atkins, J. B., *The Life of W. H. Russell* (1911)
August, T. G., *The Selling of the Empire: British and French imperialist propaganda, 1890–1940* (Westport CT, 1985).
Ayerst, D., *Guardian: Biography of a Newspaper* (1971)
——*Garvin of the Observer* (1985)
Aziz, K. K., *Britain and Muslim India: A study of British Public Opinion vis-à-vis the Development of Muslim Nationalism in India, 1857–1947* (1963)
Bagehot, W., *The English Constitution* (sixth edition, 1891)
Bakshi, S. R., *Jallianwallah Bagh Tragedy* (Delhi, 1982)
Barns, M., *The Indian Press: A History of the Growth of Public Opinion in India* (1940)
Barrier, N. G., *Banned: Controversial Literature and Political Control in British India, 1907–1947* (Columbia MO, 1974)
Bartlett, F. C., *Political Propaganda* (Cambridge, 1942)
Bayly, C., *Information and Empire: Intelligence Gathering and Social Communication in India, 1780–1870* (Cambridge, 1996)
Bean, J. M. W. (ed.), *The Political Culture of Modern Britain* (1987)
Beaverbrook, Lord, *Politicians and the Press* (1925)
——*Men and Power, 1917–1918* (1956)
——*Politicians and the War* (1960)
——*The Decline and Fall of Lloyd George* (1963)
Bell, E. H. C. M., *Life and Letters of C. F. Moberly Bell* (1927)
Beloff, M., *Britain's Liberal Empire, 1897–1921* (1987) I
Bence-Jones, M., *The Viceroys of India* (1982)
Benians, E. A., Butler, J., and Carrington, C. E. (eds), *Cambridge History of the British Empire* (Cambridge, 1959), III
Benn, C., *Keir Hardie* (1992)

BIBLIOGRAPHY

Berelson, B., and Janowitz, M. (eds), *Reader in Public Opinion and Communication* (1953)

Birkenhead, Earl of, *The Life of F. E. Smith* (1965)

Black, J. B., *Organising the Propaganda Instrument* (The Hague, 1975)

Blewett, N., *Peers, the Parties and the People* (1972)

Blumenfeld, R. D., *R.D.B.'s Diary* (1930)

Boston, R., *The Essential Fleet Street* (1990)

Bourne, H. R. F., *English Newspapers* (1887) II

Boyce, G., Curran, J., and Wingate, P. (eds), *Newspaper History: From the Seventeenth Century to the Present Day* (1978)

Boyd-Barrett, O., *The International News Agencies* (1980)

Brake, L., Jones, A., and Madden, L. (eds), *Investigating Victorian Journalism* (1990)

Brendon, P., *Life and Death of Press Barons* (1982)

Briggs, A., and Burke, P., *A Social History of the Media* (Oxford, 2002)

Bright, C., *Submarine Telegraphy* (1908)

Brock, M., and Brock, E. (eds), *H. H. Asquith: Letters to Venetia Stanley* (Oxford, 1985)

Brodrick, St John, *Relations of Lord Curzon as Viceroy of India with the British Government, 1902–1905* (1926)

Bromley, M., and O'Malley, T. (eds) *A Journalism Reader* (1997)

Brown, F. J., *Cable and Wireless Communications of the World* (1927)

Brown, J. M., *Gandhi's Rise to Power: Indian Politics, 1915–1922* (Cambridge, 1972)

——*Modern India: Origins of an Asian Democracy* (Oxford, 1985)

——*Winds of Change* (Oxford, 1991)

Brown, L., *Victorian News and Newspapers* (Oxford, 1985)

Buck, E. J., *Simla, Past and Present* (second edition, Bombay, 1925)

Buitenhuis, P., *The Great War of Words* (Vancouver, 1987)

Burk, K. (ed.), *War and the State* (1982)

Burne, O. T., *Memories* (1907)

Burnham, Lord, *Peterborough Court* (1955)

Butler, D., and Stokes, D., *Political Change in Britain* (1971)

Butler, H., *India Insistent* (1923)

Butler, I., *The Viceroy's Wife: Letters of Alice, Countess of Reading, from India, 1921–1925* (1969)

Cannadine, D., *Ornamentalism* (2001)

Carrington, C., *Rudyard Kipling* (1986)

Carthill, A., *The Lost Dominion* (1924)

Castle, K., *Britannia's Children* (Manchester, 1996)

Chamberlain, A., *Down the Years* (1935)

——*Politics from Inside, 1904–1914* (1936)

Chanda, M. K., *History of the English Press in Bengal, 1780–1857* (Calcutta, 1987)

Chapman, C., *Russell of* The Times (1984)

Chapman-Huston, D. M. (ed.), *Subjects of the Day* (1915)

Charmley, J., *Lord Lloyd and the Decline of the British Empire* (1987)

Chirol, V., *The Middle Eastern Question, or, Some Problems of Indian Defence* (1903)
——*Indian Unrest* (1910)
——*India, Old and New* (1921)
Chisholm, A., and Davie, M., *Beaverbrook: A Life* (1992)
Churchill, W., *Great Contemporaries* (1937)
Clarke, T., *My Northcliffe Diary* (1931)
——*My Lloyd George Diary* (1939)
——*Northcliffe in History* (1950)
Collins, H. M., *From Pigeon Post to Wireless* (1925)
Colvin, I., *The Life of General Dyer* (1929)
Cook, E. T., *The Press in Wartime* (1920)
Copland, I., *The Princes of India in the Endgame of Empire* (Cambridge, 1997)
Cotton, H. E. A., *The Century in India* (Calcutta, 1901)
——*Calcutta Old and New* (Calcutta, 1907)
Cotton, H. J. S., *New India, or, India in Transition* (1885; revised edition, 1907)
Coupland, R., *The Indian Problem, 1833–1935* (Oxford, 1942)
Cowling, M., *The Impact of Labour, 1920–1924* (Cambridge, 1971)
Cranfield, L., *The Press and Society* (1978)
Cross, C., *The Liberals in Power, 1905–1914* (1963)
Crowley, D., and Heyer, P. (eds), *Communication in History: Technology, Culture and Society* (New York, 1991)
Cudlipp, H., *Publish and be Damned!* (1953)
——*The Prerogative of the Harlot: Press Barons and Power* (1980)
Curran, J. (ed.), *The British Press* (1978)
Curran, J., and Seaton, J., *Power without Responsibility: The Press and Broadcasting in Britain* (1995)
Curran, J., Gurevitch, M., and Woollacott, J. (eds), *Mass Communication and Society* (1977)
Curtis, L., *A Letter to the People of India* (1916)
——*Letters to the People of India on Responsible Government* (1918)
——*Dyarchy* (Oxford, 1920)
Dangerfield, G., *The Strange Death of Liberal England* (1970)
Darwin, J., *Britain, Egypt and the Middle East: Imperial Policy in the Aftermath of War, 1918–1922* (Cambridge, 1981)
Das, M. N., *India under Morley and Minto* (1964)
Datta, V. N., and Settar, S. (eds), *Jallianwallah Bagh Massacre* (Delhi, 2000)
Dayan, D., and Katz, E., *Media Events* (Cambridge MA, 1994)
Deibert, R. J., *Parchment, Printing and Hypermedia* (1997)
Deloche, J., *Transport and Communications in India prior to Steam Locomotion* (Delhi, 1993)
Denholm, A., *Lord Ripon, 1827–1909: A Political Biography* (1982)
Desai, A. R., *Social Background of Indian Nationalism* (Bombay, 1948)
Desmond, R. W., *Windows on the World: The Information Process in a Changing Society, 1900–1920* (Iowa City, 1980)
Deutsch, K. W., *The Nerves of Government: Models of Political Communication and Control* (1963)

Dewey, C., *Anglo-Indian Attitudes: The Mind of the Indian Civil Service* (1993)

Dibblee, G. B., *The Newspaper* (1913)

Dilks, D., *Curzon in India* (1969, 1970)

——(ed.), *Retreat from Power* (1981)

Dodwell, H. H., and Sethi, R. R. (eds) *Cambridge History of India* (Delhi, 1964) VI

Donald, R., *The Imperial Press Conference in Canada* (1920)

Draper, A., *The Amritsar Massacre* (1985)

Driberg, T., *Beaverbrook* (1956)

Dutton, D., *Austen Chamberlain: Gentleman in Politics* (1985)

Edward, Prince of Wales, *Speeches by H.R.H. the Prince of Wales, 1912–1926* (n.d.)

——Duke of Windsor, *A King's Story* (1951)

Eisenstein, E., *Printing Press as an Agent of Change* (Cambridge, 1979)

Eldridge, C. C. (ed.), *Empire, Politics and Popular Culture* (Lampeter, 1990)

——*Imperial Experience* (Basingstoke, 1996)

Ellinwood, D. C., and Pradhan, S. D. (eds), *India and World War I* (Delhi, 1978)

Engel, M., *Tickle the Public: One Hundred Years of the Popular Press* (1996)

Ensor, R. C. K., *England, 1870–1914* (1936)

Farrar, M. J., *News from the Front: War Correspondents on the Western Front* (Stroud, 1998)

Fein, H., *Imperial Crime and Punishment* (Honolulu, 1977)

Ferris, P., *The House of Northcliffe* (1971)

Feuchtwanger, E. J., *Democracy and Empire* (1985)

Finkelstein, D., and Peers, D. M. (eds), *Negotiating India in the Nineteenth Century Media* (2000)

Finn, B. S., *Submarine Telegraphy: The Grand Victorian Technology* (1973)

Foot, M. R. D. (ed.), *War and Society* (1973)

Foster, R. F., *Paddy and Mr Punch* (1993)

Foxbourne, H. R., *Chapters in the History of Journalism* (1887) II

Fraser, L., *India under Curzon and After* (1911)

Fraser, L., *Propaganda* (1957)

Freedman, L., Hayes, P., and O'Neill, R. (eds), *War, Strategy and International Politics* (Oxford, 1992)

Furneaux, R., *Massacre at Amritsar* (1963)

Fyfe, H., *Northcliffe* (1930)

——*Sixty Years of Fleet Street* (1949)

Gandhi, M. K., *An Autobiography* (1927)

Garvin, K., *J. L. Garvin* (1948)

Ghosh, S., *Modern History of Indian Press* (Delhi, 1998)

Gilbert, B. B., *David Lloyd George, 1912–1916* (1992)

Gilbert, M. (ed.), *Servant of India* (1966)

Gilmour, D., *Curzon* (1995)

Godfrey, R. (ed.), *Letters from a Prince* (1998)

Gollin, A. M., *The Observer and J. L. Garvin, 1908–1914* (1960)

BIBLIOGRAPHY

Gould, J., and Kolb, W. L. (eds), *A Dictionary of the Social Sciences* (1964)

Grant, M., *Propaganda and the Role of the State in Interwar Britain* (Oxford, 1994)

Greenberger, A. J., *The British Image of India* (1969)

Greenwall, H. J., *Northcliffe* (1957)

Griffiths, P., *The British Impact on India* (1952)

Grigg, J., *Lloyd George: The People's Champion* (1978)

Gupta, P. S., *Imperialism and the British Labour Movement, 1914–1964* (1974)

Gurevitch, M. (ed.), *Culture, Society and the Media* (1982)

Hamer, D. A., *Liberal Politics in the Age of Gladstone and Rosebery* (Oxford, 1972)

Hamilton, G., *Parliamentary Reminiscences and Reflections, 1886–1906* (1922)

Hammond, J. L., *C. P. Scott* (1934)

Hardie, J. K., *India: Impressions and Suggestions* (1909)

Hardinge, Lord, *Old Diplomacy* (1947)

——*My Indian Years, 1910–1916* (1948)

Hardman, T. H., *A Parliament of the Press* (1909)

Hargrave, J., *Words win Wars* (1940)

Harris, M., and Lee, A. (eds), *The Press in English Society from the Seventeenth Century to the Nineteenth Century* (1986)

——and O'Malley, T. (eds), *Studies in Newspaper and Periodical History: 1994 Annual* (Westport CT, 1996)

Harris, W., *J. A. Spender* (1946)

Havighurst, H. W., *Radical Journalist: H. W. Massingham* (1974)

Headrick, D. R., *The Tools of Empire: Technology and European Imperialism in the Nineteenth Century* (1981)

——*The Tentacles of Progress: Technology Transfer in the Age of Imperialism, 1850–1940* (1988)

Herd, H., *The March of Journalism* (1952)

Heyer P., *Communications and History* (Westport CT, 1988)

Hibbert, C., *Edward VIII* (1976)

Hindle, W., *The* Morning Post, *1772–1937* (1937)

Hobsbawm, E. J., and Ranger, T. O. (eds), *The Invention of Tradition* (Cambridge, 1983)

Holmes, C., *Antisemitism in British Society, 1876–1939* (1979)

Horniman, B. G., *Amritsar and our Duty to India* (1920)

Hoskins, H. L., *British Routes to India* (1966)

Hudson, D., *British Journalists and Newspapers* (1945)

Hudson, M., and Stanier, J., *War and the Media* (1997)

Hughes, E., *Keir Hardie* (1956)

Hutcheson, J. A., *Leopold Maxse and the* National Review, *1893–1914* (1989)

Hutchins, F., *The Illusion of Permanence: British Imperialism in India* (Princeton NJ, 1967)

Hyam, R., *Britain's Imperial Century* (1993)

Hyams, E., *The New Statesman* (1963)

Hyde, H. M., *Lord Reading* (1967)

BIBLIOGRAPHY

Hyndman, H. M., *The Unrest in India* (1907)
Hynes, S., *The Edwardian Turn of Mind* (1968)
Inden, R., *Imagining India* (Oxford, 1990)
Indo-British Association, *The Crumbling of an Empire* (1922)
Innis, H. A., *Empire and Communications* (1950, second edition Toronto, 1986)
——*The Bias of Communication* (1951, second edition Toronto, 1995)
Israel, M., *Communications and Power: Propaganda and the Press in the Indian Nationalist Struggle, 1920–1947* (Cambridge, 1994)
Jackson, S., *Rufus Issacs* (1936)
James, L., *Times of Stress* (1929)
——*High Pressure* (1929)
Jayal, N. G. (ed.), *Indian Diary of Sidney and Beatrice Webb* (Oxford, 1987)
Jeffery, K. (ed.), *An Irish Empire? Aspects of Ireland and the British Empire* (Manchester, 1996)
Jennings, L. J. (ed.), *Correspondence and Diaries of J. W. Croker* (1884) I
Jones, A., *Powers of the Press* (Aldershot, 1996)
Jones, K., *Fleet Street and Downing Street* (1920)
Jones, R., *A Life in Reuters* (1951)
Judd, D., *Lord Reading* (1982)
Kaminsky, A. P., *The India Office, 1880–1910* (1986)
Katz, D. *et al.* (eds), *Public Opinion and Propaganda* (New York, 1954)
Kaushik, H. P., *The Indian National Congress in England, 1885–1920* (Delhi, 1972)
——*Indian National Movement: The Role of British Liberals* (Delhi, 1986)
Kaye, J. W., *A History of the Sepoy War in India* (seventh edition, 1875)
Kendle, J., *The British Empire and Commonwealth* (1972)
Kerr, I. J., *Building the Railways of the Raj* (Delhi, 1995)
Keynes, J. M., *Collected Writings* (1972) X
Kieve, J., *The Electric Telegraph* (Newton Abbot, 1973)
Kilbracken, Lord A. G., *Reminiscences* (1931)
Knightley, P., *The First Casualty: The War Correspondent from the Crimea to Vietnam* (1975)
Koss, S., *John Morley at the India Office, 1905–1910* (New Haven CT, 1969)
——*Fleet Street Radical* (1973)
——*The Pro-Boers* (Chicago, 1973)
——*The Rise and Fall of the Political Press in Britain* I (1980), II (1984)
Kumar, R., *Essays in the Social History of Modern India* (Delhi, 1983)
Kundu, K., *Rabindranath and the British Press 1912–1941* (1990)
Lago, M., and Furbank, P. N. (eds), *Selected Letters of E. M. Forster* (1985)
Lane, R. E., and Sears, D. O. (eds) *Public Opinion* (Englewood Cliffs NJ, 1964)
Lansbury, G., *The Miracle of Fleet Street* (1925)
Lambert, R. S., *Propaganda* (1938)
Lasswell, H. D., *Propaganda Techniques in World War One* (1927)
——Lerner, D., and Speier, H. (eds), *Propaganda and Communication in World History* (Hawaii, 1979)

Lavin, D., *From Empire to International Commonwealth: A Biography of Lionel Curtis* (Oxford, 1995)

Lawrence, W. R., *The India we Served* (1929)

Lee, A. J., *The Origins of the Popular Press* (1976)

Levine, N. B., *Politics, Religion and Love: The Story of H. H. Asquith, Venetia Stanley and Edwin Montagu* (New York, 1991)

Lippman, W., *Public Opinion* (New York, 1929)

Louis, Wm Roger, *et al.* (eds), *The Oxford History of the British Empire* (Oxford, 1999) III–V

Lovett, P., *Journalism in India* (Calcutta, 1926)

Lovett, V., *A History of the Indian Nationalist Movement* (1920)

Low, D. A., *Eclipse of Empire* (Cambridge, 1991)

——(ed.), *The Indian National Congress: Centenary Hindsights* (Delhi, 1988)

Low, S., *A Vision of India* (1906)

Lowell, A. L., *Public Opinion in War and Peace* (Cambridge MA, 1923)

——*Public Opinion and Popular Government* (New York, 1919)

Lowry, D. (ed.), *The South African War Reappraised* (2000)

Lucas, R., *Lord Glenesk and the* Morning Post (1910)

MacDonagh, M., *In London during the Great War* (1935)

MacDonald, R., *The Awakening of India* (1909)

MacDonald, R. H., *The Language of Empire* (Manchester, 1994)

MacKenzie, F. A., *Beaverbrook* (1931)

MacKenzie, J. M., *Propaganda and Empire* (Manchester, 1984)

——(ed.), *Imperialism and Popular Culture* (Manchester, 1986)

——(ed.), *Popular Imperialism and the Military, 1850–1950* (Manchester, 1992)

MacKenzie, N. and J., *The Diary of Beatrice Webb* (1983) II

Magnus, P., *King Edward VII* (1964)

Margach, J., *The Abuse of Power* (1978)

——*The Anatomy of Power* (1979)

Massingham, H. W., *The London Daily Press* (New York, 1892)

Mathur, L. P., *Indian Revolutionary Movements in the USA* (Delhi, 1970)

Matthew, H. C. G., *The Liberal Imperialists* (Oxford, 1973)

——*Gladstone, 1809–1874* (Oxford, 1988)

——(ed.), *Gladstone Diaries* (Oxford, 1968–1990)

——(ed.), *The Nineteenth Century* (Oxford, 2000)

Matthews, T. S., *The Sugared Pill* (1957)

Marvin, C., *When Old Technologies were New* (New York, 1988)

McCormick, D., *Masks of Merlin* (1964)

McKercher, B. J. C., and Moss, D. J. (eds), *Shadow and Substance in British Foreign Policy, 1895–1939* (Edmonton, Alta, 1984)

McKibbin, R., *The Evolution of the Labour Party, 1910–1924* (1974)

McLuhan, M., *The Gutenberg Galaxy* (Toronto, 1962)

——*The Medium is the Message* (1967)

——*Understanding Media: The Extensions of Man* (1967)

McMunn, G., *Turmoil and Tragedy in India, 1919 and After* (1935)

McQuail, D., *Mass Communication Theory* (1987)

Mehrotra, S. R., *India and the Commonwealth, 1885–1929* (1965)

Menpes, M., *The Durbar* (1903)

Messinger, G. S., *British Propaganda and the State in the First World War* (Manchester, 1992)

Metcalf, T. R., *Ideologies of the Raj* (Cambridge, 1997)

Middleton, Earl of, *Records and Reactions, 1856–1939* (1939)

Mills, J. S., *Press and Communications of the Empire* (1924)

Mills, W. H., *The* Manchester Guardian: *A Century of History* (1921)

Montagu, E. S., *An Indian Diary*, ed. Venetia Stanley (1930)

Monypenny, W. F, and Buckle, G. E., *The Life of Benjamin Disraeli* (1929)

Moore, R. J., *Liberalism and Indian Politics, 1872–1922* (1966)

——*The Crisis of Indian Unity, 1917–1940* (Oxford, 1974)

Morgan, K. O., *Consensus and Disunity: The Lloyd George Coalition Government, 1918–1922* (Oxford, 1979)

——*Keir Hardie* (1997)

Morison, S., *The English Newspaper* (Cambridge, 1932)

Morley, J., *Indian Speeches, 1907–1909* (1909)

——*Recollections* (1918)

Morris, A. J. A., *The Scaremongers: The Advocacy of War and Rearmament, 1896–1914* (1984)

Morris, B., *The Roots of Appeasement* (1991)

Morris, J., *Pax Britannica* (1968)

Mudford, P. G., *Birds of a Different Plumage* (1974)

Nanda, B. R. (ed.), *Essays in Modern Indian History* (1980)

Nandy, A., *The Intimate Enemy: Loss and Recovery of Self under Colonialism* (Delhi, 1983)

Narain, P., *Press and Politics in India, 1885–1905* (Delhi, 1970)

Natarajan, S., *A History of the Press in India* (1962)

Negrine, R., *Politics and the Mass Media in Britain* (1994)

Nevinson, H. W., *The New Spirit in India* (1908)

——*Lines of Life* (1920)

Newman, H., *Indian Peepshow* (1937)

——*A Roving Commission* (1937)

Northcliffe, Lord, *Newspapers and their Millionaires* (1922)

——*My Journey round the World* (1923)

O'Dwyer, M., *India as I Knew it, 1885–1925* (1925)

Ogilvy-Webb, M., *The Government Explains: A Study of the Information Services* (1965)

O'Malley, L. S. S. (ed.), *Modern India and the West* (1941)

Omissi, D., and Thompson, A. S. (eds), *The Impact of the South African War* (Basingstoke, 2002)

Orwell, G, *England, your England* (1953)

Owen, L., *The Real Lord Northcliffe* (1922)

Parry, B., *Delusions and Discoveries: Studies of India in the British Imagination, 1880–1930* (Berkeley CA, 1972)

Pearey, M., *An Imaginary Rebellion* (Lahore, 1920)

Pebody, C., *English Journalism and the Men who Made it* (1882)

Peele, G., and Cook, C. (ed.), *The Politics of Reappraisal, 1918–1939* (1975)

Pelling, H., *Popular Politics and Society in late Victorian Britain* (1968)

Pemberton, M., *Northcliffe* (1922)

Pemble, J., *Raj and the Indian Mutiny* (Rutherford NJ, 1977)

PEP, *Report on the British Press* (1938)

Petrie, C., *The Life and Letters of the Rt Hon. Sir Austen Chamberlain* (1940) II

Philips, C. H. (ed.), *Politics and Society in India* (1965)

Phillips, G. D., *The Diehards: Aristocratic Society and Politics in Edwardian England* (1979)

Pimlott, B., and Seaton, J., *The Media in British Politics* (Aldershot, 1987)

Pope-Hennessy, J., *Lord Crewe, 1858–1945* (1955)

Popplewell, R. J., *Intelligence and Imperial Defence* (1995)

Porter, B., *Critics of Empire* (1969)

——*The Lion's Share* (1975)

Postgate, R., *The Life of George Lansbury* (1951)

Pound, R., and Harmsworth, G., *Northcliffe* (1959)

Price, R., *An Imperial War and the British Working Class* (1972)

Price, V., *Public Opinion* (Newbury Park CA, 1992)

Pronay, N., and Spring, D. W., *Propaganda, Politics and Film, 1918–1945* (1982)

Raghavan, G. N. S., *The Press in India: A New History* (New Delhi, 1994)

Ram, R., *The Jallianwallah Bagh Massacre* (Chandigarh, 1969)

Ramsden, J., *The Age of Balfour and Baldwin, 1902–1940* (1978)

Ramusack, B. N., *The Princes of India in the Twilight of Empire* (Cincinnati OH, 1978)

Rantanen, T., *Foreign News in Imperial Russia* (Helsinki, 1990)

Ratcliffe, S. K., *Sir William Wedderburn and the Indian Reform Movement* (1923)

Read, D., *The Power of News: The History of Reuters, 1849–1989* (Oxford, 1992)

Reading, Marquess of, *Rufus Issacs* (1945) II

Reed, S., *The India I Knew, 1897–1947* (1957)

Renford, R. K., *The Non-official British in India to 1920* (Delhi, 1987)

Repington, C. A., *The First World War* (1920)

Richards, H., *The Bloody Circus: The Daily Herald and the Left* (1997)

Riddell, Lord, *Intimate Diary of the Paris Peace Conference and After* (1933)

——*Lord Riddell's War Diary* (1933)

Robb, P. G., *The Government of India and Reform, 1916–1921* (Oxford, 1976)

Rose, K., *George V* (1983)

——*Curzon: A Most Superior Person* (1985)

Rosenthal, R. (ed.), *McLuhan: Pro and Con* (New York, 1968)

Rumbold, A., *Watershed in India, 1914–1922* (1979)

Russell, A. K., *Liberal Landslide* (1973)

Russell, H., *With the Princes in the East* (1922)

BIBLIOGRAPHY

Russell, W. H., *My Indian Mutiny Diary* (1860)
Rutherford, V. H., *India and the Labour Party* (1924)
Ryan, A. P., *Lord Northcliffe* (1953)
Said, E., *Orientalism* (1978)
Saintsbury, G., *A Scrap Book* (1922)
Salehi, J., and Bulliet, R. W. (eds), *Columbia History of the Twentieth Century* (New York, 1998)
Sanders, M. L., and Taylor, P. M., *British Propaganda during the First World War* (1982)
Sarkar, R. S., *The Press in India* (Delhi, 1984)
Sarkar, S., *Modern India, 1885–1947* (1995)
Schneider, W. H., *An Empire for the Masses: The French Popular Image of Africa, 1870–1900* (Westport CT, 1982)
Scott, C. P., *The Making of the* Manchester Guardian (1946)
Scott, G., *Reporter Anonymous: The Story of the Press Association* (1968)
Scott, J. M., *Extel 100* (1972)
Scott, J. W. R., *The Story of the* Pall Mall Gazette (1950)
——*The Life and Death of a Newspaper* (1952)
Searle, G. R., *Corruption in British Politics, 1895–1930* (Oxford, 1987)
Seeley, J. R., *The Expansion of England* (1883)
Self, R. C., *The Austen Chamberlain Diary Letters* (Cambridge, 1995)
Seldon, A., and Ball, S. (eds), *Conservative Century* (1994)
Seymour-Ure, C., *The Press, Politics and the Public* (1968)
Seymour-Ure, C., and Schoff, J., *David Low* (1985)
Shattock, J., *Politics and Reviewers: The* Edinburgh Quarterly (Leicester, 1989)
——and Wolff, M. (eds), *The Victorian Periodical Press* (Leicester, 1982)
Simonis, H., *The Street of Ink* (1917)
Singh, A. K., *Indian Students in Britain* (1963)
Singh, G., Singh, P. B., Verma, D. K., and Ghai, R. K. (eds), *Jallianwallah Bagh* (Patiala, 1997)
Smith, A., *New Statesman* (1996)
Smith, V. A., *The Oxford Student's History of India* (Oxford, 1958)
——*Oxford History of India*, fourth edition, ed. P. Spear (Oxford, 1991)
Spender, J. A., *The Changing East* (1926)
——*Life, Journalism and Politics* (1927) I–II
Startt, J. D., *Journalists for Empire* (Wesport CT and Harlow, 1991)
Stead, W. T., *A Journalist on Journalism* (1893)
Steed, H. W., *Through Thirty Years, 1892–1922* (1924)
Steiner, Z., *The Foreign Office and Foreign Policy, 1898–1914* (1969)
Stembridge, S. R., *Parliament, the Press and the Colonies, 1846–80* (1982)
Stephens, M., *History of News* (1997)
Storey, G., *Reuters' Century, 1851–1951* (1951)
Storrs, R., *Orientations* (1937)
Strachey, A., *St Loe Strachey: his Life and his Paper* (1930)
Strachey, J. St Loe, *The Adventure of Living* (1922)
Stutterheim, K. von, *The Press in England* (1934)
Symons, J. D., *The Press and its Story* (1914)

Symonds, R., *Oxford and Empire: The Last Lost Cause* (1986)

Symonds, R. V., *The Rise of English Journalism* (Exeter, 1952)

Taylor, A. J. P., *English History, 1914–1945* (1965)

Taylor, H. A., *Robert Donald* (1934)

Taylor, P. J. O. (ed.), *A Companion to the Indian Mutiny* (Delhi, 1996)

Taylor, P. M., *Projection of Britain: British Overseas Publicity and Propaganda, 1919–1939* (Cambridge, 1981)

——*Munitions of the Mind* (Manchester, 1995)

Taylor, S. J., *The Great Outsiders: Northcliffe, Rothermere and the* Daily Mail (1996)

Thomas, J. A., *The House of Commons, 1906–1911* (1958)

Thomas, W. B., *The Story of the* Spectator, *1828–1928* (1928)

Thompson, A. S., *Imperial Britain* (Harlow, 2000)

Thompson, J. Lee, *Politicians, the Press and Propaganda: Lord Northcliffe and the Great War* (Kent OH, 1999)

——*Northcliffe: Press Baron in Politics, 1865–1922* (2000)

Thornton, A. P., *The Imperial Idea and its Enemies* (1959)

The Times, The History of the Times, 1785–1841 (1935) I

——*The History of the Times, 1841–1884* (1939) II

——*The History of the Times, 1884–1912* (1947) III

——*The History of the Times*, Part 1, *1912–1920*, Part 2, *1921–1948* (1952) IV

Trench, C. C., *Indian Army and the King's Enemies, 1900–1947* (1988)

Turner, J., *Lloyd George's Secretariat* (Austin TX, 1980)

——*British Politics and the Great War* (New Haven CT, 1992)

Vadgama, K., *India in Britain* (1984)

Waley, D., *British Public Opinion and the Abyssinian War, 1935–1936* (1975)

Waley, S. D., *Edwin Montagu* (1964)

Wasti, S. R., *Lord Minto and the Indian Nationalist Movement, 1905–1910* (Oxford, 1964)

Wheeler, S., *History of Delhi Coronation Durbar* (1904)

Wickwar, W. H., *The Struggle for the Freedom of the Press, 1819–1832* (1928)

Wiener, J. H., *War of the Unstamped* (New York, 1969)

——(ed.), *Innovators and Preachers: The Role of the Editor in Victorian England* (Westport CT, 1985)

——(ed.), *Papers for the Millions* (Westport CT, 1988)

Wilkinson, S., *Thirty-five Years* (1933)

Williams, D., *The India Office, 1858–1869* (Hoshiarpur, 1983)

Williams, F., *Dangerous Estate: The Anatomy of Newspapers* (1957)

——*The Right to Know* (1969)

Williams, L. F. R., *The History of the Indian Tour of HRH the Prince of Wales, 1921–1922* (Calcutta, 1922)

——*Inside both Indias, 1914–1938* (Stroud, n.d.)

Williams, R., *The Long Revolution* (1961)

——*Communications* (1976)

Williams, V., *The World of Action* (1938)

Wilson, K. M. (ed.), *British Foreign Secretaries and Foreign Policy* (1987)

——*A Study in the History and Politics of the* Morning Post, *1905–1926* (Lampeter, 1990)

——(ed.) *The Rasp of War: The Letters of H. A. Gwynne to the Countess of Bathurst, 1914–1918* (1988)

Wilson, R. M., *Lord Northcliffe: A Study* (1927)

Wilson, T., *The Downfall of the Liberal Party, 1914–1935* (1966)

——(ed.), *The Political Diaries of C. P. Scott, 1911–1928* (1970)

Wolpert, S., *Morley and India, 1906–1910* (1967)

——*An Error of Judgement* (Boston MA, 1970), also published as *Massacre at Jallianwallah Bagh* (Delhi, 1989)

——and Sisson, R. (eds), *Congress and Indian Nationalism* (1988)

Woodhead, C., *Press and Empire* (Durban, 1909)

Woods, O., and Bishop, J., *The Story of* The Times (1983)

Woods, P., *Roots of Parliamentary Democracy in India, 1917–1923* (Delhi, 1996)

Wrench, J. E., *Uphill* (1934)

——*Struggle, 1914–1920* (1935)

——*Geoffrey Dawson and our Times* (1955)

Wrigley, C., *Lloyd George and the Challenge of Labour: The Postwar Coalition, 1918–1922* (1990)

Ziegler, P., *King Edward VIII: The Official Biography* (1990)

——(ed.), *The Diaries of Lord Louis Mountbatten, 1920–1922* (1987)

Articles

Bayly, C., 'Knowing the country: empire and information in India', *Modern Asian Studies*, 27: 1 (1993), 3–43

Blewett, N., 'The franchise in the United Kingdom, 1885–1918', *Past and Present*, 32 (1965), 27–56

Boyce, D. G., 'Public opinion and historians', *History*, 63 (June 1978), 214–28

Bright, C., 'Imperial telegraphs', *Quarterly Review* (1903), 364–83

——'Imperial telegraphy at a popular tariff', *Fortnightly Review*, 507 (March 1909), 526–41

Cumpston, M., 'Some early Indian nationalists and their allies in the British Parliament, 1851–1906', *English Historical Review*, 76: 299 (1961), 279–97

Demm, E., 'Propaganda and caricature in the First World War', *Journal of Contemporary History*, 28: 1 (1993), 163–92

Ellinwood, D. C., 'The Round Table movement and India, 1909–1920', *Journal of Commonwealth Political Studies*, 9 (1971), 183–209

Fisher, M. H., 'The office of Akhbar Nawis: the transition from Mughal to British forms', *MAS*, 27: 1 (1993), 45–82

Goold, D., 'Lord Hardinge and the Mesopotamia expedition and inquiry, 1914–1917', *Historical Journal*, 19: 4 (1976), 919–45

Harding, D. W., 'General conceptions in the study of the press and public opinion', *Sociological Review*, 29: 4 (1937), 370–90

Hiley, N., 'Counter-espionage and security in Great Britain during the First World War', *English Historical Review*, 101: 400 (July 1986), 635–70

Hopkin, D., 'Domestic censorship in the First World War' *Journal of Contemporary History*, 5: 4 (1970), 151–70

Kaul, C., 'England and India: the Ilbert Bill, 1883: a case study of the Metropolitan press', *Indian Economic and Social History Review*, 30: 4 (New Delhi, 1993), 413–36

——'A new angle of vision: the London press, governmental information management and the Indian empire, 1900–1922', *Contemporary Record*, 8: 2, special issue *Empire, Competition and War: Essays on the Press in the Twentieth Century* (1994), 213–41

——'The press', in B. Brivati, A. Seldon and J. Buxton (eds), *Contemporary History Handbook* (Manchester, 1996), 298–310

——'Imperial communications, Fleet Street and the Indian empire, c. 1850s–1920s', in M. Bromley and T. O'Malley (eds), *A Journalism Reader* (1997), 58–86

——'*Round Table*, the British Press and India, 1910–22', in A. Bosco and A. May (eds), *The Round Table Movement: The Empire/Commonwealth and British Foreign Policy* (1997), 343–68

——'Popular press and empire: Northcliffe, India and the *Daily Mail*, 1896–1922', in P. Catterall, C. Seymour Ure and A. Smith (eds), *Northcliffe's Legacy: Aspects of the Popular Press, 1896–1996* (2000), 45–69

Kennedy, P. M., 'Imperial cable communications and strategy, 1870–1914', *English Historical Review*, 86: 341 (1971), 728–53

Koss, S. E., 'The destruction of Britain's last Liberal government', *Journal of Modern History*, 40: 2 (1968), 257–77

Lee-Warner, W., 'Our work in India in the nineteenth century', *Journal of the Society of Arts*, 2 (1900), 213–28

Marquis, A. G., 'Words as weapons: propaganda in Britain and Germany during the First World War', *Journal of Contemporary History*, 13: 3 (1978), 467–98

Marshall, P. J., 'No fatal impact? The elusive history of imperial Britain', *Times Literary Supplement* (12 March 1993), 8–10

——'Imperial Britain', *Journal of Imperial and Commonwealth History*, 23: 3 (1995), 379–94

McEwan, J. M., 'The press and the fall of Asquith', *Historical Journal*, 21: 4 (1978), 863–83

——'The national press during the First World War: ownership and circulation', *Journal of Contemporary History*, 17: 3 (1982), 459–86

Moore, R. J., 'Curzon and Indian reform', *Modern Asian Studies*, 27: 4 (1993), 719–40

Morgan, K. O., 'Lloyd George's premiership: a study in "Prime Ministerial government"', *Historical Journal*, 13: 1 (1970), 130–57

Morley, J., 'British democracy and Indian government', *Nineteenth Century and After*, 69 (1911), 189–209

Palmegiano, E., 'The Indian Mutiny in the mid-Victorian press', *Journal of Newspaper and Periodical History*, 7 (1991), 3–11

Peers, D. M., '"Those Noble Exemplars of the True Military Tradition": constructions of the Indian Army in the mid-Victorian press', *Modern Asian Studies*, 31: 1 (1997), 109–42

Porter, A. N., 'Sir Alfred Milner and the press, 1897–1899', *Historical Journal*, 16: 2 (1973), 323–39

Read, D., 'War news from Reuters: Victorian and Edwardian reporting', *Despatches*, 4 (autumn 1993), 72–85

Robb, P. G., 'British Cabinet and Indian reform', *Journal of Imperial and Commonwealth History*, 4: 3 (1976), 318–34

Ryland, S., 'Edwin Montagu in India, 1917–1918: politics of the Montagu–Chelmsford report', *Journal of South Asian Studies*, 3 (1973), 79–92

Sayer, D., 'British reaction to the Amritsar massacre, 1919–1920', *Past and Present*, 131 (1991), 130–64

Wadsworth, A. P., 'Newspaper circulations, 1800–1954', *Manchester Statistical Society* (1955), 1–40

Woods, P., 'The Montagu–Chelmsford reforms (1919): a reassessment', *South Asia*, 17: 1 (1994), 25–42

Unpublished doctoral theses

Gannon, F. R., 'The British Press and Germany, 1936–1939' (Oxford, 1968)

Husain, S. A., 'The Organisation and Administration of the India Office, 1910–1924' (London, 1978)

Inwood, S., 'The Role of the Press in English Politics during the First World War, with special Reference to the Period 1914–1916' (Oxford, 1971)

Kaul, C., 'Press and Empire: the London Press, Government News Management and India, *c.* 1900–1922' (Oxford, 1999)

Legg, M., 'Newspapers and Nationalism: the Social and Political Influence of the Irish Provincial Press, 1850–1892' (London, 1992) (draft copy lent by the author).

May, A. C., 'The Round Table, 1910–66' (Oxford, 1995)

Morris, A. J. L., 'A Study of John St Loe Strachey's Editorship of the *Spectator*, 1901–1914' (Cambridge, 1986)

Thomas, J. P., 'The British Empire and the Press, 1763–74' (Oxford, 1982)

INDEX

Note: 'n.' after a page reference indicates the number of a note on that page.